Marriage Bonds of Haywood and Jackson Counties, North Carolina

Compiled By: James E. and Vivian Woolley

Copyright 1978 by:

The Rev. Silas Emmett Lucas, Jr.

Please Direct All Correspondence and Book Orders to:
Southern Historical Press, Inc.
PO Box 1267
375 West Broad Street
Greenville, SC 29602-1267
or
southernhistoricalpress@gmail.com

ISBN #0-89308-107-8

INTRODUCTION

When the people of the frontier west of Buncombe County became sufficient to form a new county a bill was introduced in the North Carolina General Assembly on Dec. 23, 1808 for the formation of a new county. Beginning at the highest point on the South Carolina line where the ridge divides the waters of the French Broad River and the Tuckaseigee River, running along the ridge to Mt. Pisgah then a straight line to John C. Smather's home on Hominy Creek, then on the ridge to Newfound Gap to Herbo Mt. and Rough Knob to the Tenn. line, near Waterville Dam on Pigeon River. Thence west on said line to the Georgia line, near the city of Ducktown, Tenn. East on the Ga. and and S. C. line to the beginning.

These bonds were issued in accordance with an act of the General Assembly in the year 1778 which in part states, "That all ministers of the gospel of every denomination, having the cure of souls, and all justices of the peace in the state, are hereby authorised and empowered to solemnize the rite of matrimony, according to the rites and ceremonies of their respective Churchs, and be it further enacted. That the Clerk of each county court is hereby authorised and empowered to grant marriage licenses to any person applying for the same, First taking bond, in the name of the Governor for the time being, and his successors, with sufficient security, in the sum of five hundred pounds lawful money of the state, with condition that there is no lawful cause to obstruct the marriage for which such license is desired, to be recovered by action of debt, in any court of record having cognizance thereof, by the parties grieved which bond aforsaid shall be taken, and license granted by the clerk of the county in which the female resides."

It is from these bonds that we have the Haywood Co. part of the book, the Jackson Co. part is from clerk's register book. If "Not Returned" is stated, this does not mean or imply that the marriage was not performed, only that the minister of J.P. didn't return the bond or complete the clerk's register. (As proof a lady in Texas has sent a copy of five licenses that she found in her gr.grandfather's papers, one was not in the first book.) If a husband abandoned or refused to provide for the family, the bondsman was responsible for the family.

With the fire in Burke County in 1865 and the one in Buncombe County in 1830 all marriage bonds were destroyed. These of Haywood County are the oldest in the mountain area.

Jackson County was formed in 1851, with the area that is in the Tuckaseigee River basin with Balsam Mt. to the East and Cowee Mt on the West. Ther clerk's register is in chronological order, if the date isn't known a lot of time is spent looking for a marriage. In the second book a few pages have very dim ink and pages are getting brown reading is most difficult.

Jim & Vivian Woolley

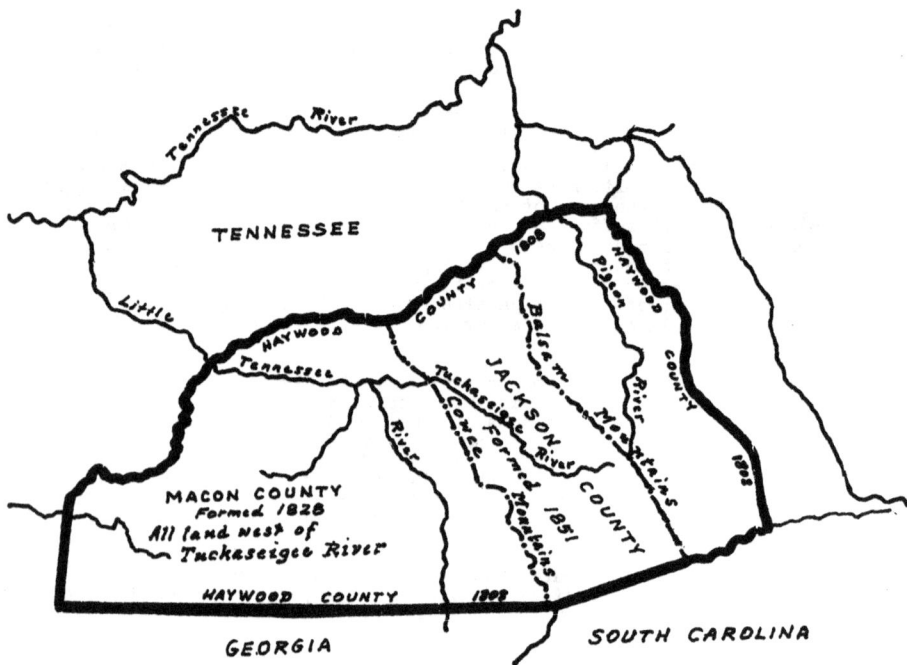

TENNESSEE

Tennessee River

Little

Tennessee

HAYWOOD

COUNTY

1808

Pigeon River

HAYWOOD COUNTY

Balsam Mountains

JACKSON COUNTY

Tuckaseigee River

Cowee Mountains

Formed 1851

River

1808

MACON COUNTY
Formed 1828
All land west of
Tuckaseigee River

HAYWOOD COUNTY 1808

GEORGIA

SOUTH CAROLINA

PREFACE

The original marriage bonds of Haywood County, North Carolina, are in the archives of the North Carolina Historical Commission, Raleigh, North Carolina. They are alphabetically by the groom and may be consulted by the public.

These bonds were abstracted and alphabetized by youth of Wake County, working on a National Youth Administration project, and the Historical Records Survey of the Work Project Administration and checked by Miss Mary Jones Jeffreys, employed by the Genealogical Society of Utah in cooperation with the North Carolina Historical Commission.

The abbreviation "col" following the name of the bride and groom means that they are Negroes.

The small -x- following a name means that the person did not sign the bond but made his mark.

Haywood County was formed in 1808 from Buncombe County

The act authorizing marriage bonds was passed in 1740 and continued in effect until 1868 when marriage licenses were authorized.

This copy made from a reel of microfilm. A few errors corrected and some additional information added when possible

MARRIAGE BONDS

GROOM	BRIDE	DATE OF BOND	BONDSMAN & WITNESS
---------------	Adalaide Osborn	10 Aug. 1862	A.J.Osborn (w) A.L.Herren
Abbott,Levi x	Dousha Anderson (d. of Josiah)	14 June 1833	D(octor) C.Howell (w) ----------
Able,James H.R.	Levada C.Kinsland	30 Sept. 1865	E.C.Johnson (w) M.C.Killian
Able,John x	Jane Moore	7 Feb. 1857	Amos Smith (w) ----------
Able,Jonathan	Sophena Green	2 Mar. 1858 M.2 Mar. 1858	Wm.H.Green (w) W.W.Medford,clk.
Able,Samuel W.	Jane Avaline Smith	3 Apr. 1829	W(illia)m Haynes (w) R.Love,clk.
Able, Wm. (H)	Miry A.Justice	25 Feb 1859 M.27 Feb. 1859 By D.R.Ford,J.P.	E.G.Johnson (w) W.W.Medford,clk.
Ables, Moses x	Casey E.Rathbone	19 Nov. 1860	George Williamson (w) Elizabeth E. Williamson
Adam,David P.	Elisabeth Wood (d.of Henry Wood)	15 July 1813	Stephan White (w) ----------
Adams,William	Carline Galeymar (d.of Asey)	11 Oct. 1838	Jacob Beck (w) Samuel Gibson
Alexander,Dan x	Sarah Sutton	22 Oct. 1825	David Colman (w) Jas.R.Love, Deputy
Alexander,John	Sariah Lard (d.of Ann)	30 Nov. 1816	Ja(me)s McKee (w) ----------
Alexander,W(illiam) P.	Altha Philips	12 Sept. 1851 M.14 Sept. 1851 By A.M.Russell,J.P.	C.B.Phillips (w) J.Keener,clk.
Alexander,J(ames) W(ashington)	Mary Ann Phillips (d.of Elisha)	20 July 1835	Jeremi(ah) Hairson (w) S.Fitzgerrald,clk.
Allen,Allonso	Magdalene Underwood	26 July 1852	J(oseph) Keener (w) ----------
Allen,David x	M.C.Mann	6 Sept. 1856 M.7 Sept. 1856 By Allen Ammons,M.G.	Wm.B. x Hawkins (w) C.T.Rogers,clk.
Allen,J(ames) J.	Sarrah M.King	28 Dec. 1844	Joseph x Sorrals (w) W.Brown
Allen,Jeramiah	Elizabeth Allen	24 Sept. 1848	J(ames) (N) Brendle (w) W. Brown
Allen,Laranzar	A.Underwood	---------- M.4 Aug. 1852 By J.F.Fincher,J.P.	---------- (w) ----------

GROOM	BRIDE	DATE OF BOND	BONDSMAN & WITNESS
Allen,Nathen	Elizabeth Farmer (d.of Mary)	9 Feb. 1836	Elias Brend(1)e (w) Wm. Welch,clk.
Allen, W(illia)m	L.C.Edmonston	14 Oct. 1856 M.14 Oct. 1856 By W.Brown,J.P.	W(alter) Brown (w) Wm.M.Rhea,C.C.C.
Alleson,Daniel	Lucenda S.Henry	6 Oct. 1840	M.S.Henry (w) Wm.Welch
Alleson,Francis P.	Mary A.Potts	4 Jan. 1841	H.L.Potts (w) Wm.Welch
Allison,Jason x	Jemima Dotson (d.of Thomas Dotson)	12 Sept. 1832	David A.Ross (w) Wm.Welch
Allison,Wm. x	Mary Williams (d.of Susanah & James Williams)	6 Feb. 1836	Edmond x Aldridge (w) F.McGee
Allman,Nathan G.	Louisa E.Rhinehart (d.of Coonrod)	7 Feb. 1839	R(obt) H.Penland (w) Wm.Welch
Allman,Peyton	Nancy Tritt (d.of John Tritt)	21 Sept. 1839	J(ohn) P.Cooper (w) Wm.Welch
Allman,W(illia)m	Mary Ingraham (d.of Delia)	17 Aug. 1837	A(rchibald) Herren (w) Wm.Welch,clk.
Allridge,Edmond	Jane Woods (d.of Laurence)	9 Jan. 1837	Jeremiah Vickers (w) M.Francis
Almsted,John	Rebecca Lenoir	16 Oct. 1868 M.17 Oct. 1868 By James A.Zachary,M.G.	(w) W.C.Brown reg. H.C.
Ammons,John	Nancy Cirby (d.of Amus)	17 June 1823	Young x Ammons (w) ----------
Ammons,Young	Ella Cabe (d.of Saml.)	14 June 1822	Charles Stiles (w) Dillard Love
Anderson,James M.	Elisabeth C.Battle	19 Dec. 1850	H.Battle (w) John S.Gibson
Anderson,James x	Nancey D.Forington	26 June 1829	John Carrel (w) Samuel Gibson,J.P.
Anderson,John	Elizabeth Dier	13 Sept. 1817	Bannister Turner (w) John B.Love
Anderson,John J.	Nancey Burnett	5 Jan. 1841	Allen Davis (w) ----------
Anderson,Johnston	Elisure Blaylock	13 May 1842	Isarael x Medford (w) ----------
Armstrong,Thos.H.	Mary Coleman (d.of George Coleman)	4 Oct. 1834	A(rchibald) Herren (w) S.Fitzgerrald,clk.
Arrington,Eli	Faney E.Eastes	24 Dec. 1847	J(ohn) N.McGree (w) ----------
Arrington,John	Rachael Johnston	23 Aug. 1858 M.24 Aug. 1858 By J.H.Noland,J.P.	James Crawford (w) W.N.Freeman,D.C.

GROOM	BRIDE	DATE OF BOND	BOND SMAN & WITNESS
Ash,David W(estley)	Delphey Jones (d.of Edward)	28 Sept. 1840	Charles Bumg(ar)ner (w) Jno B.Lobe
Balding,D(avid) B.	Harriet Caroline Byers M.	14 June 1851 15 June 1851 By H.P.Haynes,J.P.	L.S.Moody
Ball, Royal x	Elisabeth Price	20 Mar. 1828	Aaron x Price (w) Ro.Love clk.
Bandy,John	Margaret Hughes (d.of Thomas)	7 Jan. 1815	Robert Bandy (w) Ro.Love,clk.
Bannister,Austin x	Elizabeth Simmons (d.of Benjamin)	17 Apr. 1821	Ja(me)s R.Love (w) ----------
Barker,Brantley x	Marey Stillwel (d.of Samuel)	12 Apr. 1838	Jacob Stillwel (w) Samuel Gibson
Barker,Calvin x	Lidia Perry	27 Jan. 1835	Allen Fisher (w) J.Keener
Barnes,James x	Mary Ann Roof	23 Oct. 1839	William x Coldwell (w) Wm.Welch
Barnes,Thomas x	Fanney Colwell	18 Oct. 1842	Thomas Colwell (w) ----------
Barnes,Henry	Catherin Caldwell	28 June 1850	David Messer (w) ----------
Barns,John x	Elisabeth Tumberlin (d.of John)	28 Dec. 1830	Alex(ander) T.Holyday (w) ----------
Battle,W(illiam)W.	Emerline Howell (d.of Henry)	8 Jan. 1834	T(hos) J Cooper (w) S.Fitzgerrald
Battle,Watson x	Sarah Hide (d.of Benjamin)	24 Apr. 1823	G(eorge) McCracken (w) John B.Love,clk.
Beach,Eanoch x	Rebecca Dotson (d.of Thomas)	5 Oct. 1838	Jason Allison C.Bumgarn(er) (w) Wm.Welch
Beach,Enoch x	Rody Clark	21 Nov. 1843	G.S.Moody (w) ----------
Beal,John	Elisabeth Bracket (d.of Burrell)	-- Sept. 1816	Benj(ami)n Clark (w) ----------
Beaty,N(ewton) A.	Mary Long	4 Apr. 1843	T(homas) L.Potts (w) ----------
Beazley,William x	Nancy Hebberts (d.of John)	8 Sept. 1822	George McCracken (w) John B.Love,clk.
Beck,Henry J.	Jane Sims	25 Nov. 1843	Ephraim Stillwell (w) Samuel Gibson
Beck,Jacob x	Nancy Gallimore (d.of Asaph)	16 July 1824	Ralph Hughs (w) ----------
Beck,John M.	Saley Galemor (d.of Asey)	7 Dec. 1835	John x Beck (w) Samuel Gibson
Beesley,John x	Patsy Wrathbone (d.of Pernal)	17 Apr. 1834	Wm. x Wrathbone (w) S.Fitzgerrald,D C.

GROOM	BRIDE	DATE OF BOND	BONDSMAN & WITNESS
Bell,S.W.	Jane Matilda Palmer	23 Dec. 1867 M.24 Dec. 1867 By F.M.Messer,J.P.	(w) W.W.Medford,clk.
Benjamin,Wm.H.	Margaret Sharp	25 June 1858 M.26 June 1858 By J.H.Johnson,J.P.	C.C.Rogers (w) W.W.Medford,clk.
Bennet, Young x	Elvira Meece (d.of Fanny)	10 Mar. 1832	John x Anderson (w) Ro.Love
Bennett,C.M.	L.M.Colwell	3 June 1856 M.---------- By Wm.P.Gillett,J.P.	Wm.E.Smith (w) David Howell
Berry,James D.	Nancy Jones	21 Mar. 1825	W(illia)m Shelton (w) Ro.Love (w) Wm.Fox
Berry, Robert D. x	Nancy Hill (d.of Richmond)	-------1834	William x Parris (w) J.Keener
Bess,David x	Matilda Scott	17 Mar. 1845	Aaron x Roberson
Bess,Rodan	Talitha Baity	29 Aug. 1854 M.29 Aug. 1854 By H.P.Haynes,J.P.	Jonathan x Woods (w) Wm.M.Rhea,clk.
Best,Saml (s.Benedict Best)	Laura Roberson (d.of Mary Roberson widow)	3 June 1869 M.13 June 1869 By P.Holsclaw,M.G.	(w) W.C.Brown,R.D.H.C.
Bevans,James	Partheany Turner	17 Mar. 1825	William x Sorrells (w) R.Dever
Bigham,Dru(ry)	Mary Young	19 June 1858 M.19 June 1858 By R.E.Medford,J.P.	Reece Francis (w) W.W.Medford,clk.
Bigham,Thomas P.	Barbery Cooper	15 Jan. 1859 M.25 Jan. 1859 By Thos.S.Edwards,J.P.	T.B.Gaddy (w) W.W.Medford,clk.
B(i)gham,William R(illegible)	Malinda Farmer	23 Dec. 1854 M.24 Dec. 1854 By B.Turner,J.P.	T(homas) W.Farmer (w) Wm.M.Rhea,clk.
Bird,Jesse M.	Martha J.Terrill	7 July 1852 M.7 July 1852 By Thos R.Bradshaw,M.G.	Wm.G.Ingram (w) A.C.Hartgrove
Bird,Josiah A.	Sarah Hays (d.of Henry)	11 Oct. 1820	Felix H.Walker (w) ----------
Bird,J(osiah)L.	Nancey Mann (d.of David)	12 Aug. 1845	John C.Evans (w) ----------
Bird,Lauson	Adoline Boon	13 Aug. 1848	J.F.Owens (w) ----------
Blackburn,Levi x (s.of Benjamin)	Mahala Dyer	28 Apr. 1844	Milton Rhodes (w) ----------
Blalock,E.H.	Mary Campbell	18 June 1850	A.C.Hartgrove (w) ----------

GROOM	BRIDE	DATE OF BOND	BONDSMAN & WITNESS
Blalock,Francis A.x	Agness Martin	10 Mar. 1840	Isaac Ivester (w) Wm.Welch
Blalock,Isom x	Poley Buckehon (d.of Benjamin)	---Mar. 1816	William x Trull (w) James Love
Blalock,James M.x	Lucinda Cathey (d.of Widow Cathey)	28 Aug. 1837	Joseph x Brookshear (w) S.Fitzgerrald
Blalock,Willie C.x	Elizebeth Campbell (d.of Allen)	11 Sept. 1834	James Moore (w) ----------
Blaylock,Charles	Ruth Kingsland (d.of Rebecca	---June 1812	Francis Bird (w) Ro.Love,clk.
Blaylock,David x	Priselar Walker (d.of James)	22 Nov. 1836	John Gibson (w) Samuel Gibson
Blaylock,E.H.	Mary Anderson (d.of John,dec'd)	8 Sept. 1838	H(enry) E.Smith (w) N.Francis
Blaylock,William	Selena Cathey (d.of Sarah)	27 May 1837	F(rances B.Evans (w) Wm.Welch
Bolen,Jackson x	Elizabeth C.Miller	8June 1849	Thomas Henderson (w) ----------
Bolin,William	Polly Miller	11 Mar. 1853 M.13 Mar. 1853 By A.C.Hartgrove,J.P.	(w) Jospeh Keener,C.C.C.
Bonham,Jahu x	Mary Smith	28 June 1846	Green Moore (w) W.Brown
Bonham,James (s.of Jahu & Mary)	Jane Whitehead (d.of William & Polly)	20 Dec. 1870 M.22 Dec. 1870 By C.B.Mingus	(w) Joseph Liner,R.D.H.C.
Bonham,John T.	Sarah Murilla Runolds	25 Oct. 1855 M.25 Oct. 1855 By A.C.Hartgrove,J.P.	J.N.Moore (w) Wm.M.Rhea,clk.
Bonham, N.	Martha M.Sellers	26 Feb. 1859 M.27 Feb. 1859 By D.B.Ford,J.P.	Jacob Sellers (w) W.W.Medford,clk.
Boone,M.L.	Nancy M.Roger	30 Dec. 1848	J.F.Brown (w) W.Brown
Boyd,D.L.	M.J.Howell	15 Aug. 1857 M.15 Aug. 1857 By W.H.Leatherwood,J.P.	(w) W.W.Medford,clk.
Boyd,J(ames) F.	Margaret L.Jones	16 Jan. 1851	John C.Curry (w) J.Keener
Boyd,John H.H.	R.J.Brown	3 Dec. 1867	(w) W W.Medford,clk.
Bradey,Loranza Daw x.	Deborah Griffin (d.of William)	7 May 1832	William Green Sr. (w) Wm.Welch
Bradley,P(l)easant	Alisabeth Gibson (d.of John)	5 Mar. 1837	Rusel (Saton ?) (w) Samuel Gibson
Bra(d)ley,Stanford	Lydia Caroline Price	20 Jan. 1835	Soloman x Ray (w) S.Fitzgerrald,clk.

GROOM	BRIDE	DATE OF BOND	BONDSMAN & WITNESS
Bradley,Wilson	Elizabeth T.Mingus	20 Mar 1851	C.B.Mingus (w) R.V.Welch,Dep.
Bradshaw,James	Ana Lovingood (d.of Samuel)	19 Feb. 1836	Hugh Johnston (w) S.Fitzgerrald,D.clk.
Bradshaw,John	Anna Shuler (d.of George)	12 May 1834	James Bradshaw (Jr) (w) ----------
Bradshaw,Merill	Elezebeth C.Welch (d.of Widow Welch)	12 May 1834	James Bradshaw (Jr) (w) ----------
Bradshaw,William	Nancy Noland	25 May 1825	James Bradshaw (w) Ro.Love,clk.
Brannen,Joseph A.	Mary J.Love	4 Mar. 1856 M.4 Mar. 1856 By John Reynolds	(w) Wm.M.Rhea,clk.
Brannon,W(illia)m L.	Levina Hill (d.of Green)	26 Dec. 1835	David Plott (w) Wm.Welch
Brendle,Elias	Salinda Plott (d.of Henry,dec'd)	3 Nov. 1838	Enos Plott (w) ----------
Brendle,J(ames) N.	Elizabeth Cuningham	13 Nov. 1843	J(ohn) B.Allison (w) ----------
Brendle,Jospeh	Harett Long	20 Oct. 1841	Jeremiah Vickers (w) ----------
Brindle,Nicholas	Rachel Harman	3 June 1840	Jeremiah Vickers Joseph Brendle (w) M.Francis
Brittain,H(orateo) N.	Elizabeth Morrow (d.of Jane)	6 Dec. 1838	T(homas) C.Rinehardt (w) ----------
Broadway,John	Marian Earley (d.of John)	13 June 1823	Wm.Berry (w) ----------
Brock,James Thomas (s.of Thomas)	Abagill Demsey (d.of Luke)	3 Apr. 1869 M.4 Apr. 1869 By. R.L.Owen,J.P.	(w) W.C.Brown,R.D.H.C.
Brock,Jessy	Debsy Berry (d.of Jese)	30 June 1834	John Bradshaw (w) ----------
Brooks,Isaac (C)	Eloner Cuningham	12 Jan. 1849	J.N.Brendle (w) W.Brown
Brookshear,Henry x	Clarissa Parks (d.of Rachal)	17 Jan. 1820	W(illia)m Welch (w) ----------
Brookshear,Joel	Temperance Thompson (d.of William)	28 May 1832	John Moore (w) Ro.Love
Brookshier,Mannering	Patsey Brookshere (d.of James)	14 Nov. 1812	James x Brookshere (w) Ro.Love
Brookshir,James	Nancy Norton	5 Jan. 1843	Jesse x Roberson (w) ----------
Brown,Ezekiel	Margaret Plott	19 Feb. 1829	David x Plott (w) ----------

6

GROOM	BRIDE	DATE OF BOND	BONDSMAN & WITNESS
Brown,Henry x	Mary Hooper	12 May 1826	Abesolem x Hooper (w) Adam Corn
Brown,Henry	Margett An Vess	7 June 1862	J.H.Noland (w) ----------
Brown,Hugh x	Susanah Barnes (d.of Mary)	15 May 1830	Elihu x Coward (w) Wm.B.Queen
Brown,Hugh	Martha Caroline Plott (d.of Henry)	11 Aug. 1836	James x Land (w) Wm.Welch,clk.
Brown, Hugh (Jr)	Susanah Woodburn	13 Jan. 1831	John D.Brown (w) Wm.B.Queen
Brown,Jahue Chasteen (s.of Hugh,dec'd)	Lucinda Smith (d.of Thos)	24 Dec. 1868 M.28 Dec. 1868 By H.S.L.Moody,J.P.	(w) W.C.Brown,Reg. of I
Brown,James x	Mary Nelson	28 Nov. 1847	J(ohnathan) H.Woody (w) D.V.McCracken
Brown,James	Talitha Green	9 Jan. 1868 M.9 Jan. 1868 By F.M.Messer	(w) W.W.Medford,clk.
Brown,Jesse	Emoline Woods	13 Mar. 1854 M.13 Mar. 1854 By H.Rogers	John Noland (w) Wm.M.Rhea,clk.
Brown,Jesse F.	Jane Jones	19 Nov. 1848	Joshua C.Farmer (w) W.Brown
Brown,John	Margaret Eunis Potts (d.of Henry)	25 Nov. 1830	Jeremiah Vickers (w) ----------
Brown,Levi	Martha Caroline Trannwell (d.of John)	4 Nov. 1845	E.C.Chastine (w) ----------
Brown.Milton x	Kesiah Hooper (d.of Absolom)	----------	H(oloman) Battle (w) John B.Love
Brown,Mosses	Letty Green	16 Oct. 1840	W(illia)m Green (w) Wm.Welch
Brown, Phillip L.	Jane Henson	21 Jan. 1850	Jonathan D.Coward (w) S.W Gaston
Brow,Pinckney	Hannah Stewart	18 Sept. 1843	Joseph M.Cabe (w) ----------
Brown,R(obert)	Nercissa E.Green	19 Mar. 1845	D.V.McCracken (w) W.Brown
Brown,S.E.	M.E.Allison	10 Aug. 1858 M.---------- By Wm.P.Gillett	J C.Leatherwood (w) W W.Medford,clk.
Brown,Sampson	Naomi Wilson (d.of Robert)	22 Nov. 1821	Isreal Robison (w) Jos.Byers
Brown,Tho(ma)s	Elezabeth Welch (d.of Joseph)	10 Apr. 1822	Dillard Love (w) John B. Love
Brown,Thomas A.	Jane Parker	23 Aug. 1844	E(lf) G.Watson (w) ----------

GROOM	BRIDE	DATE OF BOND	BONDSMAN & WITNESS
Brown,Walter	Leuezor Dodson (d.of Daniel)	9 Jan. 1834	H.G.Woodfin (w) ----------
Brown,W(alter)	Nancy Shook (d.of David Shook)	21 Dec. 1837	William Allen (w) ----------
Brown,Will(m)(F)	Rachel Kilba (d.of Henry)	21 Jan. 1836	Elias Brendle (w) S.Fitzgerald,D.clk.
Brown,W(illiam) M.	Sarah R.Fish	17 Sept. 1865	J.M.Benners (w) ----------
Brown,Wilson	Matilda Noland	26 May 1857 M.26 May 1857 By Samuel Brown,J.P.	Samuel Brown (w) Wm.M.Rhea,clk.
Brownen,Lewis x	Elizabeth Vaughn	31 Dec. 1839	Jeremiah Vickers (w) ----------
Browning,Harvah	(Ado)line Swanger	6 May 1855 M.6 May 1855 By J.Vickers,J.P.	(w) Wm.M.Rhea,clk.
Browning,Wm.	Margret Oliver	23 Aug. 1855 M.---------- By J.F.Fincher,J.P.	J.F.Fincher (w) Wm.M.Rhea,clk.
Bruce,Herod	Polly Ann Arrington	8 July 1848	E.T(homson) x Nickle (w) W.Brown
Bryson,And(rew)	Peggy White (d.of Stephen)	1 May 1817	Dillard Love (w) ----------
Bryson,Daniel	Lucenda Jones (d.of Edward)	25 Sept. 1837	W(illia)m Allman (w) Wm.Welch
Bryson,George .x	Violet Inmon	13 May 1856 M.15 May 1856 By D.B.Ford	W.C.Blaylock (w) Wm.M.Rhea,clk.
Bryson,George x	Mary Ann Mahaffy	2 Sept. 1857 M.3 Sept. 1857 By H.P.Haynes,J.P.	John Messer (w) Wm.M.Rhea
Bryson,James (Jr.)	Anna Gross (d.of Thomas)	22 Dec. 1813	William Morrow (w) Ro.Love,clk.
Bryson,John	Mary Robinson	4 Apr. 1858 M.4 Apr. 1858 By D.B.Ford,J.P.	Jonathan x Woods (w) W.W.Medford,clk.
Bryson,John Jr. x	Peggy Ingram (d.of Colman)	8 Apr. 1816	Andrew x Ensley (w) Ro.Love,clk.
Bryson,Jno.C.	Rhoda Jane Davis	10 May 1846	J(oseph) Keener (w) ----------
Bryson,J(onathan)M.	Damaris Griffin (d.of John)	14 Mar. 1822	W(illia)m Berry (w) ----------
Bryson,Milton	Annie Duncon	26 Dec. 1850	D.G.Bryson (w) ----------
Bryson,Rob(er)t	Polly Cuningham (d.of George)	16 Dec. 1833	Jos(eph) Keener (w) Jos.Keener
Bryson,Saml.	Rebecca Caler	28 Dec. 1820	(w) John B.Love D.C.

GROOM	BRIDE	DATE OF BOND	BONDSMAN & WITNESS
Brvson Sam(uel) C.	Margart Francis	12 Dec. 1859 M.---------- By J.N.Benners,J.P.	W(illiam) Green (w) J.N.Benners
Bryson,Thos.J.	Susanah Berong (d.of Henry,Sr.)	6 Apr. 1839	S.B.Cathey (w) J.B.Allison
Bryson,W(illia)m F.	Medley Cunningham (d.of George)	31 Aug. 1821	Dillard Love (w) John B. Love
Buchanan,James Jr.	Jane Gribble	16 Nov. 1820	James Buchanan,Sr. (w) J.B.Love
Buchanan,William	Margaret Stiles (d.of John)	25 Mar. 1816	John x Stiles (w)Ro.Love,clk.
Buckhanan,M.M.	Candas E.Haynea (d.of Allen & Sousa)	6 Aug. 1868 M.6 Aug. 1868 By C.B.Mingus	(w) H.P.Haynes
Buff,Daniel x	Vianah Jones (d.of Charles)	2 May 1837	George Smith (w) ----------
Buff, James M.	Elizabeth Yarborough (d.of Elisha)	19 Dec. 1838	James N.Curry (w) Wm.Welch
Buff,John F.	Elizabeth Cogens	24 Nov. 1842	M.W.Smith (w) ----------
Buff,Martin	Nancey Lea (d.of Alford)	18 Sept. 1839	J(ohn) L.Smith (w) Wm.Welch
Bug,David	Mary McMillin (d.of Mary)	29 Dec. 1821	Elazer x Hogland (w) Wm.Welch
Bugg,H.T.	N.E.Williams	21 July 1865	J.P.Osborne (w) J.W.Killian,clk.
Bugg,Henry	Neomey Henderson	15 Sept. 1839	Joseph Cabe (w) Wm.Welch
Bugg,J.H.	H.J.Davis	5 Feb. 1868 M.6 Feb. 1868 By Joshue Inamn,J.P.	(w) W.W.Medford,clk.
Bumgarner,Ephram	Nancy Blanton	2 Mar. 1850	C(hristenbury) Blanton (w) R.A.Edmonston
Bumgarner,Hosey	Lucinda Bryson	4 Dec. 1848	J.C.Bryson (w) Allen Fisher
Burgess Richard Hugh (s.of Wilson)	Cordelia Jane Owens (d.of Adolphus)	18 Mar. 1869 M.18 Mar. 1869 By E.L.Shelton,J.P.	(w) W.C.Brown,R.D.H.C.
Burnett,A.J.	Miley Roxaner Henson	5 May 1859 M.5 May 1859 By A.J.Long,J.P.	David x Mann (w) W.W.Medford
Burnett,James M.	----------	7 Jan. 1861	F.M.Miller (w) W.W.Medford,clk.
Burn(e)tt,John G.	Mary Pless	21 July 1852 M.25 July 1852 By A.C.Hartgroves,J.P.	John F.Long (w) C.T.Rogers,D.C.

GROOM	BRIDE	DATE OF BOND	BONDSMAN & WITNESS
Burnes,James x	Mary Hall	11 Oct. 1865	L.W.Hall (w) J.W.Killian
Burns,Sam(ue)l	Elisabeth Welch (d.of William Sr.)	15 Jan. 1817	John Leatherwood (w) ----------
Burns,Uriah	Peggy Hide (d.of John)	17 Jan. 1814	Joseph Chambers (w) Ro.Love,clk.
Butler,Moses (Col) (s.of Harrison Butler)	Minda McCracken (Col) (d.of Hagar McCracken)	12 Jan. 1870 M.13 Janl 1870 By G.W.McCracken,J.P.	(w) W.C.Brown, R.D.H.C.
Byers,David McS.	Mary Caroline Henry	16 Oct. 1847	J(ohn) J.Jones (w)----------
Byers,Ephrain	Mily Ratcliff (d.of Abraham)	14 Nov. 1830	W(illia)m Sittan (w) ----------
Byers,Francis	Sarah Medford (d.of Jonas)	10 Sept. 1835	Wrily Medford (w) S.Fitzgerald,clk.
Byers,Samuel E.	Emelia McCracking (d.of Joseph)	25 Feb. 1833	P.W.Edwards (w) ----------
Cabe,Emanuel	Elizath C.Haynes	28 Oct. 1865	J.N.Benners (w) J.W.Killian,clk.
Cabe,Joseph M.	Sarah J.Howard	28 June 1853 M.---------- By Issac Clark,J.P.	J.L.Smith (w) W.Brown,D.C.
Cabe,Joseph M.	Manervey Curtice	15 Mar. 1860	Wm.W.Battle (w) W.W.Medford
Cagdale,George W.x	Sarrah Long (d.of William)	9 Feb. 1837	J(ohn) S.Long (w) ----------
Cagdale,Jackson x	Dicy J.Hunacutt (d.of Joseph)	2 Mar. 1837	Charles Long (w) ----------
Cagel,George	Syntha C.James	24 Sept. 1844	David x Messer (w) W.Brown
Cagel,W(illia)m	Escna Moore	8 Feb. 1848	James x Collwell,Jr. (w) W.Brown
Cagle,Calv(i)n	Pricilla H.Cagle	10 Nov 1865	Henry Cagle (w) J W.Killian,clk.
Cagle,H.W.	W.E.Owen	28 Mar. 1855 M.5 Apr. 1855 By J.A.McClure,J.P.	J(ohn) J.Cagle (w) Wm.M.Rhea,clk.
Cagle,Henry	Nancy Demsy	14 July 1858 M.-- July 1858 By Wm.P.Gillett,J.P.	E.H.Cagle (w) David Howell,D.C.
Cagle,Jacob	Alafar Parker	20 May 1837	Jeremiah Vickers (w) Wm.Welch
Cagle,Jacob	Martha J.Calwell	28 Aug. 1854 M.29 Aug. 1854 By J.A.McClure,J.P.	J.J Cagle (w) W.M.Rhea,clk.
Cagle,John	Lucinda Owen	11 Oct. 1855 M.---------- By P.Gillett,J.P.H.C.	L.C.Coaldwell (w) J.Vickers

GROOM	BRIDE	DATE OF BOND	BONDSMAN & WITNESS
Cagle,John Sr.	Catherine Halcombe	8 Nov. 1869 M.8 Nov. 1869 By J.H.Moody,J.P.	(w) W.C.Brown,R.D.H.C.
Cagle,Joseph	Easter Dotson	13 Apr. 1861	Riley x James (w) W.W.Medford
Cagle,Jos. C.	Mila J.Holyfield	26 Dec. 1856 M.28 Dec. 1856 By (illegible)	George x Carson (w) Wm.M.Rhea,clk.
Caldwell,James	Minervia Beach	16 Mar. 1845	E.S.Howell (w) ----------
Caldwell,Ja(me)s	Martha J.Byers	27 Jan. 1853 M.---------- By H.P.Haynes,J.P.	L(awson) C(ald)well J.Keener,clk.
Caldwell,James	Elizabeth Lacky	16 June 1858 M.---------- By C.Nelson,J.P.	(w) David Howell
Caldwell,Lawson	Addeline Owen	25 Mar. 1846	Ja(me)s Calswell (w) ----------
Caldwell,Lawson Jr.	Jane Hall	3 Feb. 1860	J.A.Caldwell (w) J C.Leatherwood
Caldwell,Reuben A.	Nicey Evans	7 Oct. 1854 M.11 Oct. 1854 By Wm.P.Gillett,J.P.	(w) Wm.M.Rhea,clk.
Caldwell,Thos.Jr.x	Rany Ball	6 Mar. 1857 M.10 Mar. 1857 By W.G.B.Garrett,J.P.	Thos.x Caldwell,Sr. (w) C.T.Rogers,D.clk.
Caldwell,W(illia)m	Nancy Black (d.of William)	22 Sept. 1810	John Battle (w) ----------
Caler,George F.	Rebecca Mahaffy (d.of William)	2 Jan. 1821	Saml. x Bryson (w) John B.Love
Calwell,Daniel x	Lucenda Roberts	1 July 1850	Henry Barns (w) S.W.Gaston,clk.
Calwell,James H.	Easter Ownens	15 Feb. 1860 M.27 Mar. 1860 By Wm.P.Gillett,J.P.	L.L.Calwell (w) J.C.Leatherwood
Camp,J.C.	Viana Morgan	15 May 1861	K.V.Rhinehardt (w) W.W.Medford
Campbell,J(ames)M.	Elizabeth Carroll (d.of John)	1 Dec. 1843	S(amuel) Sherrill (w) J.Keener
Campbell,W.A.	Martha J.Plott	4 Nov. 1863	Saml.L.Love (w) H.P.Haynes
Campbell,W(illia)m A.	Margaret Jane Bird	20 Mar. 1851 M.20 Mar. 1851 By B.turner,M.G.	J(ames) W.Terrell (w) Wm.Johnston
Canup,Jacob x	Margaret Moore	3 Oct. 1829	Wilam Caldwell (w) Ro.Love
Carrell,James	Mitilda Gibbs (d.of Hugh)	19 Aug. 1839	John S.Gipson (w) Samuel Gibson

GROOM	BRIDE	DATE OF BOND	BONDSMAN & WITNESS
Carson,Elias	Sary Ann Beaty	21 Oct. 1846	N.A.Beaty (w) W. Brown
Carson,James T.	Charlott Henson	21 Dec. 1851 M.21 Dec. 1851 By Wm.McClure,J.P.	Elias Carson (w) J.Keener clk.
Carson, Mathaw	Rody Rose (d.of Samuel)	16 Sept. 1812	John Stevenson (w) John Love,clk.
Carson,Matthew x	Elizabeth Coward	1 Apr. 1828	Jonathan Coward (Sr) (w) ----------
Carson,Shadr(a)ch	Polly Turner (d.of Nancey)	2 Mar. 1826	W(illia)m Welch (w) ----------
Carson,Willaim	Liddy Crawford (d.of Samuel)	17 June 1822	James Crawford (w) John B. Love
Carter,John	Nancy Runions	25 Oct. 1823	Israel Robeson (w) Ro.Love
Carter,Ross x	Olive Queen (d.of William)	26 Dec. 1832	Maxwell Queen (w) J.R.Love
Carter,Wilson	Jane Cantrell (d.of Moses)	-- Aug. 1816	William Welch (w) ----------
Carver,A.B.	Mary Cagle	23 Dec. 1854 M.24 Dec. 1854 By J.A.McClure,J.P.	W. Green (w) H.Rogers
Carver,David x	Orpha Hannah (d.of Alexander)	10 Mar. 1824	Jerimiah x Green (w) Wm.Welch
Carver,David x	Mahala Cooper (d.of Benjamin,dec.)	23 Feb. 1836	Lind Cooper (w) S.Fitzgerald,D.C.
Carver,Ewuel (s.of David)	Minty Roughf	9 Apr. 1845	Consent signed by David Carder (w) Robert Penland
Carver,George x	Elizabeth Cagle	23 Aug. 1856 M.14 Aug. 1856 ? By W.G.B.Garrett,J.P.	A.B.Carver
Carver,Gils x	Katharine Price	31 July 1847	Yewel P. x Carver (w) D.V.McCracken
Carver,Gils x	Mary Green	7 Feb. 1848	D.N. x Green (w) D.V.McCracken
Carver,Isral x	Marey Bradley (d.of Isac)	19 Aug. 1839	Isac x Bradley (w) Samuel Gibson
Carver, J.A.	P.E.Ruff	25 Jan. 1859 M.25 Jan. 1859 By H.Rogers, J.P.	(w) W.W.Medford,clk.
Carver,Yewel x	Kisiah A.Ruff	5 Apr. 1845	G.L.T. x Ruff (w) D.V.McCracken
Casey,Leander(Col)	Caroline Welch(Col) (d.of Joseph)	27 Nov. 1869 M. 7 Dec. 1869 By M.H.Love,J.P.	(w) W.C.Brown,R.D.H.C.
Cathey,Andrew	Mary Deaver	11 June 1828	R(euben) Deaver (w) ----------

GROOM	BRIDE	DATE OF BOND	BONDSMAN & WITNESS
Cathey,Andrew	Maria Ellison (d.of Benjamin)	31 Dec. 1833	(Wm.Cathey) (w) J.L.Chambers,clk.
Cathey,G(eorge) B.	Easter M.Worley	2 Mar. 1854 M.2 Mar. 1854 By A.C.Hartgrove,J.P.	G.W.Cathey (w) W.Brown,D.C.
Cathey,George W.	Mary C.Hartgrove	7 Jan. 1852 M.10 Jan. 1852 By A.J.Murray,J.P.	J(ohn) C.Hartgrove (w) A.C.Hartgrove
Cathey,J.L.	L.L.Hyatt	5 Aug. 1855 M.5 Aug. 1855 By A.C.Hartgrove	A.J.Long (w) Wm.M.Rgea,clk.
Cathey,James N.	Elizabeth Brown	30 Dec. 1844	Jabal F.P(a)rker (w) E.C.Chastain
Cathey,Joseph	Hannah Posey (d.of Humphrey)	7 Apr. 1815	John McClure (w) ----------
Cathey,J(oseph)	Nancy Hyatt	21 Mar. 1825	Joseph Dever (w) James R.Love,D.P.C.
Cathey,J(oseph) T.	Martha A.J.Killian	2 Mar. 1858 M.2 Mar. 1858 By Wm.Groves,M.G.	J(ohn) G.Osborne (w) W.W.Medford,clk.
Cathey,S(aml) B.	Mary Parker	8 Oct. 1840	J(ohn) S.Long (w) Wm.Welch,clk.
Cathey,William x	Hannah Dyer	10 Sept. 1825	Andrew Cathey (w) Reuban Dever
Cathey,W(illia)m B.	Leucinda Moore	12 Sept. 1846	J.Mills Shook (w) ----------
Chambers,Asa x	Elizabeth Vest	28 Aug. 1852 M.29 Aug. 1852 By J.F.Fincher,J.P.	J.M. x Chambers (w) J.Keener
Chambers,Elihu(Jr.)	Lydia Ratcliff (d.of Abraham)	28 Mar. 1824	J(oseph) Cathey (w) ----------
Chambers,J.H.	Adaline Allen	28 Dec. 1859 M.29 Dec. 1859 By R.E.Medford,J.P.	J.F.Murry (w) Wm.McClure
Chambers,James	Polly Buff (d.of Martin)	5 Apr. 1823	Samuel x Cabe (w) James R.Love
Chambers,J(esse)M.	Margaret Woods (d.of Martin)	24 Oct. 1829	W(illiam) Moody (w) N.G.Howell
Chambers,John	Rhiney Oneal	9 May 1825	Kedar Boone (w) R.Love
Chambers,John M.	Nancy Sorrells	1 Dec. 1849	John M.Queen (w) S.W.Gaston
Chambers,Jonathan	Elizabeth Moody	16 Jan. 1825	J(ohn) W.Henry (w) R.Love
Chambers, Joseph	Elizabeth Smathers (d.of Henry)	13 July 1824	N(inian) Edmonston (w) ----------

13

GROOM	BRIDE	DATE OF BOND	BONDSMAN & WITNESS
Chambers,Joseph(Jr.)	Winnei Owen	28 Jan. 1828	Barney Martin J(esse) H.Moody (w) K.Boone
Chambers,Lewis	Maryann Medford	23 Mar. 1841	J(ohn) N.McGee (w) ----------
Chambers,Martin x	Elizabeth Lowe	11 Sept. 1852 M.12 Sept. 1852 By J.L.Stephenson,M.G.	Abram x West (w) Joseph Keener,clk.
Chambers,Samuel	Sofia Hill	19 Nov. 1859 M.20 Nov. 1859 By R.E.Medford,J.P.	J.N.Ratcliff (w) W.W.Medford,clk.
Chambers,William	Jensy Hughes (d.of Saml)	17 Dec. 1817	Joseph Chambers (w) ----------
Chamder,Ja(me)s S.	Mary Steward (d.of Noah)	4 Nov. 1835	Lewis S.Deaver (w) S.Fitzgerrald,D.C.
Chastain,Benjamin	Nancy Hooper (d.of Absolem)	17 Nov. 1812	David Carson (w) Ro.Love,clk.
Chastain,John	Nancy Weatherrow	14 Dec. 1820	(w) John B.Love,clk.
Chastain,John x	Drusey Barns (d.of George)	5 Mar. 1832	Harmon Queen (w) ----------
Chastain,William x	Elizabeth Coward (d.of James)	12 Nov. 1848	J(ohnathan) D.Coward (w) A.Bumgarner,J.P.
Chasteen,Jas. x	Jane Carson (d.of David)	29 Nov. 1819	Elijah x Denton (w) ----------
Christopher,Devalt x	Malinda Holland	7 Jan. 1843	David x Layfan (w) W.Brown,clk.
Christopher,Davalt x	Elizabeth Hall	24 Aug. 1843	Jeremiah Vickers (w) ----------
Christopher,Davault x	Betsy Ann Hollen	15 Jan. 1837	John x Sellers,Jr. (w) S.Fitzgerrald
Christopher,Ephraim x	Mary Sellers	28 May 1842	John x Sellers (w) W.Brown
Christopher,J(oseph)	Jane Moore	10 Feb. 1849	Noah Rhodeamer (w) ----------
Christopher,McDonel	Margret Christopher	1 May 1864	J.M.Henderson (w) J.A.Hayaman
Cisk,James Graham (s.of Mertin & Neoma)	Fanny Elizabeth Inman (d.of Anderson & Mary)	1 May 1869 M.2 May 1869 By John C. Evans,M.G.	(w) W.C.Brown,R.D.H.C.
Cittchens,John	Elizabeth Hooper	7 Dec. 1847	Jon.A.Hooper (w) Jno.C.Bryson,J.P.
Clark,A.S.	Jane Russell	30 Apr. 1855 M. 3 May 1855 By H.Rogers,J.P.	(w) Wm.M.Rhea,clk.
Clark,Alford	Cassia McMillins (d.of Polly)	18 Jan. 1822	William Clark,(Jr.) (w) Ro.Love,clk.

14

GROOM	BRIDE	DATE OF BOND	BONDSMAN & WITNESS
Clark,C.R.	N.A.Haynes	31 July 1868 M. 6 Aug. 1868 By C.B.Mungus	(w) W.W.Medford,clk.
Clark,Carson	Huldy Noland	28 Aug. 1854 M. 28 Aug. 1854 By H.Rogers,J.P.	W(m) Green (w) Wm.M.Rhea,clk.
Clark,Dales P.	Rachel J.Ferguson	12 Apr. 1868 M.12 Apr. 1868 By G.W.McCracken,J.P.	(w) G.S.Ferguson,D.clk.
Clark, George M.	Mary Jane Murray	14 July 1862	(w) A.L.Herren,D.C.
Clark,H.F.	Leeanor Henson	9 Feb. 1850	Andrew Ferguson (w) S.W.Gaston,clk.
Clark,H(enry)L.	Martha Ann Shook	10 Sept. 1843	H(umphrey)P. Haynes (w) Wm.Welch
Clark,Henry L.	Mahala Roberson	20 Oct. 1869 M.21 Oct. 1869 By J.H.Massey	(w) W.C.Brown,R.D.H.C.
Clark,Hiram	Susanah Haynes	4 Nov. 1844	H.P.Haynes (w) ----------
Clark,Isaac x	Elizabeth Roberson	19 Dec. 1843	J.P.Roberson
Clark,Isaac (C)	Lutica Roads	7 Feb 1856 M. 10 Feb. 1856 By R.W.Patty,M.G.	Isaac Clark (w) Wm.M.Rhea,clk.
Clark,Isaac R.	Elizabeth Phillips	5 Aug. 1842	William Robinson (w) W.Brown
Clark,I(saac)R.	Catherine Renno	18 Apr. 1862	B.Best (w) A.L.Herron,D.C.
Clark,James A.	Eliza L.Killian	26 Jan. 1857 M.27 Jan. 1857 By J.Hood,M.G.	W.B.G.Garrett (w) Wm.M.Rhea,clk.
Clark,John H. x	Polly Hood (d.of Allen)	7 May 1832	Tipton Ford (w) ----------
Clark,R.M.	Mary Harbin	27 Aug. 1864	W.H.Clark (w) H.P.Haynes,J.P.
Clark,Richard	Sarah Robison (d.of Isaac)	13 Aug. 1824	William Robison (w) Wm.Welch
Clark,Robert	Cassy Gunter (d.of William)	25 May 1819	J(oseph) H.Walker (w) ----------
Clark,Robert	Margaret Stiles (d.of William)	30 Dec. 1824	Moses Clark (w) Wm.Welch
Clark,S.	E.C.Hall	3 Mar. 1860	W.G.B.Boyd (w) W.W.Medford,clk.
Clark,William Scot	Rachal Stiles (d.of Wm.)	2 Jan. 1822	Henry Clark (w) Ro.Love,clk.
Clarke,Moses	Hanah Robison	25 May 1818	Henry Clark (w) Ro.Love,clk.

GROOM	BRIDE	DATE OF BOND	BONDSMAN & WITNESS
Clayton,G(orge) W.	Arta Elvira Bryson (d.of Daniel)	9 Jan. 1840	J.S.Long (w) J.Keener
Cleaman,Billey	Sary Miller (d.of Samuel Rose)	21 Nov. 1812	Joseph Lusk (w) John Love,clk.
Cleav(an) Robert H.	Haret Cooper (d.of William)	23 Feb. 1839	James M.Battle (w) Samuel Gibson
Cline,G.W.	Nercisa Neweton	4 Jan. 1852 M.4 Feb. 1852 ? By Samuel Gibson	J.A.Cline (w) Samuel Gibson,D.C.
Cline, Jacob	Elizabeth Messor (d.of Solomon)	3 Feb. 1823	G(eorge) McCracken(Sr.) (w) John B.Love,clk.
Cline,Lawson H. x	Rebicca Mingus (d.of George)	16 Sept. 1839	L(awson) H.xLemons (w) J.Kinon Jesup
Clonts,John	Melvina Henderson	26 Sept. 1865 M.28 Sept. 1867 By C.B.Mingus	R(obert) P.Fowler ?(w) J.W.Killian
Clonts,William x	Elizabeth Wells	25 Mar. 1851 M.25 Mar. 1851 By John Killian,J.P.	James x Hill (w) J.Keener,clk.
Clonts,William R(iley)	Jane Smathers	19 Aug. 1865	F(rancis) M.Cook (w) ----------
Cobb,Alfred	Charlotte Henson (d.of Daniel)	11 Jan. 1830	E(lijah) Deaver (w) ----------
Coggins,Alfred x	G racy Nowland	17 Dec. 1842	M(athew) J.Coman (w) W.Brown
Coggins,Jonathan L.	Elizabeth King (d.of James)	31 July 1834	Richard Cox (w) S.Fitzgerrald
Coggins,Zadok	Sarah Griffith	9 Apr. 1843	Jas.B. x Tritt (w) W.Brown
C(o)l(d)well,John	Susanah Woods (d.of Lawrance)	11 Oct. 1839	L.D.x Brady (w) Wm.Welch
Coldwell, John x	Mary Loe	22 Sept. 1841	Thomas x Coldwell (w) Wm.Welch
Cole,G.W.	M.M.Johnston	26 Feb. 1857 M.26 Feb. 1857 By A.M.Russell,J.P.	G.W.Palmer (w) Wm.M.Rhea,clk.
Coleman,Mark	Nancy Welch (d.of Andrew)	25 May 1816	George Colman (w) Ro.Love
Collet,Nassaw (Col)	Ida Boyd (Col)	5 Dec. 1868 M.6 Dec. 1868 By Joshua Kinsland,J.P.	W.C.Brown,R.D.H.C.
Collins,Eli x	Rachiel Reece	24 Oct. 1845	John Chandler (w) ----------
Collins,Isaac	Lusinda Massay	2 Oct. 1858 M.---------- By N.Francis,J.P.	Saml. x Massay (w) W.W.Medford clk.

16

GROOM	BRIDE	DATE OF BOND	BONDSMAN & WITNESS
Collins,J(oseph) H.	Sarah Sherrill (d.of George)	5 Dec. 1843	S(aml) Sherrill (w) J.Keener
Colvert,Jefferson x	Ann Gribble	8 Dec. 1827	W(illia)m Welch (w) Wm.Welch
Colwell,Alfred	Elizabeth Hall	12 Sept. 1857 M.13 Sept. 1857 By C.Nelson,J.P.	(w) Wm.M.Rhea,clk.
Colwell,H.E.	Elmina Beech	9 Mar. 1858 M. ---------- By C.Nelson,J.P.	R.A.Colwell (w) W.W.Medford,clk.
Colwell,James Jr. x	M.A.Roler	16 Dec. 1847	James x Colwell,Sr. (w) D.V.McCracken
Colwell,John	Lusinda Cagle	31 Dec. 1859 M.---------- By Wm.P.Gillett,J.P.	J.H.Colwell (w) W.W.Medford,clk.
Colwell,Lawson	Emeline Howell	16 Jan. 1845	James x Colwell (w) W.Brown
Colwell,Samuel	Eady C.Colwell	23 Aug. 1851 M.---------- By Colverd Nelson,J.P.	(w) J.Keener clk.
Colwell,Thomas x	Angelline Noland	6 Jan. 1855	Thomas Milner (w) Wm.M.Rhea,clk.
Coman,M(atthaw) J.	Elizabeth Ann Fulbright	14 May 1846	J(ohn) L(ouis) Smith (w) ----------
Conley,S(amuel) W.	Mary E.Cooper	21 Oct. 1841	J(ohn) N.Shook (w) W.Brown
Conley,W(illu)m	Alisabeth Cockarham (d.of Willum)	29 July 1838	John Gibbs (w) Samuel Gibson
Conly,John W.	Levicey A.Shook (d.of Peter)	3 Oct. 1837	J.B.Sherrill (w) Wm.Welch
Connelly,John	Mary Sherrell (d.of Samuel)	28 Sept. 1824	Nath(an)l Blackburn (w) ----------
Conner,Bush (R)	Masey Coner (d.of Samuel)	23 July 1832	Samuel Conner (w) Samuel Gibson,J.P.
Cook,Abraham F.x	Lovina Price	21 Jan. 1846	Henry A.Curry (w) Wm.Welch
Cook,Charles	Polly Wooddy (d.of William)	21 Jan. 1824	Abramham Pence (w) Wm.Welch
Cook,Dan(ie)l J.	Harriet E.Colwell	24 July 1854 M.25 July 1854 By Wm.P.Gillett,J.P.	James Williamson (w) George Williamson
Cook,George x	Mary Ann Smathers	5 Aug. 1853 M.21 Aug. 1853 By A.C.Hartgrove,J.P.	Manson Smathers (w) S.E.Byers,clk.
Cook,Isaiah	Sarah E.Poteet (d.of John)	5 Feb. 1824	W(illiam) P.Poteet (w) Wm.Welch

GROOM	BRIDE	DATE OF BOND	BONDSMAN & WITNESS
Cook,J(ames) R.	Matilda C.Beasly	12 June 1858 M.20 June 1858 By J.J.Sparks,Elder	D(aniel) J.Cook (w) Geo.Williamson
Coonrod,George W. x	Chaney Williams	4 Nov. 1844	William x Price (w) W.Brown
Coonrod,James x	Elizabeth Finey	30 Mar. 1858 M.--------- By C.Nelson,J.P.	Joseph x Finey (w) W.W.Medford,clk.
Coonrod,Jno. x	Adoline Finney	23 May 1855 M.-- --- 1855 By Wm.P.Gillett,J.P.	John x Franklin (w) Wm.M.Rhea,clk.
Cooper,J.W.	Emela Henry	4 Nov. 1857 M.4 Nov. 1857 By J.Vickers,J.P.	M.C.Cooper (w) W.W.Medford,clk.
Cooper,Lind x	Wyney Smith (d.of Mat Brown)	22 Aug. 1835	J(ohn) P.Cooper (w) S.Fitzgerrald
Cooper,Lock x	Mary Snider (d.of Adam)	28 Apr. 1832	Peter x Snider (w) Ro.Love,clk.
Cooper,Robison x	Clarissa Massey	6 Oct. 1827	James Inman (w) R.Love,clk.
Cooper,Senton B.	Sarah Ray (d.of Haniah)	9 Jan. 1834	W(m) W.Battle (w) S.Fitzgerrald
Cooper,Thomas	Fanny Dever	9 Aug. 1827	Rob(er)t B.Hyatt (w) Reuben Dever
Cooper,William x	Peggy Snider (d.of Adam)	30 June 1824	N(inian) Edmonston (w) ----------
Cooper,Gorge	Kathrine Shook (d.of Jacob)	26 Mar. 1821	Montgom(er)y Bell (w) Ro.Love
Cope,Andrew	Ann Chambers (widow of J.Chambers)	2 Oct. 1837	J(ohn) L.Dilliard (w) ----------
Cope,Philip x	Temperance Underwood	25 Jan. 1839	George x Long (w) J.Keener,clk.
Copelen,Thomas Dr.	Mary A.Smith Dunken	20 Feb. 1852 M.21 Feb. 1852 By Colward Nelson,J.P.	(w) J.Keener,clk.
Corbin,John x	Nancy McClure	26 Apr. 1825	James McClure (w) R. Dever
Cornwell,Eli x	Massy Stillwell (d.of Jeremiah,dec'd)	20 Aug. 1816	Chap Langford (w) Dillard Love
Cornwell,Jesse	Rachel Cresp (d.of John Franch Hawser)	26 Sept. 1836	W(illia)m Welch (w) Samuel Gibson,J.P.
Coster,Frederick x	Margaret Coster (d.of William)	10 Sept. 1834	Thomas x Coster (w) Jos.Keener
Coward,Benjamin x	Nelley Fisher	27 Dec. 1843	James M.Hooper (w) A.D.Hooper
Coward,James	Clowy Denton (d.of Saml)	3 Jan. 1825	Saml.x Denton (w) ----------

GROOM	BRIDE	DATE OF BOND	BONDSMAN & WITNESS
Cox, Elijah	Betsey Gibson	-- Mar. 1826	Joseph x Gibson (w) ----------
Craigo,Robt.J.	Lydia Ables	2 Sept. 1826	Ja(me)s R.Love (w) Reuben Dever
Crawford,Amos A.	Mary M.Inman	25 Feb. 1855 M.25 Feb. 1855 By A.C.Hartgrove,J.P.	(w) Wm.M.Rhea,clk.
Crawford,Francis x	Elezebeth Land (d.of Widow Land)	11 Dec. 1834	G.W.Crawford (w) S.Fitzgerrald,clk.
Crawford,James	Ann Mercer (d.of Solomon)	5 Mar. 1823	H(oliman) Battle (w) ----------
Craw(f)o(r)d,James	Adaline Howell	17 Apr. 1850	C.C.Rogers (w) S.W.Gaston
Crawford,John	Elvira Henson (d.of Thomas)	30 Oct. 1845	Philip Henson (w) ----------
Crawford,John J.	Sarah Reece	7 Dec. 1851 M.7 Dec. 1851 By A.C.Hartgrove,J.P.	A.C.Hartgrove (w) J.Keener,clk.
Crawford,Joseph A.	Polly Ensley	16 June 1852	James R.Crawford (w) J.Keener,clk.
Crawford,Josiah x	Chery McCrackins (d.of Joseph)	9 Jan. 1815	Enos McHenry (w) Ro.Love,clk.
Crawford,Samuel M.	Mary Land	1 Apr. 1838	George L.Cunningham (w) J.Keener
Crawford,Thomas M.	Rachel C.Reece	17 Nov. 1855 M.18 Nov. 1855 By J.Inman,J.P.	Joshua Inman (w) J.W.Benners
Crawford,Willson x	Rachail Elizabeth Farmer (d.of James)	26 Feb. 1846	P(hilip) Henson (w) J.Keener
Creasman,John x	Morning Reddeck (d.of Wm.Ingram)	24 Sept. 1823	Russel x Miniday (w) ----------
Crisp,Alexander x	Polly Thompson (d.of Nathan)	11 Aug. 1820	Jacob x Shular (w)John B.Love
Crisp,Willum x	Nancy Caringer (d.of Danal)	24 Aug. 1837	Menas x Morgin Isaac Caringer (w) Samuel Gibson
Crye,William	Elizabeth Barker (d.of Shedrick)	10 Aug. 1822	Edmond x Barker (w) John B.Love
Crymes,W(illia)m	M.S.C.Turner	29 Dec. 1851 M.30 Dec. 1851 By Wm.Haynes,M.G.	(E.B.Herren) J.Keener (w) J.Keener,clk.
Cumming,Paxton	Priscilia E. Davidson	26 Dec. 1827	J(oseph) H.Walker (w) ----------
Cuningham,G.L.	Mary Shook	10 Feb. 1856? M.10 Jan. 1856? By W.Brown,J.P.	W(alter) Brown (w) Wm.M.Rhea,clk.

GROOM	BRIDE	DATE OF BOND	BONDSMAN & WITNESS
Cuningham,George x	Peggy Hughes	----------	Nathan Hyatt (w) R.Love
Cuningham,J.K.	Jane Medford	28 Nov. 1865	G.L.Cuningham (w) J.W.Killian,clk.
Cuningham,Lewis	Hannah Allen	15 Apr. 1845	J(ames) J.Allen (w) W.Brown
Cunningham,John x	Lucinda McMahan	2 Oct. 1845	Hiram Gunter x (w) J.Keener
Curry,John C.	Martha P.Welch	4 July 1851 M.11 Dec. 1851 By W.I.Davis,J.P.	John Turpin (w) J.Keener,clk.
Curtis,John	Mary M.Smathers	18 Oct. 1845	John C. Smathers (w) ----------
Dalrymple,Thomas	Mary Couch (d.of Thos.Milsaps.)	28 June 1820	Edward x Ferrington (w) Ro.Love clk.
Danel,William C.	Ricey Hannh ?	22 July 1865	Ricey F.Hannh ? (w) ----------
Daniels,William x	Rhoda L.Colwell	3 Dec. 1844	William x Colwell (w) W.Brown
Darnel,John	Tilletha Yarborow	10 Jan. 1844	Tho(mas) McLure (w) W.Brown
Darnell,Greenbery	Lucinda Davis	25 Oct. 1867 M.25 Oct. 1867 By A.L.Herren,J.P.	(w) W.W.Medford,clk.
Daugharty,Lemuel	Emely Gambrel	30 Dec. 1856 M.30 Dec. 1856 By R.H.Moody	E.V.Plott (w) Wm.M.Rhea,C.C.C.
Davidson,A.T.	Elizabeth A.Howell	12 Oct. 1842	J.G.Gudger (w) ----------
Davidson,H(ugh) H.	Lucinda E.Moody	27 Oct. 1840	J.R.Love (w) Wm.Welch
Davis,Andrew J(ackson)	Margaret Hyatt	15 Apr. 1860	W.A.Davis (w) W.W.Medford
D(a)vis,Asbery	Margret Campbell (d.of Allen)	15 Apr. 1858	Charles x Davis (w) Wm.Welch
Davis,F.M.	Angeline Fergason	18 Oct. 1847	J(ohn) N.McGee (w) ----------
Davis,Isham M.	Milly Allen	24 Dec. 1850	N.T.Hyatt (w) J.Keener
Davis,J.B.	Caroline Henson	1 Jan. 1861	Wm.D.Pearson (w) W.W.Medford,clk.
Davis,J.H.	Sarah Palmer	28 Sept. 1867 M.29 Sept. 1867 By S.J.Shelton,J.P.	(w) W.W.Medford,clk.

GROOM	BRIDE	DATE OF BOND	BONDSMAN & WITNESS
Davis,Jacob R.	Elisabeth Cathey	30 Dec. 1854 M.30 Dec. 1854 By J.Inman,J.P.	(w) Wm.M.Rhea,clk.
Davis,John	Nancy Gunter	23 Feb. 1843	Solomon Messer (w) Samuel Gibson
Davis,John	Mary Russel	19 Sept. 1850	C.T.Rogers (w) S.W.Gaston
Davis,John S. x	Mary Ann Elliot (d.of Lakey)	1 Feb. 1840	John x Cunningham (w) J.Keener
Davis,Joseph M.	Matilda Henson	5 Mar. 1849	Willis C. x Blaylock (w) W.Brown
Davis,Joseph Scott	Julia Ann Inmon	23 Dec. 1867 M.23 Dec. 1867 By H.G.Franklin,J.P.	(w) W.W.Medford,clk.
Davis,L.Monterville (s.of T.W.)	Mary Elizabeth Hawkins (d.of B.F. & M.A.)	13 Sept. 1869 M.----------	(w) W.C.Brown,R.D.H.C. By John Turpin,J.P.
Davis,Madison x	Ann Crawford (d.of Josiah)	21 Apr. 1838	Stanford x Bradley (w) Wm.Welch
Davis,P.L.	Margaret L.Davis	1 Apr. 1850	S.P.C.Patton (w) Allen Fisher,J.P.
Davis,Phillip x	Peggy McGee (d.of John)	30 Oct. 1834	W(illia)m Noalen (w) Wm.Welch
Davis,Phillip	Mary J.Vess	31 May 1863	William Rathbone (w) ----------
Davis,Samuel x	Sarah Presley (d.of William)	23 Oct. 1838	John x Sellers,Jr. (w) Wm.Welch
Davis,T.W.	Catherine Shook	11 May 1857 M.11 May 1857 By W.G.B.Garrett,J.P.	(w) Wm.M.Rhea,clk.
Davis,Thomas x	Caly Stiles (d.of Benjamin)	18 Dec. 1816	Thomas Davis (w) ----------
Davis,Thomas	Elizebeth Freemun	18 Jan. 1825	Thomas x Calwell (w) R. Dever
Davis,William	Rachal Massey	17 ---- 181-	Thomas x Stiles (w) ----------
Davis, Wm.A.	Elizabeth Snider	21 Feb. 1854 M.21 Feb. 1854 By Wm.McClure,J.P.	Daniel Winchester (w) W.Brown,D.C.
Davis,Willum x	Jane Gibson	22 Jan. 1841	Adam Snider Solomon x Gibson (w) Samuel Gibson,D.C.
Davis,Wilson	Hannah Campbell	1 Apr. 1843	W(illia)m Haynes (w) ----------
Dawson,Berry	Kesiah Ledbetter (d.of Matthew)	26 Nov. 1824	Jessee Underwood (w) Jno.B.Love

GROOM	BRIDE	DATE OF BOND	BONDSMAN & WITNESS
Deaver,Eligah	Arminta Kilpatrick	23 May 1846	Rufus Edmonston (w) ----------
Deaver,Gabriel	Rebecca Cathey (d.of Sarah)	17 Mar. 1832	John R.Cooper (w) ----------
Deaver,Jasper	Susaan Cooper	7 Dec. 1857 M.7 Dec. 1857 By A.C.Hartgrove,J.P.	J(oseph) J.Sorrells (w) W.W.Medford,clk.
Deaver,Joseph	Mary Mehaffy (d.of Wm.)	29 May 1834	E(benezer) McLeod (w) S.Fitzgerrald
Deaver,L(ewi)s	Mary Chandler (d.of Tunstill)	10 Aug. 1831	Ja(me)s S.Chandler (w) Ro.Love,clk.
Deaver,R.A.	Mary Hawkins	21 Oct. 1851 M.23 Oct. 1851 By A.J.Murry,J.P.	W(illia)m A.Davis (w) C.T.Rogers,D.C.
Deaver,R.L.	N.C.Henson	21 Dec. 1865	T.B.Deaver (w) J.W.Killian,clk.
Dell, (Dill)Bartlett	Nelly Parres	9 July 1841	J(ohn) L.Smith (w) Wm.Welch
Demory,Thomas (Col) (s.of Thomas)	Martha Welch(Col) (d.of Alfred)	27 Dec. 1869 M.27 Dec. 1869 By M.H.Love,J.P.	(w) W.C.Brown,R.D.H.C.
Denton,Elijah x	Jane Coward (d.of Johnathan)	11 Feb. 1820	Samuel x Denton (w) ----------
Devalt,Calvin	Nancy Killian	6 Oct. 1842	W(illia)m Green (w) ----------
Dever,Eli F.	Mary Man (d.of John)	27 July 1835	Lewis x Sorrels (w) S.Fitzgerrald,clk.
Dever,Elisah	Matilda Wilson (d.of John)	2 Sept. 1820	Josiah A.Bird (w) ----------
Dever,Nathan	Adriah Dyer	5 Apr. 1826	Thomas Cooper (w) ----------
Dickerson,James	Martha Morris	11 Apr. 1868 M.11 Apr. 1868 By R.H.Penland,J.P.	(w) J.N.Benners,clk.
Dickey,Joshua	Mary C.Killian (d.of Daniel)	16 Feb. 1837	H(enry) Plott (w) ----------
Dillard,David L.	Ede Harris (d.of Benjamin)	16 Apr. 1838	J(ohn) L.Dillard (w) ----------
Dills,Bartlett	Esther Harris (d.of Daniel)	17 June 1848	D(aniel) G.Bryson (w) J.Keener
Dills,Marin x	Liley Ensley	23 Mar. 1850	T.Berton x Gunter (w) Samuel Gibson,D.C.
Dills,W(illiam) N.	Catherine Watson	22 Oct. 1847	Eli Arrington (w) ----------
Dockrey,George x	Nancy Gipson	13 July 1847	Sollomon x Gibson (w) J.L.Smith

GROOM	BRIDE	DATE OF BOND	BONDSMAN & WITNESS
Doss,William x	Nancy Brown (d.of Polly)	30 Oct. 1809	David Miller (w) Ro.Love,clk.
Dotson,J.A.	Caroline Fincher	M.10 June 1852 By J.F.Fincher,J.P.	(w) ----------
Dotson,Jacob	Sarah E.Ferguson	27 Mar. 1840	Daniel Dotson (w) Wm.Welch
Dotson,Jacob Chyle (s.of J.K.)	Mary Avaline McFalls (d.of Arthur)	9 Oct. 1869 M.11 Oct. 1869 By E.R.Ferguson,J.P.	(w) W.C.Brown,R.D.H.C.
Dotson,John	Martha Green	20 Apr. 1861 M.21 Apr. 1861 By D.C.Howell,L.D.	D.J.Dotson (w)W.W.Medford,C.C.C.
Dotson,Thomas	Ailsy Able (d.of Widow Able)	6 Nov. 1837	H(enry) E.Smith (w) ----------
Dotson,Thomas x	Polly Yarberry	26 Oct. 1854 M.26 Oct. 1854 By Enos McCracken,J.P.	Joseph x McCraken (w) Wm.M.Rhea,clk.
Downs,Nelson M.	Louesa Jones	28 Nov. 1854 M.30 Nov. 1854 By J.N.Banners,J.P.	Thomas S Gillett (w) Wm.M.Rhea,clk.
Ducket,John x	Matilda Masson	20 Dec. 1843	J.A.McClure (w) ----------
Ducket,Westley x	Margaret Crawford (d.of Sire)	5 Jan. 1839	Benjamin Dcukett (w) Thos.Hy.Armstrong
Duckett,Adolphus	Lydia Mahaffey	6 Oct. 1867 M.6 Oct. (18)67 By T.F.Glenn,M.G.	(w) W W.Medford,clk.
Duckett,Bemjamin	Sarah Crawford (d.of Josiah)	21 Dec. 1838	Wesley x Ducket (w) Wm.Welch
Duckett,Jasper M.	R.A.Hoglin	12 Sept. 1865	J(oseph) A.Duckett (w) J.W.Killian
Duckett,John (s.of James)	Margaret Suazngin (d.of Samuel)	4 Feb. 1869 M.4 Feb. 1869 By J.W.Bird,M.G.	(w) W.C.Brown,R.D.H.C
Duckett,Thomas x	Altha Crawford	20 Dec. 1843	J.A. x McClure (w) ----------
Duncan, Isaac x	Tebitha Smith	16 Jan. 1829	William McClure (w) Reub. Deaver
Duncan,Moses x	Nancy Noland	6 Dec. 1839	Caleb Snider (w) Wm.Welch
Duncun,Moses	Nancy C.Estes	26 Mar. 1853 M.27 Mar. 1853 By B.Turner,M.G.	(w) E.P.Erwin,D.C
Dunkin,William x	Susanan Harper	6 Nov. 1845	J(ohn) R.Cooper (w) ----------
Durham,George	Susannah Wolfe	12 Apr. 1809	Caleb-Wolff(Ger) (w) R.Love,clk.

GROOM	BRIDE	DATE OF BOND	BONDSMAN & WITNESS
Dyer,John x	Rebecca Sorrels	8 Mar. 1852 M.---------- By J.F.Fincher	Elijah x Sorrels (w) E.P.Erwin
Early,Van	Nancy Hipps	11 Oct. 1868 M.11 Oct. 1868 By James H.McClure,Esqs.	(w) W.C.Brown,R.D.H.C.
Eastes,Dolphus (Ervin)	Jane Stiles	12 Jan. 1848	J.N.Brendle (w) W.Brown
Eaton,Absolam	Sarah Reeves (d.of James)	21 Mar. 1815	Lebanon Nix (w) ----------
Eaton, Lazerus x	Lydia Bugg (d.of William)	27 Sept. 1815	Henry x Bugg (w) Ro.Love,clk.
Edgerton,W(illia)m	Myra Parks	5 July 1813	John Battle (w) John Fergus
Edmonston,Benjamin R.	Caroline Strother (d.of Flowy Inman)	27 Feb. 1834	N(inian) Edmonston (w) ----------
Edmonston,N(inian)	Polly Strother (d.of Flora Inman)	14 Jan. 1823	B(enjamin) Chambers (w) ----------
Edward,B(enjamin)M.	Eliza Ratcliff	4 Sept. 1843	J(ohn) Reid (w) Wm.Welch
Edwards,J.A.	Nancy M.Tate	25 Nov. 1856 M.26 Nov. 1856 By J.F.Fincher,J.P.	J(ohn) M.Tate (w) C.T.Rogers,D.C.
Edwards, John x	Polly Truett	2 Apr. 1828	Isaac Truit (w) ----------
Edwards,P.L.	Mary Caroline Cathey	12 Nov. 1857 M.12 Nov. 1857 By A.C.Hartgrove,J.P.	J(ulius) A.Edward (w) W.W.Medford,clk.
Edwards,P.W.	Elizabeth Tritt (d.of Henry)	1 Dec. 1834	Jeremiah Vickers (w) ----------
Edwards,Thomas S.	Harriett M.Coleman (d.of George)	23 Dec. 1832	Franklin J.Coleman (w) P.W.Edwards
Edwards,Weldon	Eliza Carter	19 Apr. 1862	J(ames) S.Welch (w) A.L.Herren
Elder,B.H.	N.L.Beck (d.of John)	16 Sept. 1839	I(sac) P.Harris (w) Samuel Gibson,J.P.
Ellidge,William	Mary M.West	8 July 1860	John Smathers (w) W.W.Medford,clk.
Elliott,Isaac x	Rutha Laney	22 Oct. 1845	David x Mills (w) ----------
Elliott,John x	Hannah Ricketts	9 Aug. 1834	Oliver Painter (w) Jos.Keener
Ellis,James W.	Rachul M.Mingus	25 Feb. 1843	George Trulov (w) ----------
Ellis,Josiah x	Eve Truelove (d.of James)	13 June 1822	James Truelov (w) ----------
Ellott,Carroll x	Lusinda Hatfield (d.of Benjamin)	2 Oct. 1833	Thomas x Ellot (w) Jno.T.Chambers,clk.

GROOM	BRIDE	DATE OF BOND	BONDSMAN & WITNESS
England,Ezekial	Viny Yarborough	2 Apr. 1853 M.---------- By Colvard Nelson,J.P.	J.R.Love (w) W.Brown,D.clk.
Enloe,B(enjamin) M.	Jane Jones (d.of James)	6 Nov. 1833	J.W.Maxwell (w) S.Fitzgerrald,D.C.
Enloe,Jesse	Polly Hyde (d.of John)	4 Feb. 1816	Edward Jones (w) Ro.Love,clk.
Enloe,Wesly M.	Melinda Lolis	9 Apr. 1847	A.J.Bell (w) ----------
Enlow,A(lfred) E.	Celia E.Davidson (d.of William M.)	20 Jan. 1834	J(oseph) Keener (w) S.Fitzgerrald.D.C.
Ensley,James x	Sarah Bivens (d.of Benj.)	10 Mar. 1836	John x Morrow (w) S.Fitzgerrald,D.C.
Ensley,Willum x	Lucresse Paras	26 Nov. 1849	Marion x Dills Daneral x Shook (w) ----------
Ensley,John	Senthey Paris	10 Jan. 1845	Bartlet Dills (w) Samuel Gibson
Erwin,E(li) B.	Mariah Bonom	25 Oct. 1841	H.L.Potts (w) W.Brown
Estas,Thomas	Margret Crawford (d.of Samuel)	25 May 1823	William Carson
Estes,J(ohn) H.	Mary Patten	20 Sept. 1849	J.M.Shook (w) ----------
Evans,Jermiah	Jane Henry	9 June 1859 M.9 June 1859 By Wm.Turner,J.P.	H.F.Plott (w) W.W.Medford,clk.
Evans,F(rancis) B.	Elizabeth Mehaffey (d.of William)	5 Jan. 1839	A(ugust) C. Hartgrove (w) Wm.Welch
Evans,(Jacob) Thomas	Leuezre Moore	17 Mar. 1842	J(osiah) L.Bird (w) W. Brown
Evans,James A. x	Rosanah Wikel	16 May 1844	M.W.Smith (w) ----------
Evans,James M.	Eliza Ann Dever (d.of Richard,Dec'd)	24 July 1831	Gabriel Deaver (w) R.Love,clk.
Evans,Jesse T.	Ruthy R.Warren	26 Aug. 1865	Thomas Burnett (w) J.W.Killian,C.C.C.
Evans,Jessee	Mary Sorrels	25 Dec. 1858 M.26 Dec. 1858 By Wm.Turner,J.P.	Wm.Turner (w) W.W.Medford,clk.
Evans,John	Sussanah Bird (d.of Thomas)	28 Sept. 1811	John Woody (w) Ro.Love,clk.
Evans,John	Nancy D.Henry	24 June 1852 M.24 June 1852 By H.P.Haynes,J.P.	E.V.Plott (w) H.P.Haynes
Evans,Joseph	Julai Ann McElroy	27 Apr. 1842	A.T.Davidson (w) M.J.Coman

GROOM	BRIDE	DATE OF BOND	BONDSMAN & WITNESS
Evans,L.D.	Mary A.Ratcliff	29 Aug. 1855 M.30 Aug. 1855 By A.C.Hartgrove,J.P.	A.H.Mann (w) Wm.M.Rhea,clk.
Evans,T.J.	Margaret Tate	23 Oct. 1856 M.23 Oct. 1856 By B.Turner,M.G.	J.L.Smith (w) C.T.Rogers,D.clk.
Evans,Wm.S.	Mary C.Hyatt	12 June 1846	T.J.Dawson (w) ----------
Evens,Charles x	Mary Ratliff (d.of Abraham)	5 Oct. 1819	Eli x Bryant
Evens,Isham x	Mary Hill (d.of Richmond)	7 June 1855	Elihu Barnes (w) S.Fitzgerrald,clk.
Evens,Jacob	Harriet Terrell	10 Jan. 1865	T.G.Evans (w) ----------
Evins,Jacob,Jr. x	Sally Chambers	17 Aug. 1829	Edward Haynes (w) Jas.R.Love
Evins,Samuel	Mary McMillian (d.of Mary)	25 Dec. 1821	Henry x Hillard (w) ----------
Evins,Zachariah x	Mary Waters (d.of Micheal Waters)	29 Aug. 1817	Isham x Evins (w) ----------
Fain,A(ndrew) J.	Irenia Philips	9 Oct. 1843	J.T.Penland (w) ----------
Fair,Am(brose)	Nancy Chambers (d.of Elihu)	23 Nov. 1830	Samuel Chambers (w) ----------
Farmer,I(ra) D.	Elizabeth Moody	9 Oct. 1845	(w) ----------
Farmer,Joel L.	Sarah Ann Cathey (d.of William)	24 July 1869 M.25 July 1869 By Wm.S.Evans,J.P	(w) W.C.Brown,R.D.H.C.
Farmer,John	Ann Rinehardt	8 Feb. 1842	J(ohn) L.Smith (w) W.Brown
Faw,Abraham A.	Cathern E.Sharrel	19 June 1841	Nathl.Blackburn (w) Samuel Gibson
Fawler,J.C.	Levesa Green	10 Nov. 1858 M.15 Nov. 1858 By P.W.Edwards,J.P.	W.W.Medford,clk.
Felmet,N(athan) G(reen)	Preshus Carter (d.of Henry)	17 Aug. 1837	Jonas x Jenkins Samuel x Thomson (w) Samuel Gibson,J.P.
Fergson,A.J.	Emoline Rogers	23 Aug. 1848	F(rancis) M.Davis (w) ----------
Fergus,John x	Hannah Watson	24 Nov. 1841	Johnson x Kirkland (w) J.Keener
Ferguson,Andrew	Mily Lemming	13 Sept. 1865	J.A.Dotson (w) J.W.Killiam
Ferguson,John	Elizabeth Bradshaw (d.of James)	16 Nov. 1824	William Bradshaw (w) Jno.B.Love

GROOM	BRIDE	DATE OF BOND	BONDSMAN & WITNESS
Ferguson,N.J.	Mary C. Worley	7 Nov. 1857 M.8 Nov. 1857 By F.M.Davis,J.P.	T(hos) J.Ferguson (w) W.W.Medford,clk.
Ferguson,Robert M.	Louisa E.Murry	5 Feb. 1845	A.T.Davidson (w) W.Brown
Ferguson,Samuel	Matilda C.Lowingood (d.of Samuel)	12 Feb. 1835	Solomon x Ray (w) S.Fitzgerrald,clk.
Ferguson,Thomas	Sarah McCracken	25 Jan. 1858 M.26 Jan. 1858 By F.M.Davis,J.P.	D.A.Haynes (w) W.W.Medford,clk.
Ferguson,William	Ruth Gibson (d.of Nathan)	28 Oct. 1828	John L.Gaddis (w) Ro.Love
Ferrell,Frank	Sarah Fish	18 Jan. 1862	Luis Smith (w) W.W.Medford,clk.
Fincher,J(oseph)F.	A.Henry	10 Jan. 1855 M.11 Jan. 1855 By Jas. B.Fitzgerrald,M.G.	Geo.W.x Fincher (w) J.N.Benners
Finley,J.D.C.B.	Elizah F.Chambers	19 Nov. 1829	Henry Hice (w) ----------
Fish,Logan	Hariett A. Justes	29 Mar. 1852 M.31 Mar. 1852 By W.Green,J.P.	(w) J.Keener,clk.
Fisher,John Jackson (s.of John Sr.)	Marinda Green (d.of Silas)	11 Dec. 1868 M.13 Dec. 1868 By J.D.Wright,M.G.	(w) W.C.Brown,R.D.H.C.
Fisher,Lawson	Elizabeth Dills (d.of Bartlett)	30 June 1849	D.G.Bryson (w) ----------
Fitzgerrald,J.B.	Harret M.Grahl	16 Aug. 1843	H.H.Davidson (w) ----------
Ford,D.B.	Racheal Robeson	7 Dec. 1850	J.H.Haynes (w) Joseph Keener
Ford,John T.	Nancy Jinkens	17 Sept. 1859 M.22 Sept. 1859 By J.A.McClure,J.P.	J.A.McClu(re) (w) J.J.Sparks
Ford,Joseph	Elizare Roberson	13 Mar. 1842	Griffy McM(u)llen (w) ----------
Ford,Tipton	Elenor Howell	21 Apr. 1825	Nath(anie)l Blackburn B(enjamin) Chambers (w) ----------
Ford,W(illia)m	Sarah Besst	22 Sept. 1841	Wm.S.Smith (w) W.Brown
Foster,George	Frankey Bishop (d.of A.)	5 Dec. 1836	George x Foster (w) S.Fitzgerrald,D.C.
Foster,Wm. x	Careoline Henson (d.of Loid,Dec'd)	29 Sept. 1837	Thomas Presley (w) ----------
Foster,William J.	Margaret Brown (d.of Amos)	--Apr. 1812	Benjamin Chambers (w) ----------

GROOM	BRIDE	DATE OF BOND	BONDSMAN & WITNESS
Fouts,Jam(e)s	Rebecka Barns (d.of Thos.)	21 Jan. 1836	Elihu Barnes (W) S.Fitzgerrald,D.C.
Fowler,George Bryson	Emaline Miller	6 Sept. 1869 M.12 Sept. 1869 By P.Holsclaw,M.G.	(w) W.C.Brown,R.D.H.C.
Fraday,Henry x	Epsey Parton (d.of Benjamin)	29 Mar. 1835	Britain W. x Parton (w) S.Fitzgerrald,clk.
Francis,M.N.	Margaret Ratcliff	2 Jan. 1855 M.4 Jan. 1855 By B. Turner,M.G.	F(ranklin) Francis (w) Wm.M.Rhea,clk.
Francis,Reece	Elizabeth Morrow	31 Aug. 1841	Wm.B.Turner (w) ----------
Francis,W(illia)m	Mary Allman (d.of Gibeon)	15 Apr. 1832	Jeremiah Vickers (w) ----------
Franklin,Benyly x	Elizabeth Davis	24 Oct. 1841	Jacob K.Dotson (w) W.Brown
Franklin,D.N.	S.A.Evens	7 Jan. 1857 M.8 Jan. 1857	J.P.Long (w) C.T.Rogers,D.C.
Franklin,Eason	Margret England	15 Dec. 1840	Jacob K.Dotson (w) Wm.Welch
Franklin,Elasha x	Rhoda Ball	12 Sept. 1850	Bently x Franklin (w) ----------
Franklin,Elias x	Ann Sular	9 Oct. 1844	James Land (w) E.B.Herrin
Franklin,Henry	Mary Levisa Deaver	6 Aug. 1848	W(m) A. Campbell (w) W.Brown
Franklin,John	Elizabeth Bennett	25 Dec. 1858	H.J.Franklin (w) W.W.Medford
Franklin,Lewis x	Emeline Gaddy	10 Aug. 1848	Wm. x Stanford (w) W.Brown
Franklin,Minor x	Sarah Lovina Price	26 Feb. 1851 M.16 June 1851 By Wm.P.Gillett,J.P.	Ira D.Farmer (w) J.Keener,clk.
Frankl(in),Pary	Rachel A.Henson	8 Nov. 1856 M.---------- By A.C.Hartgrove,J.P.	R.P.Hartgrove (w) Wm.M.Rhea,clk.
Frayday,Henson S. x	Polly Hensley (d.of Wm.Hensley Alias Mathus)	1 Jan. 1833	Jeremiah Vickers (w) J.R.Love
Freeman,James N.	Nancy E.Hannh	15 Oct. 1866	R.W.Noland (w) ----------
Freeman,Joshua	Patsey Caldwell (d.of William)	11 Apr. 1815	Jonathan Philips (w) Ro.Love
Freeman,W(esley) N.	Mary L. Welch	12 May 185-- M.13 May 1852 By B.Turner,M.G.	S.T.Jones (w) J.Keener

GROOM	BRIDE	DATE OF BOND	BONDSMAN & WITNESS
Freeman, Wm. x	Rachel Evens	31 Jan. 1857 ? M. 7 Jan. 1857 ? By A.L.Herren,J.P.	M.W.Smith (w) Wm.M.Rhea,clk.
Fulbright, L(awson) H.	Elizabeth Ingrum	12 Aug. 1845	J.Johnston (w) ----------
Fulbright,Martin	Elisabeth Davis (d.of Uriah)	26 Dec. 1809	John Fulbright Adam Killion (w) ----------
Fulbright,A.C.	Sarah J.Cooper	20 Jan. 1859 M.20 Jan. 1859 By J.N.Francis,J.P.	W(m) M.L.Shook (w) W.W.Medford,clk.
Fulbright,Aron	Isebeller Haynes (d.of John)	28 Dec. 1839	Micheal V.Smith (w) ----------
Fulbright,Jes(se)	Polly Hicks (d.of David)	15 Sept. 1838	Larkin Reeves (w) Wm.Welch
Gaddis,David W. x	Rilla Angeline Evans	8 May 1848	Thos. x Green (w) Robt.V.Welch
Gaddis,J(ohn) L.	Rosannah McLeod	9 Oct. 1828	John Bradshaw (w) Reub.Deaver
Gaddy,J(eramiah)F.	Lucinda M. Anderson	4 Dec. 1847	E.H.Blalock (w) ----------
Gaddy,Thomas B.	Jane Rody Hyatt	4 Sept. 1854 M.5 Sept. 1854 By J.Inman,J.P.	(w) Wm.M.Rhea,clk.
Gadies,Elijah x	Margrett Byers	30 Nov. 1826	Nathan x Gibson (w) Jas.R.Love
Gady,Clemons A.	Martha Dyer (d.of Adra)	1 Oct. 1823	Joseph Deaver (w) Wm.Welch
Gardner,Nelson(Col)	Lucy Ratcliff(Col)	22 Dec 1869 M.23 Dec. 1869 By James A.Zachary	(w) W.C.Brown,R.D.H.C.
Gaston,T(homas)L.	M.E.Walker	12 July 1842	James T.Penland (w) ----------
Gibson,David J.	Harriet E.Johnston	5 Nov. 1850	L.P.Gudger (w) J.Keener
Gibson,Garland	Margret R.Rogers (d.of Jane)	17 Jan. 1838	John M.Griffith (w) ----------
Gibson,John	Sary Messor (d.of Solomon)	8 Jan. 1814	W(illia)m P.Foster (w) John B.Love,clk.
Gibson,John x	Mourning Carter (d.of Wm.)	14 Nov. 1834	Amber x Waldrop Solomon x Gibson (w) S.Fitzgerrald,clk.
Gibson,John x	Mary M.Warde	25 Sept. 1851 M.27 Sept. 1851 By John S.Gibson,J.P.	Wm.H(enry) Conner (w) John S.Gibson
Gibson,Joshaway x	Rachal Carenger (d. of Danal)	21 Mar. 1830	Alexander x Crisp Samuel Gibson

GROOM	BRIDE	DATE OF BOND	BONDSMAN & WITNESS
Gibson,Nathaniel x	Nancy Casy	30 Aug. 1828	David Jackson (w) Jas. R.Love
Gibson, Solomon x	Elizabeth Millsaps	30 May 1817	Gilbert Falls (w) John B.Love
Gillaspie,Harvy	Sara C.Hooper	14 May 1852 M.16 May 1852 By Thomas Henson,M.G.	N(inian) Edmonston (w) J.Keener,clk.
Gilliam, Jesse	Jenny McDowell (d.of Wm.)	25 Dec. 1810	Owen Owens (w) R.Love,clk.
Gipson,Henry	Eliza Adaline Reece	28 Mar. 1859 M.29 Mar. 1859 By P.W.Edwards,J.P.	M.W.Smith (w) W.W.Medford,clk.
Gipson,Isaac	Mary Sellwell	12 Apr. 1843	Jason Sherrill (w) Samuel Gibson
Gipson,John S.	Marth Carrel (d.of John)	29 Aug. 1839	Samuel Gibson (w) J.Keener
Gipson,Samuel W.	Nancey Conley (d.of James)	14 Mar. 1839	E(dward) G.Hyatt John S.Gipson (w) Samuel Gibson
Gorden,J.S.W.	Mary Evans	27 Nov. 1858 M.28 Nov. 1858 By A.L.Herren,J.P.	J.C.Singleton (w) W.W.Medford,clk.
Gorg,Jaremier	Nancey Forgey	2 Sept. 1840	John Stillwell Adam Snider (w) Samuel Gibson
Grahl,Abramham S.	Caroline E.Bird	25 July 1841	Aug(ustu)s Grahl (w) Wm.Welch,clk.
Grahl,Joseph B.	Jane P.Reid	26 June 1843	S.Fitzgerrald (w) J.B.Fitzgerrald
Grahl,Woodford	Miley Holder	24 Oct. 1857	John Terpin (w) W.W.Medford
Green,Alx.	Elizabeth Rogers	4 July 1853 M.5 July 1853 By W.Green,J.P.	Thos.Green (w) Wm.M.Rhea
Green,David	Anny Hubbard	12 May 1828	Peter Noland (w) R.Dever
Green,F.W.	Elizabeth Ann Able	12 Nov. 1859	John Morrow (w) W.W.Medford,clk.
Green,George x	Lucinda Messer	22 Feb. 1855 M.22 Feb. 1855 By H.Rogers,J.P.	H.Rogers
Green,James x	Mary Ann Morrow (d.of Robert)	6 Jan. 1834	William Green (w) S.Fitzgerrald
Green,James x	Peggy Noland (d.of Wm.)	30 Dec. 1836	Wm.x Wrathbone (w) S.Ftizgerrald,D.C.
Green,Jeremiah x	Nancy Wilkins (d.of Isaac)	2 Sept. 1821	H(oloman) Battle (w) ----------

GROOM	BRIDE	DATE OF BOND	BONDSMAN & WITNESS
Green,Jeremiah	Rebecca Hunter	26 Jan. 1829	James Russel (w) Ro.Love,clk.
Green,Jesse	Morning Bandey (d.of David)	26 Dec. 1837	Thomas Walker,Jr. (w) Samuel Gibson
Green,John	Sarah Messer	13 Nov. 1848 M.17 Nov. 1846 By Reuben Coffey,M.G.	Jeremiah Green (w) Walker Brown,clk.
Green,T(hadius) M.	Lowisa Shook	28 July 1865	S(amuel) B.Green (w) ----------
Green,Thomas (or William)?	Margrett Gaddes (d.of David Rogers)	3 Nov. 1836	William Green (w) ----------
Green,Thomas	Margaret Rogers	1 Oct. 1846	James Green (w) ----------
Green,Thomas	Beckneann Smith	19 Apr. 1854 M.20 Apr. 1854 By George Williamson,J.P.	Purnel Rathbone (w) Wm.M.Rhea,clk.
Green,William	Nancy Fisher	20 Sept. 1860	J.C.Fowler (w) ----------
Green,William	Rebecha Byers (d.of David)	7 Dec. 1833	Charles Justice (w) S.Fitzgerrald,D.C.
Green,William (or Thomas)?	Margrett Gaddes (d.of David Rogers	3 Nov. 1836	Thomas Green (w) ----------
Green,W(illia)m	Sarrah Clark	24 Oct. 1846	J(ohn) N.McGee (w) ----------
Green,William (Jr.)	Melenda Hix (d.of David)	12 Apr. 1832	Charles Justice (w) J.R.Love
Grible,John x	Elizabeth Ensley (d.of Andrew)	15 Nov. 1821	Thomas x Monteith (w) John B.Love
Grooms,Henry	Eliza Colwell	30 June 1858 M.---------- By Wm.P.Gillett,J.P.	G.L.Palmer (w) W.W.Medford,clk.
Guilliams,Benjamin x	Sary Beasley (d.of Joseph)	11 Sept. 1822	William x Beasley (w) Ro.Love,clk.
Gunter,A(ndrew) W(illiamson)	Mary Mills	28 Aug. 1841	John x Franklin (w) J.Keener
Gunter,George x	Sidney Watson (d.of David)	9 Jan. 1817	George x Shooler (w) ----------
Gunter,Hiram x	Alesabeth A.Cornwell	9 Aug. 1842	Solomon Messer (w) Samuel Gibson,Dp.
Gunter,Joseph	Sarah Bumgarner (d.of Henry)	17 Sept. 1839	S.W.Carson Wm.Welch
Gunter,Samuel M. x	Darcus Estes	28 Jan. 1854 M.29 Jan. 1854 By J.N.Benners,J.P.	Moses Dunkin (w) W.Brown,D.C.
Gurley,Nedom x	Sally Henson (d.of Mathias Mease)	7 Sept. 1833	William x Cooper (w) Jno.B.Love,D.C.

GROOM	BRIDE	DATE OF BOND	BONDSMAN & WITNESS
Gurley,William	Nancy Rowland (d.of William Harp)	23 May 1812	Henry Gurley (w) ----------
Hall,Elb(e)rt	Cintha Mull (d.of Peter)	24 Mar. 1838	James Hall (w) J.Keener
Hall,Enoch (Sr.)	Marinda E.Blaylock	6 Nov. 1841	Samuel W.Able (w) W.Brown
Hall,George x	Rachel T.Williams	5 Jan. 1856 M.10 Jan. 1856 By C.B.Mingus,Elder	Saml. x Hall (w) Wm.M.Rhea,clk.
Hall,George (Jr.)	Eliza Clark (d.of William)	9 May 1822	George Hall (Sr.) (w) Ro.Love,clk.
Hall,I.M.	Margaret Chambers	9 Oct. 1864	C.B.Mungus (w) H.P.Haynes,J.P.
Hall,Isaac M.	Mary E.Hawkins	30 Dec. 1841	Green Moore (w) ----------
Hall,Jesse	Necessa Stillwell (d.of Jacob)	10 Feb. 1838	Allen C.Broom (w) Wm.Welch
Hall,Jimison	Mima Reeves	1 Nov. 1849	M.M.Hall (w) S.W.Gaston,clk.
Hall,John	(Sary Phillips)	-- Sept. 1812	Reuben Phillips (w) John B. Love
Hall,La(w)son A.	Margaret Emaline Warren	1 July 1851 M.7 July 1851 By A.M.Russell,J.P.	Isaac M.Hall (w) J.Keener,clk.
Hall,Samul x	Rachul M.Clark	4 Oct. 1848	J.H.Estes (w) W.Brown
Hall,Tho(ma)s	Melinda Christopher	24 Jan. 1850	R.M.Henry (w) B.A.Edmonston,D.C.
Hall,Wm.H.	Eliza Pool	27 Feb. 1867 M. 3 Mar. 1867 By W.B.Smathers,J.P.	(w) W.W.Medford,clk.
Halscalaught,W.P.	Naoma Pharr	3 Nov. 1852 M.14 Nov. 1852 By Thomas Henson	A.J.Murry (w) J.Keener,clk.
Haly(d)ay, Alexander T.	Elisabeth Chambers (d.of Phillip)	12 June 1830	Samuel Monroe (w) Ro.Love,clk.
Hanah,Levi	Patience Ruff	13 Mar. 1842	W(illia)m Green (w) ----------
Hannah,Alexander	Prislla Rogers	25 Mar. 1856 M.30 Apr. 1856 By H.Rogers,J.P.	George Ruff (w) Wm.M.Rhea,clk.
Hannah,Alexander	Sarah Ann Lackey	25 June 1861	A.A.Robinson (w) W.W.Medford
Hannah,Benjamin x	Polly Moore	4 Mar. 1856	C.T.Rogers (w) ----------
Hannah,Evan x	Elizabeth Noland	31 Apr. 1829	David x Carver (w) Reub. Deaver

GROOM	BRIDE	DATE OF BOND	BONDSMAN & WITNESS
Hannah,James	Margaret J.Fish	30 Nov. 1859 M.30 Nov. 1859 By H.Rogers	Harvey Hannah (w) W.W.Medford,clk.
Hannah,Jeremiah	Elvira Hodge	13 Mar. 1852 M.15 Mar. 1852 By W.Green	(w) J.Keener,clk.
Hannah,Levi x	Priscilla Green (d.of Jeremiah)	------1829	James x Green (w) Ro.Love
Harben,Joseph D.	Marey E.Collel	26 July 1864	Thomas J.Rogers (w) ----------
Harbin,James W.	Polly Hall (d.of Enoch)	29 Aug. 1835	Enoch Hall (w) S.Fitzgerrald,clk.
Harbin,Carroll R.x	Polly Kirkland (d.of John)	4 Mar. 1828	William x Shelton (w) Jonathan Coward
Harbin,Eli	Elizabeth M.Collins (d.of Polly)	6 Oct. 1830	William x Cathey,Jr. (w) R. Deaver
Harell,Elihu x	Avoline White	21 Aug. 1852 M.21 Aug. 1852 By Wm.P.Gillett,J.P.	Wm.M.Rhea (w) J.Keener,clk.
Haren,Anderson x	Mary Fortner	16 Mar. 1845	G.W.Clayton (w) Samuel Gibson,J.P.
Hares,Tolever	Nancey Berry (d.of Richmond Hill)	24 Sept. 1837	J(ohn) R.Cooper Matthew Hix (w) Wm.Welch
Haris,Isaac	Sarey Beck (d.of John)	1 Dec. 1829	Jacob Beck (w) Samuel Gibson
Harrass,James x	Marth Killpatrick (widow of Leander Killpatrick)	31 Oct. 1865	Mark x Howell (w) J.W.Killian,clk.
Harres,WI(lliam) H.	Wavaline Jones (d.of J.G.)	17 Dec. 1865	W.F.Grasty (w) J.W.Killian,clk.
Harris,Terrell x	Elizabeth Duncan (d.of Isaac)	26 Sept. 1838	Caleb Snider (w) Wm.Welch,clk.
Harrison,Joseph (s.of Adam)	Haseline Medford (d.of R.E. & Rebecca)	8 Oct. 1869 M.8 Oct. 1869 By Joseph Brendle,J.P.	(w) W.C.Brown,R.D.H.C.
Hartgrove,J(ohn) C.	Jane A.Warren	4 July 1852 M.4 July 1852 By A.J.Murray,J.P.	R(ufus) P.Hartgrove (w) J.Keener,clk.
Hartgrove,L.P.	Mary Turrell	3 Mar. 1858 M.4 Mar. 1858 By A.L.Herren,J.P.	D.F.Bird (w) W.W.Medford,clk.
Hartgrove,R(ufus) P.	Rebecca C.Long	1 May 1833 M.2 May 1853 By J.N.Benners,J.P.	John F.Long (w) A.C.Hartgrove
Haston,James x	Marey Nickols	9 Apr. 1826	Edward F. x Faranton (w) Samuel Gibson,J.P.

GROOM	BRIDE	DATE OF BOND	BONDSMAN & WITNESS
Hawkins,Alston x	Manervy Davis	17 Feb. 1844	Wm.W.Battle (w) W.Brown
Hawkins,B.F.	Masind Battle	20 Dec. 1849	A.J.Murry (w) ----------
Hawkins,Elihu	Louesa Hawkins	9 Aug. 1856 M.10 Aug. 1856 3y J.N.Benners,J.P.	J(oseph) Hawkins (w) Wm.M.Rhea,clk.
Hawkins,Thos.M.	Mary Fulbright	22 Aug. 1860	J(oseph) Hawkins (w) W.W.Medford,clk.
Hawkins,W.B. x	Elizabeth M.Rogers	1 Dec. 1848	J.T.Hehaffy (w) W.Brown
Hayet,Jasper N.	Matilda Lourena Cathey	21 Dec. 1850	J.C.Hartgrove (w) J.Keener
Haynes,Allen x	Susanna Snook (granddau. of Jacob)	14 Aug. 1836	W(illia)m Moore (w) Wm.Welch,clk.
Haynes,D.A.	S.C.Mingus	5 May 1859 M.5 May 1859 By C.B.Mingus	E.F.Conner (w) H.P.Haynes,J.P.
Haynes,Eph(r)aim	Milinda Clay	15 Nov. 1825	W(illiam) Sitton (w) N.G.Howell,J.P.
Haynes,Jacob	Avalin Byers	29 Mar. 1860	S(aml) B.Green (w) W.W.Medford
Haynes,John	Rebecha Brown (d.of the Widow Rachel)	25 Feb. 1836	W(alter) Brown (w) S.Fitzgerrald,D.C.
Haynes,John H.	Violet S.Fergurson	9 Oct. 1858 M.10 Oct. 1858 By S.Walker,J.P.	G.W.McCracken (w) W.N.Freeman,D.C.
Haynes,John Monterville (s.of H.P.)	Nancy Adaline Smathers (d.of Leve & Sarah)	22 Oct. 1868 M.---------- By J.H.Massy	(w) W.C.Brown, R.D.H.C.
Haynes,Jonathan	Synthey McDowell (d.of Danl)	25 Aug. 1818	David Shook (w) ----------
Haynes,Judson P. x	Margret McCracken	17 Feb. 1840	W.G.B.Garrett (w) Wm.Welch
Haynes,Wm.	Sarah Campbell	12 Nov. 1840	John Haynes (w) ----------
Haynes,William Jr.	Elisabeth Hood (d.of John)	6 Nov. 1811	William x Haynes,Sr. (w) Ro.Love,clk.
Heartgrove,John C.	Nancy T.Henson	28 Mar. 1855 M. 1 Apr. 1855 By J.Inman,J.P.	Wm.L.Love (w) Wm.M.Rhea,clk.
Heartgrove,A.F.	Elvira Jane Henson	23 Aug. 1851 M.24 Aug. 1851 By A.J.Murray,J.P.	George W.Cathey (w) J.Keener,clk.
Hebberts,Charles	Jane Stiles (d.of Thos.)	31 July 1831	(Thos.Davis) (w) Jno.B.Love,D.C.

GROOM	BRIDE	DATE OF BOND	BONDSMAN & WITNESS
Hebberts,Elijah x	Ruth Caler	26 Oct. 1822	John x Buff (w) John B.Love
Hefley,Martin	Clerrissy Mahaffy (d.of Joseph)	13 Sept. 1817	(w) John B.Love
Henderson,James M.	Mariah Sellers	2 July 1859 M.3 July 1859 By D.B.Ford,J.P.	J.A.Williams (w) W.W.Medford
Henderson,John	Jane Hogland	18 Nov 1855 M.18 Nov. 1855 By D.B.Ford	Jonathan x.Wood (w) W.Brown
Henderson,Tho(ma)s	Elizabeth Cook	18 Sept. 1843	J.Vickers (w) W.Brown
Henderson,William	Sarah Bess	22 June 1841	Wm.S.Smith (w) Wm.Haynes
Henderson,W(illia)m	Lydia Guiliams	26 Aug. 1843	Jacob Miller (w) W.Brown
Henry,A.S.	Ailcy E.Evens	15 Oct. 1856 M.16 Oct. 1856 By E.V.Plott,J.P.	Thos.W.Davis (w) Wm.M.Rhea,clk.
Henry,Alexander	Sarah Miller	24 Feb. 1846	Ephraim Ash (w) ---------
Henry,A(lexander)	Polly Sorrels (d.of Jsoeph,dec'd)	6 Sept. 1832	T(hos) P.Noblitt (w) ----------
Henry,Lorenzo N.	Mary Malinda Moore	26 Aug. 1823	Emanuel J(efferson) (w) -----Walker
Henry,M(Ejamin)? S.	Rachael A.Penland	6 Aug. 1841	J(ohn) J.Patton (w) Wm.Welch,clk.
Henson,A.N.	Levisa Holland	21 Nov. 186(0)	Griffen Henson (w) W.W.Medford
Henson,Aaron x	Elisabeth Presley	25 Mar. 1828	James x Mann (w) ----------
Henson,Aaron,Jr.	Nancy Mann	14 Sept. 1849	Daniel x Henson,Sr. (w) ----------
Henson,Abslom	Cintha Meese	23 June 1857 M.26 June 1857 By A.C.Hartgrove,J.P.	Joshua Kinsla(n)d (w) Wm.M.Rhea,clk.
Henson,Alfred x	Ceila Brown (d.of David)	22 Aug. 1838	W(illia)m Allman (w) ----------
Henson,Allen x	Elizabeth Blaylock (d.of Isham,Sr)	18 Sept. 1821	Wyly x Henson (w) Wm.Welch
Henson,Aquilla W. x	Nancy Presley (d.of William)	18 Aug. 1838	W(illia)m A.Cobb (w) Wm.Welch
Henson,Burton	Mariah Christopher	26 Sept. 1865 M. 1 Oct. 1865 By J.Long,J.P.	Morgan Mease (w) J.W.Killian
Henson,Griffon	Mary Holland	13 May 1848	Allen x Henson,Sr. (w) R.V.Welch

GROOM	BRIDE	DATE OF BOND	BONDS & WITNESS
Henson,Henry x	Zelia Holland	31 May 1841	Daniel x Henson (w) Wm.Welch
Henson,Henry Jr. (s.of Daniel)	Mary Christopher (d.of Davault)	23 Jan. 1869 M. 3 Feb. 1869 By Joshua Kinsland,J.P.	(w) W.C.Brown,Reg. D.
Henson,J.E.	Mary Holder	29 Sept. 1856 M. ---------- By A.C.Hartgrove,J.P.	H.P.Holland (w) Wm.M.Rhea,clk.
Henson,John M.	Elizabeth Ray	2 Feb. 1828	Felix Axly (w) Ro.Love,clk.
Henson,Loyde	Sally Meace (d.of Matthias)	27 May 1818	Anthony Mees (w) Ro.Love,clk.
Henson,Nathen x	Katty Presley (d.of William)	4 Nov. 1824	Aaron x Henson (w) Ro.Love,clk.
Henson,P(hillip)	Mary Allison	31 Jan. 1852	J.B.Allison (w) ----------
Henson,Thos.x	Mary Ann Hughes	25 July 1820	John Carrell (w) John B.Love,clk.
Henson,Thomas F.	Mary L. Smathers	15 Dec. 1852 M.16 Dec. 1852 By A.C.Hartgrove,J.P.	R.P.Hartgrove (w) A.C.Hartgrove
Henson,Tho(ma)s M.	Mary Emlin Crawford	21 Dec. 1847	P(hillip) Henson (w) ----------
Henson,Wesley	Lucinda Christopher	20 Sept. 1867 M.22 Sept. 186(7) By Griffin Henson,J.P.	(w) W.W.Medford,clk.
Henson,Wiley,Jr.x	Susanah Wise (d.of Benjamin)	12 Feb. 1837	Isham Blaylock (w) S.Fitzgerrald,D.C.
Herren,G.B.	Caroline Johnston	4 Dec. 1843	H.A.Rabun (w) J.T.Penland
Herrin,Collin x	Jenny Mercer (d.of Solomon)	4 Mar. 1817	Goldman Ingram (w) Ro.Love
Herrin,E(li) B.	Jane Yarborough (d.of Elisha)	7 June 1832	Jos(eph) Keener (w) Wm.Allman
Hickey,John	Eve Caler	20 Dec. 1821	(w) ----------
Hicks,Joseph	Margaret Shook	----------	Reuben Phillips (w) ----------
Hicks,Stevenson x	Maria Ledford (d.of Ely)	23 Oct. 1833	Thomas Ferguson (w) ----------
Hill,David	Nicee McGee (d.of John)	29 Apr. 1832	Joseph Osborn (w) ----------
Hill,Joseph H.	Arriena M.Sumaker	16 Jan. 1858 M.17 Jan. 1858 By N.J.Roberts,J.P.	J.W.Brown (w) N.J. Roberts
Hill,Mikiel x	Tebithy Dunkin	11 May 1844	Daniel Farmer (w) W.Brown

GROOM	BRIDE	DATE OF BOND	BONDSMAN & WITNESS
Hill,N(oah)	Taletha Heffley (d.of Barbary)	20 July 1833	Amos Plott (w) Wm.Welch
Hill,Richmon	Cary Duckett	3 Nov. 1860	G.W.McCracken (w) W.W.Medford,clk.
Hill,Robert x	Ailsey Evans	17 Mar. 1841	Bryant x Hill (w) Wm.Welch
Hill,Thomas	Elizabeth Nicholes	22 June 1852 M.22 June 1852 By J.F.Fincher,J.P.	John P. Nochols (w) J.Keener
Hilliard,(Dr.)W.L.	Margaret E.Love	28 Dec. 1853 M. 3 Jan. 1854 By John Reynolds	Saml.L.Love (w) Wm.M.Rhea,clk.
Hinson,Absolam	Cinthia Medford (d.of Elizabeth Robison	13 Oct. 1819	Henry x Robison Willie x Hinson (w) Ro.Love,clk.
Hinson,Daniel x	Polly Presley (d.of Wm.)	9 Aug. 1831	William x Thompson (w) Ro.Love,clk.
Hinson,Willie x	Mary Meace (d.of Matthias)	18 June 1816	William Stodghill (w) ----------
Hipp.William(Jr.)	Elizah Stephenson	12 June 1858 M.---------- By C.Nelson,J.P.	Wm.Hipp (Sr.) (w) W.W.Medford,clk.
Hodge,Dempsey x	Mary or Polly Ray (d.of John)	22 Oct. 1832	Thos(ma)s N.Noland (w) Ro.Love,clk.
Hodge,Denney x	Elisabeth Thompson	9 Aug. 1854 M.9 Aug. 1854 By H.Rogers,J.P.	Absalem x Carver (w) Wm.M.Rhea,clk.
Hoglan,Andrew J.	Agness Woods (d.of Johnothan)	13 Mar. 1834	David Bugg (w) S.Fitzgerrald,D.C.
Hogland,James	Adline Bradley	4 Sept. 1860	John Bryson (w) W.W.Medford
Hogland,William K.	Letta Messer	9 Aug. 1865	A.T.Rogers (w) J.W.Killian
Holden,Henry x	Annis Mathes (d.of William)	7 Dec. 1848	Andrew x Mathes (w) A.Bumgarner,J.P.
Holden,Richard x	Barbarry Schunk (d.of Molly)	2 July 1821	Henson x Queen (w) Ro.Love,clk.
Holder,James	Letiscia Roberson	21 Sept. 1843	Isaac R.Clark (w) W.Brown
Holder,John x	Polly McMullins	22 Jan. 1829	W(illia)m Parham (w) Ro.Love,clk.
Holder,William x	Peggy Smith	10 Nov. 1834	John D.H(o)well (w) S.Fitzgerrald,clk.
Holder,W(illiam) H.	Nancy E.Morgan	29 Aug. 186-	John M.Curtis (w) J.W.Killian,clk.
Holland,Humphry P.	Rebeca Anderson	28 Feb. 1866	Morgan Mease (w) ----------

GROOM	BRIDE	DATE OF BOND	BONDSMAN & WITNESS
Holl(and),John (Jr.)	Ruth Blaylock	25 Sept. 1827	Thomas Jefferson Evans (w) ----------
Holland,Mathias x	Sarah Clark	9 May 1857 M.10 May 1857 By C.B.Mingus,M.G.	Danel x Henson (w) Wm.M.Rhea,clk.
Hollingsworth, E(noch)	Margaret Cuningham (d.of George)	1 Aug. 1812	Joseph Sorrolls (w) ----------
Hollis,F(idellia) (or Howell)	Luvisa A.Ivester	15 Mar. 1852 M.28 Mar. 1852 By A.C.Hartgrove,J.P.	Isaac Ivester (w) J.Keener,clk.
Hollon,James	Fanny Meece	19 Nov. 1817	Needom x Gurley (w) Wm.Welch
Holyfield,Samuel x	Lucenda Bryant	23 Jan. 1834	Solomon x Ray (w) S.Fitzgerrald,D.C.
Holyfield,Samuel x	Janie McClure	14 July 1851 M.14 July 1851 By J.A.McClure,J.P.	J(ermiah) Vickers (w) J.Keener,clk.
Hooper,A(ndrew) D.	E.J.Long	12 Jan. 1852 M.20 Jan. 1852 By Thomas Henson	J(ohn) B.Allison (w) J.Keener,clk.
Hooper,William	Nancy Bryson	22 June 1826	William Cathey (w) Adam Corn
Hooper,Enos x	Tildy Burrell (d.of Walles)	19 Jan. 1822	Benjamin x Chastin Jesse x Burrell (w) John B.Love,D.C.
Hoppkins,William M.	Elizabeth Russell	22 Dec. 1857 M.24 Dec. 1857 By J.H.Noland,J.P.	J.H.Noland (w) W.W.Medford,clk.
Howard,William	Nancy Clark	18 Mar. 1860	W.S. xRoberson (w) D.B.Ford
Howell,Albert	Elender Fergason	29 Apr. 1847	John D. Howell (w) ----------
Howell,Christopher	Betsy Hall (d.of George)	11 Sept. 1816	Joseph Howell (w) Dillard Love
Howell,D.S.	Mary E.Ivester	27 Aug. 1857 M.30 Aug. 1857 By A.C.Hartgrove,J.P.	A.R.Trull (w) Wm.M.Rhea,clk.
Howell,David	Neomea Edwards (d.of Thos.)	10 Oct. 1821	Jas. R.Love (w) ----------
Howell,David	M.M.Edwards	------18(63)	(w) ----------
Howell,Evan	Rody Fullbright	25 Aug. 1865	Marcus Howell (w) J.W.Killian,C.C.C.
Howell,E(van) S.	Camilla McLeod	26 Dec. 1828	Jonathan Chambers (w) Reub. Deaver
Howell,Fidellia	Luesia A.Ivester	15 Mar. 1852 M.28 Mar. 1852 By A.C.Hartgrove,J.P.	(w) J.Keener,clk.

38

GROOM	BRIDE	DATE OF BOND	BONDSMAN & WITNESS
Howell,George	Elizabeth Evans	10 Mar. 1846	T(hos) E.Bird (w) R.V.Wech
Howell,Henry x	Catherin Smith	28 Sept. 1843	Wm.W.Battle (w) Wm.Welch
Howell,J(ames) D(eberry)	Lydia Caroline Fincher	2 Jan. 1851	John Fincher (w) J.Keener
H(ow)ell,John D.Jr.	Elisabeth Ratcliff	20 Dec. 1827	David Hill (w) Ro.Love
H(o)well,Nelson	Fanny Furguson	9 Sept. 1850	John D.Howell (w) S.W.Gaston
Howell,N(elson) G.	Mary Moody (d.of John)	22 Feb. 1823	David Howell (w) Wm.Welch
Hoyles,John	Mary L.Noland	21 Feb. 1868 M.23 Feb. (1868) By Joseph Brendle	(w) J.N.Benners,Dy.clk.
Hufman,Elias	Sarah Brown	30 June 1851 M.30 June 1851 By W.L.Davis,J.P.	Elihu Coward (w) Joseph Keener,clk.
Hughes,George N.	Sarah Adam (d.of David)	5 Sept. 1808	H(olliman) Battle (w) ----------
Hughes,J(ason) W.	Marey C.Balal (d.of John)	22 Nov. 1838	Pleasant Bradley Wm.R.Killian (w) Samuel Gibson
Hunter,B(alis) J(ackson)	Margaret Louisa Angelin Fraday	31 Jan. 1852 M. 29 Feb. 1852 By Colvard Nelson,J.P.	David Messer (w) J.Keener,clk.
Hunter,Richard x	Ruthey Millender	31 Dec. 1827	William Noland (w) Reuben Dever
Hunter,Richard x	Sarah Roof	23 Oct. 1839	William x Coldwell (w) Wm.Welch
Hunycut,James x	Catharan Wilkes (d.of Isaac)	20 Dec. 1823	William x Oaks (w) J.L.Moore
Hurst,J(oseph) B.	Margaret Raby	26 Jan. 1851	Elijah Raby (w) John S.Gibson
Hyatt,Able	Sarah A.Moody	26 Oct. 1854 M.26 Oct. 1854 By J.N.Benners,J.P.	Wm.G.Moody (w) Wm.M.Rhea,clk.
Hyatt,A(ble) B.	Eliza Dobson (d.of John)	13 Aug. 1821	W(illia)m Welch (w) N.Edmonston
Hyatt,E(dward) G.	Nancy E.Howell	15 Oct. 1842	Z(achariah) B.Allen (w) ----------
Hyatt,Elish(a)	Rosanah Young	27 July 1808	Thomas Love (w) Ro.Love
Hyatt,Elisha	Cinthy Ann Shipp	28 Jan. 1825	J(onathan) M.Bryson (w) R.Dever

GROOM	BRIDE	DATE OF BOND	BONDSMAN & WITNESS
Hyatt,J.N.	Elizabeth Chambers	2 Dec. 1855 M.2 Dec. 1855 By T.S.Edwards,J.P.	Thos.B.Gaddy (w) Wm.L.Love
Hyatt,Ute	Julletta Howell	1 Dec. 1839	Z(acharia) Allen (w) Wm.Welch
Hyatt,William x	Sarah Nelson	22 Mar. 1828	N(athan) B.Hyatt,Jr. (w) ----------
Hyatte,R.A,L.	Margaret Mahaffey	4 Mar. 1852 M.4 Mar. 1852 By B.Turner,M.G.	W(illia)m Allen (w) J.Keener,clk.
Hyde,John	Polly Beck (d.of John)	15 Oct. 1818	John Leatherwood (w) John B. Love
Ingram,William	Lily Pace	25 Dec. 1822	Dillard Love (w) ----------
Ingram,W(illia)m G.	Elizabeth Bird	12 Mar. 1851 M.12 Mar. 1851 By J.A.Reagan,M.G.	J(ames) W.Terrell (w) W.Johnston
Inman,Anderson	----------	21 Feb. 1843	(Request for marriage license signed by Joshua Inman)
Inman,Benjamin x	Sarah Holder	14 Aug. 1824	James Inman (w) Wm.Welch
Inman,J(ames) A.	Mary Kerby	22 Feb. 1843	Jeramiah Liner (w) W.Brown
Inman,Joseph x	Nercisa Hill (d.of Sally)	28 Nov. 1836	Wriley Medford (w) S.Fitzgerrald,D.C.
Inman,Joshua	Polly Smith	12 Mar. 1825	John McDowell (w) R.Dever
Inman,Joshua E.	Vilinda Swanger	11 Sept. 1853 M.11 Sept. 1853 By A.C.Hartgrove,J.P.	David x Reece,Sr. (w) Joshua Inman
Inmon,Hezerkier	Martha Franklin	30 Apr. 1858 M.---------- By T.S.Edwards,J.P.	Amos A.x Crawford (w) W.W.Medford,clk.
Iveans,Isam	Martha Crofford	30 Oct. 1858	(w) W.W.Medford,clk.
Ivester,Henry (C.)	Ruthy Anderson	21 Jan. 1854 M.28 Jan. 1854 By J.Inman,J.P.	John G.B(u)rnett (w) J.Inman,J.P.
Jackson,James L.	Roxney W.Floid (d.of Henry)	23 Jan. 1836	Henry Floyd (w) Wm.Welch
James,John x	Barbary Roof	2 Aug. 1841	Robert x Ray (w) A.T.Davidson
James,M.R.M.	H.M.Owen	29 June 1867 M. 4 July 1876 ? By Wm.L.Moody,J.P.	(w) W.W.Medford,clk.
James,Riol x	Avolin Holyfield	25 Dec. 1855 M.24 Jan. 1856 By James Plemmons,M.G.	Wm. x Justice (w) Wm.M.Rhea,clk.

40

GROOM	BRIDE	DATE OF BOND	BONDSMAN & WITNESS
James R(obert) F.	M.J.Killion	4 Oct. 1853 M. 27 Oct. 1853 By Jacob Hood,M.G.	J.Vickers (w) Wm.M.Rhea,clk.
Jarrett,W(m) P.	Margaret E.Howell	24 Nov. 1857 M.24 Nov. 1857 By J.A.Reagan,M.G.	C.T.Rogers (w) W.W.Medford,clk.
Jeanes,J.J. x	Jane Henry	5 Nov. 1842	J(errimiah) Vickres (w) W.Brown
Jenkins,C.Washington	Eliza Knight	21 Dec. 1869	(w) W.C.Brown,R.D.H.C.
Jenkils,Nathen	Marey Abbot	1 Feb. 1824	Jas. M.Baits (w) ----------
Jenkins,Norris x	Sarah Ann Coldwell (d.of William,dec'd)	18 May 1838	Daniel x Williams (w) ----------
Jests,William	Elizabeth Brown	31 Jan. 1854 M.31 Jan. 1854 By H.Rogers	J.M.Tate (w) S.E.Byers,clk.
Jinkans,Richmaond	Emeline Hall	31 Dec. 1863	John Renno (w) H.P.Haynes
Jinkens,Jonas	Nancey Rosan Word	4 Jan. 1852 M.4 Jan. 1852 By Samuel Gibson	(Abram Selars) Thomas W. x Word (w) Samuel Gibson,D.C.
Jinkins,Jeremiah	Mary Gibson (d.of Joseph)	23 July 1822	James Ruddell (w) ----------
Jinkins,James	Mary Nations	30 Mar. 1852	Samuel Gibson (w) ----------
Johnson,Elijah,Jr.	Polly Riddick	27 Apr. 1825	El(ijah) Johnston Sr. W(illia)m Rogers (w) Ro.Love,clk.
Johnson,E(nuch) E.	Lydia Pharr	5 June 1853 M.12 June 1853 By C.B.Mingus,M.G.	J.D.Justice (w) A.C.Hartgrove
Johnson,Henry x	Phebe Hall	31 Mar. 1825	Enoch Hall,Jr. (w) George Hall
Johnston,Benj(ami)n	M.E.Welch	3 May 1843	J(ames) T. Penland
Johnston,Harvy x	Ellender Z. Picklesimer	12 Mar. 1851 M.13 Mar. 1851 By Peter King.J.P.	Jason x Johnston (w) R.V.Welch,Depty.
Johnston,Willis	E.J.Allison	M.12 Feb. 1853 By J.F.Fincher,J.P.	(w) ----------
Johnston,W(illia)m	Juda Wade	25 Mar. 1850	D.B.Ford (w) ----------
Johnston,W(illia)m	Lucinda Gudger (d.of James)	18 Mar. 1830	T(hompson) Allman (w) Ro.Love,clk.
Jones,Alfred B.	Matilda Bivens (d.of Benjamin)	19 Nov. 1835	G.W.Kirkland (w) S.Fitzgerrald,clk.
Jones,Burton	Centha Curry (d.of John)	23 July 1832	Joseph Turner (w) Jas. R.Love

GROOM	BRIDE	DATE OF BOND	BONDSMAN & WITNESS
Jones,Burton	Polly Russell	10 Mar. 1857 M.10 Mar. 1857 By J.N.Benners,J.P.	Moses D.Dunkin (w) Wm.M.Rhea,clk.
Jones,D(illard) E.	Rhoda Fulbright	17 Aug. 1843	M(ichael) W.Smith (w) Wm.Welch
Jones,James W. x	Nancey A.Pruett	18 Sept. 1838	J(ohn) L.Smith (w) Wm.Welch
Jones,John C.	Easter Keener	22 Oct. 1846	John A.McCluer (w) ----------
Jones,John L. x	Nancy J.Stokes	12 Jan.1843	M(ikiel) W.Smith (w) W.Brown
Jones,P.L.	Naoma Medford	17 Mar. 1866 M.17 Mar. 1866 By John Turpin,J.P.	(w) W.W.Medford,clk.
Jones,Z.P.	Mary Jane Welch	29 Jan. 1866 M.30 Jan. 1866 By Jas.R.Long.M.G.	(w) W.W.Medford,clk.
Jones,Zachariah P. x	Sarah Morrow (d.of Robert)	22 Sept. 1831	Charles x Jones Abner C.Wines (w) Ro.Love,clk.
Justice,A.H.	N.A.Allison	25 Dec. 1859 M.---------- By Wm.P.Gillett,J.P.	J(as) L.Moody (w) David Howell
Justice,A.J.	Emily McCrackin	2 Mar. 1854 M.2 Mar. 1854 By Enos McCracken	R.P.Kelly (w) W.Brown,D.C.
Justice,Charles	Matty Peck (d.of William Greene)	5 Apr. 1832	David A.Ross (w) ----------
Justice,Joseph	Nancy Clark (d.of George)	26 May 1824	Richard Clark,Jr. (w) Wm.Welch
Justice,Moses	Nancey Kilpatrick	14 Apr. 1860	W.Green (w) W.W.Medford
Kagle,Moses	Priscella Owens	27 May 1848	L(awson) C(old)well (w) Jno.Bryson
Keeler,Albert	Amanda M.Henry	24 Jan. 1857 M. 8 Mar. 1857 By W.C.B.Gerrett,J.P.	F.A.M.Boyd (w) Wm.M.Rhea,clk.
Keener,Jos(eph)	Margaret W.Cuningham (d.of George)	5 Aug. 1834	Allen Fisher (w) Uriah Keener
Kelley,Amos	Sussannah Hunter	18 July 1829	Thomas x Caldwell (w) Ro.Love,clk.
Kelly,Rufus P.	D.F.Edmonston	6 Oct. 1855 M.11 Oct. 1855 By C.B.Mingus,Elder	(w) Wm.M.Rhea,clk.
Kelly,Samuel	Polly Harry	31 Jan. 1824	W(illia)m Carpenter (w) Ro.Love,clk.
Kenyon,Edward Claton	Tempy Louesa Russell (d.of David & Elizabeth)	24 Sept. 1869 M.30 Sept. 1869 By J.D.Wright,M.G.	(w) W.C.Brown R.D.H

GROOM	BRIDE	DATE OF BOND	BONDSMAN & WITNESS
Kerklin,Hamton x	Alesabeth Haras	26 Feb. 1846	Plesant Bradley (w) Samuel Gibson
Ketron,R.G.	M.A.Rogers	13 Sept. 1843	A.T.Davidson (w) ----------
Kilbee,Henry	Ruth Land	18 Nov. 1841	James Land (w) ----------
Kilbee,Ja(me)s H.	Susanah Davis	6 Nov. 1845	Adnrew Robeson (w) ----------
Kilby,Adam	Selenda Wilson	5 Sept. 1840	J(ohn) L.Potts (w) Wm.Welch
Kilby,Wm.B.	----------	17 Dec. 1846	Adam Kilby (w) W.Brown
Killian,A.N.	Rebeca H.Holeford	6 Nov 1860	J.M.Shook (w) ----------
Killian,J(ohn) W.	Margaret Grahl	17 Nov. 1862	(w) ----------
Killpatric,L.N.	Racheal M.Smart	29 Mar. 1853 M.29 Mar. 1853 By C.B.Mingus,M.G.	J W.Killian (w) J.Keener,clk.
Kilpatrick,Jasper N.x	Mary M.Justice	6 Nov 1845	A.L.Wiett (w) W.Brown
Kilpatrick,Silas x	Jane Woods	15 Dec. 1827	Roland Osborn (w) Reubben Dever
Kilpatrick,Wm.D.	Ann Hyatt	20 Feb. 1845	A.J.Murray (w) W.Brown
Kimzey,James	Salley Russel (d.of Mathew)	18 Nov. 1823	John Kimzy
Kimzey,John x	Betty Ann Raburn (d.of Hage)	22 Oct. 1819	James McClure (w) ----------
Kimzey,William	Anna Crawford (d.of George)	6 Sept. 1817	William Crawford (w) John B. Love
King,H.P.	Nercisey Enloe	19 May 1841	Scoop Enloe (w) Samuel Gibson,J.P.
King,John	Elisabeth Clark (d.of George)	15 Feb. 1822	Henry Clark
King,Peter	Elizabeth Ann Quarry	17 Feb. 1849	(J.R.Love) (w) ----------
Kingsmore,H.L. (s.of J.H.)	L.A.Byers (d.of Samuel)	30 Sept. 1869 M.30 Sept. 1869 By C.B.Mingus	(w) W.C.Brown,R.D.H.C.
Kinsland,Jesse	Zillah Holland	26 Mar. 1827	John Stamy (w) Ro.Love,clk.
Kinsland,Jesse E.x	Sarah Roberson	15 Mar. 1856 M.16 Mar. 1856 By H.P.Haynes,J.P.	J.D.Shook (w) Wm.M.Rhea,clk.
Kinsland,Joshua	Betsey Ann Shook	29 Mar. 1828	George Smathers (w) ----------

43

GROOM	BRIDE	DATE OF BOND	BONDSMAN & WITNESS
Kinsland,Joshua	Mary Radornel	26 Feb. 1845	David x Miller (w) A.T.Davidson
Kirby,Robert C.	Lavisa Henson	22 May 1869 M.23 May 1869 By Joshua Kinsland,J.P.	(w) W.C.Brown,R.D.H.C.
Kirkpatric,Milas Elexander (s.of Silas)	Laura Ann Byers (d.of Samuel)	18 Mar. 1869 M.21 Mar. 1869 By J.D.Wright,M.G.	(w) W.C.Brown,R.D.H.C.
Kitchens,David x	Jane Picklesimer	16 Nov. 1836	David Pickelsimer (w) J.Keener,clk.
Lackey,Wiyatt x	Elezebeth Wrathbone (d.of Andrew)	23 Dec. 1833	G.W.x Parton (w) S.Fitzgerrald
Land,Aninas x	Nancy Kilbay (d.of Henry)	13 Aug. 1831	John L.Dillard Henry x Plott Jr. (w) Ro.Love,clk.
Land,Hosea x	Zipha Thomas (d.of Joseph)	17 Oct. 1810	H(oliman) Battle (w) Ro.Love,clk.
Land,James	Caroline Dunkin	20 Jan. 1842	Joseph Brendle (w) ----------
Laney,Wm.x	Caroline Biddix	11 Mar. 1846	James x Hill (w) R.V.Welch
Languy,Tolbert (s.of Tolbert,Sr.)	Harritt Patton (d.of Jeremiah)	17 Oct. 1868 M.17 Oct. 1868 By James A.Zachary,M.G.	(w) W.C.Brown,Reg.Deed
Lankford,Champion	Elisabeth Reed	16 Nov. 1812	James x Reed
Lawless,Welson	Anne Newton	27 May 1826	J(oseph) H.Walker (w) Samuel Gibson
Layfawn,Monrow	Mary Right	11 Nov. 1858 M.19 Dec. 1858 By J.H.Johnson,J.P.	Robt. Sharp (w) W.W.Medford,clk.
Layfon,Julius	Mercilla Bond	14 Nov. 1854 M.14 Nov. 1854 By Isaac Clark	(w) J.Keener,clk.
Layfond,Wi-liam	Elvina Howard	17 Aug. 1860	Monroe Layfond (w) W.W.Medford,clk.
Leatherwood,William	Elisabeth Nelson (d.of David)	30 Mar. 1833	W(illia)m Moody (w) ----------
Leatherwood,Jasain	Matilda Arrington	27 Sept. 1858 M.---------- By Wm.McClure,J.P.	Philip x Noland (w) W.W.Medford,clk.
Leatherwood,Jasper Newton (s.of John & Margaret)	Lonsom E.McGee (d.of Jesse & Lucinda)	29 Jan. 1870 M.30 Jan. 1870 By J.H.Moody,J.P.	(w) W.C.Brown,R.D.H
Leatherwood,Neeley (s.of Samuel)	----------	31 Jan. 1827	(Request for License signed by Samuel Leatherwood)
Leatherwood,Nicholas x	Caroline Dotson	1 Feb. 1827	John Chambers,Jr. John M.Hinson (w) Ro.Love,clk.

GROOM	BRIDE	DATE OF BOND	BONDSMAN & WITNESS
Leatherwood,Samuel	Tersa Janes (d.of Peggy)	19 Jan. 1839	John H.Moody (w) ----------
Ledbetter,Coalmon	Lucrecea Long	4 Jan. 1847	Jonathan Ledbetter (w) ----------
Ledford,Jason	Betsey Bradley (d.of James)	22 Jan. 1824	John Colbert (w) J.L.Moore
Ledford,L.E.	Martha Russel	16 Feb. 1856 M.21 Feb. 1856 By W.G.B.Garrett,J.P.	(w) Wm.M.Rhea,clk.
Ledford,Spencer	Cassey Hix (d.of David)	14 Aug. 1833	Wm.K(elly) McGee (w) Wm.Welch
Lee,H.C.	M.M.Henry	15 Sept. 1857 M.15 Sept. 1857 By E.V.Plott,J.P.	(w) Wm.M.Rhea,clk.
Lee,Robert J.	Rebecca A.Evans	14 Dec. 1858 ? M.14 Dec. 1857 ? By E.V.Plott,J.P.	Elias Lee
Lefon,Benjamin x	Mary Clingman (d.of Micheal)	6 Apr. 1821	William Lafon (w) ----------
Leming,John	Mariah Morrow	22 Dec. 1860	P.M.Rich (w) W.W.Medford,clk.
Leming,Robert	Manerva Hawkins	16 May 1858 M.16 May 1858 By Wm.M.Turner,J.P.	Leander Liner (w) W.W.Medford,clk.
Lemming,Tho(ma)s	Sarah Stephenson	29 Dec. 1828	James Bradshaw (w) Wm.Welch
Lem(o)nes,Lawson H.	Clarissa Mingus (d.of George)	1 Jan. 1839	George Menges (w) ----------
Lenoir,Erwin (Col) (s.of Jesse & Elizabeth) (42 Yrs. old)	Candis Huskey (Col) (30 Yrs. old)	3 Oct 1867 M.6 Oct. 1867 By Isaac M.Hall	(w) W.W.Medford,clk.
Lenoir,James A. (Col)	Cilvey L.Collett (Col)	17 Nov. 1867 M.17 Nov. 1867 By A.H.Mann,J.P.	(w) W.W.Medford,clk.
Levaskue,Jesse	Sally Bryson	8 Mar. 1825	John Cuningham Tho(ma)s Rogers (w) ----------
Levey,Thorton	Lucinda Hall	16 Sept. 1851 M.18 Sept. 1851 By Colvard Nelson,J.P.	(w) Keener,clk.
Linder,Leander	Morning McDaniel	16 Apr. 1859 M.17 Apr. 1859 By R.E.Medford,J.P.	(w) W.W.Medford,clk.
Liner,James	Darcus Fulbright	11 Apr. 1840	Wriley Medford (w) Wm.Welch
Liner,Jermiah	Angelin Turner	23 Mar. 1843	P.L.Davis (w) W.Brown

45

GROOM	BRIDE	DATE OF BOND	BONDSMAN & WITNESS
Liner,John	Sarah Gray (d.of Gray of Tennessee)	14 Dec. 1837	Wriley Medford (w) S.Fitzgerrald
Liner,Leander	Nancey Nelson	31 July 1860	John C.Curry (w) W.W.Medford
Liner,W(m)	Malvina Cockraham	11 Mar. 1849	W.Tur(n)er (w) R.V.Welch,D.C.
Loftin,Joseph x	Rachel Chambers	21 May 1810	Joshoua x Kinworthey (w) Ro.Love,clk.
Logens,Simeon	Hester C.Mull	3 Dec. 1850	J(ohn) W.Killian (w) J.Keener
Londa,Burell H.x	Sarah Wrathbone (d.of Andrew)	19 Nov. 1832	Richard x Hunter (w) Wm.Welch
Long,A.J.	Jemimah L.Cathy	8 Nov. 1856 M.---------- By A.C.Hartgrove,J.P.	R.P.Hartgrove (w) Wm.M.Rhea,C.C.C.
Long,Henry (G)	Arta Wood (d.of Henry)	10 May 1837	S.Ftizgerrald (w) J.A.B.Fitzgerrald
Long,J.R.	S.J.Fitzgerrald	30 May 1854	J.N.Benners (w) Wm.M.Rhea,clk.
Long,John A.	Frances Roads	31 Dec. 1828	David x Mann (w) Reub. Deaver
Long, J(ohn) F.	Clarissa A.Hartgrove	12 Jan. 1853 M.16 Jan. 1853 By J.Trull	A.H.Mann (w) J.Keener,clk.
Long,Jonathan	Naoma Burnett	26 Nov. 1857 M.29 Nov. 1857 By A.C.Hartgrove,J.P.	J.L.Mann (w) W.W.Medford,clk.
Long,Joseph F.	Elvina S.Mull	25 Dec. 1857 M.27 Dec. 1857	J(oseph) J.Sorrels (w) W.W.Medford,clk.
Long,Michal	Elizabeth Hooper	31 Aug. 1850	A.C.Brown (w) S.W.Gaston,clk.
Loves,J.P.	Mahala Massay	5 Aug. 1865	D.H.Shook (w) J.W.Killian,clk.
Love,Robert	Sarah Welch	26 May 1868 M.28 May 1868 By R.A.Medford,J.P.	(w) J.N.Benners,D.C.
Love,Wm.Levi	Pholley J.Mills	19 Dec. 1853 M.19 Dec. 1853 By J.N.Benners,J.P.	J.N.Benners (w) W.Brown,D.C.
Lovingood,W(ashington)	Nancy Weeks	23 Jan. 1825	Drury Weeks (w) Ro.Love
Lundy,Hyram B.	Riler Brown	3 Feb. 1853 M.3 Feb. 1853 By H.Rogers,J.P.	Harvey x Hannah (w) J.Keener,clk.
Lusk,Joseph G.	Margrett Russel (d.of David)	13 Oct. 1832	John Brown (w) ----------
McBee,Ganen C.	Sarah Love	12 Dec. 1820	(w) Ro.Love,clk.

GROOM	BRIDE	DATE OF BOND	BONDSMAN & WITNESS
McBee,L(emuel) J.	Mary A.Love	22 July 1844	G.C.McBee (w) ----------
M(c)Carley,Thornton	Mary McAby	30 Aug. 1845	James McAbee (w) ----------
McClurer,Thomas J.	Delpha Snider	10 July 1859 M.10 July 1859 By D.B.Ford,J.P.	Riley Medford (w) W.W.Medford,clk.
McClure,Andrew x	Mary Street	30 May 1829	Charles x Jones (w) Reub. Deaver
McClure,Andrew Jr.x	Peggy Irons (d.of William)	-- Feb. 1816	James McClure (w) ----------
McClure,Jason x	Margaret Stephenson	2 Feb. 1828	Andrew McC(1)ure (w) ----------
McClure,Jesse x	Nancy White	18 Sept. 1828	Jason x McClure James Bradshaw (w) Ro.Love,clk.
McClure,John A.	Lueasey Jan McCracken	9 Oct. 1849	Wm.S.x Roberson (w) S.W.Gaston
McClure,Joseph x	Catherin Ducket	2 Aug. 1845	Merrill Bradshaw (w) ----------
McClure,Joseph x	Jain Bradshaw	20 July 1847	Andrew McClure (w) McCracken
McClure,Joseph (s.of Joseph,dec'd)	Nancy Moore (d.of Widow Margarett)	1 Mar. 1869 M.2 Mar. 1869 By F.M.Messer,J.P.	(w) W.C.Brown,R.D.H.C.
McClure,Thomas	Sarah Crawford (d.of Josiah Kerby)	25 Oct. 1823	W(illia)m Kimzey (w)H.Posey
McClure,Thomas	Sarah Wilson	22 Sept. 1845	Joseph L.Rinehardt (w) ----------
McClure,William	Leana Kendle (d.of Sarah)	11 Dec. 1821	Thomas McClure (w) Wm.Welch
McClure,W(illiam) R.	Jane Stephenson (d.of Katharine)	9 June 1833	John Justicse (w) Ro.Love,clk.
McClure,William R.	Mary McCracken	2 May 1857 M.2 May 1857 By J.A.McClure,J.P.	J C.Cagle (w) Wm.M.Rhea,clk.
McConnell,William,Sr.	Esther Tompson (d.of Nathan)	6 Nov. 1823	David McConnell (w) Dillard Love
McCracken,D.V.	Mary E.Slate	28 Mar. 1847	Allen Haynes (w) ----------
McCracken,Enos	Charlottee Rogers	11 Dec. 1839	W.G.B.Garrett (w) Wm.Welch
McCracken,H(yram)	Mary Howell	2 Aug. 1845	James Moore (w) ----------
McCracken,J(ames) M.	Elizabeth A. Penland	22 Mar. 1856 M.23 Mar. 1856 By A.T.Rogers,J.P.	A.T.Rogers (w) Wm.M.Rhea,clk.

GROOM	BRIDE	DATE OF BOND	BONDSMAN & WITNESS
McCracken,Joseph	Eliza McFalls	26 June 1858	J.J.Sparks (w) W.W.Medford
McCracken,Joseph F.	Juliann Howell	19 Oct. 1854 M.19 Oct. 1845 By Enos McCracken,J.P.	James McCracken (w) W.Brown,D.C.
McCracken,W(m)L.	Eliza Howell	21 May 1857 M.22 May 1857 By J.J.Sparks,M.G.	J.J.Sparks (w) Wm.M.Rhea,clk.
McC(r)ack(in),Acton	Josey Poteet (d.of John)	2 Jan. 1831	F(ra)n(cis) McGee (w) ----------
McDaniel,Stephen L.x	Nancy T.Owen	24 Jan. 1846	J.B.Leatherwood (w) ----------
McDowell,George x	Eleanor Write	6 De.c 1834	W(m) B.Morgan (w) J.Keener
McDowell,John	Elizabeth Calwell (grandd. of Alexander)	6 Oct. 1815	Nathl.Blackburn (w) ----------
McDowell,Wm.	Elisabeth McDowell	3 June 1820	Ebenez(er) Newton (w) ----------
McElroy,W(illia)m	Jane Mitchell	1 Aug. 1861	A.J.Robinson
McFalls,William (J)	Margaret Sanford	27 July 1858 M.29 Aug. 1858. By H.Rogers,J.P.	(w) J.Keener,clk.
McGee,Jesse	Lucinda -----	18 Oct. 1844	Thomas Smith (w) ----------
McGee,John Noland (s.of J.N. dec'd)	Harriett Howell (d.of John D.)	23 Oct. 1869 M.24 Oct. 1869 By E.R.Ferguson,J.P.	(w) W.C.Brown,R.D.H.C.
McGee,W(illia)m Kelly	Nancy Ledford (d.of Eli)	27 Dec. 1830	Robert Ferguson (w) Ro.Love,clk.
McHenry,John	Jane Henry (d.of John)	25 Sept. 1821	James Chambers (w) John B.Love
McKenny,Allison D.	Faney E.Hyatt	7 Dec. 1845	J.B.Leatherwood (w) ----------
McKleroy,Henry x	Miley McClure	13 May 1848	John x Queen (w) W.Brown
McLure,James H.	C.E.McCracken	23 Oct. 1856	J.J.Sparks (w) C.T.Rogers,clk.
McMulan,Joseph (Jr.)	Milly Waters (d.of Micheal)	6 Oct. 1817	Isham x Evins (w) ----------
McMullen,Griffy	Sarah Trull	1 Feb. 1842	David Hill (w) ----------
McNabb,W(illia)m	Elizabeth F. Leatherwood	2 Nov. 1840	J(ohn) B.Leatherwood (w) Wm.Welch
MePeters,Jonathan	Rachal Reed (d.of Saml.)	12 Aug. 1814	John McFarland (w) ----------
McFalls,Ar(t)er	Rachul Barnes	16 Apr. 1846	Samul x Nowland (w) ----------

GROOM	BRIDE	DATE OF BOND	BONDSMAN & WITNESS
McWilliamson, Alex(ander)	Rachael Roberts	29 Mar. 1853	(C.H.Penland) (w) J.Keener
Mehaffey,Francis Marion x	Martha Warren	23 July 1851 M.---------- By Wm.Haynes	William Mahfy (w) R.V.Welch
Maha(ff)ey,R(obert)A.	Sophronia Hawkins	8 Jan. 1852 M.8 Jan. 1852 By A.J.Murray,J.P.	R.A.Deaver (w) J.Keener,clk.
Mah(a)ffey,William	Elazabeth Snider (d.of Adam)	17 May 1819	Andrew x Snider (w) ----------
Mahaffey,Wm.N.	Violett Campbell	28 July 1857 M.29 July 1857 By A.C.Hartgrove,J.P.	(w) Wm.M.Rhea,clk.
Mahaffey,(Wm.) R(ufus)	Eliz.E.Jones	13 Nov. 1856 M.13 Nov. 1856 By J.A.Benners,J.P.	J(as) Sorrls (w) Wm.M.Rhea,clk.
Mahaffy,J.H. x	Elizabeth Smith	3 Jan. 1844	William x Mahaffy (w) ----------
Mahaffy,John	Mima Henson	5 Sept. 1857 M.6 Sept. 1857 By A.C.Hartgrove,J.P.	(w) Wm.M.Rhea,clk.
Mahaffy,Joseph x	Sally Roberson	19 Dec. 1853 M.11 June 1854 D.B.Ford,J.P.	Richard x Roberson (w) Wm.M.Rhea,clk.
Man,John x	Eby Bryson (d.of Andrew)	30 ----1815	Heder x Watson (w) ----------
Man,William x	Elizabeth Morrow	30 Jan. 1842	Stephen x Smith (w) W.Brown
Mann,A.H.	M.E.Burnett	14 Feb. 1856 M.17 Feb. 1856 By A.C.Hartgrove,J.P.	D.F.Bird (w) Wm.M.Rhea,clk.
Mann,Andrew x	Sarrah Blackburn	27 Apr. 1844	James H. x Kilbee (w) ----------
Mann,David x	Lucretia Harman	16 Aug. 1826	Joseph Dever (w) Ro.Love,clk.
Mann,David R.	Rebea Anderson	9 Jan. 1860	Wm.S.Evans (w) ----------
Mann,James	Polly Rease	23 June 1829	(w) Reub Deaver,Dept.
Mann,John Taylor (s.of William)	Catherine Elizabeth Crawford (d.of John & Sarah)	25 Sept. 1869 M. 7 Oct. 1869 By Wm.S.Evans,J.P.	(w) W.C.Brown,R.D.H.C.
Martin,William	Rebacka Jenkens	19 July 1840	J(ohn) S.Gibson G.W.Wright (w) Samuel Gibson,D.C.
Mason,Aaron L.	Mary Ann Thompson	29 Oct. 1860	W(illia)m J.Wilson (w) W.W.Medford
Mason,David	Mary Stevenson (d.of Widow Stevenson)	6 Dec. 1835	James Bradshaw (w) S.Fitzgerrald,D.C.

GROOM	BRIDE	DATE OF BOND	BONDSMAN & WITNESS
Mason,E(ph) R.W. x	M.A.M.Gregory	22 Aug. 1865	John L.Grahl (w) J.W.Killian
Mason,John	Sarah Hall	25 Aug. 1846	David Mason (w) ----------
Massa,D.A.	Mary Medford	9 June 1859 M.9 June 1859 By Wm.Haynes,J.P.	D.J.Dotson (w) David Howell
Massay,Jeremiah	Sarah Brown	6 Dec. 1869 M.---------- By J.H.Massey	(w) W.C.Brown,R.D.
Massay,J(ohn) E.	Sarah Massey	31 Oct. 1856 M.31 Oct. 1856 By J.F.Fincher,J.P	W.W.Medford (w) W.M.Rhea,clk.
Massay,Lebo	Susanah Evins alias Tindell	3 Apr. 1829	N(inian) Edmonston (w) ----------
Massay,Samuel	Navvy Massay	16 Dec. 1857 M.---------- By Noah Francis,J.P.	J.N.Ratcliff (w) W.W.Medford,clk.
Massay,W(m) M(cd)	Neoma Medford	2 Dec. 1853 M.2 Dec. 1853 By J.F.Fincher,J.P.	Wm.L.Davis (w) W.Brown,D.C.
Massey,Jacob x	Elizabeth Shook	3 July 1845 M. ---------- By W.Osborn,J.P.	John x Snider (w) Wm.Welch,D.C.
Massy,James x	Patsy Parham (d.of Wm.)	1 Apr. 1835	Jeremiah Vickers (w) S.Fitzgerrald,clk.
Massy,Tillit	Caroline Inman	30 Oct. 1846	Alfred Smathers (w) ----------
Mathes,Frances A.	Carline Coggins	11 Jan. 1850	J.L.Smith (w) S.W.Gaston
Mathus,David x	Elizabeth Jones	10 Oct. 1839	Ira x Ledbetter (w) J.Keener
Mathus,Joel x	Jane Clark (d.of John)	11 Feb. 1822	Richmand Carrel (w) Wm.Welch
Mathus,Peter Sr. x	Easter Caroline Parker (d.of Solomon)	11 Aug. 1839	Isaac N.Keener (w) J.Keener
Mauney,Hoza	Maryan C. Hill	15 Jan. 1853 M.16 Jan. 1853 By H.P.Haynes,J.P.	Wm.Moody (w) H.P.Haynes
Mauney,Larcan	Eliza Cagle	7 Feb. 1861	Wm.L.Moody (w) W.W.Medford
M(a)xwell,J.W.	Elvira Enlow	20 Jan. 1834	B.M.Enloe (w) ----------
Meace,George x	Betsey Starr	14 Aug. 1829	John R. x Cooper (w) Ro.Love,clk.
Meace,Peter x	Nancy Robison (d.of Henry)	5 Dec. 1829	David Hill (w) Ro.Love,clk.

GROOM	BRIDE	DATE OF BOND	BONDSMAN & WITNESS
Medford,E.B.	Mary Evans	16 Aug. 1854 M.---------- By J.F.Fincher,J.P.	N.L. (e) Davis (w) Wm.M.Rhea,clk.
Medford,Isreal x	Nancy Moor	24 Sept. 1813	Johnah x Medford (w) Wm.Welch,Jr.
Medford,Isreal	Mary A.Blaylock	2 Aug. 1842	Johnson Anderson (w) ----------
Medford,L.D. x	Martha Fullbright	9 Apr. 1857 M.9 Apr. 1857 By J.F.Fincher,J.P.	J(onathan) x Michel (w) Wm.M.Rhea,clk.
Medford,Lebo	Mary Malinda Massey	7 Jan. 1852 M.7 Jan. 1852 By W.L.Davis,J.P.	A(ndrew) Holder (w) J.Keener,clk.
Medford,N(icholas)	Sarah Fulbright	13 Sept. 1840	M(icheal) W.Smith (w) Wm.Welch,clk.
Medford,W.W.	Caroline Tate	18 May 1857 M.19 May 1857 By J.B.Finchers,J.P.	Lo(uranz)o(d) Medford (w) Wm.M.Rhea,clk.
Meece,A.D.	Elizabeth Barnes	21 June 1852 M.22 June 1852 By Colvard Nelson,J.P.	Jas. Calwell (w) J.Keener,clk.
Meece,George	Elizabeth A.Hall	12 June 1846	W.L.Davis (w) ----------
Meece,John Pinckney	Mary Hall	20 Feb. 1855 M.22 Feb. 1855 By A.C.Hartgrove	Saml.x Chambers (w) J.N.Benners
Meese,D.F.	Catherine Anderson	6 Jan. 1863 M.6 Jan. 1863 By C.B.Mingus	(w) W.W.Medford,clk.
Melton,John	Jane Gibson	21 Nov. 1858 M.21 Nov. 1858 By R.E.Medford,J.P.	B(raxton) P. Mull (w) W.W.Medford,clk.
Mesar,Johnx	Minervey Standcele	15 Sept. 1837	Rob(er)t Laney Wellum x Ensley Rachal x Mesor John Gibson (w) Samuel Gibson
Messer,Christain S. x	Jane Barnet Freeman (d.of Joshoway)	24 Feb. 1835	Georg x Price (w) ----------
Messer,David x	Polly Gilleland (d.of Robert)	19 Dec. 1832	Thomas x Connup (w) Ro.Love,clk.
Messer,David x	Lucinda Flemings	25 Mar. 1851 M. 8 Sept. 1852 By Colvard Nelson,J.P.	Moses x Messer (w) J.Keener,clk.
Messer,David	Elisabeth Boyeed	20 Dec. 1865	James F. Green (w) H.Rogers
Messer,Eli x	Elizabeth Price	11 June 1853 M.12 June 1854 ? By Colvard Nelson,J.P.	Thomas x Colwell (w) Wm.M.Rhea,clk.

GROOM	BRIDE	DATE OF BOND	BONDSMAN & WITNESS
Messer,Franklin	Jain Noland	13 Apr. 1857 M.13 Apr. 1857 By J.H.Noland,J.P.	J(ames) H.Noland (w) Wm.M.Rhea,clk.
Messer,George x	Nancey Coldwell (d.of William)	10 Apr. 1822	Thomas x Coldwell (w) Wm.Welch
Messer,Henry	Adoline McCracken	11 Dec. 1856 M.11 Dec. 1856 Enos McCracken	J(ohn)A.Smart (w) Wm.M.Rhea,clk.
Messer,Joseph	Nancy Ensley (d.of Andrew)	24 Feb. 1835	W(illiam) B. Morgan (w) J.Keener
Messer,Joseph	Celia Roberson	12 Nov. 1848	B(arnard) Fulbright Jr (w) ----------
Messer,Joseph A.	Nancy Cashion	29 Jan. 1850	Phillip x Noland J.N.Brendle (w) R.A.Edmonston,D.C.
Messer,Lawson	Avonline Smith	12 Oct. 1856 M.18 Oct. 1856 By H.Rogers,J.P.	(John Messer) (w) Wm.M.Reha,clk.
Messer,M.W.	Sarah Ann Burgess	30 Jan. 1858 M.31 Jan. 1858 By Young Bennett,J.P.	J.A.Messer (w) W.W.Medford,clk.
Messer,Patton	Cathorine Rhea	25 Dec. 1853 M.25 Dec. 1853 By Geo.Williams,J.P.	William(o) Mess(er) (w) W.T.Rogers
Messer,Samuel x	Polly Swanger	24 Mar. 1857 M.---------- By Wm.P.Gillett,J.P.	Wm.P.Gillett (w) Wm.M.Rhea,clk.
Messer,Saml.	Rapsey Elvira Price	30 July 1867 M. 5 Aug. 1867 By C.Nelson,J.P.	(w) W.W.Medford,clk.
Messer,Strawther x	Matilda Franklin	16 Apr. 1856 M.---------- By Colvard Nelson,J.P.	Aaron Price (w) Wm.M.Rhea,clk.
Messer,Thomas x	Mary Price (d.of Richard)	12 Feb. 1823	William x Caldwell,Jr. (w) David Russell,J.P.
Messer W(illiam) O.	Elizabeth SMith	8 Oct. 1852 M.9 Oct. 1852 By W.Green,J.P.	John A.Smith (w) C.T.Rogers,D.ck.
Messor,Federick x	Anna Hunter	17 Oct. 1828	Thos. x Colwell (w) ----------
Middleton,Nathun	Mary Pickelsimer	23 Jan. 1845	James M.Hooper (w) Wm.Hooper
Middleton,John	Miama Denton (d.of Saml.)	19 Dec. 1815	Benja.Stiles (w) ----------
Miler,M(arcus) M.	Francis E.McDaniel	28 Oct. 1857 M.28 Oct. 1857	H.F.Plott (w) W.M.Freeman,D.C.
Milican,John P. x	Sarah Snider	14 Aug. 1850	Thomas Smith (w) S.W.Gaston,clk.

GROOM	BRIDE	DATE OF BOND	BONDSMAN & WITNESS
Miller,David x	Anny Loranse (d.of Joseph)	7 Dec. 1842	Daniel x Sigmon (w) R.Dever
Miller,David x	Cassander Wallace (d.of John)	20 Sept. 1834	Jacob x Snider (w) S.Fitzgerrald,D.C.
Miller,Georg	Anna Alexander (d.of Daniel)	20 Jan. 1824	Coonard Sillers (w) Wm.Welch
Miller,Jacob	Matilda Justice	21 Nov. 1844	John Rhodarmel (w) -----------
Miller,J(acob) A.	Viana A.Evins (d.of Jacob)	12 July 1838	Hiram Drum (w) Ro.Love,clk.
M(il)ler,J(ames) L.	Elizure Miller	2 Nov. 1848	N.A.Smathers (w) ----------
Miller,S.H.	M.J.Keener	16 Oct. 1852 M.16 Oct. 1852 By J.F.Finchers,J.P.	M.B.Chapman (w) C.T.Rogers,D clk.
Miller,Tillmon	Sarah Wynes	4 Jan. 1841	Joseph Cabe (w) ----------
Mills,David x	Malenda Elliott (d.of Jason)	29 July 1837	Alfred Quee(n) (torn) (w) ----------
Mills,Reuben, x	Amelia Elliott (d.of Jason)	26 Oct. 1839	Alfred Queen (w) Wm.Welch
Mills,Thomas x	Elmina Pannel	24 Jan. 1850	Marian x Gunter (w) R.A.Edmonston,D.C.
Millsaps,John A. x	Marey T. Gibson	6 Apr. 1843	Isaac Gipson (w) Samuel Gibson
Millsaps,Joseph x	Rachel Grantham (d.of Aron Coxes)	7 June 1823	John Massey (w) John B.Love
Millsaps,Peter	Nancey Philips	1 May 1826	Th(o)ma(s) Milsaps (w) Samuel Gibson
Milner,S.F.	T.G.davis	25 Nov. 1865	W.H.Dotson (w) J.W.Killian,clk.
Milner,Thomas	Matilda Hollyfield (d.of Widow Hollyfield)	20 Nov. 1833	Thos.A.Noland (w) S.Fitzgerrald,D.C.
Minges,Abraham	Rebecca Stillwell (d.of Jeremiah,dec'd)	9 Aug. 1816	Champ Lnagford (w) ----------
Mingus,C.B.	Mary Jane Osborn	27 Mar. 1858 M.28 Mar. 1858 By A.L.Herren,J.P.	(w) W.W.Medford,clk.
Mingus,Ephram	Sophia Ellis (d.of Charles)	13 June 1814	Saml. Stilwell (w) ----------
Mingus,George E.	Susanah E.J.Herrill	27 Mar. 1850	Wm.Mingus (w) S.W.Gaston
Mingus,John x	Poly Enloe (d.of Abraham)	14 Apr. 1822	John Battle (w) John B.Love
Mingus,L(awson) A.	Salley Brice (d.of William)	31 Mar. 1839	Peter x Meace (w) ----------

GROOM	BRIDE	DATE OF BOND	BONDSMAN & WITNESS
Mingus,Richard	Jane C. Collins	24 Sept. 1849	Henry J.Beck (w) ----------
Mitchel,Jonathan	Sarah Jane Fullbright	6 May 1857 M.6 May 1857 By J.F.Fincher,J.P.	J.L.Smith (w) Wm.M.Rhea,clk.
Mitchell,B(urton)	Caroline Tate	8 Nov. 1851	A(ndy) Holder (w) J.Keener
Mitchell,Christopher	Isirmiah Jones	17 Apr. 1858 M.18 Apr. 1858 By Wm.Turner,J.P.	R.H.Leming (w) W.W.Medford,clk.
Money,Isaac	Emily Armstrong	26 Feb. 1850	N.G.Howell (w) R.A.Edmonston
Monroe,Daniel P.	Carey A.Dodson	22 Feb. 1831	W(illiam) E.Davidson (w) Ro.Love
Monroe,Samuel B.	Sarah Caroline Norress (d.of Susan,Wife of Samuel,dec'd)	16 Feb .1830	E(phraim) L(ogan) Moody (w) Ro.Love,clk.
Monteath,Samuel	Mary Fisher	8 Nov. 1838	James M.Keener (w) ----------
Monteath,Wm.B.	Mary Parris (d.of David)	26 Sept. 1857	J.S.Long (w) J.Keener
Monteith,Thomas	Hariett McClure	7 Mar. 1855 8 Mar. 1855 M. J.N.Benners,J.P.	Wm.P.Arrington (w) Wm.M.Rhea,clk.
Moody,A(ndrew) J.	Sarah Wood (d.of Lawrence)	8 Sept. 1832	Samuel B. Monroe (w) ----------
Moody,F.W.	Erena T. Howell	17 May 1845	I(ra) D.Farmer (w) W.Brown
Moody,Harlen	Elezebeth McClure (d.of Thomas)	24 Apr. 1834	John H. Moody (w) S.Fitzgerrald,clk.
Moody,J.B.	Soosan Sparks	19 June 1858 M.20 June (1858) By J.Vickers,J.P.	W.L.Wilson (w) David Howell
Moody,J(ames) L.	Nancy Aveline Henry	6 Mar. 1850	Alfred B. x Michel (w) S.W.Gaston,clk.
Moody,Joseph	Arta Crawford	30 Oct. 1858	Phillip x Noland (w) W.W.Medford
Moody,Parris Layfayett (s.of Wm.L.)	Elvira Fulbright (d.of Jacob)	13 Aug. 1870 M.14 Aug. 1870 By M.H.Love,J.P.	(w) W.C.Brown,R.D.H.C
Moody,Ruben	Polly Leatherwood	30 Jan. 1826	Strother Moody (w) Ro.Love,clk.
Moody,Wm. x	Belinda McCamish	24 Feb. 1823	John T.Chambers Sr. (w) Jas. R.Love
Moody,Wm.L.	Mursey Ann Plott (Merza)	21 Dec. 1847 M.23 Dec. 1847	J.B.Leatherwood (w) W.Brown
Moony,Char(le)s	Louisa Dotson (d.of Daniel)	18 Dec. 1838	Jacob K.Dotson (w) Wm.Welch

GROOM	BRIDE	DATE OF BOND	BONDSMAN & WITNESS
Moore,A.C.	Edney McDaniel	24 Jan. 1846	P.W.Edwards (w) ----------
Moore,Archie Levi	Rebecca Harvel	13 Feb. 1868 M.13 Feb. 1868 By J.INman,J.P.	(w) J.N.Benners,Dy.Clk
Moore,F.E.	E.C.Harben	4 Feb. 1852 M.---------- By A.C.Hartgrove,J.P.	G.B.Cathey (w) C.T.Rogers,D.clk.
Moore,George	Susanah Rhodearmel (d.of Wid.Rhodearmel)	12 Aug. 1836	Micheal Smith (w) S.Fitzgerrald,clk.
Moore,James	Sarah P.Bonham	18 Aug. 1844	A.C.Hartgrove (w) ----------
Moore,John	Mary Franklin	24 Dec. 1848	Jason (c) Allison (w) W.Brown
Moore,Levy x	Ruthy Calwell	19 Nov. 1827	John Moody (w) K.Boone
Moore,Micheal	Delitha Darnel	18 June 1850	Wm.P.Gillett (w) ----------
Moore,W.H.	A.E.Worley	27 ------1865	G.W.Moore (w) J.W.Killian
Moore,William x	Sarha Franklin	18 Oct. 1848	K(indred) Reeves (w) ----------
More,S.B.	Celia More	4 Sept. 1855 M.26 Sept. 1855 By Wm.P.Gillett,J.P.	Wm.M.Rhea,clk.
Moreland,James S.	Rhodey Lee	17 Dec. 1829	James Chambers (w) Reub.Deaver
Moren,Wm.	H.A.McCluer	8 July 1859 M.9 July By R.H.Moody	J(ohn) W.Austin (w) W.W.medford,clk.
Morgan,E.W.	Nancy E.Smathers	13 Feb. 1854 M.16 Feb. 1854 By A.C.Hartgrove,J.P.	J.N.Benners (w) Wm.M.Rhea,clk.
Morris,Jas,H.W. x	Mary Browning	26 May 1854 M.27 May 1854 By Wm.McClure,J.P.	Wm.B. xHawkins (w) Wm.M.Rhea
Morris,Wm.B.	Margret E. Dawson	13 Oct. 1849	Isaac Rhinehart (w) S.W.Gaston
Morrow,A.C.	Adaline Rinehart (d.of Isaac)	13 Dec. 1838	T(homas) C.Rinehardt (w) Wm.Welch
Morrow,Andrew x	Cleracy M.Massey	9 Mar. 1848	Lebo x Medford (w) ----------
Morrow,James x	Harett Ross	9 Apr. 1853 M.10 Apr. 1853 By J.F.Finchers,J.P.	Wm.W.Battle
Morrow,John x	Polly Bivans	8 Feb. 1826	Lewis x Sorrells (w) Ro.Love,clk.

GROOM	BRIDE	DATE OF BOND	BONDSMAN & WITNESS
Morrow,J(ohn) P.	Catharine Buff (d.of Martin,dec'd)	19 Nov. 1832	James x Trulove (w) Wm.Welch
Morrow,Morgan x	Hanah Davis (d.of Aron)	12 Jan. 1836	Lewis x Sorrels (w) S.Fitzgerrald,D.C.
Morrow,William	Case Holifield	12 Apr. 1860	T.W.Smith (w) W.W.Medford
Moss,Howell x	Jenny Rogers	10 Jan. 1827	Alex(ander) M.Moss (w) ----------
MucElroy,Jesse x	Elizabeth Michel	26 Aug. 18(5)7 M.26 Aug. 1857 By J.F.Finchers,J.P.	John M.Queen (w) Wm.M.Rhea,clk.
MucElroy,John F. x	Sally Sorrols	18 Aug. 1855 M.19 Aug. 1855 By B.Turner,M.G.	A.A. x Roberson (w) Wm.M.Rhea,clk.
Muckelroy,A.B.	Mandy L.Smith	18 Jan. 1853	W(illiam) Rineherdt (w) J.Keener
Muckleroy,David	Margaret Battle	27 Nov. 1856 M.---------- By J.N.Banners,J.P.	C.T.Rogers (w) Wm.M.Rhea,clk.
Muckleroy,James x	Lidea Medford	-----18(54)	Alvers A. x Roberson (w) W.Brown
Mulins,Ase	Peggy Watts (d.of Jacob)	8 June 1816	Jacob x Gilder (w) Ro.Love,clk.
Mull,J.B.	Manervy Hawkins	28 Dec. 1858 M.28 Dec. 1858 By Wm.P.Gillett,J.P.	J.H.Mull (w) W.W.Medford,clk.
Mull,Jacob O.	Ruth Harris (d.of Benjamin)	24 Nov. 1838	James R.Love (w) Wm.Allman
Mull,Jacob O.	Jane Davis	1 Aug. 1842	Alston x Panter (w) W.Brown
Mull,Sherreod D.	Margaret Brookshear (d.of Benjamin)	14 Nov. 1821	Asa Wilson (w) Wm.Welch
Munrow,Paxton	Soauer Anderson	17 Feb. 1853 M.17 Feb. 1853 By H.P.Haynes,J.P.	(w) J.Keener,clk.
Munteeth,Samuel x	Sarah McClure	15 Jan. 1850	Philip x Noland (w) ----------
Murry,A.J.	M.E.Bonham	27 Apr. 1864	Wm.Renno (w) H.P.Haynes
Murray,E.P.G.	N.L.Singleton	15 Aug. 1860	W.H.Hartgrove (w) W.W.Medford,clk.
Murry,Wm.S.	Armina L.Murry	29 Jan. 1868 M.29 Jan. 1868 By H.P.Haynes,J.P.	(w) W.W.Medford,clk.
Nations,Spencers x	Eliza Lollis (d.of Sarah)	10 Feb. 1839	J.W.King W(esley) M.Enloe (w) Samuel Gibson
Nelson,David Jr.	Ann Jones (d.of John)	5 Aug. 1835	James Nelson (w) S.Fitzgerrald

GROOM	BRIDE	DATE OF BOND	BONDSMAN & WITNESS
Nelson G.H.(olland)	Nancey Leatherwood	30 Oct. 1858 M. 7 Nov. 1858 By E.V.Plott,J.P.	T.A.White (w) W.W.Medford,clk.
Nelson,Hugh	Polly Owens	12 Jan. 1829 M.---------- By Paxton Cumming,M.G.	(w) Reub Deaver
Newton,Samuel	Sarey Ebline Newton (d.of John McFarlin)	24 May 1836	Henry Plemons (w) Samuel Gibson
Nicholds,C.C.	Mary Evans	4 June 1859 M.5 June 1859 By Jas. B.Fitzgerrald,M.G.	D.A.Nicholds (w) W.W.Medford,clk.
Nicholes,James	Esther McClure	11 Feb. 1847	John x McClure (w) W.Brown
Nichols,David P. x	Alief Evans	24 July 1850	Leander Liner (w) S.W.Gaston
Nichols,John P.	Elizabeth Wilson	16 May 1850	J(ames) R.Trulove (w) S.W.Gaston,clk.
Nickis,James	Lucinda Liner	5 Apr. 1842	George Trulove (w) J.Vickers
Nicks,Joseph D. x	Sarah Garrett	8 Aug. 1840	Alfred x Wines (w) Wm.Welch
Nite,David	Nancy Buge	24 Aug. 1857 M.24 Aug. 1857 By H.Rogers,J.P.	H.Rogers (w) Wm.M.Rhea,clk.
Noblitt,Thomas	Jane Valenda Corbin	17 Jan. 1828	B(enjamin) Chambers (w) Wm.Welch
Noland,Alen x	Mary A. Parmer	6 Jan. 1848	Jesse McGee (w) ----------
Noland,Allen	Caroline Rhea	22 Aug. 1852 M.22 Aug. 1852 By J.A.McClure,J.P.	John Noland (w) C.T.Rogers,D.C.
Noland,J.H.	Mary A.Messer	27 Apr. 1859 M.---------- By C.Nelson,J.P.	(w) W.W.Medford,clk.
Noland,John	Lavina Woods	22 Dec. 1851 M.23 Dec. 1851 By W.Green,J.P.	(w) J.Keener,clk.
Noland,Joseph N.	Josephine Howell	18 Oct. 1867 M.18 Oct. 1867 By W.H.Leatherwood,J.P.	(w) W.W.Medford,clk.
Noland,Lewis x	Nancey Stinson (d.of Catherin)	18 Oct. 1836	William x Wrathbone (w) Wm.Welch
Noland,Philip x	Polly McClure	15 Jan. 1850	Samuel x Menteth (w) -----------
Noland,R.B.	M.M.Rogers	5 Nov. 1851 M.5 Nov. 1851 By W.Green,J.P.	(w) J.Keener,clk.

57

GROOM	BRIDE	DATE OF BOND	BONDSMAN & WITNESS
Noland,Rily (s.of Willis)	Caroline Rogers (d.of Powers)	25 Sept. 1869	(w) W.C.Brown,R.D.H.C.
Noland,R(obt) W.	Jane Lusk	22 Apr. 1857 M.22 Apr. 1857 By J.H.Noland,J.P.	J(ames) H.Noland (w) Wm.M.Rhea,clk.
Nola(n)d,Tho(ma)s A.	Eliza Franklin (d.of Benyly)	20 May 1837	Elisha Yarborough (w) Wm.Welch
Noland,Willis x	Malenda Green (d.of William)	26 Dec. 1831	David Green (w) J.R.Love
Norris,Ephram	Elviry E.Rhods	6 Sept. 1847	Nathan Queen (w) W.Brown
Norris,Moses x	Rebeca Reece	6 Apr. 1847	J.F. x Queen (w) W.Brown
Norris,Samuel	Anna Partin (d.of Benjamin)	17 Dec. 1814	John Cuningham (w) R.Love,clk.
Norvill,John W.	Polly Ann Gaddy	23 May 1846	Amos Smith (w) ----------
Nunly,John	Mary Smathers	8 Mar. 1859 M.8 Mar. 1859 By E.D.Brendle	J.S.Mehaffey (w) W.W.MEdford,clk.
Oak,David x	Polly Lovel (d.of George)	------1817	Natham x Gibson (w) ----------
Oaks,W(illia)m	Arlotte Caldwell (d.of Henry)	15 Feb. 1817	Owen Owens (w) Ro.Love
Odum,Jesse	Mary C. NOblitt	18 Sept. 1846	J.N.Brendle (w) ----------
Ogel,Eligey x	Alisabth Coner	13 Aug. 1840	Henry Floy(d) (w) Samuel Gibson
Ogel,Willum x	Gane Conar (d.of Samuel)	22 Apr. 1836	Samuel x Coner (w) Samuel Gibson
Osbon,Ervin (col)	Martha Cathey (col)	5 Dec. 1868 M.6 Dec. 1868 By B.Nelson,M.G.	(w) W.C.Brown,R.D.H.C.
Osborn,Adoniram Judson	Mary Plott	23 July 1865 M.25 July 1865	R.G.A.Love W.W.Stringfield (w) J.W.Killian,clk.
Osborn,Enoch Morgan (s.of Jonathan)	N.Emiline Howell (d.of David)	12 Aug. 1851 M.12 Aug. 1851 By U.Keener,M.G.	E.G.Hyatt (w) David Howell
Osborn,Judson Psoey (s.of Jonathan)	Charrity Patton	26 Nov. 1845	J.M.Patton (w) Wm.Haynes
Osborn,Roland (s.of JOnathan)	Jane O. Cathey (d.of Jamima,Widow)	25 May 1830	Thompson Allman (w) Reub Deaver,D.C.
Osburn,John (s.of Jonathan)	Violet Cathey	29 Nov. 1827	R(obert) B.Hyatt (w) Reuben Dever
Osburn,Sherwood (s.of Jonathan)	Polly Cathey (d.of George)	27 Mar. 1821	David Howell (w) R.Love,clk.

GROOM	BRIDE	DATE OF BOND	BONDSMAN & WITNESS
Owen,D.A.	Martha Janes Rice	9 Aug. 1860 M.9 Aug. 1860 By Wm.Hicks,M.G.	R.L.Owen (w) W.W.Medford,clk.
Owen,Doctor J.	Vianna Birchfield	24 Apr. 1869 M.25 Apr. 1869 By H.S.L.Moody,J.P.	(w) W.C.Brown,R.D.H.C.
Owen,Jezekiah	Lucinda McCamish	21 Mar. 1826	Henderson McCamish (w) K.Boone
Owen,James	Elizabeth Parker (d.of Wm.S.)	5 Nov. 1838	William S.Parker (w) J.Keener
Owen,R.L.	Margaret Murry	25 Apr. 1853 M.26 Apr. 1853 By H.P.Haynes,J.P.	W(m) E.Rice (w) H.P.Haynes
Owen,Reubin	Elmira Davis	16 Oct. 1850	Hezekiah Allison (w) J.Keener
Owens,J.C. x	Martha Crage	24 Dec. 1859 M.---------- By C.Nelson,J.P.	M.xGrant (w) David Howell
Owens,J.F(ranklin)	Jula Ann McDaniel	5 Dec. 1849	L(awson) C(al)well (w) S.W.Gaston
Owens,William	Margaret Tilly (d.of Lazerus)	3 Aug. 1810	Benjamin Davis (w) R.Love,clk.
Oxoner,Henry	Elisabeth Gregg	24 Apr. 1860	Phillip x Noland (w) W.W.Medford
Oyster,McDaniel x	Madeby Allen (d.of Alonza)	29 Oct. 1865	Richard x Robison J.W.Killian
Painter,Oliver	Francis Crawford (d.of Saml.)	23 Dec. 1834	Saml. x Painter (w) J.D.Dilliard
Palmer,George H.	Catherin Owens (d.of Owen Owens)	13 June 1819	David Coleman (w) ----------
Palmer H.C.	R.A.L.Sutherlin	17 Aug. 1861	J.M.Tate (w) ----------
Palmer,Jesse	Deborah Hall	7 Aug. 1826	George Hall Sr. Enoch Hall Asqr.
Palmer,Jesse	Mary Ann Rogers	15 Feb. 1854 M.15 Feb. 1854 By Wm.P.Gillett,J.P.	R.A.Colwell (w) W.Brown
Palmer,Thomas	Rebecca Vandeever	7 Mar. 1819	Joseph Young (w) ----------
Paress,Alfred	Fandy Gibson	2 Mar. 1842	John Gibson (w) ----------
Parker,Daniel x	Marinda Brown	11 Jan. 1845	Sam(ue)l Higdon (w) Enos Hooper
Parker,Hiram	Vira Londay	18 Oct. 1851 M.24 Oct. 1851 By H.Rogers,J.P	(w) J.Keener,clk.
Parker,John	Nancy Phillips	28 Nov. 1844	Edward Hooper (w) H.Coward

GROOM	BRIDE	DATE OF BOND	BONDSMAN & WITNESS
Parker,John P.	Nancy Queen	18 July 1850	Joseph C.Dowson (w) S.W.Gaston
Parker,W(illia)m Jr.	Lucinda Queen (d.of Wm.B.)	11 Oct. 1839	W(illia)m B.Queen (w) ----------
Parks,J.F.	----------	17 Mar. 1852	J.Keener (w) ----------
Parris,David x	Elizabeth Gunter	16 Oct. 1839	Samuel Paris (w) J.B.Allison
Parris,David H.	Mahala Elliott	23 Sept. 1834	W(illia)m Stanfield (w) J.Keener
Parris,John	Hannah Ensly (d.of William)	6 Jan. 1840	Joseph Keener (w) ----------
Parton,Brittian W.x	Nancy Allison (d.of Joshuae)	18 Nov. 1833	Hollingsworth Moode (w) J.T.Chambers,clk.
Parton,Charles M.	Mary Sitton	15 Mar. 1840	S(tephen) W.Gaston (w) ----------
Parton,Thomas	Nancey Rathbone	1 Sept. 1864	H.T. x Smith,Jr. (w) W.W.Medford,clk.
Patters(on),John	Sally Hix (d.of David)	8 Feb. 1833	David x Hix (w) Ro.Love,clk.
Patterson,Robert x	Margaret Withrow (d.of John)	7 Dec. 1836	J.D.Dillard (w) J.Keener
Patton,L(orenzo) D.	Rebecca Love	3 Jan. 1828	N(imrod) S.Jarrett (w) Jno.B.Love
Paxton,C(harles) M.D.	Elisabeth Mann	------1843	J(ohn) B.Allison (w) ----------
Pence,Abraham x	Frankey Davis (d.of William)	21 Sept. 1824	Nicholas x Massey (w) Wm.Welch
Penland,G(eorge) N.	Tellitha Ensly Shook	8 Feb. 1849	Rolen x McClure (w) W.Brown
Penland,R(obert) H.	Sarah Sitton	8 Dec. 1840	H.L.Potts (w) ----------
Perry,Hardy x	Martha Barker (d.of Edmund)	30 Aug. 1834	W(illia)m Stanfield (w) J.Keener,D.C.
Philip,	Elizabeth Patton	1 Oct. 1843	J(ohn) B.Allison (w) ----------
Philips,Wm.	Nancy Parker (d.of Solomon)	26 Dec. 1833	Hugh Rogers (w) J.Keener
Pickens,Andrew	Delila A.Edward	17 Sept. 1840	William S.Bird (w) Wm.Welch
Picklesimer,A(braham)	Morning Barns (d.of George)	10 Sept. 1828	(Saml.D.Bragg) (w) J.B.Love
Pinion,James x	Avaline Young	19 Oct. 1852 M.19 Oct. 1852 By Wm.McClure,J.P.	Isham M.Davis (w) J.Keener,clk.

GROOM	BRIDE	DATE OF BOND	BONDSMAN & WITNESS

Pinner,Leander Nelson Susan Adaline Holland 26 June 1869 (w) W.C.Brown,R.D.
(s.of Leander Pinner & (d.of Jeremier York M.27 June 1869
  Eliza Williams   By Joshua Kinsland,J.P.

Plemmons,William   Elizabeth Colwell 19 Jan. 1847   James Plemmons
    Jefferson   (w) ----------

Pless,Asbery   Elizabeth L.Burnett 3 Aug. 1856   John G.Burnett
                                    M.4 Aug. 1856 (w) Wm.W.Rhea,clk.
                                    By A.C.Hartgrove,J.P.

Pless,Henry   Harriett M.Burnett 10 Dec. 1858 J.A.Burnett
                                    M.12 Dec. 1858 (w) W.W.Medford,clk.
                                    By Thos.S.Edwards,clk.

Pless,Posey   Nancy Z.Ivester   14 Apr. 1854   John G.Burnett
                                    M.16 Apr. 1854   (w) J.Ammon
                                    By A.C.Hartgrove,J.P.

Plott,David   Sarah Turner   17 Aug. 1830   Ezekiel Brown
(s.of Henry & Lydia) (d.of Nancy Widow)   (w) Reub. Deaver

Plott,Enos   Elizabeth Tritt   23 Sept. 1841 Jeremiah Vickers
(s.of Henry & Lydia) (d.of ARchibald)   (w) W.Brown,clk.

Plott,George   Rebeckak Land   8 Feb. 1821   David How(ell)
(s.of Henry & Lydia) (d.of Isaac)   (w) ----------

Plott,Henry Jr.   Eliza Allen   12 Dec. 1839   W(alter) Brown
(s.of Henry & Lydia)   (w) Wm.Welch

Plott,Henry B   Cordelia Fulbright7 Jan. 1869   (w) W.C.Brown,R.Deeds
(s.of John & Louesa)(d.of Jacob)   M.7 Jan. 1869

Plott,John Milas   Elisabeth Propst 5 Nov. 1859   Elias Lee
(s.of Amos)   M.7 Nov. 1859 (w) W.W.Medford,clk.
                                    By Wm.Turner,J.P.

Plott,John   Leuza Reaves   6 Jan. 1838   Kindred Reeves
(s.of Henry & Lydia) (d.of Jack)   M.8 Jan. 1838 (w) Wm.Welch

Plott,Jonathan   Elezabeth C.Harmon 30 May 1835   Ezekeel Brown
(s.of Henry & Lydia)   M. 2 June 1835 (w) S.Fitzgerrald.clk.

Postell.Thomas   Pollev Stords   6 Aug. 1822   John x Creesmon
                    (d.of Jacob)   (w) Dillard Love

Poston.Robert   Atheline Pless   20 Aug. 1847   Henrv Jackson Davis
                                                     (w) W.Brown

Poston.Robert   Delila E.Curtice 14 July 1858   Henry Pless
                                    M.18 July 1858 (w) W.W.Medford,clk.
                                    Bv John Trull

Poteet,William   Elisabeth Allen   15 July 1824   Isaiah Cook
                    (d.of William)   (w) ----------

Potts,H.L.   Eve Davison   31 July 1843   T.L.Potts
                                                     (w) ----------

Presley,James x   Catharine Stephenson 12 Dec. 1855 John Justice
                                    M.13 Dec. 1855 (w) C.T.Rogers
                                    By W.G.BGarrett,J.P.

Presley,Thomas   Jemima Henson   1 Jan. 1833   Wm.A(lford) Cobb
                    (d.of Daniel)   (w) J.R.Love

61

GROOM	BRIDE	DATE OF BOND	BONDSMAN & WITNESS
Prossley,David x	Emoline Henson	20 Apr. 1854 M. 4 May 1854 By A.C.Hartgrove,J.P.	M.B.Chapman (w) Wm.M.Rhea,clk.
Pressley,W(illiam)	Barbary Smathurs	9 May 1860	Phillip x Noland (w) W.W.Medford,clk.
Pressley,Franklin	Elizabeth Meece	15 Apr. 1858 M.18 Apr. 1858 By A.L.Herren,J.P.	(w) W.W.Medford,clk.
Price,Albert x	Sarah E.Evens	1 Apr. 1854	Aaron Price (w) Wm.M.Rhea,clk.
Price,Aron	Nancey Ann Williams	14 Dec. 1849	John x Stephenson (w) ----------
Price,James x (s.of Richard)	Nancy Caldwell (d.of James)	17 Apr. 1829	Aaron x Price (w) Reub.Deaver
Price,James W. x	Elazebeth Barnes (d.of Joseph)	5 Aug. 1835	George x Price (w) S.Fitzgerrald
Price,John x	Syntha Kilpatrick (d.of Lewis)	25 Sept. 1837	Silas Kilpatric (w) Wm.Welch
Price,John x	Mary Wyatt	12 Sept. 1854 M.14 Sept. 1854 By H.Rogers,J.P.	John Wiatt (w) Wm.Love
Price,John x	Nancy Noland	31 Dec. 1856	John x Franklin (w) Wm.Rhea,clk.
Price,Josiah	Cathreine Cagle	16 Aug. 1859 M.17 Aug. 1859 By J.C.Leatherwood	(w) J.J.Sparks
Price,Merriton R. (s.of William)	Charity Jane Messer (d.of Moses)	24 Dec. 1870 M.25 Dec. 1870 By E.L.Shelton,J.P.	(w) Joseph Liner,R.D.
Price,Richard x	Lydia Messer	11 Feb. 1825	George x Messer (w) R.Dever
Price,Richard x	Mariah Barnes (d.of Joseph)	1 Dec. 1834	George x Price (w) S.Fitzgerrald,clk.
Price,William x	Mary Calwell (d.of James)	15 Dec. 1834	George x PRice (w) S.Fitzgerrald,clk.
Price,William Thomas (s.of John)	Jane Jarrett (d.of John)	3 Apr. 1869 M.4 Apr. 1869 By F.M.Messer,J.P.	(w) W.C.Brown,R.D.
Queen,Franklin	Esabel Mann	1 Oct. 1844	Stephen Smith (w) W.Brown
Queen,Harmon or Hiram	Polly Brock	1 Feb. 1824	William Queen (w) Wm.Welch
Queen,James	Keziah A.Haynes	22 Sept. 1845	H.P.Haynes (w) Wm.Haynes
Queen,John x	Mary Martin (d.of Robert)	20 Jan. 1838	William Blalock (w) Wm.Welch

GROOM	BRIDE	DATE OF BOND	BONDSMAN & WITNESS
Queen,John M.	Sarah C.Morrow	24 Sept. 1852 M.24 Sept. 1852 By J.F.Finchers,J.P.	Wm.(M) Medford (w) W.Brown
Queen,Maxuel x	Mary Hampton	29 Oct. 1853 M.29 Oct. 1853 By J.F.Fincher,J.P.	John M.Queen (w) W.Brown
Queen,Nathan	Jane Rhodes	18 Feb. 1847	Rufus A.Edmonston (w) ----------
Queen,R(obert) H.	Nancy E.Franklin	18 Aug. 1853 M.18 Aug. 1853 By Joshua Inman,J.P.	N.S.Queen (w) A.C.Hartgrove
Queen,S.P.	Martha McMillion	12 Sept. 1867 M.12 Sept. 1867 By D.B.Ford	(w) W.W.Medford,clk.
Queen,Samuel	Susan Rinehardt	19 June 1843	John x Farmer (w) W.Brown
Queen,Timothey	Mary Ann State	4 Dec. 1816	Saml. x Queen
Queen,Timothy x	Polly Blaylock (d.of Isom,dec'd)	9 Sept. 1838	Charles x Davis (w) M.Francis
Queen,W(illia)m	Ely Bryson (d.of John)	17 Oct. 1829	James Quen (w) Jno.B.Love
Raburn,Hodg Jr.	Edy Howell	9 Nov. 1827	Tho(ma)s Raburn (w) Ro.Love,clk.
Ratcliff,Jeremiah	Abby Chambers (d.of Elihugh)	10 Oct. 1824	John x Reeves (w) Wm.Welch
Ratcliff,J(eremiah) Jr.	L.J.Battle	14 Feb. 1861	R.G.A.Love (w) W.W.Medford
Ratcliff,N(ewton)	Mary Rogers	7 Dec. 1851 M.7 Dec. 1851 By B.Turner,M.G.	F.Mosses Ratcliff (w) C.T.Rogers
Rathbone,A.J.	Loucinda A. Justis	2 July 1847	William x Rathbone (w) D.V.McCracken
Rathbone,Daniel x	Nancy Carver	21 Dec. 1841	David x Carver (w) W.Brown
Rathbone,Hewet	Margaret Frady	19 Jan. 1842	Reuben Moody (Sr.) (w) ----------
Rathbone,Hyam	Elaiza Dempsy	1 Apr. 1852 M.1 Apr. 1852 By H.P.Haynes,J.P.	(w) David Howell
Rathbone,Jacob	Tempy Jestice	6 Aug. 1853 M.7 Aug. 1853 By W.Green,J.P.	Wm.Rathbone x (w) Wm.M.Rhea
Rathbone,Jefey	Margaret Fish	4 Sept. 1852 M.5 Sept. 1852 By W.Green,J.P.	(w) J.Keener,clk.
Rathbone,Manson x	Fany Quellins	23 Mar. 1855 M.23 Mar. 1855 By H.Rogers,J.P.	H(yrum) Rogers (w) Wm.M.Rhea,clk.

GROOM	BRIDE	DATE OF BOND	BONDSMAN & WITNESS
Rathbone,Purnel Jr.	Jane S.Williamson	27 July 1854 M.27 July 1854 By H.Rogers,J.P.	James Williamson (w) George Williamson
Rathbone,W(illia)m	Jane Russel	23 Sept. 1854 M.23 Sept. 1854 By H.Rogers,J.P.	Daniel Rathbone (w) H.Roger
Rathbone,William H.	Melvina Spivy	3 Feb. 1868 M.4 Feb. 1868 By F.M.Messer,J.P.	(w) W.W.Medford,clk.
Ratliff,F.M.	Margrett Rogers	30 Jan. 1855 M. 1 Feb. 1855 By B.Turner,M.G.	J.M.Shook (w) Wm.M.Rhea,clk.
Ray,Joseph	Elizure Murrey	28 Nov. 1841	J(ohn) L.Smith (w) ----------
Ray,Robert x	Rhewhamer Green (d.of William)	20 Dec. 1854	Lewis x Noland (w) S.Fitzgerrald,clk.
Ray,Solomon x	Mary Furgoson (d.of William)	18 Mar. 1835	A(lezander) Henry (w) S.Fitzgerrald,clk.
Rayney,Albert	Talitha Turner	10 Oct. 1857	J.M.Tate (w) W.N.Freeman
Reece,Enoch x	Sarah Halk (d.of James)	20 May 1819	Jeremiah x Nations (w) ----------
Ractor,James Nicholas (s.of McCager)	Rachael Williamson (d.of George & Elizabeth)	16 Aug. 1869 M.17 Aug. 1869 By J.D.Wright,M.G.	(w) W.C.Brown,R.D.
Reease,Henry	Liew Cindy Hudgins	7 Feb. 1828	Henry x Willson (w) ----------
Reece,Daniel x	Nancy Mann	11 Mar. 1849	David x Reece (w) W.Brown
Reece,David x	Cassey Inman (d.of Widow Inman,dec'd)	6 May 1837	Wm.Allman (w) ----------
Reece,David Jr. x	Mary Kilba	6 Aug. 1839	James H. x Kilba (w) Wm.Welch,clk.
Reece,James	Mary J.Mann	1 Apr. 1865 M.3 Apr. 1865 By J.Inman,J.P.	(w) W.W.Medford,clk.
Reece,Jeremiah	Louisa Sorrels	28 Feb. 1861	James Wilson (w) W.W.Medford,clk.
Reece,John	Aliff C.Evans	18 July 1852 M.18 July 1852 By A.C.Hartgrove,J.P.	R(ufus) Hartgrove
Reece,Wm. x	Nancy E. Moore	5 Sept. 1852 M.5 Sept. 1852 By J.Inman,J.P.	Robert x Queen
Reed,George	Sary Cornwell (d.of Jessee)	8 June 1813	Robert Reed (w) ----------

GROOM	BRIDE	DATE OF BOND	BONDSMAN & WITNESS
Reed,James	Rachel Ward	11 Nov. 1809	John Colom Danl Cathey (w) Wm.McCutchen (w) Robert Love
Reeves,A(lbert)	Rabecca Liner	10 Mar. 1849	J.M.Tate (w) R.V.Welch,D.C.
Reeves,Gilbert	Neomy Long (d.of James R.)	1 May 1836	Kindred Reeves (w) Wm.Welch
Reeves,Gilbert	Rebecca Harman	30 May 1840	Kindred Reeves (w) M.Francis
Reeves,Kindred	Rebekah Queen	7 Oct. 1845	Franklin Frances (w) ----------
Reeves,M(incher) L.	Nancy Angeline Welch	17 Aug. 1849	P(hilip) W.Turner (w) R.V.Welch
Reeves,William Thomas (s.of Kindred)	Cordelea Sammantha Garrett (d.of W.G.B.)	11 Mar. 1869 M.---------- By J.H.Massey	(w) W.C.Brown,R.D.
Reid,James T.	Luisind Stynes or Luisa	6 Dec. 1851 M.14 Dec. 1851 By A.M.Russell,J.P.	J.L.Lafong (w) C.T.Rogers,clk.
Renno.John	Tellitha Osborne (d.of Ephraim)	31 Jan. 1847	J(ames) M.Patton (w) ----------
Renno.kJohn	Jane Moore	5 June 1858 M.---------- By T.S.Edwards,J.P.	John G.Osborne (w) W.N.Freeman,D.C.
Renno.Wm.	Matilda Jane Clark	3 Oct. 1852 M.3 Oct. 1852 By H.P.Haynes,J.P.	A(nderson) Renno (w) H.P.Haynes
Reno,Hardy x	Zelphia Jonson (d.of Polly)	23 Nov. 1815	Enoch Hall (w) ----------
Rey(n)olds,John H.	Sary A.Ferguson	26 Dec. 1860	Wm.M.Penland (w) ----------
Rhea,J.M.	Tynie Right	11 Sept. 1860	L.D.Medford (w) ----------
Rhea,William M.	Emely Nowland	9 June 1847	J(ohn) N.McGee (w) W.Brown
Rhinehardt,James	Martha Evens	18 May 1855	R.B.Johnston (w) Wm.M.Rhea
Rhinehart,Coonrod x	Harriett Evins (d.of Jacob)	9 Aug. 1821	Thomas G.Evins (w) ----------
Rhindhart,Isaac	Mary C.Rhinehardt	18 Oct. 1850	Joseph Rhinehardt (w) J.Keener
Rhinehart,Thomas C.	Hannah Morrow (d.of Robert)	2 June 1836	J(ohn) R.Cooper (w) ----------
Rhinhart,Jacob	Matilda Battle	6 June 1857 M.7 June 1857 By A.L.Herren,J.P.	W.L.Davis (w) Wm.M.Rhea,clk.

GROOM	BRIDE	DATE OF BOND	BONDSMAN & WITNESS
Rhinhart,William	Mary Rhinehardt	12 July 1856 M.13 July 1856 By R.B.Johnston,J.P.	Wm.L.Davis (w) Wm.Rhea,clk.
Rhineheardt,Joseph	Mary Bettle	26 Nov. 1851	J.N.Benners (w) J.Keener
Rhoads,Samuel B.	Syntha C. Mull	29 Nov. 1848	N(athan) S.Queen (w) W.Brown
Rhodeamer,Philip	Malinda Christopher	27 Nov. 1865 M.27 Nov. 1865 By J.A.Hagaman,M.G.	W.K.Rhodearner (w) J.W.Killian,clk.
Rhodes,Milton	----Norris	27 Jan. 1844	N(athan) Deaver (w) W.Brown
Rhodes,Standfird	Celia Evins (d.of Jacob)	1 Jan. 1811	Abr(aham) Rhodes (w) Ro.Love,clk.
Rice,F.E.	M.A.Penland	12 Mar. 1856 M.13 Mar. 1856 By W.G.B.Garrett,J.P.	David Howell (w) Wm.M.Rhea,clk.
Rice,J.M.	S.E.Bennett	1 May 1867 M.5 May 1867 By S.J.Shelton,J.P.	(w) W.W.Medford,clk.
Rice,J(eremiah) D.	Sarah Moody	11 Dec. 1827	Nicholas x Ferguson (w) Ro.Love,clk.
Rice,Samuel	Eliza Leatherwood (d.of Samuel)	31 Jan. 1833	J(ohn) B.Leatherwood (w) ----------
Rich,John	Elizabeth Evans	10 Jan. 1865 M.11 Jan. 1865 By James Parks,J.P.	(w) W.W.Medford,clk.
Reid,John	Mariann Grahl	9 Oct. 1845	J.L.Bird (w) ----------
Rinehart,F.M.	Z.A.Rineheart	30 Aug. 1858 M.31 Aug. 1858 By Jas.B.Fitzgerrald,M.G.	Wm.(M) Grahl (w) W.W.Medford,clk.
Roberds,W(illia)m V.	Sary A.Rogers (d.of John)	14 May 1849	C.C.Rogers (w) ----------
Roberson,Aaron x	Mary Wines	5 Sept. 1844	Jasper x Underwood (w) W.Brown
Roberson,John	Mary Clark	5 Jan. 1854 M.8 Jan. 1854 By D.B.Ford	A.R.Robeson (w) Wm.M.Rhea,clk.
Roberson,John P. x	Jane M.Clark	24 Mar. 1847	Wm.S. x Roberson (w) W.Brown
Roberson,Joseph S.	Nancy M.Scott	22 June 1847	Wm.S. xRoberson (w) ----------
Robers(on),M(iller)	Mahala Medford	13 Feb. 1856 M.13 Feb. 1856 By J.F.Fincher,J.P.	E(lias) Medford (w) Wm.M.Rhea,clk.
Roberson,Nathan	Bettyann Hoglend	19 Sept. 1842	David Hill (w) ----------

GROOM	BRIDE	DATE OF BOND	BONDSMAN & WITNESS
Roberson,Richard x	Polly Underwood	14 Sept. 1850	E.D.Underwood (w) ----------
Roberson,Richard x	Manervy Kinsland	23 Jan. 1861	W.M.x Kinsland (w) D.B.Ford
Roberts,James x	Nancey Messor	29 Jan. 1860 M.29 Jan. 1860 By Geo.Williamson,J.P.	Levi Shelton (w) Geo.Williamson
Roberts,Jessee	Elisabeth Duckett	22 June 1861	A.M.Morton (w) W.W.Medford
Roberts,N.J.	Jane Clark	25 Nov. 1854 M.25 Nov. 1854 By Geo.Williamson,J.P.	M.V.Roberts (w) George Williamson
Robertson,Jessee x	Sarah Hawkins (d.of Josha)	16 Dec. 1823	James x Robertson William x Lowry (w) John Moore
Robertson,William S.	Sarah McCracken	24 Sept. 1852 M.30 Sept. 1852 By J.A.McClure,J.P	(w) C.T.Rogers,D.C.
Robeson,A.R.	Nancy Kinsland	1 Apr. 1852 M.4 Apr. 1852 By D.B.Ford,J.P.	J. x Wood (w) J.Keener,clk.
Robinson,A.A.	Faney Monroe	12 Mar. 1858 M.13 Mar. 1858 By R.E.Medford,J.P.	Joseph Evans (w) Medford,clk.
Robinson,Alexander	Margaret Cline	31 Jan. 1828	Abel B.Hyatt (w) Ro.Love,clk.
Robinson,Isaac	Rahcheal Holder (d.of Wm.)	11 Oct. 1839	George H.Clark (w) Wm.Welch
Robinson,J(ames) A.	Charity M.Ford	27 Aug. 1865	W(m) H.Holder (w) J.W.Killian
Robinson,Ruben	Agia Hogline	20 July 1860	Joseph M.Cabe (w) D.B.Ford
Robinson,Rubin	Rebeca Howard	12 Mar. 1860	J.Bryson (w) W.W.Medford,clk.
Robinson,William	Keziah C. Shook	18 Jan. 1840	William Robenson (w) Wm.Welch
Robinson,Wm.C	Elizabeth Roberson	18 Mar. 1844	Isaac Clark (w) ----------
Robison,Aron Jr. x	Aggy Woods (d.of Johnothan)	11 Mar. 1834	Gorge H.Clark (w) S.Fitzgerrald,D.C.
Robison,I(saac) L.	Maryann G.Robers	31 Aug. 1865	J.R.Clark (w) J.W.Killian,clk.
Robison,Jessee x	Honar Brookshare (d.of Benjamin)	19 Jan. 1824	Stephen Piercy (w) Wm.Welch
Robison,John x	Anne McMullin (d.of Saml.)	21 Dec. 1819	Samuel x McMullin

GROOM	BRIDE	DATE OF BOND	BONDSMAN & WITNESS
Robinson,J(oseph) J.	Susan Lucinda Bumgerner	26 Aug. 1851 M.27 Aug. 1851 By A.Fisher	W.A.Robison (w) J.Keener,clk.
Robinson,Richard x	Mary Ratcliff (d.of Abarham)	20 Dec. 1819	Aaron x Robinson (w) ----------
Robison,Samuel x	Nancy Kilbay	12 Apr. 1828	Thomas Cathey (w) Ro.Love,clk.
Rogers,A.(N)	Telitha Hall	23 Dec. 1852 M.23 Dec. 1852 By B.F.Wells,M.G.	John J.Cole (w) A.C.Hartgrove
Rogers,C.C.	Surlinda Plott	4 Apr. 1854 M.5 Apr. 1853 By Enos McCracken,J.P.	A.T.Rogers (w) J.Keener,clk.
Rogers,C.C.	Emeline Smathers	26 Oct. 1858 M.26 Oct. 1858 By H.Rogers,J.P.	H.M.Rogers (w) W.W.medford,clk.
Rogers,Cyrus x	Peggy McCrackin	6 Jan. 1827	Russel x McCrackin (w) Ro.Love,clk.
Rogers,George	Elizabeth Cabe (d.of Samuel)	10 Feb. 1821	James McClure,Jr.
Rogers,H.M.	M.E.Howell	19 Oct. 1865	C.C.Rogers (w) J.W.Killian,clk.
Rogers,H(iram) R.	Elender Fergason	15 Aug. 1846	C.C.Rogers (w) ----------
Rogers,Hugh	Anne Bryson (d.of John)	7 Feb. 1823	Tho(ma)s Rogers (w)John B.Love,clk.
Rogers,Hugh	Katharine Cathey (d.of George dec'd)	6 Sept. 1830	Sherwood Osbun (w) Ro.Love,clk.
Rogers,J.C.	B.A.Snider	28 June 1861	J.N.Davis (w) W.W.Medford
Rogers,J.R.	----------	7 Jan. 1860	P.L.Mintz (w) H.Rogers
Rogers,John	Marget P.Penland (d.of Robert)	5 May 1855	W(illia)m Allman (w) F.McGee
Rogers,Mathew	Mary Smith	1 Nov. 1826	Ja(me)s Rogers (w) Reuben Dever
Rogers,Matison	Mary Dotson	14 Oct. 1853 M.14 Oct. 1853 By J.F.Finchers,J.P.	(w) J.Keener,clk.
Rogers,Nicholas P. x	Matilda Noland (d.of Peter)	3 Mar. 1837	R(obert) H.Penland (w) W.Welch
Rogers,Posey J.	M.L.Rinehardt	5 Aug. 1842	Green Moore (w) W.Brown
Rogers,Robert	Sussannah Smith (d.of Lewis)	23 Feb. 1832	Jeremiah Vickers (w) ----------

GROOM	BRIDE	DATE OF BOND	BONDSMAN & WITNESS
Rogers,R(obert) W.	Francis Russell	2 Sept. 1858 M.2 Sept. 1858 By James Green,J.P.	C.T.Rogers (w) W.N.Freeman,D.C.
Rogers,Thomas (Jr.)	Elizabeth Rexter (d.of William Rexter)	11 Dec. 1821	Matthew Rogers (w) Wm.Welch
Rogers,W.J.	Lusinda Liner	4 Sept. 1863	J.N.Ratcliff (w) W.W.Medford,clk.
Roland,Malachia	Sally Caler (d.of Jacob)	13 Feb. 1817	James Love (w) Ro.Love
Rose,Wm.B.	Delila E.Henson	23 Dec. 1857 M.27 Dec. 1857 By A.C.Hartgrove,J.P.	N.S.Green (w) W.W.Medford,clk.
Ross,D(avid)	Ruth Liner (d.of John)	28 Dec. 1837	H(enry) J.McClure (w) ----------
Ruff,George x	Anna Green	28 Apr. 1856 M. 4 May 1856 By James Plemmons,M.G.	Alexander x Hana(h) (w) Wm.M.Rhea,clk.
Ruff,Miner	Sarah Cagle	20 Nov. 1856 M.20 Nov. 1856 By W.G.B.Garrett,J.P.	George Ruff (w) Wm.M.Rhea,clk.
Ruff,Sillas P.	Eliza Hannah	8 Nov. 1856 M.16 Nov. 1856 By H.Rogers,J.P.	George Ruff (w) Wm.M.Rhea,clk.
Rusel,Loran(z)o	Hannah E.Down	12 Jan. 1847	Thomas P.Ruse(l) (w) ----------
Russel,James	Elizabeth Penland	14 Feb. 1829	William Noland (w) ----------
Russel,John H. x	Matilda Cross	2 Dec. 1839	Marville Sitton (w) Wm.Welch
Russel,Robe(r)t	Polly Allen (d.of Joseph)	22 Dec. 1823	Ric(har)d Clark (w) Ro.Love,clk.
Russel,Thos.B.	Polly M.Turner (d.of Bannister)	23 May 1839	J(as.) R.Love (w) ----------
Russell,A.M.	Hannah Philips	2 Dec. 1844	Tho(ma)s Russell (w) ----------
Russell Robert (s.of David & Elizabeth)	Sarah Adaline Williamson (d.of George & Elizabeth)	16 Aug. 1869 M.17 Aug. 1869 By J.D.wright,M.G.	(w) W.C.Brown,R.D.H.C.
Rutherford,James x	Barbary Mull (d.of Peter)	20 May 1822	George x Heffly (w) Wm.Welch
Sanford,Mathis x	Cathrin Evens	11 Dec. 1856 M.11 Dec. 1856 By J.A.McClure,J.P.	Robt.Hill (w) Wm.M.Rhea,clk.
Sanford,William	Mary Elmyra Crawford	18 Feb. 1851	C(olumbus) C.Rogers (w) Wm.Johnston

GROOM	BRIDE	DATE OF BOND	BONDSMAN & WITNESS
Satterfel,John W.	N.J.Abbot	18 Sept. 1867 M.18 Sept. 1867 By J.A.Hagaman,M.G.	(w) W.W.medford,clk.
Sawyer,Joel	Esther Thompson (d.of Nathan)	20 Nov. 1823	A(lezander) x Crisp (w) ----------
Sawyer,Lewis	Sarah Miller (d.of Saml.Rose)	22 Mar. 1822	Joseph Sorrels (w) ----------
Scot,David	Levinah Griffith	10 Sept. 1845	Jaco(b) Dotson (w) ----------
Scott,H.P. x	----------	21 Aug. 1850	C.B.Philips (w) S.W.Gaston,clk.
Seay,Benjamin	Sarah C.Low	22 Mar. 1860	H(enry) J.Dotson (w) W.W.Medford
Seay,Daniel x	Lourena J.Jones	26 Aug. 1856 M.28 Aug. 1856 By E.V.Plott,J.P.	John C.Curry (w) Wm.M.Rhea,clk.
Seay,James	Eliza Gillett	10 Dec. 1851 M.11 Dec. 1851 By J.L.Stephenson,J.P.	(w) J.Keener,clk.
Seay,Thornton	Lucinda Hill	16 Sept. 1851	Thomas Smith (w) J.Keener
Seller,Isaac	Jane Gibson (d.of Joseph)	28 Nov. 1821	John Gipson (w) ----------
Seller,Jacop	Rachel Bonham	25 Mar. 1854 M.26 Mar. 1854 By A.C.Hartgrove,J.P.	David Sharp (w) J.Inman
Sellers,Abram	Mary Mingus (d.of Abram)	21 Oct. 1837	Elbert Hall (w) J.Keener
Sellers,Conrad	Sarah Dotson (d.of Thos.)	21 Apr. 1834	Abram Fulbright (w) S.Fitzgerrald,D.C.
Sellers,Coonrad x	Arta Prince	24 Aug. 1839	John x Sallers,Jr. (w) Wm.Welch,clk.
Sellers,John	Martha Henson	12 Mar. 1859 M.12 Mar. 1859	(w) W.W.Medford,clk.
Sensabaugh,Leon F.	Mary C.Fitzgerald (or Molly)	21 Apr. 1858 M.4 May 1858 By J.R.Long	Sam.C.Bryson (w) W.W.Medford,clk.
Sharel,Moses L. x	Sary Camel (d.of Masey)	29 Nov. 1838	Andrew Cambel (w) Samuel Gibson
Sherp,David	Anny Sellers	18 Jan. 1850	Ira D.Farmer (w) S.W.Gaston
Sharp,Edward	Elon Miller	23 Feb. 1860	David Sharp (w) W.W.Medford
Sharp,J.P. x	Mary A.Miller	27 Oct. 1855 M. 6 Nov. 1855 By A.M.Russell,J.P.	H.Allison (w) Wm.M.Rhea,clk.

GROOM	BRIDE	DATE OF BOND	BONDSMAN & WITNESS
Sharp,John F.	A.C.Davis	6 Oct. 1857	J.A.McClure (w) W.W.Medford
Sharp,Wilson x	Mary M. Christopher	2 Aug. 1849	Robert x Sharp (w) W.Brown
Sharp,Elijah x	Sary Young	9 July 1853	Lewis x Young (w) C.T.Rogers
Sheels,Robert x	Elise E.Flaued	2 Jan. 1844	Rufus G. x Flaued Samuel Gibson
Shelton,E.L.	Mary C.Davis	29 Dec. 1851 M. 1 Jan. 1852 By W.L.Davis,J.P.	(w) Joseph Keener,clk.
Shelton,J.James	Gemima Hooper	14 Mar. 1844	Benjamin C.Hooper (w) A.D.Cathey
Shelton,Levi x	Mahala Colwell	26 Mar. 1855 M. 1 Apr. 1855 By J.H.Noland,J.P.	Wm. x Colwell (w) Wm.M.Rhea,clk.
Shelton,T.W.	Martha A.Tritt	5 Mar 1859 M.5 Mar. 1859 By J.N.Benners,J.P.	(w) W.W.Medford,clk.
Shepherd,Wiley x	Sary Woody (d.of James)	31 May 1815	John x Woody (w) ----------
Sherrill,Benj(amin)	Zelphe M.Enloe (d.of Ab.)	14 Sept. 1835	J.W.King (w) Samuel Gibson,D.C.
Sherrill,J(ames) B.	Marey Hyatt	14 Oct. 1840	J.P.Harriss (w) Samuel Gibson
Sherrill,Ute	Issabelae Enloe	16 Aug. 1829	Samuel Sherrill (w) Samuel Gibson
Sherrill,W.J(utson)	Sophia Henry	7 Nov. 1853 M.7 Nov. 1853 By Wm.P.Gillett,J.P.	John Gambrel (w) Wm.M.Rhea,clk.
Sherrill,Wilson	Elisabeth Enloe (d.of Abramham)	25 Sept. 1818	Asa Enloe (w) Ro.Love,clk.
Shook,D.H.	Mary Shelton	15 Dec. 1857 M.17 Dec. 1857 By W.G.B.Garrett,J.P	G.N.Penland (w) W.W.Medford,clk.
Shook,D.W.	Sarah A. Morrow	24 Nov. 1849	J.Keener (w) S.W.Gaston,clk.
Shook,Daniel x	Sarah Gunter	14 Jan. 1848	Samul x Hooper (w) Jno. C.Bryson
Shook,J.M.	Sophia Patton	19 Sept. 1850	J(ohn) H.Estes (w) S.W Gaston,clk.
Shook,J.M.	Margaret A.Killian	10 June 1856 M.10 June 1856 By Jas.B.Fitzgerrald,M.G.	J(ohn) W.Killian (w) Wm.M.Rhea,clk.
Shook,J(acob) D.	Mary Snider	7 Apr. 1853 M.7 Apr. 1853 By C.B.Mingus.M.G.	C.B.Mingus (w) W.Brown,D.C.

GROOM	BRIDE	DATE OF BOND	BONDSMAN & WITNESS
Shook,R.M.	Catherine cooper	3 Jan. 1858 M.3 Jan. 1858 By W.Brown,J.P.	W(illiam) M.L.Shook (w) W.W.Medford,clk.
Shook,Wm.M.J.	Sarah Shook	13 Nov. 1859 M.13 Nov. 1859 By C.Ledbetter,J.P.	(A.J.Morrow) (w) W.W.Medford,clk.
Shooler,David x	Rachel White (d.of Stephen)	27 Aug. 1815	James Love (w) John B. Love
Shooler,John x	Elizabeth Green Hughes	14 July 1808	John Hughes (w) John Fergus
Shooler,John H.	Nancy Fisher (d.of James)	19 Mar. 1840	Saml.Panter (w) J.Keener
Shooler,William	Nancey Davis	3 Dec. 1850	Thos.A.Noland (w) J.Keener
Shuler,Price	Nancey Bradshaw	10 May 1835	Merrill Bradshaw (w) Samuel Gibson,D.C.
Shults,W.E. (Ger.) Of Mississippi	Franis Bugg	24 Nov. 1865	Henry x Harass (w) J.W.Killian
Siler, David W.	Louisa C. Osborn	9 Oct. 1856 M.14 Oct. 1856 By C.D.Smith,M.G.	Wm.M.Rhea,clk.
Siler,John	Polly Caraline McKee	19 Mar. 1833	Jas. Robeson (w) M.Edwards
Siler,T(hos) S.	Josephine Herren	15 Dec. 1856 M.16 Dec. 1856 By R.H.Moody	J.L.Welch (w) Wm.M.Rhea,clk.
Simonds,William R.	Susannah Sorrells (d.of Mildred)	22 Apr. 1836	A(lexander) Henry (w) Wm.Welch,clk.
Simons,John x	Mary Honeycut (d.of Lewis)	3 Mar. 1822	Dillen Woodfin (w) Wm.Welch
Singleton,Anderson	Margaret Cathey	28 May 1868 M.28 May 1868 By A.J.Long,J.P.	(w) W.W.Medford,clk.
Singleton,Saml.P. x	Eliza J.Blaylock	28 Sept. 1861	E.P.G.Murray (w) A.J.Long,J.P.
Sitser,David	Sarah Mooney	3 Aug. 1860	H.C.Lee (w) W.W.Medford
Sitten,James	Caroline Leatherwood	21 Aug. 1867 M.22 Aug. 1867 By Wm.L.Moody,J.P.	(w) W.W.Medford,clk.
Sitton,Jacob x	Ann Ray (d.of Hanahiah)	11 Feb. 1830	David Hill (w) Ro.Love,clk.
Sitton,William	Polly McClure	31 Oct. 1821	W(illia)m Clark,Jr. (w) Wm.Welch
Slate,John Jr.	Mary Haynes (d.of Wm.)	17 Dec. 1833	James H. Potts (w) S.Fitzgerrald,D.C.

GROOM	BRIDE	DATE OF BOND	BONDSMAN & WITNESS
Slate,Joseph	Betty Ann Smith (d.of Col.Jacob)	18 July 1829	W(illia)m Haynes (w) ----------
Salte,W.W.	Rebeca M. Mingus	24 Mar. 1859 M.24 Mar. 1859 By H.P.Haynes,J.P.	R.C.Osborn (w) H.P.Haynes,J.P.
Smart,John x	Kisiah Messer	3 Dec. 1856 M.5 Dec. 1856 By H.Rogers,J.P.	G.V.McCracken (w) Wm.M.Rhea,clk.
Smathers,C.L.	----------	-- Sept. 1865	D.H.Shook (w) J.W.Killian
Smathers,Charles	Margret Cook (d.of George)	20 Dec. 1838	John Bonham (w) Wm.Welch
Smathers,G.M.	Jesephene McDaniel	29 Mar. 1862	J.D.Justice (w) ----------
Smathers,Georg(F)	Eve Kinsland	17 May 1825	Nath(anie)l Blackburn (w) Adam x Snider
Smathers,Henry	Catherine Fulbrite	26 Dec. 1816	Henry Fulbrite (w) ----------
Smathers,I(saac)	Catherine Snider	21 Dec. 1826	John x Snider (w) ----------
Smathers,Isaac,Sr.	Polly Miller	3 May 1825	Henry Miller,Jr. (w) R.Dever
Smathers,James	Dosha Sharp	30 Jan. 1854 M. 2 Feb. 1854 By A.C.Hartgrove,J.P.	E.W.Morgan (w) W.Brown
Smathers,Jese	Mary A.Hefley (d.of Mary)	23 July 1836	George F.Smathers (w) S.Fitzgerrald
Smathers,Jesse,Jr.	Mary S.Henson	28 July 1860	J.H.Johnson (w) W.W.Medford
Smathers,J(ohn) C.	Lucinda Elizabeth Johnston	1 May 1848	J.F.Brown (w) W.Brown
Smathers,L.W.S.	Sarah Waltriss	11 Feb. 1868 M.13 Feb. 1868 By Joseph Brendle	(w) W.W.Medford,clk.
Smathers,Levi x	Sarah Cook (d.of George)	19 Mar. 1836	Jesse Smathers (w) S.Fitzgerrald,D.C.
Samthers,Manson	Polly Kinsland	24 Jan. 1851	N.A.Smathers (w) Wm.Johnston
Smathers,Manson	Susson Welch	21 Aug. 1853 M.21 Aug. 1853 By A.C.Hartgrove,J.P.	N.A.Smathers (w) A.C.Hartgrove
Smathers,Nelson	Margaret Henderson	7 Apr. 1847	David x Miller (w) A.C.Hartgrove
Smathers,Phillip	Julila D. Miller	13 Mar. 1855 M.13 Mar. 1855 By J.Inman,J.P	(w) Wm.M.Rhea,clk.
Smith,Burton	Sarrah Rogers	30 Sept. 1846	John N.McGee (w) ----------

73

GROOM	BRIDE	DATE OF BOND	BONDSMAN & WITNESS
Smith,Henry	Katty Carver	4 Oct. 1824	Peter Noland William Noland (w) ----------
Smith,Henry	Rutha Owens	------185-- M.13 Mar. 1857 By J.A.McClure,J.P.	(w) Wm.M.Rhea,clk.
Smith,Jacob	Rebecca Justice	25 Dec. 1828	Nathaniel Blackburn (w) Reub Deaver
Smith,James x	Katharine Minges	20 Mar. 1828	Charles x Jones (w) Ro.Love,clk.
Smith,James P.	Rachel Morrow	27 Aug. 1857 M.27 Aug. 1857 By J.A.McClure,J.P.	(w) David Howell
Smith,John A.	Sarrah Fish	22 Aug. 1845	John N.McGee (w) ----------
Smith,John L.	Harriette Evans	9 Jan. 1849	Alfred Webb (w) S.W.Green
Smith,Lewis x	Mary Fish	6 Aug. 1852 M.6 Aug. 1852 By W.Green,J.P.	David x Messer (w) C.T.Rogers,D.C.
Smith,M.W.	Duricea Jones	26 Sept. 1845	J.R.Cooper (w) W.Brown
Smith,Noah x	Susan C,Mull	16 Dec. 1841	John Brown (w) ----------
Smith,Silas	Every Whitehead	14 Jan. 1861	W.H.Bengamine (w) W.W.Medford,clk.
Smith,Stephen	Sarrah Mann (d.of John)	8 July 1837	Joseph Chambers (w) S.Fitzgerrald,D.C.
Smith,Thomas	Jane Nichols	25 Sept. 1834	Jesse C. Cockerham (w) J.Keener
Smith,Thomas	Isabell Smith	15 Oct. 1859 M.20 Nov. 1859 By J.A.McClure,J.P.	(w) W.W.Medford,clk.
Smith,W.A. x (of Tennessee)	Sarah J.Henson	26 Sept. 1865	W.J. x Sellers (w) J.W.Killian
Smith,William x	Sharlot Clark (d.of Mary)	18 May 1838	William Robison (w) Wm.Welch
Smith,William	Nancy Rhea	20 Mar. 1845	J.N.McGee (w) ----------
Smither,JOhn x	Ruth Liner	20 Oct. 1829	John x Snider (w) Wm.Welch
Snider,Adam	Delpha Massey	1 Oct. 1846	Andy Holder (w) ----------
Snider,Adam,Sr. x	Lidia Smith	7 Nov. 1840	William Mahafy (w) Wm.Welch
Snider,Andrew x	Hannah Hall	11 July 1829	Adam x Snider (w) ----------

GROOM	BRIDE	DATE OF BOND	BONDSMAN & WITNESS
Snider,Andrew x	Elisabeth Snider (or Hise)	23 Dec. 1829	Jacob x Snider (w) Ro.Love,clk.
Snider,Caleb	Sarah McGee (d.of John)	8 Feb. 1837	Drury (S) Kilpatrick (w) Wm.Welch
Snider,Georg	Margaret Emeline Haynes	23 Sept. 1845	H.P.Haynes (w) Wm.Haynes
Snider,H.L(eander)	Mornign McDaniel	16 Apr. 1859	Henry Liner (w) W.W.Medford
Snider,John x	Katherine Smathers	21 Dec. 1826	I(saac) Smathers (w) ----------
Snider,Peter x	Sarah Shook (d.of David)	15 June 1838	Samuel Ferguson (w) ----------
Sorrell,Joseph	Hannah Trulove	17 July 1851 M.24 July 1851 By B.Turner,M.G.	W(illia)m B.Turner (w) R.V.Welch,D.C.
Sorrells,Mitchell x	Alvira Truelove	18 Jan. 1832	Jeremiah x Vickers (w) --------
Sorrells,William	Jane Morrow	21 June 1825	Bannister x Turner (w) R.Dever
Sorrels,W(illia)m	Ruth Ross	11 Oct. 1855 M.11 Oct. 1855 By J.Vickers,J.P.	A(cayus) Francis (w) J.Vickers
Sorrels,Elijaha x	Milla Smathers	2 Feb. 1850	James x Wilson (w) S.W.Gaston
Sorrels,Joseph	Barbary Snider	8 Sept. 1859 M.8 Sept. 1859 By R.E.Medford,J.P.	R.E.Medford,C.C.C. (w) W.W.Medford,C.C.C.
Sorrels,Lewis	Rebecca Morrow (d.of Robert)	18 May 1822	B(anister) Turner (w) Wm.Welch
Sorrols,Henry, Jr.	Adra Cathey	12 Nov. 1856 M.12 Nov. 1856 By B.Turner,M.G.	Joseph J.Sorrels (w) Wm.M.Rhea,clk.
Southeland,Caswell	Patsey Carter (d.of Henry)	26 July 1837	I(saac) P. Harris Ch. x Nations J.W.king (w) Samuel Gibson
Sparkes,J.J.	Marth J.Rogers	5 May 1856	H.McCracken (w) C.T.Rogers
Stafford,William x	Eda Ludise Wilson	20 Oct. 1847	B.B.Edmonston (w) Jno.C.Bryson
Stalup,Thomas x	Jane Starns	29 Dec. 1850	A.N.Cockerham (w) ----------
Stamey,Able x	Caroline Pharr (d.of Joseph)	4 June 1838	Joseph Chambers (w) Wm.Welch
Stamey,John	Nancy Kerns	16 May 1826	Jesse Kinsland (w) Jas.R.Love

GROOM	BRIDE	DATE OF BOND	BONDSMAN & WITNESS
Stamey,John x	Clarissa Massey (d.of Jeremiah)	15 July 1845	R.E(ldrige) Medford (w) Wm.Welch
Stamey,William (s.of Able & Caroline)	Racheal Davis	4 Nov. 1868 M.-------1868 By P. Holsclaw,M.G.	(w)W.C.Brown,R.D.H.C.
Standridge,Jesse	Betsey Bradley (d.of Joseph)	11 Apr. 1823	,,J(onethan) Phillips (w) ----------
Stanford,John x	Tempy Mills	11 Aug. 1852 M.11 Aug. 1852 By W.R.Crawford,J.P.	A.W.Gunter (w) Wm.R.Crawford
Stanford,Mathes x	Elizabeth Darnal	17 June 1850	Wm.X Dunken (w) S.W.Gaston,clk.
Starkey,Wm. x	Malinda Collins (d.of Elisabeth Kirkland)	23 May 1821	Benj(ami)n Clark (w) Wm.Welch
Starnes,Jacob	Levina Dotson	5 Nov. 1844	D.M. x Dotson (w) W.Brown
Stepenson,John	Margaret Bradshaw	11 Feb. 1840	Andrew Ferguson (w) _eremiah Vickers
Stephens,John	Casia Allison (d.of Hezekiah)	27 Feb. 1814	John Duff (w) Ro.Love,clk.
Stephenson,James x (s.of Catharine)	Rebacca Bradshaw	18 July 1840	Thomas x Burchfield (w) J.R.love
Stern,Benjamin	Sophia Snider (d.of Adam)	28 Oct. 1820	Adam x Snider
Stevson,John	Margerit Bird (d.of James)	11 Feb. 1840	(Consent for license signed by James Bird and witnessed by G.Wright)
Stewart,Dillard x	Sarah Wallis (d.of John)	17 Aug. 1834	David x Miller (w) S.Fitzgerrald
Stiles,Charles	Kisiah McConnel (d.of William)	24 Apr. 1813	Zachariah Cabe (w) Ro.Love,clk.
Stiles,John x	Lucy Beasely (widow)	27 Jan. 1820	Daniel McDowell (w) ----------
Stiles,John	Polly Cogdall (d.of Elijah)	19 Sept. 1822	James Buchanan (w) Ro.Love,clk.
Stiles,Tho(ma)s	Polly Ann Winchester	26 Mar. 1852 M.26 Mar. 1852 By Wm.McClure,J.P.	James Winchester (w) Ro.Love,clk.
Stilwell,Willum H. x	Merear Welch (d.of John)	17 Feb. 1836	Abram Sellers (w) Samuel Gibson
Stillwell,Jacob x	Elizabeth Mingus (d.of Jacob)	15 Sept. 1817	Saml.Stillwell (w) ----------
Stiwell,Alfred	Adaline Rogers	2 Oct. 1865	P.A.Calhoun (w) J.W.Killian
Stilwell,E(phram) P.	Jane A.Beck (d.of John)	19 Aug. 1839	James Conley Samuel Gibson

GROOM	BRIDE	DATE OF BOND	BONDSMAN & WITNESS
Stines,W(illiam A.	Telitha Smathers	23 Feb. 1851 M.23 Feb. 1851 By B.Turner,M.G.	M.H.Dawson (w) J.Leener,clk.
Strettle,Alfred	Eliza.Russell	25 July 1851 M.25 July 1851 By J.S.Gibson,J.P.	(w) J.Keener
Styles,Elijiah x	Lucy Bird	7 Sept. 1850	Dolphes (E.) Eastes (w) S.W.Gaston
Surett,Henry J.	Milley Tate	26 Jan. 1861	J(ames) W.Holder (w) D.R.Ford
Swanger,Amen	Elviry Messer	12 Feb. 1847	John Swanger Leigh Inman (w) ----------
Swanger,Green B. x	Rebeca Morrow	22 Jan. 1856 M.22 Jan. 1856 By J.F.Fincher,J.P.	Wm. x Swanger (w) Wm.M.Rhea,clk.
Swanger,John	Matilda Bullen	15 Oct. 1842	Thomas x Burchfield (w) W.Brown
Swanger,J(oseph) x	Matilda Crawford	18 Sept. 1852 M.19 Sept. 1852 By J.Inman,J.P.	Logan x Inman (w) C.T.Rogers,D.C.
Swanger,Robert x	Darcus Allen	7 Feb. 1866	G.B. x Swanger (w) ----------
Swanger,W(illia)m	Elmina JOnes	6 May 1858 M.---------- By J.N.Benners,J.P.	D(avid) M.Vess (w) W.W.Medford,clk.
Swangir,James (s.of Samuel)	Arbazemia Rogers (d.of Cyrus)	16 Sept. 1869 M.16 Sept. 1869 By G.W.McCracken,J.P.	(w) W.C.Brown,R.D.H.C.
Swearingham,Samuel x	Elisabeth Cantrell (d.of Moses)	23 Sept. 1816	James Cantrel (w) Ro.Love.clk.
Tate,John M. x	Talitha E. Murrey	21 Dec. 1857	K(indred) Reeves (w) Wm.M.Reha,clk.
Tate,John P.	Martha A.Allison	6 Apr. 1854	M.B.Chapman (w) Wm.M.Rhea,clk.
Tate,(L.M.) ?	W.A.Shook	15 Jan. 1856 M.15 Jan. 1856 By W.G.B.Garrett,J.P.	(w) Wm.M.Rhea,clk.
Tatham,John	Jane Russell (d.of Mathew)	26 Feb. 1820	(Thomas Tatham) (w) ----------
Taylor,Hamilton	Any Evins	8 Nov. 1825	Robeson x Cooper (w) Wm.Welch
Teague,A.J.	Fany Ferguson	2 Jan. 1856	G.L.Kirkpatri(c)k (w) Wm.M.Rhea,clk.
Teague,George	Marinda Crawford	25 Feb. 1857 M.26 Feb. 1857 By Enos McCracken,J.P.	B.C.Duckett (w) Wm.M.Rhea,clk.

GROOM	BRIDE	DATE OF BOND	BONDSMAN & WITNESS
Teague,Jas.Willson	Martha A.Killpatrick	6 Nov. 1851 M.12 Nov. 1851 By Enos McCracken,J.P.	(w) J.Keener,clk.
Terpin,James H. x	Nancey Hughes	30 Dec. 1842	George Cooper Samuel Gibson
Terrell,Wm.S.	Mary L.Kirkpatrick	3 Aug. 1865	Jas. W.Terrell (w) J.W.Killian
Thomas,J.G.	Adaline Henson	17 Feb. 1860	Griffen Henson (w) W.W.Medford
Thomas,Wm.H.	Sarah J(ane) Love	29 June 1857 M.30 June 1857 By B.Turner,M.G.	(R.G.A.Love) (w) Wm.M.Rhea,clk.
Thompson,Benjamin x	Elixabeth Carter	29 Mar. 1842	M.W.Smith (w) W.Brown
Thompson,James	Betsey Wilkins (d.of John)	30 Jan. 1824	William x Oakes (w) Ro.Love,clk.
Thompson,James x	Melinda Henson	6 June 1851 M.4 (?) June 1851 By Wm.Haynes	David Haynes J.Keener,clk.
Thompson,Jasin	Celia Holland	3 Mar. 1860	P.B.Hood (w) W.W.Medford
Thompson,Jesse	Rachel Welch (d.of Thomas)	25 Feb. 1825	Nathan Thompson (w) Ro.Love,clk.
Thompson,Thomas	Nancy Enloe	7 Jan. 1815	Asaph Enloe (w) ----------
Thompson,William x	Ann N.Wilson	3 Sept. 1837	Alexander x Thompson (w) Wm.Welch,clk.
Tow,Joseph x	E.Bardin	23 July 1847	James x Mathes (w) J.Keener
Tritt,James B. x	Nancy A.Bumgarner	15 Oct. 1844	Henry Tritt,Jr. (w) W.Brown
Tritt,Lafayatt x	Manervy Henson	11 Nov. 1852 M.11 Nov. 1852 By A.C.Hartgrove,J.P.	T(homas) B.Gaddy (w) A.C.Hartgrove
Trul,Absalm	Sary Gurly (d.of Isom)	1 Dec. 1812	W(illia)m Dever (w) ----------
Trull,B.R.	Violet Henson	14 Dec. 1865 M.26 Dec. 1865 By A.J.Long,J.P.	Issac Harkins (w) J.W.Killian,clk.
Trull,D.S.	Neoma Mahaffey	11 Feb. 1854 M.12 Feb. 1854 By A.C.Hartgrove,J.P.	A.J.Murray (w) W.Brown,D.C.
Trull,Layney S. x	Rasannah Simmons (d.of Benjamin)	3 Feb. 1832	Benjamin Simmons (w) Ro.Love,clk.
Trulove,George x	Jane Robison (d.of Izeral)	24 Sept. 1834	James x Trulove (w) S.Fitzgerrald,C.C.
Trulove,George	Fanny Whitson	15 Feb. 1844	A.M. Sorrels (w) ----------

GROOM	BRIDE	DATE OF BOND	BONDSMAN & WITNESS
Trulove,James R.	Rosanah Chambers	21 Jan. 1845	George Trulove (w) ----------
Trulove,J(ames) R.	Martha Ann M.Webb	24 July 1847	James x Trulove (w) W.Brown
Turner,Banister	Susanah Hefney	31 Aug. 1814	Elijah Dever (w) John B.Love,Dep.C.
Turner,Joseph	Sarah Tritt (d.of Henry)	4 Nov. 1834	Jeremiah Vickers (w) S.Fitzgerrald,clk.
Turner,Philip	S.E.A.Welch	22 Jan. 1850	Joseph Rinhart (w) J.Keener
Turner,William B.	Temperance Marlow	22 Aug. 1841	Jeremiah Vickers (w) W.Welch,clk.
Turpin,John	Almira Jones (d.of Charles)	9 Jan. 1849	J(ohn) L.Smith (w) R.V.Welch
Underwood,Barrett x	Polly Daily (d.of Edmund)	25 May 1820	Elijah Underwood (w) ----------
Underwood,Bennett x	Elizabeth Mathis (d.of John)	11 Aug 1823	Barrett x Underwood (w) John B.Love
Underwood,Fulden x	Elizabeth Land (d.of James)	17 Sept. 1821	Elijah Underwood (w) John B.Love,D.C.
Vess,A.J.	Ruth E.Parmer	25 Aug. 1850	J(oseph) Keener (w) S.W.Gaston,clk.
Vess,Abraham x	Melissa Macabee	8 Mar. 1856	David Vess (w) ----------
Vess,George N.	Mary Allison	9 Jan. 1857 M.9 Jan. 1857 By J.F.Fincher,J.P.	John x Stamy (w) Wm.M Rhea,clk.
Vess,James	Francis Keerly	13 June 1857 M.14 June 1857 By Samuel Brown,J.P.	Samuel Brown (w) Wm.M.Rhea,clk.
Vest,David x	Mintha McBee	5 Apr. 1856 M.6 Apr. 1856 By C.T.Rogers,J.P.	Abreham x Vest (w) C.T.Rogers,D.C.
Vick,Noah	Eliza M.Wines	23 Sept. 1859 M.24 Sept. 1859 By D.B.Ford	T.J.Vick (w) W.W.Medford,clk.
Vickers,J(eremiah)	Jane Janes? (o)	3 Nov 1855 M.4 Nov.1855 By R.B.Johnston,J.P.	R.B.Johnston (w) WM.M.Rhea,clk.
Waldrop,Ambrose x	Franky Gibson (d.of Nathan)	3 Sept. 1834	Solomon x Gibson (w) S.Fitzgerrald,clk.
Waldroup,Abner	Elizabeth Rite (d.of Jesse)	20 Oct. 1834	Hugh C.Jones (w) J.Keener
Wall,James x	Mahaily Cooper (d.of Nancy)	29 Mar. 1832	George x Cooper (w) Ro.Love

GROOM	BRIDE	DATE OF BOND	BONDSMAN & WITNESS
Walker,J(oseph H.	Elvirie Davidson (d.of William M.)	4 July 1821	Abel B.Hyatt (w) ----------
Ward,H.L.	Elisabeth Price	1 Apr. 1852 M.1 Apr. 1852 By Colvard Nelson,J.P.	(w) David Howell
Warren,A.M.	Matilda -----	20 Nov. -----	J.R. x Scott (w) M.C.Killian
Warren,John	Elizabeth Brookshear (d.of Benjamin)	14 Jan. 1831	Balers Brookshere Archibald Magruder Osborne
Warren,William B.	Marow M.Evans	18 Mar. 1847	John C.Evans (w) ----------
Warren,Wm.K. x	Racheal Holder	30 July 1855 M. 1 Aug. 1855	Francis M.Mahaffy (w) Wm.M.Rhea,clk.
Watson,James x	Barbary Parker	28 May 1832	George x Watson (w) W.H.Thomas
Watson,John	Peggy Hickey (d.of Sarah Groce)	31 Jan. 1851	William Cathey (w) ----------
Watson,Thomas	Sally Morrow (d.of John)	17 Mar. 1817	Adam Hiden Watson (w) Ro.Love,clk.
Watts,R.	Virlinsha Sherrill	8 Oct. 1852	J(ames) W.Terrell (w) C.T.Rogers,D.C.
Webb,Irving	Prudence Carter	31 Aug. 1848	Hiram Webb (w) ----------
Welch,Edward	Christence Love	8 Apr. 1868 M.---------- By James A.Zachary	(w) J.N.Bennerd,D.C.
Welch,James	Mary Groce (d.of Thomas)	---Aug. 1815	(Andrew Welch) (w) ----------
Welch,J(ames) R.	Adaline Plott	16 Aug. 1858 M.17 Aug. 1858 By J.N.Benners,J.P.	W.N.Freeman (w) R.V.Welch
Welch,James T.	Chairity Ratcliff	12 June 1858 M.12 June 1858 Wm.Turner,J.P.	John C.Curry (w) W.W.Medford,clk.
Welch,Josiah B(radshaw)	Marey Cornwell (d.of Eley)	3 Apr. 1836	Willium H. x Stilwell (w) Samuel Gibson
Welch,R.V.	Mary Caroline Love	27 Oct. 1858 M.27 Oct. 1858 By R.H.Moody	(w) W.W.Medford,clk.
Welch,W(illia)m	Maryann Love (d.of Robt.)	7 May 1820	James R.Love (w) ----------
Welch,Wm.W(ashington)	Alisabethe McGalon (d.of Alexander)	28 Mar. 1836	James x Britt (w) Samuel Gibson,J.P
Well,Andrew	Eliza Evans	18 Oct. 1845	E(li) F.Deaver (w) W.Brown

GROOM	BRIDE	DATE OF BOND	BONDSMAN & WITNESS
Wells,Benjamin F.	Sarah E.Penland	31 May 1841	David Ring (w) Wm.Welch
Well,J.M.	Mary E.Long	20 Jan. 1848	Thomas N.Long (w) ----------
Wells,Jersey Anderson (x)	Artemiser Caroline Guiett	9 Feb. 1837	T(hos) G.Evans (w) S.Fitzgerrald,D.C.
Wells,John F.	Laura E. Edwards	6 Feb. 1868 M.6 Feb. 1868 By T.F.Glenn,M.G.	(w) Saml.L.Love,Dep.C
West,Isaac	Jane Wade	8 Dec. 1854 M.10 Dec. 1854 By Enos McCracken,J.P.	B.H.West (w) Wm.M.Rhea,clk.
West,John S.	Mahaley Robison	6 Oct. 1827	Henry Clark (w) Wm.Welch
West,William	Elizabeth Scott	9 Jan. 1853 M.9 Jan. 1853 By Isaac Clark	(w) J.Keener
West,Wm.	Polley Blalock	24 Apr. 1866	Isaac West (w) W.W.Medford,clk.
White,David	Percilla E.Cummons	20 Sept. 1842	J(ames) T.Penland (w) ----------
White,J.M. Jr.	Sarah A.E.Nelson	8 Nov. 1856 M.---------- By C.Nelson,J.P.	Carson x Clark (w) Wm.M.Rhea,clk.
White,James M.	Elender Stephenson (d.of Widow Cathern)	26 Mar. 1834	Alston Cooper (w) S.Fitzgerrald,D.C
White,Robert S.	Ellender Ferguson (d.of Robert,dec'd)	22 Apr. 1830	Andrew Ferguson (w) Reub Deaver
Whitehead,Henry x	Jane Meeze	7 Mar. 1852 M.7 Mar. 1852 By D.B.Ford	J. x Woods (w) C.T.Roger,D.C.
Whitehead,James	Caroline Holder (d.of Wm.)	18 May 1849	Wm.x Wines (w) W.Brown
Whitehead,Thomas	Elizabeth Carver	13 Oct. 1858 M.---------- By J.N.Benners,J.P.	M.H.Love (w) W.W.Medford,clk.
W(hite(head,W(illiam)	Mary Thompson	6 Mar. 1852 M.7 Mar. 1852 By D.B.Rogers	D.B.Ford (w) C.T.Rogers,D.C.
Whiteside,John B. (of Buncombe,Co.)	Catharine Patton	9 July 1836	John Osborn (of Buncomb,Co.) (w) A.Herren
Whitlock,William	Caroline Mathus	30 May 1859 M.---------- By C.Nelson,J.P.	(w) W.W.Medford,clk.
Whits(on),Jas.M.	Martha Mitchel	15 Dec. 1855 M.20 Dec. 1855 By E.V.Plott,J.P.	H.G. x Sorrels (w) Wm.M.Rhea,clk.

GROOM	BRIDE	DATE OF BOND	BONDSMAN & WITNESS
Whitson,John x	Fanny Sorrells (d.of Milly)	7 Apr. 1833	Jeremiah Vickers (w) ----------
Wickel,Samuel	Ester Bandy	6 Oct. 1823	Lewis Smith (Ger.) (w) Ro.Love,clk.
Wiett,J.L.	Anne Smith	14 Oct. 1847	Allen Haynes (w) ----------
Wiggins,Abraham Jr. x	Peggy Dever	11 Mar. 1826	David x Nelson (w) Ro.Love,clk.
Wiggins,John	Polly Dobson (d.of Joseph)	4 May 1818	Andrew Welch (w) ----------
Wiggins,W(illia)m	Ester Dillard	10 Jan.1814	Andrew Welch (w) Ro.Love,clk.
Wike,Andrew	Meriah Fulbright (d.of Barnett)	15 Feb. 1838	John Wike (w) ----------
Wike,Jacob	Malinda Moss (d.of William)	17 Oct. 1838	J.B.Lewis J.B.Allison
Wike,Philip	Sarrah Hughs	20 Mar. 1847	J(ohn) L.Potts (w) W.Brown
Wikle,George	Rebcca Murray (d.of James)	18 Jan. 1824	John Stiles,Jr. (w) Wm.Welch
Wikle,John	Barbarry Buff	26 Dec. 1825	James Truelove (w)R.Love,clk.
Wilbar,Daniel F.	Evie Norwood	6 July 1861	John T.O.Wilbar (w) W.W.Medford,clk.
Wilber,J(ohn) T.O.	Martha Moody	16 Nov. 1859 M.16 Nov. 1859 By R.H.Moody,clk.	J.R.Wilber (w) W.W.Medford,clk.
Wilkins,David x	Susanah Oaks (d.of William Sr.)	11 Jan. 1817	William x Oaks (w) James Moore
Wilkins,William	Ulviry Clark	3 Oct. 1827	W(illia)m (B) Woody (w) Rob.B.Love,clk.
Williams,Benson x	N.M.Ramsey	31 July 1840	Jason Allison (w) Wm.Welch
Williams,Calvin	Polly Ann Gribble (d.of James)	3 Jan. 1834	Carles Bumgarner (w) J.L.Chambers,clk.
Williams,Elijah	Elizabeth M.Owens	14 July 1845	J.D.Rice (w) ----------
Williams,George W. x	Hariett A.Allison	25 Oct. 1856 M.26 Oct. 1856 By W.G.B.Garrett,J.P.	J.C.Allison x (w) Wm.M.Rhea,clk.
Williams,J.A.	Mary Bonham	19 Nov. 1859 M.---------- By D.B.Ford,J.P.	A.B.Meece (w) W.W.Medford,clk.
Williams,James	Susannah Cline (d.of Rossannah Buff)	13 July 1814	John Buff (w) ----------

GROOM	BRIDE	DATE OF BOND	BONDSMAN & WITNESS
William,James x	Mary Shunk (d.of Mary)	30 Jan. 1831	James Chastain John Williams (w) Wm.B.Queen
Williams,J(ame)s	Ruth Cole	14 Sept. 1857 M.14 Sept. 1857 By D.B.Ford,J.P	W(illia)m Renno (w) C.T.Rogers,D.C.
Williams,James N.	Jane Owen	24 Oct. 1857 M.29 Oct. 1857 By F.M.Davis,J.P.	G.H.Nelson (w) W.W.Medford,clk.
Williams,James S. x	Martha C Clark	22 Nov. 1855 M.25 Nov. 1855 By C.B.Mingus,Elder	George Hall (w) Wm.M.Rhea,clk.
Williams,John O.	Souzan Jans	14 Feb. 1839	J.M.Childres (w) Sauel Gibson
Williams,Nimrod J.	Margaret Young	22 May 1853 M.22 May 1853 By J.N.Benners,J.P.(w) W.Brown,D.C.	Thos. x Young H.L.(eander) Snider
Williams,W.H.	C.T.Abbet	4 July 1860	S.Clark S.E.Love (w) ----------
WilliamsWilliam x	Passey Williams (d.of Jorden)	18 Dec. 1821	Josha Allison (w) Wm.Welch
Williamson,James	Margaret M.Russell	28 Mar 1858 M.28 Mar. 1858 By N.J.Roberts,J.P.	A.M.Williamson (w) N.J.ROberts,J.P.
Willis,Isaac W.	Jane M.Herrell	3 May 1850	Jacob K.Dotson (w) S.W.Gaston
Willson,Asaph	Sussannah Brittian	5 Feb. 1822	M(inian) Edmonston (w) ----------
Willson,Elijah D.	Rachil Robinson	6 Feb. 1858 M.7 Feb. 1858 By Wm.M.Roberson,J.P.	John P.Robinson (w) W.W.Medford,clk.
Willson,J(ames)	Martha A.Killpatrick	6 Nov. 1851	G.L.Kilpatrick (w) J.Keener
Wilson,Henry x	Sarah Moss (d.of Wm.)	1 Nov 1823	Wm.Moss (w) John B.Love
Wilson,James x	Eliza Sorrells	13 Jan. 1850	Wm.Allen (w) S.W.Gaston
Wilson,W.J.A.	Mary M.CAthy	M.2 Nov. 1851 By B.Turner,M.G.(w) J.Keener,clk.	J.N.Benners
Wilson,William x	Elizabeth Doogen	2 Sept. 1826	David x Leadford (w) Adam Corn
Winchester,Daniel Jr.	Aylsee C.Cunningham	15 Mar. 1855 M.15 Mar. 1855 By J.N.Benners,J.P.	J.N.Benners (w) Wm.M.Rhea,clk.
Winchester,James	Racheal Rinhardt	22 July 1858 M.22 July 1858 By A.L.Herren,J.P.	(w) W.W.Medford,clk.

GROOM	BRIDE	DATE OF BOND	BONDSMAN & WITNESS
Winchester,Jones	Sarah Ann Noblitt	24 Nov. 1846	James Land (w) ----------
Wines,Alford x	Sarah Stanford	1 Feb. 1848	Jessee McGee (w) D.V.McCracken
Wines,Alfred B. x	Susan Magnes	20 May 1841	William x Holder (w) Wm.Welch,clk.
Wins,W(illiam)	Lamsy F.Wade	3 Aug. 1849	D.B.Ford (w) R.V.Welch
Wise,W(illia)m C.	Katherine Chandler (d.of Tunstill)	26 Jan. 1833	John Hollan (w) Ro.Love,clk.
Withrow,David	Rebecha Patterson (d.of James)	8 May 1835	Robert x Patterson (w) S.Fitzgerrald,D.C.
Wood,Benjn. x	Polly Bennett (d.of Hardiman)	14 Mar. 1831	Thomas x Bugg (w) R.Deaver
Wood,Johnathan x	Elizabeth Bess	2 Feb. 1855 M.2 Feb. 1855 By H.P.Haynes,J.P.	D.B.Ford (w) Wm.M.Rhea,clk.
Wood,Levi M.	Mary M. Hooper	20 Feb. 1843	James M. Hooper (w) Wm.Hooper,J.P.
Wood,Robert	Francis Hyatt (d.of Mashack)	8 Sept. 1830	Robert B. Hyatt (w) ----------
Wood,Samuel x	Betsey Benitt (d.of Hardiman)	5 Sept. 1835	A(ndrew) J.Hogland (w) S.Fitzgerrald,clk.
Wood,Thomas x	Synthey Bryson (d.of Peggy Wood)	15 June 182(2)	James Allen (w) JOhn B.Love,clk.
Woodey,Beverly x	Dilla Ellis (d.of Charles)	11 Aug. 1821	David x Nelson (w) ----------
Woodfin,Nicholas	Peggy Battle (d.of Littleberry)	10 Oct. 1815	W(illia)m Coleman (w) R.Love,clk.
Woodring,Daniel x	Elizabeth Brown (d.of David)	14 Feb. 1830	John x Wike (w) ----------
Woodring,Noah x	Eve Fulbright	5 May 1840	Jeremiah Vickers (w) Wm.Welch
Woods,James x	Eleanor Phillips (d.of Daniel)	10 Jan. 1839	Josiah x Waston (w) J.B.Allison
Woods,William x	Mary London (d.of Rody)	18 Dec. 1838	J.B.Lewis (w) J.B.Allison
Wooten,William Rily (s.of Eber. & Elizabeth)	Angeline Tompson (d.of Nancy)	21 June 1869 M.21 June 1869 By Wm.S.Evans,J.P.	(w) W.C.Brown,R.D.H.C.
Wootten,John B. (s.of Eber.)	Rebeca Tompson (d.of Alexander)	5 Aug. 1869 M.5 Aug. 1869 By D.B.Nelson,M.G.	(w) W.C.Brown,R.D.H.C.
Wootton,Lazers	Elisabeth Thompson	17 Sept. 1859 M.28 Sept. 1859 By Wm.S.Evans,J.P.	(w) W.W.Medford,clk.

GROOM	BRIDE	DATE OF BOND	BONDSMAN & WITNESS
Warthbone,A.H. x	Sarah Caroline Partin	23 May 1851 M.---------- Colvard Nelson,J.P.	R.G.A.Love (w) J.Keener,clk.
Wrathbone,John x	Margret Yarborough (d.of Elisha)	30 June 1836	Daniel Allison (w) Wm.Welch,clk.
Wrathbone,Purnel	Polly Pestal	18 Sept. 1818	Peter Noland (w) ----------
Wrathbone,Silas x	Martha Lusk	1 Mar. 1856 M.4 Mar. 1856 By H.Rogers,J.P.	Wesley x Wrathbone (w) Wm.M.Rhea,clk.
Wrathbone,Westley x	Carrandra Kilpatrick (d.of a widow)	16 May 1832	David Green (w) ----------
Wriden,James	Leoma More	15 Dec. 1859 M.---------- By Wm.P.Gillett,J.P.	James x Colwell (w) David Howell
Wright,G(eorge) W.	Mary Gibson (d.of Nathaniel)	25 Apr. 1831	Thomas Ferguson (w) J.R.Love
Wright,George W. Jr.	Jane Harris	26 Aug. 1856 M.27 Aug. 1856 By H.Rogers,J.P.	---------- (w) Wm.M.Rhea,clk.
Wright,J.D.	Hariet M.McCracken	13 Oct. 1865	A.A.Moody (w) J.W.Killian
Write,James	Martha Abells (d.of Thos.)	16 Mar. 1827	Jacob Smith (w) ----------
Wyatt,Wm.	Casa Cogdell (d.of Elijah)	22 Feb. 1834	John L.Dillard (w) ----------
Yarberry,Elisha	Oney Lacky	29 Nov. 1852 M.29 Nov. 1852 By H.P.Haynes,J.P.	(w) J.Keener,clk.
Yarberry,Richard x	Elizabeth Roden	31 May 1828	Haney x Ray,Sr (w) Wm.Welch
Yarbery,Elish	Anna Plmans	31 Aug. 1859 M. 1 Sept. 1859 By S.Walker,J.P.	David Messer (w) David Howell
Yarborough,W.A.	Charity Woods	30 Sept. 1867	(w) W.W.Medford,clk.
Yarbrough,George W.	Nancy Underwood	1 May 1847	Isaac Rhinehart (w) ----------
Yearborough,Miner x	Cathrine Smith	25 Jan. 1850	Wm.x McFalls (w) S.W.Gaston
Yoder,David x	Fanney Guilliams	5 Apr. 1826	John Hollan (w) Wm.Welch,clk.
Young,B(erry) L.	Sarah Peoples	17 Nov. 1827	W(illia)m R.Clark (w) Ro.Love,clk.
Young,James	Elizabeth Allen	22 Sept. 1856 M.23 Sept. 1856 By R.B.Johnston,J.P.	Jeremiah Allen (w) Wm.M.Rhea,clk.

GROOM	BRIDE	DATE OF BOND	BONDSMAN & WITNESS
Young,Joseph	Sally Picklesimer	13 Oct. 1831	W(illia)m R.Clark w) Ro.Love,clk.
Young,Joseph	Emily Mandyvine Kinsland	22 Apr. 1868 M.22 Apr. 1868 By Joseph Brown	(w) Jn.N.Benners,D.C.
Young,Thomas x	----------	12 Jan. 1850	J(ames) N.Brendle (w) S W.Gaston,clk.
Zachariah,M.	E.Keener	9 Feb. 1852	T.S.Addington (w) C.T.Rogers,D.C.
Zachary,James A.(col) (s.of Allen McFall)	Laura Welch (col) (d.of Lewis)	12 Jan. 1869 M.---------- By D.W.Wells,M.B.?	(w) W.C.Brown,Reg.Deeds

BRIDE		PAGE	BRIDE		PAGE
Beaty,	Sary Ann		Blaylock	Elisure	
Beck,	Jane A.			Eliza J.	
	N.L.			Elizabeth	
	Polly			Marinda E.	
	Sarey			Mary A.	
Beech,	Elmina			Polly	
Benitt,	Betsey			Ruth	
Bennett,	Elizabeth		Bond,	Mercilla	
	Polly,		Bonham,	M.E.	
	S.E.			Mary	
Berong,	Susanah			Rachel	
Berry,	Debsy			Sarah P.	
	Nancy		Bonom,	Mariah	
Bess,	Elizabeth		Boon,	Adoline	
	Sarah		Boyd,	Ida	
Besst,	Sarah		Boyeed,	Elizabeth	
Bettle,	Mary		Bracket,	Elizabeth	
Biddix,	Caroline		Bradley,	Adaline	
Birchfield,	Vianna			Betsey	
Bird,	Caroline E.			Marey	
	Elizabeth		Bradshaw,	Elizabeth	
	Lucy			Jain	
	Margaret Jane			Margaret	
	Margerit			Nancey	
	Sussanah			Rebecca	
Biship,	Frankey		Brice,	Salley	
Bivans,	Polly		Brittian,	Sussannah	
Bivens,	Matilda		Brook,	Polly	
	Sarah		Brookshare,	Honar	
Black,	Nancy		Brookshear,	Elizabeth	
Blackburn,	Sarrah			Margaret	
Blalock,	Polley		Brookshere,	Patsey	
Blanton,	Nancy		Brown,	Ceila	

BRIDE		PAGE	BRIDE		PAGE
Brown,	Elizabeth		Burnett,	M.E.	
	Elizibeth			Nancey	
	Margaret			Naoma	
	Marinda		Burrell,	Tildy	
	Nancy		Byers,	Avaline	
	R.J.			Harriet Caroline	
	Rebecha			L.A.	
	Riler			Laura Ann	
	Sarah			Margrett	
Browning,	Mary			Martha J.	
Bryant,	Lucenda			Rebecha	
Bryson,	Anna		Cabe,	Elizabeth	
	Arta Elvira			Ella	
	Eby		Cagle,	Cathreine	
	Ely			Eliza	
	Lucinda			Elizabeth	
	Nancy			Lusinda	
	Sally			Mary	
	Synthey			Pricilla H.	
Buckehon,	Poley			Sarah	
Buff,	Barbarry		Caldwell,	Arlotte	
	Catharine			Catherine	
	Polly			Nancy	
Buge,	Nancy			Patsey	
Bugg,	Francis			Ruthy	
	Lydia		Caler,	Eve	
Bulle,	Matilda			Rebecca	
Bumgarner,	Nancy A.			Ruth	
	Sarah			Sally	
	Susan Lucinda		Calwell,	Elizabeth	
Burges,	Sarah Ann			Martha J.	
Burnett,	Elizabeth L.			Mary	
	Harrett M.		Camel,	Sary	

BRIDE		PAGE	BRIDE		PAGE
Cammpbell,	Elizebeth		Cathey,	Rebecca	
	Hannah			Sarah Ann	
	Margret			Selena	
	Mary			Violet	
	Sarah		Cathy,	Mary M.	
	Violett			Matilda Lourena	
Cantrell,	Elisabeth			Pllly	
	Jane		Chambers,	Abby	
Carenger,	Rachel			Ann	
Caringer,	Nancey			Elisabeth	
Carrol,	Martha			Elizabeth	
Carroll,	Elizabeth			Elizah F.	
Carson,	Jane			Margaret	
Carter,	Eliza			Nancy	
	Elizabeth			Rachel	
	Mourning			Rosanah	
	Patsey			Sally	
	Preshus		Chandler,	Katherine	
	Prudence			Mary	
Carver,	Elizabeth		Christopher,	Lucinda	
	Katty			Malinda	
	Nancy			Margret	
Cashion,	Nancy			Mariah	
Casy,	Nancy			Mary	
Cathey,	Adra			Mary M.	
	Elisabeth			Melinda	
	Jane O.		Cirby,	Nancy	
	Jemimah		Clark,	Elisabeth	
	Katharine			Eliza	
	Lucinda			Jane	
	Margaret			Jane M.	
	Martha			Matilda Jane	
	Mary Caroline			Martha C.	

BRIDE		PAGE	BRIDE		PAGE
Clark,	Mary		Colwell,	Rhoda L.	
	Nancy		Conar,	Gane	
	Rachul M.		Coner,	Alisabeth	
	Rody			Masey	
	Sarah		Conley,	Nancey	
	Sarrah		Cook,	Elizabeth	
	Sharlot			Margret	
	Ulviry			Sarah	
Clay,	Milinda		Cooper,	Barbery	
Cline,	Margaret			Catherine	
	Susannah			Haret	
Clingman,	Mary			Mahaily	
Cockarham,	Alisabeth			Mahala	
	Malvine			Mary E.	
Cogdall,	Polly			Sarah J.	
Cogdell,	Casa			Susaan	
Cogens,	Elizabeth		Corbin,	Jane Valenda	
Coldwell,	Nancey		Cornwel,	Alesabeth A.	
	Sarah Ann		Cornwell,	Marey	
Cole,	Ruth			Sary	
Coleman,	Harriett M.		Coster,	Margaret	
	Mary		Couch,	Mary	
Collell,	Marey E.		Coward,	Elizabeth	
Collett,	Cilvey L.			Jane	
Collins,	Elizabet M.		Crage,	Martha	
	Jane C.		Crawfor,	Matilda	
	Malinda		Crawford,	Altha	
Colwell,	Eady C.			Ann	
	Eliza			Anna	
	Elizabeth			ARta	
	Fanney		Catharine	Elizabeth	
	Harriet E.			Francis	
	L,M.			Liddy	
	Mahala			Margaret	

91

BRIDE		PAGE	BRIDE		PAGE
Crawford,	Margret		Davis,	Manervy	
	Marinda			Margaret L.	
	Mary Elmyra			Mary C.	
	Mary Emlin			Nancey	
	Sarah			Racheal	
Cresp,	Rahcel			Rhoda Jane	
Crofford,	Martha			Susanah	
Cross,	Matilda			T.G.	
Cummons,	Percilla E.		Davison,	Eve	
Cuningham,	Elizabeth		Dawson,	Margret E.	
	Eloner		Deaver,	Mary	
	Margaret			Mary Levisa	
	Margaret M.		Dempsy	Elaiza	
	Polly		Demsey,	Abagill	
	Aylsee C.		Demsy,	Nancy	
	Medley		Denton,	Clowy	
Curry,	Centha			Miama	
Curtice,	Delila E.		Dever,	Eliza Ann	
	Manervey			Fanny	
Dailey,	Polly			Peggy	
Darnel,	Elizabeth		Dier,	Elizabeth	
Darnel,	Delitha		Dillard,	Ester	
DAvidson,	Celia E.		Dills,	Elizabeth	
	Elvirie		Dobson,	Eliza	
	Priscillia E.			Polly	
Davis,	A.C.		Dobson,	Carey A.	
	Elisabeth			Leuezor	
	Elizabeth		Doogan,	Elizabeth	
	Elmira		Dotson,	Caroline	
	Frankey			Ester	
	H.J.			Jemima	
	Hanah			Levina	
	Jane			Louisa	
	Lucinda			Mary	

BRIDE		PAGE	BRIDE		PAGE
Dotson,	Rebecca		Enloe,	Poly	
	Sarah			Zelphe M.	
Down,	Hannah E.		Enlow,	Elvira	
Ducket,	Catherin		Ensley,	Elizabeth	
Duckett,	Cary			Liley	
	Elisabeth			Nancy	
Duncan,	Elizabeth			Polly	
Duncon,	Annie		Ensly,	Hannah	
Dunken,	Mary A.Smith		Estes,	Darcus	
Dunkin,	Caroline			Nancy C.	
	Tebithy		Evans.	Ailsey	
Dyer,	Hannah			Alief	
	Mahala			Aliff	
	Martha			Eliza	
Earley,	Marian			Elizabeth	
Eastes,	Faney E.			Harriette	
Edmonston,	D.J.			Marow M.	
	L.C.			Mary	
Edwards,	Delila A.			Nicey	
	Laura E.			Rebecca A.	
	M.M.			Rilla Angeline	
	Neomea		Evens,	Ailey E.	
Elliott,	Amelia			Cathrin	
	Mahala			Martha	
	Malenda			Mary	
	Mary Ann			Rachel	
Ellis,	Dilla			S.A.	
	Sophia			Sarah E.	
Ellison,	Maria		Evins,	Amy	
England,	Margret			Celia	
Enloe,	Elisabeth			Harriett	
	Issabelae			Susanah	
	Nancy			Viana A.	
	Nercisey		Farmer,	Elizabeth	

BRIDE		PAGE	BRIDE		PAGE
Farmer,	Malinda		Fraday,	Anelin	
	Rachail Elizabeth		Frady,	Margaret	
Ferguson,	Ellender		Francis,	Margart	
Fergason,	Angeline		Franklin,	Eliza	
Fergurson,	Violet S.			Martha	
Ferguson,	Ellender			Mary	
	Fany			Matilda	
	Rachel J.			Nancy E.	
	Sarah E.			Sarah	
	Sary A.		Freeman,	Jane Barnet	
Fincher,	Caroline		Freemun,	Elizabeth	
	Lydia Caroline		Fulbright,	Darcus	
Finey,	Elizabeth			Elizabeth Ann	
Finney,	Adoline			Elvira	
Fish,	Margaret			Eve	
	Margaret J.			(Jane) Cordelia	
	Mary			Mary	
	Sarah			Meriah	
	Sarah R.			Rhoda	
	Sarrah			Sarah	
Fisher,	Mary		Fullbright,	Martha	
	Nancy			Rody	
	Nelley			Sarah Jane	
Fitzgerald,	Mary C. (or Molly)		Fulbrite,	Catherine	
	S.J.		Furgoson,	Mary	
Flaued,	Elsie E.		Furguson,	Fanny	
Flemings,	Lucinda		Gaddes,	Margrett	
Floid,	Rexney W.		Gaddy,	Emeline	
Ford,	Charity			Polly Ann	
Forgey,	Nancey		Galemor,	Saley	
Forington,	Nancey D.		Galeymar,	Carline	
Fortner,	Marey		Gallimore,	Nancy	
Fraday,	Margaret Louisa		Gambrel,	Emely	

94

BRIDE		PAGE	BRIDE		PAGE
Garrett,	Cordelea Samantha		Gribble,	Ann	
	Sarah			Jane	
Gibbs,	Mitildea			Polly Ann	
Gibson,	Alisabeth		Griffin,	Damaris	
	Betsey		Griffith,	Levinoh	
	Fandy		Grifith,	Sarah	
	Franky		Groce,	Mary	
	Jane		Gross,	Anna	
	Marey T.		Gudger,	Lucinda	
	Mary		Guiett,	Artemiser Caroliner	
	Ruth		Guilliams,	Lydia	
Gilleland,	Polly		Guilliams,	Fanney	
Gillett,	Eliza or Louiza		Gunter,	Elizabeth	
Gipson,	Nancy			Cassy	
Gragg,	Elizabeth			Nancey	
Grahl,	Harret M.			Sarah	
	Margaret		Gurly,	Sary	
	Maria-n		Halk,	Sarah	
Grantham,	Rachel		Halcombe,	Catharine	
Gray,	Sarah		Hall,	Betsy	
Green,	Anna			Deborah	
	Letty			E.C.	
	Levesa			Elizabeth	
	Malenda			Elizabeth A.	
	Marinda			Emeline	
	Martha			Hannah	
	Mary			Jane	
	Nercissa E.			Lucinda	
	Priscilla			Mary	
	Phewhamer			Phebe	
	Talitha			Polly	
	Sophena			Sarah	
Gregory,	M.A.M.			Telitha	
			Hampton,	Mary	

BRIDE		PAGE	BRIDE		PAGE
Hannah,	Eliza		Haynes,	Margaret Emeline	
	Orpha			Mary	
Hannh,	Mancy E.			N.A.	
	Ricey			Susanah	
Haras,	Alesabeth		Hays,	Sarah	
Harben,	E.C.		Hebberts,	Nancy	
Harbin,	Mary		Heffley,	Taletha	
Harman,	Lucretia		Helfey,	Mary A.	
	Rachel		Hefney,	Susanah	
	Rebecca		Henderson,	Margaret	
Harmon,	Eliezebeth C.			Melvina	
Harper,	Susanah			Neomey	
Harris,	Ester		Henry,	A.	
	Jane			Amanda M	
	Ruth			Emela	
	Ede			Jane	
Harry,	Polly			Lucenda S.	
Hartgrove,	Clarissa A.			M.M.	
	Mary C.			Mary Caroline	
Harvel,	Rebecca			Nancy Aveline	
Hatfield,	Lusinda			Nancy D.	
Hawkins,	Louesa			Sophia	
	Manerva		Hensley,	Polly	
	Manervy		Henson,	Adaline	
	Mary			Careoline	
	Mary E.			Caroline	
	Mary Elizabeth			Charlott	
	Sarah			Charlotte	
	Sophronia			Delila E.	
Haynes,	Candas E.			Elvira	
	Elizath			Elvira Jane	
	Isebellar			Emoline	
	Keziah A.			Jane	

96

BRIDE		PAGE	BRIDE		PAGE
Henson,	Jemima		Hogland,	Jane	
	Lavisa		Hoglend,	Bettyann	
	Manervy		Hoglin,	R.A.	
	Martha		Hogline,	Agia	
	Mary S.		Holder,	Caroline	
	Matilda			Mary	
	Melinda			Miley	
	Miley Roxaner			Racheal	
	Mima			Rahcheal	
	N.C.			Sarah	
	Nancy T.		Holeford,	Rebeca H.	
	Rachel A.		Holifield,	Case	
	Sally		Holland,	Celia	
	Sarah J.			Levisa	
	Violet			Malinda	
Herrell,	Jane M.			Mary	
Herren,	Jospehine			Susan Adaline	
Herrill,	Suanah E.J.			Zelia	
Hickey,	Peggy			Zillah	
Hicks,	Polly		Hollen,	Betsy Ann	
Hide,	Peggy		Hollyfield,	Matilda	
	Sarah		Holyfield,	Avolin	
Hill,	Levina			Mila J.	
	Lucinda		Honeycut,	Mary	
	Mary		Hood,	Elisabeth	
	Maryan C.			Polly	
	Nancy		Hooper.	Elizabeth	
	Nercisa			Gemima	
	Sofia			Kesiah	
Hipps,	Nancy			Mary	
Hix,	Cassey			Mary M.	
	Melenda			Nancy	
	Sally			Sara C.	
Hodge,	Elivra		Howard,	Elvina	

97

BRIDE		PAGE	BRIDE		PAGE
Howard,	Rebeca		Hyatt,	Ann	
	Sarah J.			Faney E.	
Howell,	Edy			Jane Rody	
	Elenor			L.L.	
	Adaline			Marey	
	Eliza			Margaret	
	Elizabeth A.			Mary C.	
	Emeline			Nancy	
	Emerline			Francis	
	Erena T.		Hyde,	Polly	
	Harriett		Ingraham,	Mary	
	Juliann		Ingram,	Peggy	
	Julletta		Ingrum,	Elizabeth	
	M.E.		Inman,	Caroline	
	M.J.			Cassey	
	Margaret E.		Fanny	Elizabeth	
	Mary			Mary M.	
	N.Emiline		Inmon,	Julia Ann	
	Nancy E.			Violet	
	Josephine		Irons,	Peggy	
Hubbard,	Anny		Ivester,	Mary E.	
Hudgins,	Liew Cindy			Luesia A.	
Huges,	Nancey			Nancy Z.	
Hughes,	Elizabeth Green,		James,	Syntha C.	
	Jensy		Janes, ? (o)	Jane	
	Margaret			Tersa	
	Mary Ann		Jans,	Souzan	
	Peggy		Jarrett,	Jane	
Hughs,	Sarrah		Jenkens,	Rebecka	
Hunacutt,	Dicy J.		Jestice,	Tempy	
Hunter,	Anna		Jinkens,	Nancy	
	Rebecca		Johnston,	Caroline	
	Sussannah			Harriet E.	
Huskey,	Candis			Lucinda Elizabeth	

BRIDE		PAGE	BRIDE		PAGE
Johnston,	M.M.		Kilbay,	Nancy	
	Racheal		Killian,	Eliza L.	
Jones,	Almira			Margarett A.	
	Ann			Martha A.J.	
	Delphey			Mary C.	
	Duricea			Nancy	
	Eliz.E.		Killion,	M.J.	
	Elizabeth		Killpatrick,	Marth	
	Elmina			Martha A.	
	Isirmiah		Kilpatrick,	Arminta	
	Jane			Carrandra	
	Louesa			Nancey	
	Lourena			Syntha	
	Lucenda		King,	Elizabeth	
	Margaret L.			Sarrah M.	
	Vianah		Kingsland,	Ruth	
	Wavaline		Kinsland,	Emily Mandyvine	
	Nancy			Eve	
Jonson,	Zelphia			Levada C.	
Justes,	Hariett A.			Manervy	
Justice,	Mary M.			Nancy	
	Matilda			Polly	
	Miry A.		Kirkland,	Polly	
	Rebecca		Kirkpatrick,	Mary L.	
Justis,	Loucinda A.		Knight,	Eliza	
Keener,	E		Lackey,	Sarah Ann	
	Easter		Lacky,	Elizabeth	
	M.J.		Land,	Oney Elezebeth	
Keerly,	Francis			Elizabeth	
Kendle,	Leana			Mary	
Kerby,	Mary			Rebeckak	
Kerns,	Nancy			Ruth	
Kilba,	Mary		Laney,	Rutha	
	Rachel		Lard,	Sariah	

BRIDE		PAGE	BRIDE		PAGE
Lea,	Nancey		Love,	Mary Caroline	
Leatherwood,	Caroline			Mary J.	
	Eliza			Rebecca	
	Elizabeth F.			Sarah	
	Nancey			Sarah J(ane)	
	Polly		Lovel,	Polly	
Ledbetter	Kesiah		Lovingood,	Ana	
Ledford,	Maria		Low,	Sarah C.	
	Nancy		Lowe,	Elizabeth	
Lee,	Rhodey		Lowinggood,	Matilda C.	
Lemming,	Mily		Lusk,	Jane	
Lenoir,	Rebecca			Martha	
Liner,	Lucinda		McAby,	Mary	
	Lusinda		McBee,	Mintha	
	Rebecca		McCamish,	Belinda	
	Ruth			Lucinda	
Loe,	Mary		McClurer,	Elezebeth	
Lolis,	Melinda			H.A.	
Lollis,	Eliza		McClure,	Esther	
Londay,	Vira			Hariett	
London,	Mary			Janie	
LOng,	E.J.			Miley	
	Harett			Nancy	
	Lucrecea			Polly	
	Mary			Sarah	
	Mary E.		McConnel,	Kisiah	
	Neomy		McCracken,	Adoline	
	Rebecca C.			C.E.	
	Sarrah			Hariet	
Loranse,	Anny			Lueasey Jan	
Love,	Christence			Margret	
	Margaret E.			Mary	
	Mary A.			Minda	
	Maryann		McCraken,	Sarah	

BRIDE		PAGE	BRIDE		PAGE
McCrackin,	Emily		Mahaffey,	Neoma	
	Peggy		Mahaffy,	Clerrissy	
McCracking,	Emelia			Mary Ann	
McCrackins,	Chery			Rebecca	
McDaniel,	Edney		Man,	Mary	
	Francis E.		Mann,	Elisebeth	
McDaniel,	Jesephene			Esabel	
	Jula An			M.C.	
	Morning			Mary J.	
McDowell,	Elizabeth			Nancey	
	Jenny			Nancy	
	Synthey			Sarrah	
McElroy,	Julia Ann		Marlow,	Temperance	
McFalls,	Eliza		Martin,	Agnes	
	Mary Avaline			Mary	
McGalon,	Alisabethe		Massay,	Lusinda	
McGee,	Lonsom E.			Mahala	
	Nicee			Navvy	
	Peggy			Clarissa	
	Sarah			Cleracy	
McKee,	Polly Caraline			Delpha	
McLeod,	Camilla			Mary Malinda	
	Rosannah			Rachal	
McMahan,	Lucinda			Sarah	
McMillian,	Mary		Masson,	Matilda	
McMillin,	Mary		Mathes,	Annis	
McMullins,	Cassia		Mathis,	Elizabeth	
McMillion,	Martha		Mathus,	Caroline	
McMullin,	Anne		Meace,	Mary	
McMullins,	Polly			Sally	
Macabee,	Melissa		Medford,	Cinthia	
Magnes,	Susan			Haseline	
Mahaffey,	Lydia			Jane	
	Margaret			Lidea	

101

BRIDE		PAGE	BRIDE		PAGE
Medford,	Mahala		Miller,	Polly	
	Mary			Sarah	
	Maryann			Sary	
	Naoma		Mills,	Mary	
	Neoma			Pholley H.	
	Sarah			Tempy	
Meece,	Elizabeth		Millsaps,	Elizabeth	
	Elvira		MIngus,	Clarissa	
	Fanny			Elizabeth	
Meese,	Cintha			Elizabeth T.	
Meeze,	Jane			Mary	
Mehaffey,	Elizabeth			Rachul M.	
Mehaffy,	Mary			Rebeca M.	
Mercer,	Ann			Rebicca	
	Jenny			S.C.	
Messer,	Charity Jane		Mitchel,	Martha	
	Elviry		Mitchell,	Jane	
	Kisiah		Monroe,	Faney	
	Letta		Moody,	Elizabeth	
	Lucinda			Ludinda E.	
	Lydia			Martha	
	Mary A.			Mary	
	Sarah			Sarah	
Messor,	Elizabeth			Sarah A.	
	Nancey		Mooney,	Sarah	
	Sary		Moor,	Nancy	
Michel,	Elizabeth		Moore,	Escna	
Millender,	Ruthey			Jane	
Miller,	Elizabeth C.			Leucinda	
	Elizure			Leuezre	
	Elon			Margaret	
	Emaline		Mary Malinda		
	Julile D.			Nancy	
	Mary A.			Nancy E.	

BRIDE		PAGE	BRIDE		PAGE
More,	Celia		Nelson,	Mary	
	Leoma			Nancey	
Morgan,	Nancy E.			Sarah	
	Viana			Sarah A.E.	
Morris,	Martha		Neweton,	Nercisa	
Morrow,	Elizabeth		Newton,	Anne	
	Hannah			Sarey Ebline	
	Jane		Nicholes,	Elizabeth	
	Mariah		Nichols,	Jane	
	Mary Ann		Nickols,	Marey	
	Rachel		Noblitt,	Mary C.	
	Rebeca			Sarah Ann	
	Rebecca		Noland,	Angelline	
	Sally			Elizabeth	
	Sarah			Huldy	
	Sarah A.			Jain	
	Sarah C.			Mary L.	
Moss,	Malinda			Matilda	
	Sarah			Nancey	
Mull,	Barbary			Nancy	
	Cintha			Peggy	
	Elvina		Norress,	Sarah Caroline	
	Hester C.		Norris,	----------	
	Susan C.		Norton,	Nancy	
	Syntha C.		Norwood,	Evie	
Murray,	Mary Jane		Nowland,	Emely	
	Recca			Gracy	
Murrey,	Elizure		Oaks,	Susanah	
	Talitha E.		Oliver,	Margret	
Murry,	Armina L.		Oneal,	Rhiney	
	Louisa E.		Osborn,	Adalaide	
	Margaret			Louisa C.	
Nations,	Mary			Mary Jane	
Nelsons,	Elizabeth		Osborne,	Tellitha	

103

BRIDE		PAGE	BRIDE		PAGE
Owen,	Addaline		Partin,	Anna	
	H.M.		Patten,	Mary	
	Jane		Patterson,	Rebecha	
	Lucinda		Patton,	Catharine	
	Nancy T.			Charrity	
	W.E.			Elizabeth	
	Winnei			Harritt	
Owens,	Catharin			Sophia	
	Cordelia Jane		Peck,	Matty	
	Elizabeth M		Penland,	Elizabeth A.	
	Polly			Elizabeth	
	Prisclla			M.A.	
	Rutha			Marget P.	
Owens,	Easter			Rachael A.	
Pace,	Lily			Sarah E.	
Palmer,	Jane Matilda		Peoples,	Sarah	
	Sarah		Perry,	Lidia	
Pannell,	Elmina		Pestal,	Polly	
Paras,	Lucresee		Pharr,	Caroline	
Parham,	Patsy			Lydia	
Paris,	Senthey			Naoma C.	
Parker,	Alafar		Philips,	Altha	
	Barbary			Hannah	
	Easter Caroline			Irenia	
	Elizabeth		Phillips,	Eleanor	
	Jane			Elizabeth	
	Mary			Mary Ann	
	Nancy			Nancey	
Parks,	Clarissa			Nancy	
	Myra			Sary	
Parmer,	Mary A.		Pickelsimer,	Mary	
	Ruth E.		Picklesimer,	Ellender E.	
Parres,	Nelley			Jane	
Parris,	Mary			Sally	

BRIDE		PAGE	BRIDE		PAGE
Pless,	Atheline		Queen,	Lucinda	
	Mary			Nancy	
Plmans,	Anna			Olive	
Plott,	Adaline			Rebekah	
	Margaret		Raburn,	Betty Ann	
	Martha Caroline		Raby,	Margaret	
	Martha J.		Radornel,	Mary	
	Mary		Ramsey,	N.M.	
	Merza Ann		Ratcliff,	Chairity	
	Salinda			Elisabeth	
	Surlinda			Eliza	
Pool	Eliza		.	Lucy	
Posey,	Hannah			Lydia	
Poteet,	Josey			Margaret	
	Sarah E.			Mary	
Potts,	Margaret Eunis			Mary A.	
	Mary A.			Mily	
Presley,	Elisabeth		Rathbone,	Casey E.	
	Katty			Nancey	
	Nancy		Ratliff,	Mary	
	Polly		Ray,	Ann	
	Sarah			Elisabeth	
Price,	Elisabeth			Mary or (Polly)	
	Elizabeth			Sarah	
	Katharine		Rease,	Polly	
	Lovina		Reaves,	Leuza	
	Lydia Caroline		Reddeck,	Morning	
	Mary		Reddicks,	Polly	
	Rapsey Elvira		Reece,	Eliza Adaline	
	Sarah Lovina			Rachel C.	
Prince,	Arta			Rachiel	
Propst,	Elisabeth			Rebeca	
Pruett,	Nancey A.			Sarah	
Quarry,	Elizabeth Ann		Reed,	Elisabeth	

BRIDE		PAGE	BRIDE		PAGE
Roler,	M.A.		Sellers,	Mary	
Roof,	Barbary		Sellwell,	Marey	
	Mary Ann		Sharp,	Dosha	
	Sarah			Margaret	
Rose,	Rody		Sharrel,	Cathern	
Ross,	Harett		Shelton,	Mary	
	Ruth		Sherill,	Virlinsha	
Roughf,	Minty		Sherrell,	Mary	
Rowland,	Nancy		Sherrill,	Sarah	
Ruff,	Kisiah A.		Shipp,	Cinthy Ann	
	P.E.		Shook,	Betsey Ann	
	Patience			Catharne	
Ru(n)ions,	Nancy			Elizabeth	
Runolds,	Sarah Murilla			Kathrine	
Russel,	Jane			Keziah C.	
	Margrett			Levicey A.	
	Martha			Lowisa	
	Mary			Margaret	
	Salley			Martha Ann	
Russell,	Eliza			Mary	
	Elizabeth			N.A.	
	Francis			Nancy	
	Jane			Sarah	
	Margaret M.			Susanna	
	Polly			Tellitha Ensly	
	Tempy Louesa		Shuler,	Anna	
Sanford,	Margaret		Shunk,	Mary	
Schunk,	Barbarry		Simmons,	Elizabeth	
Scott,	Elizabeth			Rasannah	
	Matilda		Sims,	Jane	
	Nancy M.		Singleton,	N.L.	
Sellers	Anny		Sitton,	Mary	
	Mariah			Sarah	
	Martha M.		Slate,	Mary E.	

BRIDE		PAGE	BRIDE		PAGE
Smart,	Rachael M.		Snider,	Barbary	
Smathers,	Elizabeth			Catharine	
	Emeline			Delpha	
	Jane			Elazabeth	
	Katherine			Elisabeth	
	Mary			Elizabeth	
	Mary Ann			Mary	
	Mary L.			Peggy	
	Mary M.			Sarah	
	Milla			Sophia	
	Nancy Adaline		Sorrells,	Nancy	
	Nancy E.			Eliza	
	Telitha			Fanny	
Smathurs,	Barbary			Sussannah	
Smith,	Anna		Sorrels,	Louisa	
	Avoline			Mary	
	Beckneann			Polly	
	Betty Ann			Rebecca	
	Catherin		Sorrols,	Sally	
	Cathrine		Sparks,	Soosan	
	Elizabeth		Spivy,	Melvina	
	Isabell		Standcele,	Minervey	
	Jane Avaline		Stanford,	Sarah	
	Lidia		Starns,	Jane	
	Lucinda		Starr,	Betsey	
	Mandy L.		State,	Mary Ann	
	Mary		Stephenson,	Catharine	
	Mary			Elizah	
	Peggy			Jane	
	Polly			Margaret	
	Sussannah			Sarah	
	Tebitha		Stephenson,	Elender	
	Wyney		Syevenson,	Mary	
Snider,	B.A.		Steward,	Marey	

108

BRIDE		PAGE	BRIDE		PAGE
Stewart,	Hannah		Thompson,	Mary Ann	
Stiles,	Caly			Polly	
	Jane			Temperance	
	Margaret		Tilly,	Margaret	
	Rachal		Tompson,	Angeline	
Stillwel,	Marey			Esther	
Stillwell,	Massy			Rebeca	
	Necessa		Trannwell,	Martha Caroline	
	Rebecca		Tritt,	Elizabeth	
Stinson,	Nancey			Martha A.	
Stokes,	Nancy J.			Nancy	
Stords,	Polly			Sarah	
Street,	Mary		Truelove,	Alvira	
Strother,	Caroline			Eve	
	Polly		Truett,	Polly	
Stynes,	Luisind (or Luisa)		Trull,	Sarah	
Suazngin,	Margarett		Trulove,	Hannah	
Sular,	Ann		Tumberlin,	Elisabeth	
Sumaker,	Arriena M,		Turner,	Angelin	
Sutherlin,	R.A.L.			Partheany	
Sutton,	Sarah			Polly	
Swanger	(ado) Line			Polly M.	
	Polly			S.C	
	Vilinda			Sarah	
Tate,	Caroline			Talitha	
	Margaret		Turrell,	Mary	
	Milley		Underwood,	A.	
	Nancy M.			Magdalene	
Terrell,	Harriet			Nancy	
Terrill,	Martha J.			Temperance	
Thomas,	Zilpha		Vandeever,	Revecca	
Thompson,	Elisabeth		Vaughn,	Elizabeth	
	Esther		Vess,	Margett An	
	Mary			Mary J	

BRIDE		PAGE	BRIDE		PAGE
Vest,	Elizabeth		Welch,	Merear	
Wade,	Jane			Nancy	
	Juda			Nancy Angeline	
	Lamsy F			Rachel	
Walker,	M.E.			S.E.A.	
	Priselar			Sarah	
Wallace,	Cassander			Susson	
Wallis,	Sarah		Wells,	Elizabeth	
Waltriss,	Sarah		West,	Mary M.	
Ward,	Rachel		White,	Avoline	
Warde,	Mary M.			Nancy	
Warran,	Jane A.			Peggy	
Warren,	Margaret Emaline			Rachel	
	Martha		Whitehead,	Every	
	Ruthy R.			Jane	
Waters,	Mary		Whitson,	Fanny	
	Milly		Wikel,	Rosanah	
Watson,	Catharine		Wilkes,	Catharen	
	Hannah		Wilkins,	Betsey	
	Sidney			Nancy	
Watts,	Peggy		Williams,	Chaney	
Weatherrow,	Nancy			Mary	
Webb,	Martha Ann M.			N.E.	
Weeks,	Nancy			Nancey Ann	
Welch,	Caroline			Passey	
	Elezebeth C.			Rachel T.	
	Elezabeth		Williamson,	Jane S.	
	Elizabeth			Rachael	
	Luara			Sarah Adaline	
	M.E.		Wilson,	Ann N.	
	Martha			Eda Ludisa	
	Martha P.			Elizabeth	
	Mary Jane			Matilda	
	Mary L.			Naomi	

BRIDE		PAGE	BRIDE		PAGE
Wilson,	Sarah		Wrathbone,	Elezebeth	
	Selenda			Patsy	
Winchester,	Polly Ann			Sarah	
Wines,	Eliza M.		Write,	Eleanor	
	Mary		Wyatt,	Mary	
Wise,	Susannah		Wynes,	Sarah	
Withrow,	Margaret		Yarberry,	Polly	
Wolfe,	Arta		Yarborough,	Elizabeth	
	Elizabeth			Jane	
	Sarah			Margret	
Woodbun,	Susanah			Viny	
Woody,	Sary		Yarborrow,	Tilletha	
Wooddy,	Polly		Young,	Avaline	
Woods,	Aggy			Margaret	
	Agness			Mary	
	Charity			Rosanah	
	Emoline			Sary	
	Jane		NOSURNAME	Matilda	
	Lavina				
	Margaret				
	Susanah				
Word,	Nancey Rosan				
Worley,	A.E.				
	Easter M.				
	Mary C.				

This work has suffered greatly in the multiple transcriptions of the original particularly in the interpretations of the recorders' then uncertain spelling of both given and surnames. While this indexer does not profess to have made no errors herself, after a one by one examination of the names, she does suggest an exhaustive study of this index. Listing as it does SOME parents, bondsmen, witnesses, court officials, persons officiating at the marriages and fewer than ten brides who were omitted from the BRIDES INDEX, combined with the first 86 pages of spouses, it approximates a "census" of the adult population of Haywood County.

JACKSON COUNTY
MARRIAGES

Able,Henry--23   Aug.5,1896   E.B.McDade   J.P.
  Sheppard,Sophia--23   At Dillsboro,
                        Wit; F.M.Cathey, W.A.Enloe

Adam,-- 25 (Red)   July 17,1875   T.K.Welch   J.P.
  Sih, Yet--20 (Red)   At T.K.Welch's
                        Wit; Will West, Alex Hornbuckle

Adam, B. --   Sept.19,1857   -----   --
  Evitt,Cleninda--   At ----

Adam,W.H.--19   Dec.10,1897   T.B.Queen   J.P.
  McMahan,Syntha--16   At T.B.Queen's
                        Wit; W.S.McMahan,John McMahan, Wm.Sutton
                        He From Swain,Co.

Adams,Banister--62   Mar.20,1894   John Bumgarner   J.P.
  Wilks,Mary K.--30   At Cullowhee
                        Wit; Nute Fox, Allie Wilks,N.E.Bumgarner

Adams,Harrison--20   Oct.19,1894   Lee Hooper   J.P.
  Pressley,Queen--17   At Cullowhee
                        Wit; Ann Dills,Thomas Pressley,John Ashe

Adams,McDonnel--22   Feb.15,1881   C.B.Fugate   M.G.
  Davis,Allie--18   At W.B.Davis'
                        Wit; David Norton, P.N.Adams

A-haw-ne-tok--22 (Red) July 24,1874   T.K.Welch   J.P.
  Elizabeth--19 (Red) At T.K.Welch's
                        Wit; Will West

Aheris,L.M.--   Aug.18,1853   J.C.Galloway   M.G.
  Barton,J.B.   -----------

Akin,Andrew J.--20   July 18,1886   J.R.Crawford   J.P.
  Cogdille,Callie M.--18 At B.F.Akin's
                        Wit; B.F.Akin, Wm.Ensley

Akin,Benjamin--22   Mar.25,1880   E.D.Brendle   B.M.
  Ensley,Josephine--18 At W.Ensley's
                        Wit; W.T.Ensley, S.A.Ensley

Akins,John--21   License Issued--Sept.8,1880
  Cowan,Nancy--25   Not Returned

Alexander,C.R.--18   Oct.5,1896   T.J.Mathis   J.P.
  Brown,Nelie--16   At Canada Ts.
                        Wit; F.R.Huffman, J.M.Wood

Alexander,Elijah--29   July 27,1882   H.M.Bennett   M.G.
  Robison,Eliza--21   At Ellen Hamp. Robison's
                        Wit; Ellen Bennett, J.B.Rochester

Alexander,E.F.--   Oct.6,1859   D.H.Cennomur   Clg.
  Green,Mary--   ----------

Alexander,Geo.H.--33   Aug.3,1894   J.A.Marshall   M.G.
  Pickelsimer,R.Zella--20 At Cashier, Transylvania Co.
                        Wit;E.F.& D.M.and W.H.Alexander

```
Alexander,John--              Feb.23,1856            Allen Fisher    J.P.
Ash, Katherine--              -----------

Alexander,John H.--16         July 22,1883           L.W.Hooper      M.G.
   Shelton,Margaret J.--18    At Rockey Hollow Church
                              Wit; J.A.Galloway, C.L.Hooper

Alexander,R.S.--21            Oct.25,1898            T.J.Mathis      J.P.
   Brown,Annie--18            At Canada  Ts.
                              Wit;F.S.Fortner,S.E.Hamilton,J.C.Massen-
                                                                  gale.

Alexander,Samuel--24          July 3,1881            B.N.Queen       B.M.
   Ash,Melvina--22            At B.N.Queen's
                              Wit; T.J.Bryson, B.N.Queen

Alexander,Samuel M.--20       Feb.3,1879             B.N.Queen       B.M.
   Coward, Rachel--22         At Matilda Coward's
                              Wit; Thos. Brown, J.Alexander

Alexander,W.L.--21            Feb.11,1891            Henry Jackson   J.P.
   Shelton,Annie--17          At River  Ts.
                              Wit; A.M.Brown, J.P.Jackson,J.W.Shelton

Alexander,Wm.P.--24           Mar.15,1883            H.M.Bennett     M.G.
   Cabe, Susan B.--18         At Thos. Cabe's
                              Wit; H.H.Taylor, M.Moody
                              He From Ocona,Co. S.C.

Allen,George--32  (Col)       License Issued  Oct.24,1888
   Love, Hattie--21 (Col)     NOT RETURNED

Allen,Jerry C.--24            Apr.30,1886            W.Ensley        B.M.
   Fisher,Alice--21           At Mont Farmer's
                              Wit;W.H.Allen, R.W.Fisher

Allen,Lawrencce--31           Aug.6,1900             R.A.Painter     J.P.
   Sutton,Alice--20           At Sylva  Ts.
                              Wit; R.J.Crawford, M.L.Knight

Allen,L.W.--28                License Issued  Dec.16,1898
   Sutton,Alice--19           NOT RETURNED

Allen,Mikel--21  (Col)        Apr.22,1881            G.W.Spake       M.M.
   West,Gustus--17 (Col)      At Dol Addington's
                              Wit; Dol Addington, B.Sherrill

Allen,Nathan--60              Jan.13,1878            G.W.Spake       M.M.
   McConnell,Malinda--39      At Mrs.McConnell's
                              Wit;R.F.McFee, W.P.Allman

Allen,Nathan--65              Oct.16,1879            E.D.Brendel     B.M.
   Hall, Jency--58            At James Parris'
                              Wit; R.M.Parris, J.M.Parris

Allen,Philander C.--40        Feb.25,1883            W.P.Jones       J.P.
   Wilke,Menervia I.--28      At Phillip Wike's
                              Wit; J.S.Fullbright, W.H.Bumgarner

Allen,Pierce--28              Nov.27,1894            A.H.Sims        B.M.
   Reed,Alice--31             At Sylva, N.C.
                              Wit; A.W.Farmer,R.Q.Phillips,J.L.Fisher

Allen,Robert--19              Feb.9,1900             R.A.Painter     J.P.
   Sparks,Emma--19            At C.C.Love's
                              Wit; D.L.Love,A.J.Love,W.B.Love
```

```
Allen,Sherman--22           Jan.3,1889          A.D.Hooper    J.P.
   Coward,Hattie--18        At Cullowhee, N.C.
                            Wit; Bowman Davis

Allen,Walton C.--21         Mar.14,1880         W.Ensley      B.M.
   Angil,Ann--21            At L.M.Angel's
                            Wit; W.J.Fisher, H.P.Brendle

Allen,W.B.--                Sept.17,1871        D.D.Davis     J.P.
   Bumgarber,C.A.--         ------------

Allen,W.B.--22              Feb.28,1895         A.H.Sims      B.M.
   Mooney,Ida--20           At Sylva, N.C.
                            Wit; Judson Allen,Fred Mooney,Callie Sims

Allen,W.E.--                Sept.19,1869        A.Zachery     -----
   Gibson,Margaret--        At----------

Alley,J.F.--22              Mar.20,1890         Javan Davis   -----
   Bowlick,Lon--            At Cashiers Valley  Ts.
                            Wit; E.M.Alley,M.D.Edwards,W.B.Picklesimer

Alley,J.H.Jr.--32           June 7,1892         B.G.Wilds     M.G.
   Hooper,Pauline--25       At J.M.Hooper's
                            Wit; Javan Davis,Cassie Hill, Pauline Davis

Allison,Andrew B.--27       Sept.20,1883        W.C.Carden    M.G.
   Woodfin,Hattie--30       At J.W.Terrell's
                            Wit; J.W.Terrell

Allison,C.B.--26            Lic.Issued-Sept.2,1891-B.G.Wild   M.G.
   Keener,Alice Belle--17   At -------
                            Wit; T.B.Allison,W.T.Fisher,J.W.Keener

Allison,F.P.--              Aug.20,1871         J.R.Long--P.E.of M.E.C.S.
   Coats,Martha A.--        At---------

Allison,J.C.--22            Feb.21,1896         L.M.Dillard   J.P.
   Heaton,Minnie Gertrude--20- At Cashier  Ts.
                            Wit;W.R.Zachary,M.A.Sharrall,Nannie A.Zach
                                                              ary.

Allison,Joseph--            Oct.13,1870         J.M.Candler   J.P.
   Ash,Martha--             At --------

Allison,Lee--22             June 22,1892        J.C.Watkins   J.P.
   Munday,Hattie--22        At Dillsboro, N.C.
                            Wit; R.P.Potts,Mrs.S.R.Davis,Lola Sherrill
                            He From McDowell Co.N.C.

Allison,Monterville--       Oct.26,1859         W.H.Higdon    J.P.
   Wilson,Jane--            At --------

Allison,Oatus M.--22        Jan.2,1883          D.H.Ash       J.P.
   Hall,Cordellia--16       At J.L.Hall's
                            Wit;C.M.Buchanan,J.J.Buchanan

Allison,Samuel--            Sept.30,1860        L.G.Ward      J.P.
   Paris,Elizabeth--        At ---------

Allison,S.N.--              Sept.28,1870        T.H.Edwards   Elder
   Zachary,S.C.--           At ---------

Allison,Samuel N.--38       Dec.29,1882         L.M.Dillard   J.P.
   Bryson,Elizza J.--33     At E.J.Bryson's
                            Wit;W.B.Davis, H.R.B.Lindon
```

Allison,W.C.--22 Miller,Tennie--18	Feb.24,1897 At Shoal Creek Ts. Wit;Vergia Cooper,J.B.Sherrill,A.S.Patterson	J.J.Gray	M.G.
Allman,Issac--57 (Col) Hall,Eda--67 (Col)	Dec.21,1885 At Webster,N.C. Wit; Julia Wild, John M.Long	J.A.Wild	J.P.
Allman,John C.--23 Clayton,Hattie--22	Jan.12,1900 At Wm.Clayton's Wit;J.H.Terrey,Delos D.Hooper,H.C.Crumley	W.E.Conner	B.M.
Allman,John G.-- Bryson,R.J.--	Sept.21,1868 At ---------	Thom.Wilson	J.P.
Allman,William P.--27 Stillwell,Bettie--20	Apr.25,1883 At J.F.Stillwell's Wit; Juliet Buchanan, J.H.Rogers	D.G.Bigham	J.P.
Ammons,James G.--24 Shelton,Lydia S.--21	Mar.19,1878 At S.P.Shelton's Wit;J.E.McLain, W.A.Queen	W.Zachary	-----
Ammons,John-- Higdon,Martha--	Feb.23,1858 At --------	J.L.Buchanan	J.P.
Ammons,J.G.-- Cowan,Laura--	Apr.14,1872 At --------	J.S.Woodard	M.G.
Ammons,J.G.--41 Dills,Laura L.--31	Nov.5,1890 At Savannah Ts. Wit; R.N.Deitz, C.L.Dills, J.G.Buchanan.	A.W.Davis	J.P.
Ammons,S.W.-- Childers,Nancy--	Apr.17,1859 At --------	W.M.Buchanan	J.P.
Anderson,Ervin--38 (Col) Love,Laura--20 (Col)	License Issued, Aug.15,1901 NOT RETURNED		
Anderson,R.-- Hall,Sarah--	Jan.30,1870 At --------	E.P.Stillwell-J.P.	
Angel,J.E. Conley,Elmina--	Sept.15,1869 At ---------	G.W.Spake	Cleg.
Angel,Lee--24 (Col) Gibson,Georgia Ann--18 (Col)	Jan.16,1892 At Webster Ts. Wit;C.B.Bowman, Amanda Powell	W.C.Vanhook	M.G.
Arington,Thos-- Williams,Polly--	July 30,1871 At ---------	P.G.Green	M.G.
Armstrong,Charley--30 Hawkins,Rosa Ann--16	May 15,1894 At Webster, N.C. Wit; W.E.Moore, J.C.McLain, F.W.Stiles He From New Castle, Pa.	R.B.Shelton	M.G.
Arneeh,Will West--22 (Red) Ecua,Dina E.--17 (Red)	Mar.29,1875 At The Church Wit;Enola & Jessee Reed	J.R.Long	M.M.
Arrington,Dexter--22 Hill,Nancy--20	Aug.26,1900 At On the Rail Road Wit; H.L.Babb, J.P.Davis, J.E.Fisher	T.F.Arrington	B.M.

Arrington,Elbert--40 Blanton,Catherine--40	Apr.24,1884 At Nancy Blanton's Wit; James Henry	A.J.Hall	J.P.
Arrington,Eli--21 Allen,Pattie--19	Mar.20,1892 At Scotts Creek Wit; J.W.Blanton,T.C.Welch, V.C.Welch BOTH From Haywood,Co.N.C.	Henry D.Welch-	M.G.
Arrington,James R.--20 Lemons,Martha--19	Dec.21,1878 At S.Enloe's Wit; J.B.Sherrill, S.Jenkins	J.W.Bird	J.P.
Arrington,T.F.-- Arington,Polly--	July 24,1870 At ---------	A.J.Hall	J.P.
Arrington,Thomas P.--26 Reed,Artie--24	Dec.31,1884 At A.V.P.Bryson's Wit; A.V.P.Bryson, Jessee Bryson	M.W.Bryson	J.P.
Ash,Asberry B.--18 Brooks,Mary J.--18	Sept.30,1881 At D.H.Ash's Wit; D.C.Jones, W.T.Brooks	D.H.Ash	J.P.
Ash,A.J.-- Bryson,Litticia L.--	Mar.6,1855 At -------	Allen Fisher	J.P.
Ash,Charles C.--25 Enloe,A.J.--	Nov.1,1874 At -------	T.K.Welch	J.P.
Ash,Clingman--17 Watson,Nancy A.--16	Nov.25,1883 At Robert Watson's Wit;G.E.Painter, S.F.Bryson	O.B.Coward	J.P.
Ash,Coleman-- Parker,Jane--	Aug.25,1857 At --------	J.Wike	J.P.
Ash,Coleman--28 Shular,Mary--48	Apr.3,1881 At Scoop Enloe's Wit; Mary Knight, Scoop Enloe	J.O.Wallace	J.P.
Ash,Hiram-- Ash,Sarah--	Nov.16,1856 At --------	Peter King	J.P.
Ash,Hiram G.--20 Pruit, Harriet--19	Apr.1,1883 At R.H.Brown's Wit;R.H.Brown, William Painter	G.W.Spake	M.M.
Ash,Hix-- Painter,Harriett--	Oct.20,1863 At --------	Wm. Wilson	J.P.
Ash,Jessee-- Merrill,Mary--	Dec.12,1857 At --------	--------	----
Ash,John--19 Melton,Margaret--18	Oct.21,1880 At Gilbert Meltons' Wit; W.A.Queen, W.B.Queen	B.N.Queen	B.M.
Ash,John M.--32 Shular,Martha J.--21	May 23,1877 At E.M.Shular's Wit; Robt.Ash, John Shular	J.R.Crawford	J.P.
Ash,Robert--27 Higdon,Alis--20	Mar.14,1883 At V.Higdon's Wit; V.S.Higdon, Elizabeth Higdon	D.G.Bigham	J.P.

Ash,William--20 Hooper,Sarah A.--16	Aug.24,1882 R.L.Watson J.P. At A.D.Hooper's Wit; M.B.Hooper, Andrew Bryson	

Ash,William--20
  Hooper,Sarah A.--16
Aug.24,1882   R.L.Watson   J.P.
At A.D.Hooper's
Wit; M.B.Hooper, Andrew Bryson

Ash,William--
  Mathis,Sarah--
June 23,1872   E.D.Brendle   Elder
At ---------

Ash,Wm.W.--
  Stiles,Samantha--
July 11,1861   Elcanat Ash   J.P.
At ---------

Ashe,C.A.--55
  Brown,Martha E.--27
Nov.9,1890   M.C.Warlick   M.G.
At Canada Ts.
Wit; S.B.Melton, H.Warlick, E.Brown

Ashe,C.C.--40
  Strutton,Mary--51
May 1,1890   W.Ensley   M.G.
At Webster Ts.
Wit; J.N.Candler,J.D.Coward,S.H.Bryson

Ashe,Charlie--18
  Tilly,Mandiney--18
Feb.25,1886   A.D.Hooper   J.P.
At L.H.Tillt's
Wit; J.B.Rochester, J.W.Tilly

Ashe,Clingman--24
  Stuart,Ida--20
License Issued Oct.31,1888
NOT RETURNED

Ashe,C.W.--22
  Holder,Lillie--19
Jan.25,1891   A.J.Long Sr.   J.P.
At Webster, N.C.
Wit;J.V.Ashe,J.W.Robison,James Holder

Ashe,Hampton P.--25
  Tilly,Margaret--23
Sept.27,1886   A.D.Hooper   J.P.
At L.H.Tilly's
Wit;J.B.Rochester, J.W.Tilly

Ashe,Henry--26
  Slatton,Neddie--18
Dec.25,1893   F.P.Hooper   J.P.
At Hamburg Ts.
Wit;A.T.Parton, T.B.Wilson, M.B.Hooper

Ashe,James R.--24
  Cowan,Lillie--16
Mar.5,1891   B.G.Wild   M.G.
At Webster, N.C.
Wit; C.M.Buchanan, T.B.Cowan

Ashe,John--23
  Cowan,Jane--20
Apr.10,1892   T.F.Deitz   M.G.
At Sanannah Ts.
Wit; R.N.Deitz,J.L.Buchanan,C.C.Higdon

Ashe,John--33
  Parker,Victoria--19
Dec.24,1893   J.C.Wood   J.P.
At Canada Ts.
Wit;S.M.Parker,A.J.Parker,G.W.Shook

Ashe,John--24
  Bumgarner,Ellen--20
Nov.9,1893   J.P.Brendle   J.P.
At Webster, N.C.
Wit;E.D.Franklin,R.C.Bumgarner,Sallie Long

Ashe,John N.--27
  Middleton,Elzy Magdaline--20-At David Middleton's
July 8,1900   J.H.Owens   B.M.
Wit; John Ashe,A.J.Parker,F.M.Ashe

Ashe,John W.--26
  Tilley,Margaret--22
Oct.2,1898   J.P.Brendle   J.P.
At Webster, N.C.
Wit;John W.Ashe, J.C.Davis, Fred Brendle

Ashe,Joseph L.--28
  Philips,Harriett--18
Issued Mar.31,1894-- Returned Not Executed
VOID

Ashe,Lewis--21
  Jones,Ellen--18
Oct.5,1891   T.F.Deitz   M.G.
At Savannah Ts.
Wit; L.D.Hall, W.C.Buchanan, W.A.Wilson

```
Ashe,Marion--19            Jan.31,1892      W.A.Queen    M.G.
  Middleton,Sallie--20     At River  Ts.
                           Wit; M.J.Watson,E.M.Watson,J.Middleton

Ashe,Marve--25             Jan.24,1897        J.H.House    J.P.
  Nations,Bennie--21       At Barker's Creek  Ts.
                           Wit; James Nations, B.P.Bradley

Ashe,M.N.--19              Oct.21,1884        A.J.Hall    J.P.
  Painter,Lena--18         At R.S.Painter's
                           Wit; Ellis Painter, E.M.Painter

Ashe,M.N.--28              Jan.28,1894        H.M.Bennett   M.G.
  Rhodes,Martha A.--20     At; Cullowhee Ts.
                           Wit; W.C.Norton,David Coward,J.R.Long

Ashe,R.C.--21              Dec.10,1888        B.N.Queen    B.M.
  Woodring,Callie--16      At Hamburg  Ts.
                           Wit; D.M.Presley, Miss Ava Wilson

Ashe,Rufus--26             Sept.13,1888       B.H.Jones    J.P.
  Wilson,Polina--19        At B.H.Jone's
                           Wit; W.H.Jones, W.R.Thompson

Ashe,Silvanas--26          Issued  June 10,1901
  Phillips,Hattie--18      Not Returned

Ashe,W.D.--21              Sept.5,1895        Wm.Bumgarner J.P.
  Moore,Mary--18           At Barker  Ts.
                           Wit;R.G.Bumgarner,J.R.Ensley,M.M.Buchanan

Ashe,W.I.--25              Apr.17,1898        J.P.Brendle   J.P.
  Extine,Amanda J.--24     At Sylva  Ts.
                           Wit; E.L.Ashe, C.J.Franklin

Ashe,William A.--22        Aug.16,1885        A.J.Hall     J.P.
  Slaton,Laura--           At John Alaton's
                           Wit; Jack Wike, John Slaton

Austin,John--30  (Col)     Aug.19,1899        L.A.Bailey   B.M.
  Norman,Lizzie--19 (Col)  At The Church
                           Wit; A.M.Bobo, W.H.Williams, Lee Howell

Ayers,Bake--57             June 2,1887        C.A.Bird     J.P.
  Falen,Margaret--45       At Falen's
                           Wit; H.F.Gibbs, M.J.Conley

Baker,Harrison S.--24      Aug.31,1876        J.W.Bird     J.P.
  Keener,Hattie--23        At Sarah Keener's
                           Wit; J.W.Terrell, J.S.Keener
                           He From Haywood,Co.N.C.

Baker,Jessie W.--21        No Information
  Conner,Dovey--19

Baker,Robert--19           Dec.5,1880         H.S.Baker    J.P.
  Fowler,Sarah--17         At B.F.Fowler's
                           Wit; James Martin, L.J.Baker

Bailey,John--22            Sept.25,1889       W.Ensley     M.G.
  Cope,Mary J.--20         At Sylva, N.C.
                           Wit; W.W.Cope, W.A.Bailey, T.C.Young

Bailey,J.H.--23            May 28,1893        S.C.Allison  J.P.
  Bumgarner,Tennessee--16  At  Barker Creek
                           Wit; Lizzie Brown, J.P.Robinson
```

Baird,Robert--31 Barker,Lucinda--35	Apr.16,1893 H.C.Conner J.P. At Savannah Ts. Wit;Jno.S.Keener,Z.V.Brooks,N.N.Frady He From Rabun,Co.Ga.	
Balard,Alonza--25 Wilson,Stella--20	Aug.9,1900 J.C.Henderson J.P. At Wm.A.Wilson's Wit; W.G.Wilson,A.L.Wilson He From South Carolina	
Baley,W.P.-- Woodard,M.M.--	Jan.9,1871 P.G.Green M.G. At -------	
Banter,George--21 Mathis,Medar--17	Oct.29,1899 J.C.Wood J.P. At John Mathis' Wit; W.U.Mathis,W.H.Phillip,W.S.Brown	
Bard,Coleman--20 Fox,Emly--22	May 18,1901 Nathan Coward J.P. At Webster, N.C. Wit; Robt.L.Madison,Mrs.W.O.Cary,Sopha C. Coward.	
Barker,Ira B.--25 Conner,Oma--14	July 31,1881 C.S.Buchanan B.M. At W.S.Barker's Wit; Sarah A.Conner,Caroline Barker	
Barker,Jessee--23 Buchanan,Jane--23	Oct.14,1882 D.H.Ash J.P. At C.S.Buchanan's Wit; G.W.Pangle,Silas Sutton	
Barker,John-- Sutton,Cherryan--	Oct.31,1855 L.G.Ward J.P. At --------	
Barker,John-- Barker,Mary--	Aug.18,1864 E.C.Ash J.P. At --------	
Barker,John--29 Davis,Carrie S.--20	July 1,1888 W.R.Barnett M.G. At D.D.Davis' Wit; Thos.A.Cox, M.E.Cox He From Hamilton, Ind.	
Barker,John M.-- Barker,Margaret M.--	Dec.5,1871 J.L.Buchanan M.G. At -------	
Barker,M.M.--20 Brooks,Mary--23	Jan.28,1888 E.C.Ash J.P. At E.C.Ash's Wit; A.B.Ashe,M.M.Barker Jr.	
Barker,Micaja M.--31 Upten,Dulcena S.--21	Feb.13,1881 T.M.Frizell J.P. At G.W.Dillard's Wit; A.J.Long,A.D.Cagle,W.Dillard	
Barker,William R.--23 Allen,Sarah J.--23	May 1,1881 G.W.Spake M.M. At Nation Allen's Wit; A.J.Long, Nation Allen	
Barnes,A.C.--22 Harris,Belle--21	Dec.23,1897 J.B.Ensley J.P. At Ben Harris' Wit; S.M.Rhea,D.G.Bryson, J.O.Fisher	
Barnes,Allen--25 Mathis,Sarah--22	Sept.4,1882 Lewis Queen M.G. At Jevan Parker's Wit; J.R.Queen, Javan Parker	

Barnes,Henry G.--18　　　　Aug.18,1889　　　S.H.Bryson　　J.P.
　　Duncan,Nancy E.--21　　At J.F.Arrington's
　　　　　　　　　　　　　　Wit; T.G.Bryson, John Queen

Barnes,John--24　　　　　　Oct.14,1881　　　J.C.Watkins　　J.P.
　　Watson,Aveline--23　　At Clerk's Office
　　　　　　　　　　　　　　Wit; W.A.Dills, W.P.Allman

Barnes,John H.--24　　　　Mar.15,1900　　　J.R.Crawford　J.P.
　　Frizzell,Laura--26　　At J.R.Crawford's
　　　　　　　　　　　　　　Wit; Robt.Nichols, Wilson Paterson

Barnes,Lee--21　　　　　　　Apr.17,1898　　　V.F.Brown　　J.P.
　　Slatton,E.M.--16　　　At D.F.Slatton's
　　　　　　　　　　　　　　Wit; West Conner,M.H.Powell,C.B.Webster

Barron,Franklin--22　　　June 11,1874　　　P.G.Green　　B.M.
　　Ash,Allow C.--14　　　At Sydney Ash's
　　　　　　　　　　　　　　Wit; Sydney Ash, W.T.Stiles

Battle,Wm.F.--19　　　　　Sept.24,1891　　　J.A.Williams　B.M.
　　Hughes,Luzena--19　　At Qualla Ts.
　　　　　　　　　　　　　　Wit;W.B.Terrell,M.L.Hipps, C.A.Bird

Battles,J.F.--　　　　　　Nov.12,1871　　　T.H.Welch　　J.P.
　　Keener,M.A.--　　　　At --------

Baty,W.L.--　　　　　　　　May 1,1856　　　N.B.Thompson　J.P.
　　Cooper,Lucinda--　　At -------

Beach,W.C.--27　　　　　　Sept.18,1889　　　B.G.Wild　　M.G.
　　Wilson,Maggie--18　　At Webster, N.C.
　　　　　　　　　　　　　　Wit; J.E.McLain, J.W.Fisher,W.E.Moore
　　　　　　　　　　　　　　He From Burke,Co.N.C.

Bean,John--35　　　　　　　NO DATE
　　Bryson,Candas--25　　At ----
　　　　　　　　　　　　　　Wit; W.E.Bryson, L.W.Crawford
　　　　　　　　　　　　　　He From Buncombe,Co.N.C.

Beard,Freeman--26　　　　Dec.7,1879　　　Tho.J.Bryson　J.P.
　　Brown,Haseltine--26　At John Brown's
　　　　　　　　　　　　　　Wit; J.R.Crawford, John Brown

Beard,James--　　　　　　Apr.14,1866　　　H.M.Cook　　J.P.
　　Parris,E.J.--　　　　At --------

Beasley,James D.--20　　Jan.3,1886　　　Wm.Bumgarner　J.P.
　　Davis,Mary E.--20　　At A.J.Parris'
　　　　　　　　　　　　　　Wit; John Davis, A.J.Parris

Beasley,Joseph M.--20　Mar.23,1875　　　E.C.Ash　　J.P.
　　Green,Margaret M.--19　At Joseph Green's
　　　　　　　　　　　　　　Wit; S.H.Messer, M.R.Buchanan

Beck,A.L.--24　　　　　　　Dec.20,1883　　　T.J.Love　　J.P.
　　Hall,Syntha E.--16　　At A.J.Hall's
　　　　　　　　　　　　　　Wit; Joseph Hoyle, M.M.Robinson

Beck,Andrew--24　　　　　　Aug.8,1879　　　G.W.Moody　　J.P.
　　Gunter,Alice--18　　　At Qualla Ts.
　　　　　　　　　　　　　　Wit; R.L.Hyatt, O.A.Hyatt, W.A.Hyatt

Beck,Joseph--24　　　　　Mar.25,1886　　　W.P.Jones　　J.P.
　　Snider,Lure--18　　　At F.N.Snider's
　　　　　　　　　　　　　　Wit;Wm.Bumgarner,Russell Sutton
　　　　　　　　　　　　　　He From Swain, Co.N.C.

Beck,S.A.--28
Jones,Clarissa--20

Dec.3,1899   W.C.Buchanan J.P.
At John Jones'
Wit; B.H.Hughs, R.L.Cabe, Cole Thompson

Beck,Samuel--22
Long,Mollie J.--20

Nov.20,1879   Tho.M.Frizzell J.P.
At A.J.Long's
Wit; A.J.Long, Samuel Buchanan

Beck,Samuel--21
Frizzell,Eva M.--21

June 10,1883   D.G.Bigham J.P.
At W.M.Frizzell's
Wit; W.M.Frizzell,Wilburn Beck

Beck,S.T.--
Conner,C.P.--

Sept.5,1869   Merrit Rickmon M.G.
At --------

Beck,Ste.--
Dawson,Eliza--

Apr.20,1856   J.B.Sherrill J.P.
At --------

Beck,Stephen J.--46
Wilson,Arminda E.--27

Aug.2,1883   A.B.Clements M.G.
At Alfred Wilson's
Wit; Zeb V.Watson, T.H.Franks

Beck,Wilburn--21
Bryson,Dollier A.--19

July 8,1883   D.G.Bigham J.P.
At P.P.Buchanan's
Wit; S.M.Beck, W.M.Frizzell

Belt,Jerry--26
Hawkins,Lillian--24

Sept.11,1898   R.L.Phillips J.P.
At Sam Hawkins'
Wit; J.H.Hawkins, J.T.Henson, A.E.Edwards
He From Haywood,Co.N.C.

Benfield,Wm.--22
Boid,Sarah--18

Mar.1,1899   T.F.Deitz B.M.
At M.C.Deitz's
Wit; T.M.Deitz, Sam Morgan, Nancy Deitz
He From Macon,Co.N.C.

Benjamin,W.E.--27
Jones,Lula--16

Sept.20,1893   J.P.Painter M.G.
At Barker Creek
Wit; J.M.Painter, H.Dills, Lel.Jones
He From Haywood,Co.N.C.

Bennet,John--
Graham,Lucinda--

July 20,1854   Allen Fisher J.P.
At ---------

Bennett,A.M.--27
Hyatt,Mary C.--22

Jan.1,1889   G.H.Church B.M.
At Qualla Ts.
Wit; Ransom Hyatt, J.S.Elmore, Laura Hyatt
He From Swain, C. N.C.

Bennett,Haynes A.--21
Presley,Ella--21

Dec.9,1900   H.M.Bennett M.M.
At H.M.Bennett's
Wit; E.J.Bennett, C.S.Bennett

Bennett,H.H.--24
Adams,Sarah A.--27

May 18,1892   W.C.Norton J.P.
At Cullowhee N.C.
Wit; John Bumgarner,Allen Wilks

Bennett,H.H.--16
Fox,Amanda--15

Apr.12,1885   E.P.Gibson M.G.
At Cullowhee N.C.
Wit; Jane Mathis, John Fox

Bennett,H.M.--
Bryson,E.J.--

Nov.25,1862   F.M.Fanning M.G.
At --------

Bennett,John--19
Coggins,Belle--18

Feb.3,1897   N.J.Fox J.P.
At Cullowhee N.C.
Wit; Isaac Love, N.J.Fox, J.A.Adams

```
Bennett,Montraville--        Apr.3,1866        A.D.Hooper    J.P.
   Crawford,Martha--         At -------

Berry,Ellis--20              June 2,1883       W.W.Reed      M.G.
   Woodruff,Ella--24         At W.W.Reed's
                             Wit; C.T.Reed, Charles Jones

Biddix,John--22              Sept.25,1890      T.M.Frizzell  J.P.
   Gibson,Sallie--18         At Qualla Ts.
                             Wit; J.C.Fisher, E.L.Farley R.E.Turpin

Bigham,D.G.--                Dec.7,1870        Thos.Wilson   J.P.
   Wilson,Mollie--           At -------

Bingham,B.G.--30             June 9,1899       P.P.McLean  L.C.of M.E.C.S.
   Cooper,Florence--19       At Qualla Ts.
                             Wit;R.H.Hyatt,E.L.McKee
                             He.From Swain,Co.N.C.

Birchfield,Henry--           Aug.20,1853       E.C.Newton    J.P.
   Lawless,Kathrine--        At --------

Birchfield,Samuel--          Aug.27,1853       M.Coleman     J.P.
   Lawless,Polly--           At --------

Birchfield,Wm.A.--           Mar.27,1871       I.T.S.Sherrill  Elder
   Jenkins,L.J.--            At --------

Bird,-- (Red)                Apr.23,1871       I.T.S.Sherrill  Elder
   Annie or Aisley--(Red)    At --------

Bird,--- (Red)               Apr.15,1871       T.K.Welch     J.P.
   Lucy-- (Red)              At --------

Bird,Charles A.--24          Oct.16,1877       J.W.Bird      J.P.
   Terrell,Sarah E.--16      At J.W.Terrell's
                             Wit; G.C.Hall, Hattie Woodfin

Bishop,Daniel--24            Sept.19,1886      J.A.Galloway  M.G.
   Phillips,Sallie--20       At A.J.Phillips'
                             Wit; Robert Coward, John Brown

Bishop,Daniel F.--21         Nov.4,1899        A.B.Henson    B.M.
   Painter,Alice--23         At Samuel Painter's
                             Wit; S.C.C.Cook, W.L.Painter,A.B.Bishop

Bishop,Frank--21             Sept.23,1900      J.D.Sitton    B.M.
   Bishop,Octa--18           At Bride's Fathers
                             Wit; J.M.Corbin, Bob Brown, H.G.Crisp

Bishop,Hugh--                Oct.15,1870       W.C.Berry     M.G.
   Woodard,J.E.--            At --------

Bishop,John B.--             Oct.19,1871       Wm.C.Berry    M.G.
   Franks,Mary--             At --------

Blakeny,Junison--22  (Col)   May 28,1893       F.W.Wallace   M.G.
   Love,Hattie--18   (Col)   At Scotts Creek
                             Wit;Scinda,Rosa Love, Sol. Dorsey
                             He From Rabun,Co.Ga.

Blankenship,E.M.--27         June 17,1896      J.M.Worley    J.P.
   Farley,Lula E.--17        At Qualla Ts.
                             Wit; D.G.Bigham, Nora C.Worley, Mary Bigham

Blantin,J.M.--25             Dec.25,1894       Josehp Hoyle  J.P.
   Farly,M.B.--21            At Scotts Creek
                             Wit; J.M.Crawford, J.Y.Hooper, E.D.Franklin
```

```
Blanton,A.R.--              Jan.6,1864        E.D.Brendle   Elder
  Watson,A.M.--             At -------

Blanton,Alvin R.--         Oct.19,1856       Allen Fisher  J.P.
  Henry,Lelah--            At --------

Blanton,Ellis--30          Aug.19,1891       W.W.Reed      M.G.
  Barker,Virginia--21      At Scotts Creek
                           Wit; Jerry Blanton,Amanda Blanton,J.Reed

Blanton,J.E.--26           Mar.17,1889       A.B.Henson    B.M.
  Fisher,Mary C.--19       At Scotts Creek
                           Wit; J.L.Ballard, J.K.Mills, R.H.McKay

Blanton,J.R.--20           Apr.26,1885       A.J.Hall      J.P.
  Mills,Mary--20           At T.B.Mills'
                           Wit; W.B.Love, T.B.Mills

Blanton,Jermiah--          Apr.7,1858        Wm.R.Crawford J.P.
  Crawford,Mary--          At -------

Blanton,Jermiah W.--52     Sept.28,1885      A.J.Hall      J.P.
  Wood,Amanda--22          At J.K.Mills'
                           Wit; J.K.Mills, John Dills

Blanton,Marcus L.--20      Nov.14,1873       L.G.Ward      J.P.
  Ward,Martha E.--22       At Walace Ward's
                           Wit; ------

Blanton,Robert L.--27      Feb.24,1901       Albert Brown  J.P.
  Brown,Mollie--29         At Wattie Brown's
                           Wit; J.B.Price, J.H.Parker

Blanton,W.H.--29           Issued-Sept.27,1901
  Jenkins,Lizzie--24       LICENSE NOT RETURNED

Blanton,W.H.--20           Aug.18,1892       J.A.Galloway  M.G.
  Normon,Emma--21          At Scotts Creek
                           Wit; R.V.Normon, M.J.McKay, C.N. ?

Blanton,William R.--       Mar.14,1869       A.J.Hall      J.P.
  Ensley,T.P.--            At ----- (He son of Riley & Nancy Blanton,
                           she Dau.of Wm.& C.Ensley)

Blythe,David--35  (Red)    July 17,1898      J.W.Bird      M.M.
  Jackson,Nanie--27 (Red)  At J.W.Bird's
                           Wit;Jessee Bird, L.C.Reid, Sophia Bird

Boggs,John S.--30          July 12,1892      George H.Bell M.G.
  King,Harriett C.--17     At Webster  N.C.
                           Wit; E.R.Hampton,B.H.Woodfin,W.D.Foster
                           He From Buncombe,Co.N.C.

Bogle,Laurence P.--26      Oct.19,1898       T.E.Wagg--M.M.E.C.S.
  McLain,H.Frances--21     At Webster  N.C.
                           Wit;Jas.W.Terrell,W.V.Honeycutt,T.B.Allison

Bolen,W.H.--               Dec.16,1869       W.R.Crawford  M.G.
  Arington,Elmira--        At --------

Boon,C.C.--25              Nov.18,1882       J.O.Wallace   J.P.
  Holden,Drusella--21      At John Holden's
                           Wit; C.C.Martin, Martha Holden

Boon,C.C.--37              Apr.22,1895       G.W.Spake     M.M.
  Waycaster,Roxie--21      At Dillsboro,N.C.
                           Wit; Wm.Forly, Thomas Farly
```

```
Bowman,George--23              July 23,1882        J.T.Stuart    J.P.
   Jennings,Martha--28         At John Jennings'
                               Wit;J.F.Watson, J.R.Taylor
                               He From Macon, Co.N.C.

Boyd,W.L.--                    Nov.8,1866          E.C.Ashe      J.P.
   Dalton,Elmena--             At -------
Bracken,Floyd--26              Jan.8,1893          W.C.Dunn      M.G.
   Owen,Adline--21             At Canada, Ts.
                               Wit; J.A.Hoxit, J.R.Owen, W.L.Owen
                               He From Transylvina,Co. N.C.

Bracken,J.F.--19               Jan.2,1898      James A.Galloway  J.P.
   Owens,Linda--23             At Canada, Ts.
                               Wit;E.C.McCall,John Galloway,Julas Kitchen

Bradley,AndrewG.--23           Feb.13,1874         F.M.Nations   J.P.
   Conner,Manervia--19         At J. Hughs'
                               Wit; Silas Bradley, J.H.Hughs

Bradley,Green--42  (Col)       Nov.28,1893         A.M.Parker    J.P.
   Fretwell,Emma--19 (Col)     At Sylva, N.C.
                               Wit;J.C.Love, L.A.Powell

Bradley,Harrison--25           Feb.15,1876         D.G.Fisher    J.P.
   Bryson,Angeline--18         At D.G.Fisher's
                               Wit; E.J.Fisher

Bradley,J.E.--27               Feb.21,1898         H.M.Bennett M.M.E.C.S.
   Mathis,Cannie--21           At Wm.Painter's
                               Wit;James Painter,Wm.Painter,Mahala Painter
                               He From Madison,Co.N.C.

Bradley,J.H.--23               June 2,1889         W.P.Jones     J.P.
   Raby,Mary--17               At Barker Creek Ts.
                               Wit; J.F.Jones, E.B.McDade,F.M.Nations

Bradley,Jasper--               July 13,1865        --------
   McMahan,Sarah--             At ---------
Bradley,Jasper--41             Apr.10,1892         W.W.Rhinehart J.P.
   Hall,Rachel P.--33          At Savannah  Ts.
                               Wit; R.W.Hall, M.C.Hall, J.H.Allison
                               He From Swain, Co.N.C.

Bradley,Phillip--21            Dec.5,1897          T.C.Jones     J.P.
   Mathis,Pattie--18           At James Mathis'
                               Wit; Thomas Segle,A.L.Nations,L.B.Nations

Bradley,Samuel--22             Aug.1,1896        Thomas L.Brown J.P.
   Jones,Josie--18             At Barker Creek  Ts.
                               Wit;J.R.Gunter, J.C.Nations

Bradley,Thomas--64             Mar.30,1890        J.L.Buchanan  M.G.
   Johnson,M.E.--45            At Savannah  Ts.
                               Wit;R.W.Hall, M.S.Bradley, J.B.Barker
                               He From Swain, Co.N.C.

Bradley,Wm.F.--24                 June 3,1883       W.P.Jones     J.P.
   Cockerham,Charlotte R.--19-At  A.N.Cockerham's
                               Wit; J.B.Gibson, J.H.Moody

Bradshaw,William--             July 27,1869        Wm.B.Garrett J.P.
   Anderson,Mary--             At ---------
```

Bramlet,Robert--23 Turpin,Charlotte--18	Apr.4,1897 L.Bumgarner J.P. At Barker Creek Ts. Wit; H.C.Stiles,F.N.Bumgarner,J.B.Bumgarner
Branton,J.A.-- Stiles,Caroline--	Sept.20,1857 W.R.Crawford J.P. At ---------
Branton,William R.--24 Davis,Martha--24	June 29, 1884 H.S.Baker J.P. At William Davis' Wit; Sarah Gibbs, W.D.Davis
Brendle,Elias D.--16 Parker,Jane--15	License Issued Nov.2,1895 NOT RETURNED -- Both From Swain, Co. N.C.
Brendle,Henry Plott--26 Davis,Sarah A.--19	Oct.18,1875 J.B.Allison J.P. At D.F.Brown's Wit; D.F.Brown
Brendle,Joseph H.--28 Tritt,Sarah G.--19	Apr.7,1887 J.H.Weaver M.G. At A.C.Tritt's Wit; E.H.Brendle, John Tritt He From Swain, Co.N.C.
Brendle,W.M.--45 Barn,Lyddia--30	June 3,1899 Nathan Coward J.P. At Nathan Coward's Wit; Felix E.Alley,T.B.Allison,C.C.CCowan He From Swain, Co.N.C.
Bridges,Wm.G.--22 Sellers,Fannie--19	Jan.26,1898 G.W.Moody J.P. At Merriet Seller's Wit; J.B.Farmer,W.W.Bridges,J.E.Bridges
Briggs,William R.--20 Gibson,M.E.--19	License Issued Aug.17,1886 Not Returned
Brinkley,J.R.-- Mingus,Sarah--	Jan.2,1870 G.W.Spake M.M. At -------
Brinkley,John-- Buchanan,Mary--	Apr.14,1856 Peter King J.P. At --------
Brody,John-- Nations,Nancy--	Jan.4,1866 I.C.Brooks J.P. At -------
Brogden,Henry--20 Watson,Eliza--21	May 20,1875 J.G.Ammons J.P. At David Bigham's Wit; D.G.Bigham, M.A.Bigham
Brom,Samuel M.--28 Ashe,Jane--18	License Issued Apr.14,1900 NOT Returned
Brooks,J.C.--28 Zachary,T.L.--21	Aug.12,1895 T.Baxter White J.P. At Cashiers Wit; Bessie Grinshaw,Ciscly Hampton,J.W.Br- He From Central, S.C. ock.
Brooks,William G.--21 Frady,May F.--15	June 4,1886 B.F.Barron J.P. At Sarah Frady's Wit; J.B.Barker, Ira Frady
Brooks,Christopher C.--19 Estis,Samantha A.--21	Mar.3,1888 E.C.Ashe J.P. At A.B.Ashe's Wit; A.B.Ashe, W.W.Estis
Brooks,Coleman--19 Green,Mariah--18	Aug.24,1890 H.C.Cannon J.P. At Savannah Ts. Wit; A.W.Buchanan, Wm.Buchanan, Meritt- Green.

Brooks,Coleman--21   June 5,1895 W.E.Conner M.G.
 Hensley,Sinda--21   At Savannah Ts.
          Wit; I.B.Barker,S.B.Buchanan, W.Tatham

Brooks,Dill--20   Aug.23,1899 R.A.Painter J.P.
 Williams,Martha J.--18 At P.B.Williams'
          Wit; Cash Dillard, Mark Cabe, I.J.Moore

Brooks,Issac--   Dec.14,1856 Wm.R.Buchanan J.P.
 Roberts,Racheal-- At --------

Brooks,Joe--22   Aug.25,1898 Thomas Queen J.P.
 Cunningham,Peggy--21 At Near Henry Sutton's
          Wit; T.Buchanan, W.C.Queen, Kid McMahan

Brooks,John--28   Jan.31,1887 W.H.T.Dillard J.P.
 Ensley,Elizabeth J.--28 At Lucinda Brooks'
          Wit; James I.Norman, Hiram Raines

Brooks,John W.--18   Feb.8,1874 E.C.Ashe, J.P.
 Buchanan,Martha C.--20 At C.S.Buchanan's
          Wit; G.W.Green, J.W.Morgan

Brooks,Samuel--21   Apr.26,1896 L.L.Brown J.P.
 Dills,Pollie--21   At Barker Creek Ts.
          Wit; C.S.Brooks, T.S.Brooks

Brooks,S.H.--   Feb.11,1864 W.R.Crawford Elder
 Henry,Matilda--   At --------

Brooks,Swanson --22 Mar.31,1888 J.L.Buchanan B.M.
 Ashe,Ida--18   At J.L.Buchanan's
          Wit; N.L.Sutton,W.H.Buchanan,J.H.Green

Brooks,T.D.--23   Mar.10,1895 J.P.Brendle J.P.
 Deitz,Hattie--16   At Cullowhee
          Wit; John V.Ashe,Phillip Henson,Ben Buchan

Brooks,Thomas--   Dec.10,1871 Sol.Messer J.P. an.
 Green,Malvina--   At --------

Brooks,Thomas--22   License Issued May 31,1901
 Gunter,Polly Ann--19 NOT RETURNED

Brooks,William--38   May 10,1900 W.E.Conner B.M.
 Ward,Pollie--35   At Hetty Beck's
          Wit;T.M.Ward,M.L.Blanton,N.C.Blanton

Brooks,William--22   Mar.12,1884 E.C.Ash J.P.
 Bradley,Mandy--17 At A.B.Ash's
          Wit; A.B.Ash, John Bradley

Brooks,Zebulon V.--24 License Issued Apr.27,1883
 Frady,Martha A.--15 NOT RETURNED

Brooks,Z.V.--35   Mar.19,1893 H.C.Cannon J.P.
 Buchanan,Margaret--40 At Savannah Ts.
          Wit; Wesley Allison, Jno.A.Cannon

Broom,Jefferson--25   Jan.16,1887 W.S.Queen J.P.
 Fortner,Sarah--19   At E.W.Fortner's
          Wit; D.N.Mathis, J.C.Franklin

Broom,William R.--22 Sept.9,1887 R.A.Sitton J.P.
 Jones,Emma L.--18   At River Ts.
          Wit; D.W.Middleton

Brown,A.D.--19   License Issued Jan.19,1889
 Watson,Hannah A.--19 NOT executed because they are too near
          related.

Brown,A.M.--37 Feb.12,1893 B.N.Queen B.M.
 Slatton,Victoria--18 At River Ts.
  Wit; D.H.Fox, W.E.Price,F.M.Twilley

Brown,Alna E.--23 Dec.8,1898 J.J.Gray Meth.Min.
 Price,Lula E.--25 At Dillsboro, N.C.
  Wit; Jno.H.Wilson,J.W.Price,C.B.Allen

Brown,Alonzo--21 Jan.2,1890 John P.Stewart J.P.
 Moody,Loucinda--18 At Hamburg Ts.
  Wit; J.I.Stewart, M.L.Coggins

Brown,Andrew--22 June 6,1878 B.N.Queen B.M.
 Shelton,Sarah--16 At W.L.D.Broom's
  Wit;W.A.Queen, S.C.Queen

Brown,Andrew J.--39 Nov.17,1889 C.L.Hooper J.P.
 Shelton,Brilliann--26 At River Ts.
  Wit; A.M.Brown,J.W.West, John Wike Jr.

Brown,Andy--24 July 1,1894 T.L.Jemison J.P.
 Hedden,Etta--19 At Hamburg Ts.
  Wit;C.M.Jemison,J.G.Collins,W.W.Montieth

Brown,Bartlet A.--22 July29,1878 G.W.Hooper J.P.
 Coward,Folba M.--18 At Matilda Coward's
  Wit; J.F.Coward,L.D.Brown

Brown,B.M.--21 Jan.9,1895 A.D.Davis B.M.
 Yarborough,Arrizena--17 At Cullowhee Ts.
  Wit; J.B.Bishop, J.B.Buchanan,L.P.Buchanan

Brown,Candler--18 Oct.8,1897 M.C.Walrick's
 Ashe,Laura--24 At M.C.Walrick's
  Wit; J.T.Alexander, M.M.Ashe

Brown,Cute--24 Oct.25,1894 N.A.Orr M.G.
 Cantrell,Ann--15 At Canada Ts.
  Wit; R.J.Orr, Rubrn Brown, Mealus Brown

Brown David W.--21 Dec.24,1872 F.M.Nations M.G.
 Davis,Mary Ann--20 At A.Nation's
  Wit; --------

Brown,E.N. License Issued Dec.31,1892
 Cook,Laura--22 NOT RETURNED

Brown,E.N.--25 Jan.7,1894 A.C.Queen M.G.
 Cook,Laura--24 At Caney Folk
  Wit;J.F.Shelton,P.Parker, N.J.Hooper

Brown,E.W.--23 Mar.6,1873 B.N.Queen B.M.
 Bryson,Sarah--20 At R.H.Brown, E.C.Chastian

Brown,F.M.-- Feb.1,1866 S.P.C.Shelton J.P.
 Potts,S.C.-- At -------

Brown,Horrace A.--21 Aug.23,1878 B.N.Queen B.M.
 Woodard,Darcus L.--16 At J.T.Woodard's
  Wit; J.Y.Blythe, C.C.Hooper

Brown,H.C.-- Sept.4,1870 N.W.Vaughan M.G.
 Monteith,M.E.-- At --------

Brown,H.G.-- Feb.7,1858 Jacob Wike J.P.
 Potts,M.L.-- At -------

Brown,H.M.--20
  Buchanan,Francis--19

Feb.17,1901   J.D.Sitton   B.M.
At Bride's Fathers
Wit, W.D.Bishop,G.H.Crisp,Jno.Bishop

Brown,H.R.--
  Bishop,P.L.--

Apr.16,1866   W.Zachy   J.P.
At --------

Brown,J.M.--
  Potts,Margaret--

Sept.17,1856   B.N.Queen   B.M.
At ---------

Brown,J.M.--22
  Moody,Rhoda--18

Nov.13,1892   John P.Stewart J.P.
At Hamburg Ts.
Wit;J.T.Hoxit,J.M.Henderson,J.M.Davis

Brown,James W.--21
  Shook,Samantha A.--19

Mar.24,1876   M.M.Brown   B.M.
At Daniel Shook's
Wit; J.M.Shook, James Shook

Brown,Jessie--21
  Cabe,Mary--19

Jan.16,1873   P.G.Green   B.M.
At T.B.Cabe's
Wit;L.P.Brown, M.L.Dills

Brown,John--19
  Slaton,Olivene--18

Sept.19,1880   T.J.Bryson   J.P.
At T.J.Bryson's
Wit; H.B.Bryson, D.E.Bryson

Brown,John D.--26
  Ensley,Candis--27

Sept.21,1897   J.D.Sitton   J.P.
At John Ensley's
Wit;H.E.Shelton,Tinie Hoxit,Docia Ensley

Brown,John Jr.--
  Woods,Anna--

July 13,1860   J.Wike   J.P.
At ---------

Brown,John Jr.45
  Alexander,Sarah--22

Apr.30,1886   J.A.Wild   J.P.
At Register's Office
Wit; A.J.Long Jr.

Brown,John O.--20
  Mathis,Roda--18

Sept.16,1880   D.D.Davis   J.P.
At ---------
Wit; D.F.Brown, Sophia Brown

Brown,John R.--22
  Brown,Laura--24

Mar.22,1883   T.J.Bryson   J.P.
At J.M.Brown's
Wit; Lizzie J.Brown, J.M.Brown

Brown,Julius M.--23
  Middleton,Chloe--24

Feb.10,1884   B.N.Queen   B.M.
At Polly Middleton's
Wit; Lizzie J.Brown, D.W.Middleton

Brown,Levi--47
  Hooper,Sousan--25

Nov.23,1874   G.W.Hawkins   J.P.
At John Hooper's
Wit; C.L.Hooper, J.A.Hooper

Brown,Levi--21
  Shelton,Isabella--17

Jan.1,1899   J.W.Thomas   J.P.
At Susan Brown's
Wit;J.H.Painter,Wrought Brown,W.E.Shelton

Brown,M.A.--21
  Shelton,Sophiah--18

Jan.29,1893   J.C.Wood   J.P.
At Canada Ts.
Wit;N.H.Brown,S.E.Hamilton,J.B.Crawford

Brown,Melus--19
  Mathis,Texata--18

June 15,1893   M.C.Warlick   M.G.
At Canada Ts.
Wit; Sue E.Robinson,J.W.Chalham

Brown,Melvin--20
  Hoxit,Jane--18

Nov.14,1887   David Fisher   M.G.
At Martha Hoxit's
Wit; T.A.Fisher, Thomas Smith

Brown,M.M.--
Hooper,Catherine--
Apr.13,1876   ---------
At ---- This marriage in front of book # 2
Wit; H.A.Brown,

Brown,R.H.--27
Crawford,I.B.--22
Oct.12,1894   J.C.Wood   J.P.
At Canada Ts.
Wit; J.W.Phillips,Arty Phillips,L.M.Wood

Brown,R.M.--20
Brown,L.I.--18
Dec.16,1894   James A.Galloway   J.P.
At Canada Ts.
Wit; J.A.Brown, J.J.Powell,A.L.Brown

Brown,Talor--
Watson,Elizabeth--
Oct.11,1869   Melton Brown   J.P.
At --------

Brown,Thomas--49
Grant,Elvira--27
Aug.20,1882   Levi Brown   J.P.
At Levi Brown's
Wit; S.H.Brown, J.M.Brown

Brown.Thomas D.--20
Cowart,Rutha--18
Sept.8,1872   E.D.Brendle   B.M.
At The Church
Wit; ----------

Brown,Thomas L.--25
Cockerham,Ida J.--22
Jan.20,1881   J.E.McLain   J.P.
At Barker Creek Church
Wit; S.W.Cooper

Brown,Thomas M.--19
Cathey,Lavada--18
Sept.11,1875   John H,Mathis   J.P.
At John H.Mathis'
Wit; S.H.Mathis, Margaret Brown

Brown,T.M.--39
Queen,Sytha--20
June 23,1895   J.H.Owen   M.G.
At Canada Ts.
Wit; J.A.Brown,J.D.Owen,J.M.Brown

Brown,T.M.--44
Reed,Rosa--19
Oct.14,1900   J.M.Thomas   J.P.
At Near My House
Wit; John Galloway,Willie Reed,Hattie Blan
                                         ton.

Brown,Virgil F.--25
Hooper,Dora--19
Mar.18,1888   L.W.Hooper   J.P.
At Susan Hooper's
Wit; John A.Woodring,A.W.Brown

Brown,Wm.A.--22
Coats,Lula C.--20
May 4,1873   J.R.Long   M.M.
At F.P.Allison's
Wit; Javan Davis, John E.McLain

Brown,W.C.--23
Coward,Arlesie--20
Feb.6,1898   R.R.Coward   J.P.
At Javan Coward's
Wit E.M.Coward,A.N.Henson,J.F.Coward

Brown,Willie E.--23
Hedden,Minnie--19
Oct.8,1899   Elbert Watson   J.P.
At Elbert Watson's
Wit;Maggie Raby,Ratchel Wilson,Victor Hend-

Brown,Wm.L.--
Brown,Mahala--
Mar.30,1862   E.C.Chastain, J.P.erson
At --------

Brown,W.W.--28
Wilson,N.J.--27
Apr.26,1897   J.D.Sitton   J.P.
At Cullowhee Ts.
Wit; W.J.Hughes,A.C.Queen, M.H.Golden

Brown,William W.--25
Parker,Mary H.--25
Nov.4,1882   Lewis Queen   M.G.
At J.H.Parker's
Wit; J.M.Parker, T.H.Quuen

Browning,Cling--18   Aug.27,1893   John A.Hooper J.P.
  Mills,Sarah--15   At Cashier Ts.
                    Wit; H.T.Mills, T.I.Mills, W.T.Mills

Browning,Marion--20   Sept.12,1884   H.Conner   J.P.
  Williams,Sarah--18   At John Cabe's
                    Wit; J.N.Wilson, J.B.Woodard

Broyles,John L.--30   June 1,1886   R.A.Owens   M.M.
  Allison,Lillie R.--25 At Webster, N.C.
                    Wit; J.A.Wild, L.C.Hall
                    He from Buncombe,Co.N.C.

Bruce,Albert--22   Dec.2,1900   J.B.Ensley   J.P.
  Grasty,Lillie--19   At Beta, N.C.
                    Wit; D.G.Bryson, M.L.Ensley, E.R.Aiken

Bryson,A.B.--27   License Issued Oct.15,1898
  Fisher,Maggie--21   Returned NOT Executed

Bryson,A.B.--22   Aug.24,1892   J.T.Carson   M.G.
  Crawford,H.C.--16   At Scotts Creek Ts.
                    Wit; C.R.Dean, G.C.Crawford, A.M.B.

Bryson,Abram--25 (Col) Nov.23,1893   A.M.Parker   J.P.
  Bryson,Larcena--16 (Col) At Sylva, N.C.
                    Wit; J.K.Allen, W.E.Allen
                    He From Swain, Co.N.C.

Bryson,Albert N.--23   Sept.12,1872   H.M.Bennett M.M.
  Wike,Mariah--19   At Andrew Wike's
                    Wit; ----------

Bryson,Aldine S.--21   Oct.29,1879   Wm.Bumgarner J.P.
  Messer,Charlotte--18 At John Messer's
                    Wit; W.B.Sherrill, W.H.Green

Bryson,Alexander--24   Jan.22,1885   C.L.Woodring J.P.
  Collins,Julia L.--18 At J.T.Collins'
                    Wit; R.L.Bryson, A.B.Billingsly

Bryson,Alexander--35   July 2,1891   C.P.Bryson   J.P.
  Taylor,Dora--23   At Hamburg Ts.
                    Wit; J.M.Moss, J.R.Taylor, J.C.Owens

Bryson,Alfred F.--21   Nov.8,1883   D.G.Bigham   J.P.
  Frady,Mary M.--18   At Solomon Frady's
                    Wit; M.H.Morris, J.S.Frady, S.M.Beck

Bryson,Allen F.--40   Jan.26,1888   J.S.Leopard J.P.
  Leopard,Martha--27   At Thos.N.Leopard's
                    Wit; Jessee Owen, Western Bryson

Bryson,A.M.--23   Jan.16,1897   J.T.Carson   J.P.
  Norman,J.E.--19   At Caney Fork Ts.
                    Wit; A.C.Bryson, H.M.West, T.G.Norman

Bryson,Andrew C.--24   Apr.15,1894   T.V.Henderson J.P.
  Stewart,Etta--22   At Mountain Ts.
                    Wit; H.Wike, A.C.Stewart,W.R.Stewart

Bryson,Andrew V.P.--30 July 29,1877   G.W.Spake   M.M.
  Conley,Canney--19   At M.W.Bryson's
                    Wit; G.W.Dillard, M.W.Bryson

Bryson,Arrelius--21 (Col) Nov.25,1900   R.A.Painter J.P.
  Pickens,Florence--18   At Sylva, N.C.
                    Wit; Tom Pickens, Phelix Love

-20-

Bryson,Coleman-- Henson,Aliss Jane--	Feb.9,1869 At-- He son of Robert & Mary Bryson. Wit;-- She Dau.of Thomas Henson.	A.J.Hall	J.P.
Bryson,Columbus--24 Philips,Artie--23	Feb.5,1878 At William Watson's Wit; J.M.Davis	R.L.Watson	J.P.
Bryson,David E.--21 Cathey,Martha A.--18	Feb.26,1875 At D.H.Mathis' Wit; A.W.Cathey, D.H.Mathis	J.A.Galloway	J.P.
Bryson,D.G.Jr.--21 Frizzle,Hattie--18	May 5,1895 At Dillsboro, N.C. Wit; Mrs.J.J.Mason, J.Y.Sims	A.H.Sims	B.M.
Bryson,D.L.--25 Henson,L.E.--18	Dec.24,1891 At Scotts, Creek Wit; R.W.Fisher, D.G.Bryson, H.M.Gray	R.R.Fisher	J.P.
Bryson,Elbert B.--19 Jennings,Susan O.--17	Oct.29,1885 At J.B.Jennings' Wit; J.C.Evitt, John Carroll	J.P.Stuart	J.P.
Bryson,Fernando--36 Montieth,Clemintine--35	Nov.14,1899 At Clemintine Montieth's Wit; J.B.Buchanan,R.W.Deitz, J.W.Beck	A.W.Davis	B.M.
Bryson,F.M.-- Ensley,F.C.--	Oct.15,1863 At --------	W.R.Crawford	Elder
Bryson,George W.--47 (Col) Gaddis,Nancy L.--27 (Col)	Jan.16,1882 At J.C.Watkins' Wit; Samuel Smith,Joseph Hix	J.C.Watkins	J.P.
Bryson,George W.--44 McCall,Mary--24	Dec.7,1884 At William McCall's Wit; S.C.McCall, W.L.McCall	J.L.Owens	M.G.
Bryson,Goleman--23 Ward,Donia--21	Mar.13,1898 At Thomas Henson's Wit; A.B.Bryson, W.W.Ensley, H.M.West	A.B.Henson	B.M.
Bryson,Harry B.--28 Brown,Margaret--30	Dec.26,1875 At J.H.Mathis' Wit; T.S.Fortner, S.H.Goldel	J.H.Mathis	J.P.
Bryson,H.L.--20 Crawford,O.C.--18	Oct.24,1892 At Scotts Creek Ts. Wit; S.W.Crawford,Gol.Bryson,L.C.Bryson	J.T.Carson	J.P.
Bryson,Hoile--26 Wilson,Beulah--22	Oct.15,1900 At School House Wit; Robt.Knight,Bub Wilson,Miles Holden	John Bumgarner	J.P.
Bryson,Hugh R.--26 Presley,Martha E.--22	Mar.10,1887 At Cullowhee Wit; Lewis Tilley, Get Tilley	A.D.Hooper	J.P.
Bryson,James--21 Tatham,Sarah--18	Feb.7,1892 At Savannah Ts. Wit; J.F.Sutton, M.A.Taylor	T.F.Deitz	M.G.
Bryson,James B.--31 Gibson,Rachel--30	Dec.18,1884 At Rachel Gibb's Wit; W.J.Miller, J.R.Ensley	Wm.Bumgarner	J.P.

```
Bryson,James B.--27        Nov.9,1897        J.J.Gray      M.M.
  Davis,Pauline--19        At East Laporte, N.C.
                           Wit; R.F.Allison, W.A.Davis, Thadeus Bucha
                                                                  anan

Bryson,James R.--30        Dec.21,1899       Elbert Watson  J.P.
  Fowler,Mary--19          At Taylor Fowler's
                           Wit;B.J.Moody,J.F.McCall,Miles Nichololson

Bryson,Javan--21           Mar.15,1900       J.W.Conner     J.P.
  Moody,Samantha--18       At Nancy Moody's house
                           Wit;Walter Coggins,T.B.Sims,D.G.Moody

Bryson,J.B.--              Mar.31,1853       Jacob Wike     J.P.
  Morgan,Nancy--           At --------

Bryson,J.B.--              Apr.10,1870       E.H.Cagle      J.P.
  ----------               At --------

Bryson,J.T.--42            Nov.22,1891       Lee Hooper     J.P.
  Leopard,Sarah F.--37     At Cullowhee
                           Wit; E.V.Richards,F.I.Lacy, W.F.Coggins

Bryson,John--22  (Col)     Mar.26,1899       W.E.Bryson     J.P.
  Babb,Jane--18  (Col)     At Joseph Babb's
                           Wit; Thos.Pickens, Acrum Babb

Bryson,John B.--20         Jan.13,1895       T.L.Jemison    J.P.
  Buchanan,Mira--17        At Cullowhee, N.C.
                           Wit; Boone Bryson,Sallie Bryson,Ben Buchan
                                                                   an.

Bryson,John C.--16  (Col)  Dec.22,1887       John T.Wike    J.P.
  Coward,Stella--18 (Col)  At Alfred Coward's
                           Wit; Wm.Norton, Bowman Davis

Bryson,John F.--25         May 6,1877        J.R.Crawford   J.P.
  Shular,Maggie--18        At E.M.Shular's
                           Wit; Lee Shular, John Shular

Bryson,Merit W.--27        Nov.6,1881        R.L.Watson     J.P.
  Presley,Jane--22         At L.C.Presley's
                           Wit; B.N.Henson, William Crawford

Bryson,M.W.--              Nov.18,1865       J.M.Harris     Elder
  Conley,Mary E.--         At --------

Bryson,M.W.--50            Aug.16,1890       B.G.Wild       M.G.
  York,Mary N.--35         At Scotts Creek Ts.
                           Wit; J.W.Fisher,J.M.York

Bryson,N.E.--              May 1,1869        E.P.Stillwell  J.P.
  Frizell,Elizabeth Ann--  At-- He son of James & Margaret Bryson.
                           Wit;-- She Dau.of Jason & Margaret Frizell

Bryson,Nelson--29          Jan.26,1901       J.R.Crawford   J.P.
  Henson,Mary--33          At Margaret Henson's
                           Wit; Oscar Fisher, Edward Fisher

Bryson,Pender A.--21       Jan.1,1885        W.A.Dills      J.P.
  Ensley,Sarah--18         At Wilson Ensley's
                           Wit; James Bryson, A.L.Ensley

Bryson,Preston--22         June 5,1881       C.B.Fugate     M.M.
  Hill,Maggie--22          At W.R.Hooper's
                           Wit; Mattie A.Bennett, Ellen Bennett

Bryson.Robert--            Mar.3,1870        A.J.Hall       J.P.
  Ensley,Juda--            At--------
```

Bryson,Robert H.--28 Hooper,Marinda--18	Dec.3,1874 At Rebecca Mathis' Wit; W.Knight, G.W.Bryson	Thomas Wilson J.P.
Bryson,Robert L.--22 Nicholson,Alice J.--15	Aug.26,1885 At W.R.Hooper's Wit; R.N.Long, Lee V.Hooper	J.A.Hooper J.P.
Bryson,R.M.--23 Bennett,M.E.--28	Nov.26,1890 At Cashier Valley Wit; E.H.Bell, D.R.Bryson, C.D.Bell	T.R.Zachary J.P.
Bryson,S.C.-- Moss,Margaret C.--	Dec.24,1865 At --------	S.P.C.Shelton J.P.
Bryson,S.H.-- Crawford,Sina--	Apr.6,1864 At -------	E.D.Brendle J.P.
Bryson,Simon P.-- Love,Molley--	Nov.28,1869 At --------	E.D.Brendle Elder
Bryson,Sterling--24 York,Maggie--18	July 12,1891 At Webster, N.C. Wit; M.D.Cowan,W.L.Cowan, A.B.Fullbright	B.G.Wild, Min.M.E.C.S.
Bryson,T.C.--24 Henson,Loreaney P.--16	Dec.3,1889 At Scotts Creek Ts. Wit; A.B.Henson, J.T.Carson, C.R.Dean	H.M.Bright J.P.
Bryson,T.C.--24 Dills,Tiney--17	Dec.6,1893 At Sylva Ts. Wit; C.W.Allen, H.C.Cowan, J.C.Buchanan	A.B.Henson B.M.
Bryson,Thaddeus G.-- Ensley,Hannah--	Jan.17,1869 At --------	A.J.Hall J.P.
Bryson,Tilen--21 Warren,Ida--30	Nov.28,1897 At Balsam, N.C. Wit; A.E.Galloway,H.J.Barnes,W.L.Fisher	A.C.Bryson J.P.
Bryson,W.C.--21 Holland,Connie--14	June 16,1888 At H.P.Holland's Wit; W.T.Fisher, A.J.Montieth	C.L.Woodring J.P.
Bryson,William D.--23 Bumgarner,Melvina--23	Sept.26,1878 At Hosea Bumgarner's Wit; Polk Gibson, Louisa Bryson	D.D.Davis J.P.
Bryson,W.E.--21 Queen,Maybelle--19	Oct.23,1890 At Scotts Creek Wit; R.R.Fisher, John L.Snider	S.R.Cook J.P.
Bryson,Wm.F.--16 Tatham,T.C.--18	Feb.26,1893 At Savannah Ts. Wit; Amos Cabe,Rufus Gribble,A.F.Bryson	T.F.Deitz M.G.
Bryson,W.J.--21 Leopard,Martha--16	Oct.19,1897 At Taylor Bryson's Wit; J.T.Potts, Alice Potts	B.Norton J.P.
Bryson,William R.--19 Woodring,Alice--21	Sept.22,1885 At A.Woodring's Wit;G.E.Painter, W.B.Rogers	J.E.Moss J.P.
Bryson,William R.--21 Parris,Laura--18	Dec.30,1886 At J.M.Parris' Wit; W.H.Montieth, J.M.Parris	A.J.Hall J.P.

Bryson,William S.--19   Nov.2,1879   Wm.Wilson   J.P.
Hooper,Roda J.--19   At A.D.Hooper's
Wit; Hosea Bumgarner, Enos Wilson

Bryson,Willie S.--28   Feb.26,1893   T.B.McCurdy   M.G.
Hooper,Stella--25   At Cullowhee   Ts.
Witl C.A.Wallace, J.H.Clayton,J.N.Bryson

Bucha ?,Montrivill--   Apr.3,1866   A.D.Hooper   J.P.
Crawford,Martha--   At -------

Buchanan,Ben F.--23   Feb.18,1900   W.L.Henson   J.P.
Coward,Fannie M.--23   At W.L.Painter's
Wit;J.H.Long,Claralou Norton,W.L.Painter

Buchanan,Benjamin--21   Nov.24,1881   D.H.Ash   J.P.
Elmore,Josie L.--19   At D.H.Ash's
Wit; A.B.Ash, G.W.Green

Buchanan,B.S.--   Apr.15,1860   W.A.Buchanan   J.P.
Buchanan,Margaret--   At --------

Buchanan,Charles--19   Sept.10,1891   J.L.Buchanan   M.G.
Green,Hester--20   At Webster,   Ts.
Wit; S.B.Buchanan, J.A.Parker

Buchanan,Coleman--20   Oct.5,1890   C.S.Buchanan   M.G.
Cabe,Cordelia--18   At Savannah   Ts.
Wit; B.G.Buchanan,E.M.Cabe,J.H.Buchanan

Buchanan,Columbus--21   May 31,1891   J.W.King   J.P.
Bumgarner,Leona--18   At Webster   Ts.
Wit; J.W.Beck, E.L.Gribble, M.Harris

Buchanan,Columbus--22   June 2,1889   E.C.Ashe   J.P.
Green,Emiline--21   At Savannah   Ts.
Wit; A.B.Ashe, J.H.Green, G.W.Green

Buchanan,C.M.--   Aug.26,1866   W.J.Buchanan   J.P.
Clement,T.--   At --------

Buchanan,Daniel D.--22   Dec.22,1881   S.C.Owen   M.G.
Davis,Nancy A.--22   At M.A.Davis'
Wit; D.W.Zachary,Bragg Hooper

Buchanan,Emulus O.--18   Jan.1,1884   G.W.Spake   M.M.
Cagle,Cordelie--16   At E.H.Cagle's
Wit; Harvey Cagle, Richard Hall

Buchanan,Erastus--19   Mar.23,1894   J.C.Reed   J.P.
Brooks,Dorkie--19   At Savannah
Wit; Richard Hall, B.B.Green, Lillie Green

Buchahan,F.P.--   Apr.22,1866   J.B.Sherrill J.P.
Beck,S.J.--   At --------

Buchanan,James--22   Jan.13,1892   T.H.Deitz   M.G.
Presley,Nancy--22   At Cullowhee   Ts.
Wit; R.N.Deitz,A.A.Deitz,J.N.Buchanan

Buchanan,James M.--   Nov.12,1871   J.L.Buchanan   M.G.
Briggs,Elminy--   At --------

Buchanan,James M.--54   Nov.2,1891   A.W.Davis   M.G.
Reed,Sarah J.--33   At Savannah   Ts.
Wit; L.D.Hall,J.B.Buchanan,N.E.Buchanan

Buchanan,James W.--20   Nov.23,1882   G.W.Spake   M.M.
Dills,Almer--20   At M.L.Dills'
Wit; W.W.Rhineheart, Wm.Self

```
Buchanan,John--25          Nov.161890        J.L.Buchanan      M.G.
  Beasley,Caldonia--15     At Savannah
                           Wit; James Sutton, Silas Buchanan

Buchanan,John C.--26       Dec.24,1896        A.B.Thomas        M.G.
  Rogers,Druscilla--19     At Webster Ts.
                           Wit;P.A.Calhoun,W.A.Stillwell,J.A.Stillwell

Buchanan,John S.--22       Mar.23,1884        B.F.Barron        J.P.
  Tatham,Lilla--17         At T.N.Tatham's
                           Wit; Jessee Jones, Sydney Ashe

Buchanan,J.D.--            Apr.4,1861         J.L.Buchanan      Elder
  Harris,E.C.--            At -------

Buchanan,J.F.--            Mar.13,1870        P.G.Green         M.G.
  Wilson,Matilda P.--      At --------

Buchanan,J.G.--18          Dec.21,1891        T.H.Deitz         M.G.
  Cabe,Elmina--20          At Sylva, N.C.
                           Wit; R.N.Deitz, C.L.Dills, J.Cabe

Buchanan,J.M.--            Oct.4,1870         J.L.Buchanan      M.G.
  Dills,Susanah--          At -------

Buchanan,J.M.--            May 27,1859        W.H.Higdon        J.P.
  Buchanan,Louisa--        At --------

Buchanan,Joseph--19        Nov.9,1893         A.W.Davis         M.G.
  Cabe,Hester--18          At Savannah Ts.
                           Wit; N.E.Buchanan,Robt.Cabe,Granderson Buchanan

Buchanan,J.R.Jr.--25       Mar.11,1900        Thadeus F.Deitz   B.M.
  Woodard,Sallie--30       At J.T.Woodard's Res.
                           Wit; L.D.Hall, Pink Collins, Wm. Silas

Buchanan,J.Webb--50        May 26,1892        B.G.Wild          M.G.
  Gribble,Margaret--37     At John Gribble's
                           Wit; Cordella Buchanan,E.L.Gribble,Lou Young

Buchanan,Leander--20       July 1,1875        E.C.Ash           J.P.
  West,Mary--19            At A.C.Ash's
                           Wit; W.Walker, R.W.Hall

Buchanan,Leander,--26      June 21,1883       D.G.Bigham        J.P.
  Frady,Rebecca M.--16     At Soloman Frady's
                           Wit; A.F.Bryaon,Linch Frady

Buchanan,L.L.--18          Jan.17,1895        J.P.Brendle       J.P.
  Frizell,Florence--17     At Webster
                           Wit; J.W.Bumgarner,N.B.Ashe, W.H.Brendle

Buchanan,L.P.--14          Dec.26,1897        A.W.Davis         B.M.
  Brogdon,Cora--18         At Savannah Ts.
                           Wit; James Franks,J.B.Buchanan, R.N.Deitz

Buchanan,M.--31            Jan.2,1894         R.H.Parker,    P.E.M.E.C.S.
  Leatherwood,Laura Bell--19 At Webster Ts.
                           Wit; Eva McLain,Frank McLain, Lula Terrell

Buchanan,Mack--27          Jan.20,1900        J.B.Raby          J.P.
  Harris,Mary--22          At Wilmont, N.C.
                           Wit; I.F.Jones

Buchanan,Mart R.--25       Oct.11,1873        P.G.Green         J.P.
  Green,Meriah--20         At G.W.Green's
                           Wit; S.J.Green, J.A.Green

Buchanan,Monroe--23        Apr.27,1898        W.D.Frizell       J.P.
  Paxton,Maggie--18        At Webster Ts.
                           Wit; W.A.Long, L.L.Buchanan, J.W.Frizell
```

Buchanan,Nathan--17   Dec.31,1891   T.H.Deitz   M.G.
  Bryson,Charlotte--18   At Cullowhee Ts.
                             Wit; C.C.Higdon, R.L.Cunningham

Buchanan,Nathan--   Oct.5,1856   Joseph L.Buchanan M.G.
  Dills,Martha--   At -------

Buchanan,Robert G.--21   Apr.3,1879   B.H.Jones   J.P.
  Deitz,Martha T.--18   At Amos Cabe's
                             Wit; N.P.Jones, J.F.Thompson

Buchanan,Rufus--19   Aug.30,1876   E.C.Ash   J.P.
  Wilson,Violet J.--18   At Manson Wilson's
                             Wit; W.M.Wilson, J.F.Buchanan

Buchanan,Samuel--19   "NEVER MARRIED" license returned
  Mills,Fancy--18   -----

Buchanan,Samuel C.--25   Nov.5,1899   Elbert Watson J.P.
  Robinson,Bertha--20   At T.A.Robinson's
                             Wit; J.M.Alexander,Emma Watson,Maggie Raby

Buchanan,Silus B.--   Dec.24,1868   J.P.Buchanan J.P.
  Brooks,E.E.--   At --------

Buchanan,Thomas--21   Jan.27,1895   W.C.Buchanan J.P.
  Lewis,Hattie--21   At Savannah
                             Wit;W.D.Rogers,Henry Hall,Henry Buchanan

Buchanan,Thomas J.--   Nov.26,1868   J.L.Buchanan J.P.
  Cabe,Sarinda--   At --------

Buchanan,Tyler--28   May 23,1901   W.D.Frizell J.P.
  Blanton,Vilantie--19   At Edna Gipson's
                             Wit;Ida Gipson,Gracy Gipson,Lillie Gipson

Buchanan,W.--   Apr.22,1880   S.C.Owens   M.G.
  Allen,Harriet C.--   At C.A.Ash's
                             Wit; -------

Buchanan,Wm.--20   Sept.15,1878   E.C.Ash   J.P.
  Ash,Rua E.--23   At Malinda Ash's
                             Wit; J.R.Ash, C.C.Higdon

Buchanan,Wm.B.--   Nov.25,1865   J.C.Brooks   J.P.
  Brooks,Emiline--   At --------

Buchanan,W.C.--18   Oct.3,1886   J.A.Hooper   J.P.
  Cabe,Rachel M.E.--15   At Thos.Cabe's
                             Wit; S.E.Wilson, T.S.Montieth

Buchanan,William C.--17   Nov.27,1887   B.F.Barron   J.P.
  Guilliam,Salena--18   At John Buchanan's
                             Wit; T.N.Tatham, R.G.Buchanan

Buchanan,William H.--23   Sept.16,1888   E.H.Cagle   J.P.
  Sutton,Rebecca J.--23   At James Sutton's
                             Wit; S.M.Brooks, N.L.Sutton

Buchanan.William L.--20   Sept.27,1891   T.F.Deitz   M.G.
  Stiles,Etta--17   At Savannah
                             Wit; L.D.Hall, W.C.Buchanan, W.A.Wilson

Buchanan,William N.--   Jan.7,1869   J.L.Buchanan J.P.
  Stiles,Margaret--   At -------

Buchanan,W.Nute--40   Dec.11,1888   J.L.Buchanan B.M.
  Hall,Margaret--39   At Savannah
                             Wit; A.W.Davis,W.V.Buchanan,L.A.Buchanan

Buckham,Joseph R.-- Frizel,Mary M.--	Apr.16,1853 At --------	William Hidgon J.P.
Bumgarner,A.C.-- Alley,M.J.--	Feb.26,1871 At --------	T.H.Edwards J.P.
Bumgarner,Adolphus-- Herrel,Phebe--	Dec.30,1855 At --------	Peter King J.P.
Bumgarner,Adolphus-- Herrell,Frances--	Oct.7,1868 At -------	James Mahoney Clegʻ.ᴸ
Bumgarner,Anthany-- Parker,Charity--	Mar.3,1872 At -------	H.H.Gibbs J.P.
Bumgarner,Boman--24 Stewart,Laura--21	Oct.10,1872 At M.M.Stewart's Wit;A.C.Stewart,T.V.Henderson,J.B.Bumgarneɪ	R.H.Stewart J.P.
Bumgarner,C.A.--20 Fisher,Pollie--20	June 7,1896 At Barker Creek Ts. Wit; L.E.Suttlemyer	J.B.Raby J.P.
Bumgarner,Charles C.--22 Holden,Susan--19	Sept.22,1889 At Cullowhee Ts. Wit;W.M.Bryson,J.Bumgarner, W.H.Bryson	W.C.Norton J.P.
Bumgarner,Eb A.--21 Shelton,Oeta--18	July 9,1899 At Whiteside Cove Wit;H.B.Picklesimer,E.A.Picklesimer,T.Grim- shaw	M.P.Alexander B.M.
Bumgarner,Elbert N.--22 Hooper,Lizzie--20	Oct.23,1879 At A.D.Hooper's Wit; W.S.Bryson,A.C.Bumgarner	Wm.Wilson J.P.
Bumgarner,F.--20 Sutton,Hattie--16	Oct.27,1892 At Dillsboro Ts. Wit;J.K.Keener,J.H.Bailey, G.C.Ensley	J.W.Buchanan J.P.
Bumgarner,Fidil--26 Parton,Rixie--19	June 2,1900 At Lige Keener's Wit; J.E.Keener,C.Sutton, G.T.Keener	L.B.Watson B.M.
Bumgarner,George--28 Baily,Mary J.--22	Sept.21,1881 At John Dills' Wit; J.M.Robinson, J.W.Robison	J.E.McLain J.P.
Bumgarner,George--21 Moss,Dorthula--17	Dec.23,1886 At Wm.Moss' Wit; T.L.Jemison, E.F.Watson	Elbert Watson J.P.
Bumgarner,Herchel--21 Dillard,Bessie--18	License Issued Oct.16,1901 NOT RETURNED	
Bumgarner,H.F.-- Farley,Emeline--	Nov.14,1861 At --------	W.H.Conner Elder
Bumgarner,H.T.--21 Kirby,Artie L.--24	Mar.4,1898 At White Side Cove Wit; Cora Alley,Z.B.Alley,A.E.Cobb	McD.Edwards J.P.
Bumgarner,James--23 Jones,Melvina--17	Dec.24,1892 At Sylva, N.C. Wit; J.F.Rogers, J.D.Sitton	A.M.Parker J.P.
Bumgarner,J.B.--21 Stewart,Sallie--23	Oct.6,1898 At Mountain Ts. Wit; W.J.Henderson,Sallie S.Stewart,John A.	John J.Moss J.P.

Bumgarner,J.Carson--24　　June 3,1897　　　Felix E.Alley　J.P.
　Kirly,Emily--18　　　　　At Cashier Ts.
　　　　　　　　　　　　　　Wit;Felix Alley,E.A.Bumgarner,L.D.Watson

Bumgarner,John--　　　　　Aug.2,1863　　　　W.H.Conner　　J.P.
　Parker,Clerica T.--　　At -------

Bumgarner,John--31　　　　Oct.25,1891　　　J.P.Stewart　　J.P.
　Holden,Amanda--25　　　At Cullowhee
　　　　　　　　　　　　　　Wit; C.Bumgarner,Coleman Bryson,M.Holden

Bumgarner,John W.--21　　Dec.21,1880　　　F.M.Frizell　　J.P.
　Long,Mary L.--18　　　　At A.J.Long's
　　　　　　　　　　　　　　Wit;W.B.Frizell, W.D.Allen

Bumgarner,J.P.--21　　　　Apr.29,1894　　　J.P.Painter　　M.G.
　Hill,Maude--15　　　　　At Qualla Ts.
　　　　　　　　　　　　　　Wit; W.D.Hill, C.A.Moody,C.A.Bumgarner

Bumgarner,Lindsey--24　　Aug.3,1891　　　　A.M.Parker　　J.P.
　Calhoun,Ermma A.--20　At Sylva, N.C.
　　　　　　　　　　　　　　Wit;J.E.Ensley, H.M.Snyder

Bumgarner,N.W.--　　　　　Oct.25,1871　　　E.D.Brendle　　Elder
　Parris,Margaret T.--　At --------

Bumgarner,R.C.--22　　　　Jan.17,1895　　　J.P.Brendle　　J.P.
　Shular,M.C.--20　　　　At Scotts Creek
　　　　　　　　　　　　　　Wit; J.W.Bumgarner,W.A.Henson,E.D.Franklin

Bumgarner,W.H.--　　　　　Sept.15,1871　　W.B.Allen
　Allen,S.J.　　　　　　　At ---------

Bumgarner,William--20　　Apr.7,1880　　　J.C.Watkin　　J.P.
　Bumgarner,Francis--20　At W.D.Frizell's
　　　　　　　　　　　　　　Wit; W.D.Frizell, R.S.Long

Burchfield,John H.--26　July 30,1882　　John H.Reed　　J.P.
　Robison,Rachel C.--26　At John Bumgarner's
　　　　　　　　　　　　　　Wit; John T.Reed, Charles Bumgarner
　　　　　　　　　　　　　　He From Swain, Co. N.C.

Burgus,Eli--　　　　　　　Aug.30,1881　　　E.H.Ash　　　J.P.
　Partin,Martha--　　　　At E.H.Ash's
　　　　　　　　　　　　　　Wit; James M.Candler, R.A.McMahan

Burnes,William M.--26　　Mar.24,1889　　　A.B.Thomas　　B.M.
　Gibson,Laura--20　　　　At Sylva, Ts.
　　　　　　　　　　　　　　Wit; A.M.Parker,T.G.Fisher,S.Waldroop Jr.

Burreasr,L.B.--23　　　　Aug.29,1895　　　W.T.Fisher　　J.P.
　Ashe,Sarah--50　　　　　At Webster Ts.
　　　　　　　　　　　　　　Wit; Gordon Stanford,Robt.Watson,J.R.Long

Burrell,Mark--21　　　　　Oct.17,1881　　　B.N.Queen　　B.M.
　Broom,Sarah--22　　　　At W.L.D.Broom's
　　　　　　　　　　　　　　Wit; W.A.Queen, Jefferson Broom

Burris,William--21　　　July 23,1876　　D.G.Fisher　　J.P.
　Strutton,Catherine--22　At George Pruit's
　　　　　　　　　　　　　　Wit; W.B.Love, James Pruit

Byers,Jefferson L.--20　Feb.22,1886　　　John S.Kein　　J.P.
　Sellers,Ruth N.--20　　At Katherine Sellers'
　　　　　　　　　　　　　　Wit; S.C.Cope, Wm.Cope

Byllingsley,Andrew W.--24　Feb.28,1884　　C.B.Fugate　　M.G.
　Bryson,Annie Bell--　　At S.Bryson's
　　　　　　　　　　　　　　Wit; W.C.Long, E.N.Holden

Cabe,Amos--	Dec.10,1862	W.H.Buchanan J.P.
Green,Jo Annah--	At --------	
Cabe,Amos--	Mar.14,1866	E.C.Ash J.P.
Deitz,Mary--	At --------	
Cabe,Fidily--18	June 18,1898	J.W.Cowan J.P.
Frizzle,Martha--19	At Mr.Mashburn's	
	Wit; S.A.Grant,R.M.Frady, E.H.Loudermilk	
Cabe,Floyd--19	Aug.7,1873	M.W.Bryson J.P.
Young,Mary--25	At In Road	
	Wit; J.A.Mitchell	
Cabe,Jessie--21	Nov.12,1899	W.C.Buchanan J.P.
Sutton,Lou--16	At Jerome Sutton's	
	Wit; John C.Jones,B.H.Hughes,Robt.Tatham	
Cabe,Joel--	Dec.29,1859	W.H.Buchanan J.P.
Green,Nancy--	At --------	
Cabe,John--22	Mar.2,1873	P.G.Green B.M.
Cocherham,Raline--15	At Manson Wilson's	
	Wit; Manson Wilson,A.L.Wilson	
Cabe,Joseph H.--20	Nov.10,1880	J.L.Buchanan M.G.
Wilson,Violet--20	At Thomas Cabe's	
	Wit; J.A.Buchanan, M.E.Buchanan	
Cabe,Josh--26	Jan.13,1880	W.W.Reed B.M.
Barron,Perthinia--23	At G.W.Barron's	
	Wit; John Cabe, B.F.Barron	
Cabe,Julius--21	Oct.25,1894	W.C.Buchanan J.P.
Green,Lillie--21	At Savannah	
	Wit;J.R.Tatham,J.H.Cabe, J.E.Buchanan	
Cabe,Leander--21	Nov.26,1873	M.W.Bryson J.P.
Cunningham,Margaret--24	At Sol. Frady's	
	Wit; ---------	
Cabe,Lee--44	License Issued Apr. 29,1899	
Buckner,Hanner--28	At -----------------	
Cabe,Mitchall--21	Dec.18,1879	J.B.Allison J.P.
Ash,Callie--15	At Syndny Ash's	
	Wit; O.M.Allison, S.W.Allison	
Cabe,Nathan--25	Sept.15,1878	E.C.Ash J.P.
Wilson,Mary Ann--20	At D.F.Hall's	
	Wit; J.W.Fisher, D.F.Hall	
Cabe,R.L.--23	Jan.10,1890	A.M.Parker J.P.
Reynolds,Oma--16	At Sylva, Ts.	
	Wit; G.P.Austin, F.M.Tompkins, E.M.Cabe	
Cabe,Robert L.--20	Oct.29,1886	B.F.Barron J.P.
Buchanan,Sarah J.--25	At W.H.Buchanan's	
	Wit; D.J.Tatham, James Cabe	
Cabe,Thomas--	Aug.12,1866	W.H.Buchanan J.P.
Buchanan,Margaret--	At --------	
Cabe,William--19	Aug.2,1892	J.A.Wild J.P.
Frady,Rabecca--15	At Webster Ts.	
	Wit; G.W.McConnell,Julius Snider,Steve Wood	
Cabe,William--20	Dec.25,1895	A.W.Davis B.M.
Frady,Ella May--16	At Cullowhee	
	Wit; J.R.Buchanan,J.W.Frizzel,J.L.Frizzel	

Cagle,Allen D.--25   Mar.15,1888   W.Ensley   M.G.
Montieth,Celinda J.--   At J.A.Montieth's
Wit; Harrison Bradley, A.H.Sims

Cagle,E.P.--19   Jan.26,1891   J.W.Buchanan J.P.
Keener,Eliza--22   At Dillsboro Ts.
Wit; J.W.Cagle, A.A.Massie, W.A.Sutton

Cagle,H.S.--   Mar.15,1869   E.H.Cagle   J.P.
Barker,Rachel--   At --------

Cagle,John W.--21   License Issued Mar.24,1885
Hall,Sarah L.--   Not Returned

Cagle,Robert--   Oct.9,1870   E.H.Cagle   J.P.
Allison,Sallie--   At -------

Cain,Andrew C.--23   License Issued Apr.16,1887
Young,Mary--23   NOT Returned

Calhoun,Geo.--21   Dec.2,1896   S.D.Sutton   J.P.
Bryson,Sina--18   At Scotts Creek Ts.
Wit; S.R.Cook, J.S.Calhoun, E.N.Smith

Calhoun,J.L.--24   ---- 18,1901   R.A.Painter   J.P.
Dotson,Eliza--22   At Sylva, N.C.
Wit; R.L.Davis, Geo.Calhoun, W.D.Edwards

Calhoun,John S.--22   Apr.12,1891   J.R.McKay   J.P.
Cook,Julia--20   At Scotts Creek
Wit; W.A.McKay, R.H.McKay

Calhoun,P.A.Jr.--23   Aug.17,1893   John S.Smiley J.P.
Stillwell,Emma Jane--16 At Webster, N.C.
Wit; G.N.Cowan,H.N.Mashburn,A.R.Stillwell

Calie,William--18   Sept.13,1896   D.H.Ashe   J.P.
Blackwell,Anna--19   At Webster Ts.
Wit; J.H.Cabe, T.J.Cabe, D.C.Hall

Camp,Joseph R.--24 (Col) Dec.20,1877   M.M.Brown   M.G.
Davis,Hattie--19 (Col)   At Silas Davis'
Wit; ---------

Campbell,D.C.--24   Nov.30,1899   C.M.Carpenter M.G.
Cogdille,Hattie--20   At John Cogdille's
Wit;Charley Hill,R.G.A.Campbell,G.S.Hill
He From Haywood,CO.N.C.

Campbell,Thos.D.--26   Dec.22,1898   J.P.Calhoun   J.P.
Sitton,Lela--17   At John Sitton's
Wit; S.L.Nicholson,John R.Long,David Frank lin.
He From Iredell,CO.N.C.

Campbell,Z.W.--23   Jan.5,1890   B.N.Queen   M.G.
Wilson,Darthula--18   At Hamburg Ts.
Wit; A.E.Pinkard,H.A.Brown,C.L.Woodring

Candler,Charley Z.--24   License Issued Aug.28,1901
Thomas,Annie--23   NOT Returned

Cann,John C.--24   Feb.14,1877   C.B.Fugate   M.G.
Alley,Sarah E.--22   At John Alley's
Wit; M.F.Bumgarner, A.C.Bumgarner
He From Rabun Co.Ga.

Cannon,E.B.--22   Nov.8,1883   J.O.Shelly   M.G.
  Monday,Laura B.--19 At Near Webster
                       Wit; J.T.Sherrod,D.G.Boyd,F.H.Leatherwood
                       He From Knox Co.Tenn

Cannon,Henry--   Apr.12,1871   G.W.Spake   M.G.
  Allison,R.A.--   At --------

Cannon,John W.--30   Feb.27,1881   G.W.Spake   M.G.
  Hannah,Julia--25   At A.M.Parker's
                       Wit; A.M.Parker, Wm.Beard

Cannon.Owen R.--23   Feb.10,1881   T.M.Frizell   J.P.
  Rochester,Sally M.E.--23 At R.E.Beard's
                       Wit;R.E.long, J.W.Cannon

Carbus,Thomas--26   Mar.1,1874   A.H.Wilson   J.P.
  Parson,America--19   At Rebecca Pearson's
                       Wit; John Stuart,D.Norton

Carpenter,J.M.--20   Aug.21,1890   J.G.Ammons   M.G.
  Stillwell,Belle--19 At Webster Ts.
                       Wit; H.C.Cowan,J.Davis, Geo.Davis

Carpenter,T.A.--32   Mar.29,1889   A.H.Sims   B.M.
  Stillwell,Cordilia--22 At Webster Ts.
                       Wit; G.N.Cowan,L.D.Hall,G.W.Davis

Carpenter,Thos.A.--26 June 24,1883   A.B.Clemenes   M.G.
  McLain,Laura A.--16 At J.E.McLain's
                       Wit; W.D.Terrell, James H.Cathey

Carrell,J.B.--   Jan.6,1856   J.B.Sherrill   J.P.
  Floyd,Jain--   At -------

Carroll,Alfred E.--20 Aug.30,1888   John P.Carroll J.P.
  Wilson,Ella J.--23   At Emaline Wilson's
                       Wit; J.B.Stewart, M.M.Pierson

Carroll,Joseph--39   Mar.23,1873   Hosa Bumgarner J.P.
  Lusk,Airy--30   At John Stuart's
                       Wit; ---------

Carroll,Thomas E.--21 Dec.4,1881   J.P.Stuart   J.P.
  Leopsrd,Ellen L.--21 At John Carroll's
                       Wit; R.A.Carroll, Sarah Stuart

Carson,J.L.--21   July 14,1896   J.T.Carson   J.P.
  Jones,Mary C.--22   At Dillsboro Ts.
                       Wit; William Montieth,Samuel Jones,J.R.Jon.

Carter,Thomas B.--17   Aug.3,1879   E.D.Brendle   B.M.
  Beck,Roxie--16   At Samuel Beck's
                       Wit; P.P.Buchanan,Samuel Beck
                       He From Rabun Co.Ga.

Carver,Benjamin--   June 22,1862   W.H.Conner   Elder
  Watson,Becersisa--   At ---------

Carver,James--20   Oct.16,1884   J.G.Ammons   M.G.
  Tilly,Elizabeth--24 At John Tilly's
                       Wit; Hugh S.Rogers, John Tilly

Carver,John D.--26   June 16,1886   J.O.Wallace   J.P.
  Kite,Mary E.--21   At W.J.Jones'
                       Wit; A.J.Gibbs, Wm.McLonghlin

Carver,Silas J.L.--27 Oct.30,1885 A.B.Clements M.G.
 Henson,Maggie A.--17 At M.Henson's
  Wit;J.B.Gibson,A.J.Carver

Case,F.G.--29 Aug.10,1891 P.P.McLean M.G.
 Stallcup,Mary--18 At Qualla Ts.
  Wit;E.L.McKee,R.H.Zachary,W.A.Sprinkle
  He From Swain,Co.NShe from Swain,Co.N.C.

Casey,William-- (Col) Jan.14,1869 C.C.Spake J.P.
 Thomas,Manda-- (Col) At --------

Casy,John--26 (Col) Feb.19,1899 Rev.T.R.Hacket Meth. Min.
 Davis,Sallie--19 (Col) At Thos.Davise's
  Wit; J.H.Hooper, Edward Love, David Love

Cathey,Alfred W.--24 Aug.22,1875 John Mathis J.P.
 Beard,Lydia M.--15 At Church
  Wit. Robert Moffitt,L.M.Cathey

Cathey,B.H.-- Jan.11,1866 L.G.Ward J.P.
 Conley,M.C.-- At --------

Cathey,Elonzo R.--19 Aug.3,1879 E.D.Brendle B.M.
 Clemmens,Charity T.--18 At Samuel Beck's
  Wit; S.J.Beck, G.B.Davis
  He From Swain,Co. N.C.

Catey,James--21 July 22,1887 C.A.Bird J.P.
 Caler,Maggie--23 At Under Apple Tree
  Wit; M.C.Ayers,D.A.Martin

Cathey,James T.--18 Nov.27,1881 T.J.Bryson J.P.
 Brown,Carrie--18 At D.E.Bryson's
  Wit;A.S.Queen,R.C.Bryson

Cathey,John A.--21 Mar.2,1889 John H.Mathis J.P.
 Mathis,Bethena--17 At Canada Ts.
  Wit; A.C.Queen,Levi Brown,J.A.Galloway

Chambers,James A.--24 May 9,1881 J.B.Raby J.P.
 Conner,Julia E.--19 At J.B.Raby's
  Wit; Ida Raby

Chastain,E.C.-- Dec.1,1858 Jacob Wike J.P.
 Boon,E.E.-- At -------

Chastain,Edward-- Oct.2,1856 B.N.Queen B.M.
 Watson,R.C.-- At -------

Chastain,Ezekiel--24 Sept.14,1878 W.A.Brown J.P.
 Stephens,Raa--18 At H.Stephens'
  Wit; W.W.Brown, Vance Stephens

Chastain,James--25 Sept.10,1899 E.F.Pell J.P.
 Rochester,Nettie--18 At Bride's fathers (A.Rochester)
  Wit; W.H.Robinson,J.O.Price, E.G.Robinson

Chastain,James--25 Mar.19,1901 E.F.Pell J.P.
 Handcock,Emma--19 At Hamp Robinson's
  Wit;Mariah Nicholoson,Julia Dunn,Lizzie Robison. Ro

Chastain,Jessee E.--23 Sept.18,1877 Lewis Queen J.P.
 Moore,Mary E.--18 At John Brown's
  Wit; ---------

Chastain,John-- Mar.7,1864 Jacob Wike J.P.
 Shook,Rebecca-- At -------

```
Chastain,John--                Sept.1,1864        J.Wike       J.P.
  Mathis,Mary A.--             At --------

Chastain,Junius M.--24         Dec.24,1878        W.A.Brown    J.P.
  Wilson,Sarah L.--19          At William Wilson's
                               Wit; O.B.Cowan, Enis Wilson

Chastain,R.C.--24              Feb.13,1898        E.F.Pell     J.P.
  Rochester,Hattie--18         At Elmina Rochester's
                               Wit;T.A.Robinson,W.H.Robinson,C.W.Paxton

Chastain,Robert--23            Aug.18,1881        W.S.Brown    J.P.
  Woodring,Sarah--23           At Charles Woodring's
                               Wit; Elihu Coward, Wm.Coward

Chastain,Robert M.--18         Nov.25,1882        J.E.McLain   J.P.
  Jones,Melvina--21            At Leanard Jones'
                               Wit;R.L.Jones'

Chasteen,George W.--           Dec.21,1862        E.C.Chastain J.P.
  Grigs,Marinda--              At --------

Cheoih,James--                 May 28,1869        G.W.Spake    M.G.
  Gibbs,Susan--                At ----
                               He son of an Unknown Cherokee.
                               She Dau.of an Unknown Slave.

Childers,John--25              Apr.9,1884         D.H.Ash      J.P.
  Sutton,Sarah A.--24          At James Sutton's
                               Wit; M.Sutton, H.D.Childers
                               He From Swain Co.N.C.

Childers,M.E.--19              Dec.22,1895        T.L.Brown    J.P.
  Sutton,Lillie--17            At Dillsboro,  N.C.
                               Wit; R.C.Parris,W.J.Sutton, Sam Brooks

Childers,Reubun A.--25         Dec.20,1887        C.A.Bird     J.P.
  Hays,Maud--18                At Marion Green's
                               Wit; J.H.Boyd, C.C.Martin

Christy,Thomas J.--25          Oct.23,1888        W.R.Barnett  M.G.
  Bryson,Corall--25            At J.H.Bryson's
                               Wit; W.R.Johnston, F.T.Smith
                               He From Macon Co. N.C.

Clark,Will A.--29              Oct.2,1892         Henry D.Welch M.G.
  Sutton,M.M.--21              At Scotts Creek  Ts.
                               Wit; V.C.Welch, N.M.Welch
                               He From Knoxville,Tenn.

Clarke,JohnJ.--25              Dec.3,1890         R.Brown  Pres.Min.
  Bright,Belle--21             At Scotts Creek  Ts.
                               Wit; Nora Welch, Mattie Jones,L.E.Perry
                               He From Buncombe Co.N.C.

Clayton,Daniel J.--24          Oct.31,1882        W.H.T.Dillard J.P.
  West,Mollie--22              At J.B.Clayton's
                               Wit; J.V.Clayton, J.P.Calhoun

Clayton,T.C.--22               Oct.11,1896        A.H.Sims     M.G.
  Allman,Maggie--18            At Sylva Ts.
                               Wit; Thomas Love,Mattie Benet,John Allamn

Clayton,Wm.A.--                Jan.17,1872        E.D.Brendle  Elder
  Cogdill,Mary A.--            At --------
```

Clayton,W.T.--23   Dec.17,1897   S.H.Queen   J.P.
  Cook,Dora M.--18   At Samuel Cook's
                          Wit; W.L.Thurber,G.W.Clayton,J.T.Henson

Cline,David--   Dec.23,1855   N.B.Thompson J.P.
  Jenkins,Jane--   At --------

Cline,John W.--   Nov.3,1868   Wm.B.Garrett J.P.
  Shular,Sarah Angaline-- At -------

Cline,W.P.--   (No date) Executed By I.T.S.Sherrill B.M.-This
  McKee,Harriet--   marriage is Recorded in book-A- page 74.
                            The one before Feb.26,1871--The one after
                            Mar.26,1871

Cline,William R.--45   Sept.22,1897   H.H.Hude   B.M.
  Wood,Dovey V.--22   At ---------
                          Wit;Josephine Fuller, Lee Fuller
                          He From Swain Co. N.C.

Clure,J.T.--22   Mar.29,1881   C.S.Buchanan
  Green,C.E.--22   At Joseph Green's
                          Wit; W.T.Brooks, Leander Buchanan

Cobb,Earl--25   Nov.1,1896   J.S.Leopard   J.P.
  Mathis,Ella--24   At Mountain Ts.
                          Wit; A.M.Moore, J.H.Long, A.V.Mathis

Cobb,Roland--21   Jan.3,1880   J.N.Cathey   J.P.
  Parker,Ann--21   At A.W.Parker's
                          Wit; J.H.Parker, J.T.Cathey

Cocherham,T.W.--   Jan.22,1871   P.G.Green   M.G.
  Baily,Jane--   At --------

Cocherham,W.C.--   Sept.3,1871   J.S.Woodard   M.G.
  Baley,N.E.   At --------

Cochiham,Ross--23   May 10,1875   T.K.Welch   J.P.
  Darcus,-- --20 (Red)   At T.K.Welch's
                          Wit; Ross Smith, E.A.Hyatt

Cockerham,Jessee B.--27   Sept.4,1887   A.H.Sims   M.G.
  Wilson,Laura--16   At Near Baptist Church
                          Wit; E.L.McKee, J.M.Long

Cogdelle,Samuel--23   Sept.26,1897   S.H.Green   J.P.
  Allman,Lula--22   At John Allman's
                          Wit; W.E.Bryson, J.B.Queen, T.J.Love

Cogdill,John--   Jan.9,1866   A.Fisher   J.P.
  Cook ,S.G.--   AT -------

Cogdill,John --26   Jan.27,1899   S.H.Queen   J.P.
  Alman,Mary--18   At J.B.Queen's
                          Wit;J.B.Queen, F.D.Parris

Cogdill,Johnny--21   Jan.9,1890   J.R.McKay   J.P.
  Brooks,Pattie--21   At Sylva. Ts.
                          Wit; W.A.McKay, L.C.Murry

Cogdill,J.M.---   Mar.25,1864   W.R.Crawford   Elder
  Cook,Mary A.--   At --------

Cogdill,Robert--18   May 4,1890   S.R.Cook   J.P.
  Bradshaw,Maggie--21   At Scotts Creek Ts.
                          Wit; L.D.Queen,R.L.Cook, Bill Hall

Cogdille,G.L.--21 Henry,Thersa--18	Aug.15,1896 At Scotts Creek Ts. Wit; J.M.Hoyle, W.D.Henry, A.C.Calhoun	J.P.Calhoun	J.P.
Cogdille,Lee W.--26 Clayton,Artilia--25	Oct.9,1898 At ------- Wit; T.C.Clayton, D.J.Clayton	S.H.Queen	J.P.
Cogdille,William--17 Wilson,Mollie--17	.Oct.2,1879 At Brunettee Wilson's Wit; Wm.Wilson, J.F.Buchanan	G.W.Spake	M.M.
Coggins,Charlie--21 Wilks,Margaret--18	Aug.14,1898 At Allen Wilks'Home Wit; W.F.Moody,W.A.Leopard,Willey Leopard	J.W.Leopsrd	J.P.
Coggins,Edward--21 Bryson,Martha J.--26	Apr.1,1885 At ------- Wit; W.F.Coggins, J.A.Henson	J.B.Sutard	J.P.
Coggins,Francis P.--20 Bryson,Mary A.--18	Jan.28,1879 At Lettie Mathis' Wit; L.Mathis, Peter Mathis	D.D.Davis	J.P.
Coggins,Francis P.--22 Wilks,Amanda--21	Apr.2,1877 At Josiah Watson's Wit; B.N.Watson, Thos.Dills	R.L.Watson	J.P.
Coggins,Marcus L.--22 Moody,Lou--17	Oct.17,1885 At Nancy Woodring's Wit; N.G.Fox, J.T.Moody	C.L.Woodring	J.P.
Coggins,R.H.--22 Zachary,Mary T.--19	May 10,1874 At M.Zachary's Wit; C.Bryson, John Keener	C.W.Wiggins	M.M.
Cole,George M.--22 Zachary,Sarah A.--22	Nov.25,1877 At Alex Zachary's Wit; J.P.Slaton, A.Zachary	C.P.Bryson	J.P.
Collins,Eli-- Jenkins,Nancy--	July 27,1869 At ---------	Wm.B.Garrett	J.P.
Collins,Joseph A.--34 McKee,Hattie V.--17	Nov.9,1875 At R.F.McKee's Wit; J.C.Watkins, L.C.Hall	J.W.Bird	M.M.
Collins,S.S.--35 Pinson,Mrs.M.E.--27	Mar.12,1892 At Barker Creek Wit; Mary L.Bradley Both From Swain,CO.N.C.	S.C.Allison	J.P.
Colnquatag,Joe-- (Red) Anna ------ (Red)	Apr.30,1871 At --------	W.H.Conner	M.G.
Conley,Bengeman S.-- Lester,Sousan--	May 29,1871 At --------	T.H.Welch	J.P.
Conley,Jessee-- Hughes,Ruanna--	Jan.3,1861 At -------	L.G.Ward	J.P.
Conley,Manley-- Enloe,R.A.--	License Issued Oct.29,1868 NOT Returned		
Conley,W.D.-- Hicks,May	Oct.23,1866 At --------	W.H.Hicks	J.P.
Conner,B.M.-- Harris,Emeline--	Jan.8,1871 At -------	Stephen J.Beck	J.P.

Conner,Doctor F.--21   Apr.9,1876   John E.McLean J.P.
York,Margaret--20   At In Road
Wit; A.K.Bradley, J.R.Beck
He From Swain, Co.N.C.

Conner,Francis--20   Nov.15,1877   J.C.Watkins J.P.
Cope,Margaret C.--18   At John J.Cope's
Wit; L.C.Shoffield, L.H.Leatherwood

Conner,Henry--21   License Issued Sept.9,1901
Cunningham,Dovey--19   NOT Returned

Conner,H.Y.--42   License Issued Jan.17,1894
Smathers,Mary--20   Returned-- NOT Executed

Conner,J.D.--21   Jan.26,1896   W.S.Conner B.M.
Dills,Candas--22   At Dillsboro Ts.
Wit; Thomas Queen,B.F.Fowler,L.L.Sitton

Conner,Joseph--27   May 3,1898   W.D.Frizell J.P.
Moody,Lecie--19   At Stephens Wood's
Wit; Stephens Wood, Mont Davis,Mary Wood

Conner,J.S.--60   Jan.26,1896   G.C.Sherrill J.P.
Hornbuckle,Minda--50   At Qualla
Wit; G.C.Sherrill,S.Sherrill,M.Sherrill

Conner,M.L.--   Feb.11,1864   W.H.Conner J.P.
Teeters,Mary--   At --------

Conner,R.C.--55   Nov.16,1895   Thomas Queen J.P.
Davis,Martha Jane--45   At Dillsboro
Wit; W.D.Sitton,J.L.Gibson,J.A.Gibson

Conner,Symms--21   License Issued Aug.21,1883
Harris,Mary C.--17   NOT Returned

Conner,Vestel--22   License Issued July 8,1901
Mathis,Laura--18   NOT Returned

Conner,Wiley--21   Dec.9,1883   E.D.Brendle B.M.
Beck,Clarinda A.--18   At S.J.Beck's
Wit; C.T.Cathey, S.J.Beck
He From Swain,Co. N.C.

Conroy,Frank J.--33   Sept.15,1892   J.A.Deal Min.P.E.C.S.
Davies,Ella Maia--27   At Cullowhee Ts.
Wit; W.W.Helm, J.F.Hays, M.Buchanan
He From New Castel, Pa.

Cook,E.A.--   Mar.3,1858   J.Wike   J.P.
Wood,A.M.--   At --------

Cook,James--24   Dec.25,1882   W.J.Parker J.P.
Stephens,Susan--18   At W.J.Hooper's
Wit; H.J.Hooper, J.H.Smith

Cook,James A.--20   Nov.8,1877   S.H.Bryson J.P.
Deen,Sarah A.--18   At John Cogdill's
Wit; John Cogdill, Joseph Queen

Cook,Lee--22   Aug.11,1898   J.D.Sitton J.P.
Queen,Elvina--35   At Bride's Residence
Wit; J.E.Long, S.C.Wood,W.D.Mills

Cook,Marcus--19   Oct.1,1873   Wm.Estes   J.P.
Lemmons,Martha--18   At James Farly's
Wit; S.F.Cook, Wm.Gunter

Cook,Marvel R.--48
Fulbright,Barbary--41

July 22,1877   G.W.Spake   M.M.
At Eli Fulbright's
Wit; Eli Fulbright, D.Fulbright

Cook,Robert L.--18
Pannel,Hannah J.--17

Nov.27,1884   J.R.Crawford   J.P.
At M.J.Pannel's
Wit; J.B.Queen, John Snider

Cook,Robert L.--21
Bumgarner,Annie--19

Feb.18,1900   J.R.Crawford   J.P.
At W.Bumgarner's
Wit; John Bumgarner,A.B.Moore, Ed.Austin

Cook,Samuel--24
Parker,Bessie--17

Jan.7,1900   W.F.Cook   B.M.
At Rebecca Parker's
Wit; S.L.Parker, M.A.Parker, J.H.Shular

Cook,S.F.--
Shelton,Martha A.--

Oct.9,1853   L.C.Hooper   J.P.
At -------

Cook,S.R.--
Bennett,N.R.--

Sept.25,1865   J.M.Harris   Elder
At ---------

Cook,Thomas--35
Brown,Mattie--16

License Issued Dec.6,1899
NOT Returned

Cook,William F.--20
Parker,Aled--17

Mar.11,1886   Bragg Hooper   J.P.
At John Smith's
Wit; W.C.Long, J.H.Smith

Cooper,J.B.--
Conley,R.J.--

Sept.10,1865   W.L.Norris   J.P.
At ---------

Cooper,Leander--
Paris,Mary T.--

Dec.30,1861   F.M.Fanning   M.G.
At -------

Cooper,Lee W.--23
Long,Laura Bell--15

Feb.12,1891   P.P.McLean   M.G.
At Sylva Ts.
Wit; Z.V.Watson,J.E.Diverbliss,R.M.Davis

Cooper,William W.--19
Gipson,Sarah A.--19

Nov.13,1875   J.B.Allison   J.P.
At L.M.Angel's
Wit; Berry Cooper, L.M.Angel

Cope,A.C.--29
Barnes,F.I.--21

Sept.3,1896   J.S.Leopard   J.P.
At Hamburg Ts.
Wit; R.A.Brown,H.T.Conner, M.G.Daves

Cope,Andrew C.--21
Bryson,Emma--19

Jan.29,1887   T.M.Frizell   J.P.
At N.E.Bryson's
Wit; J.W.Montieth, T.B.Dillard

Cope,Coleman--22
Queen,I.--17

Oct.9,1887   S.P.Cook   J.P.
At John Cogdill's
Wit; John Cogdill, William Cope

Cope,C.M.--20
Gunter,Alice--16

Sept.16,1894   Joseph Hoyle   J.P.
At Scotts Creek
Wit; W.D.Mills,J.M.Lindsey,A.T.Harrell

Cope,Engehart--21
Higdon,Mollie--18

Sept.17,1899   D.C.Jones   J.P.
At W.H.Higdon's
Wit; R.L.Collins,James M.Cabe,J.B.Buchanan

Cope,Henry A.--20
Parker,Polly L.--17

Feb.9,1888   John H.Mathis J.P.
At Bride's Fathers
Wit; D.W.West, W.L.Cope

Cope,James--18
White,----- 18

Dec.28,1883   W.H.Hooper   J.P.
At W.M.Hooper's
Wit; J.A.Woodring, Lizzie Wilson

Cope,James--30   Aug.19,1897   V.F.Brown   J.P.
    Bradley,Fannie--25   At River Ts.
       Wit; H.V.Conner, A.C.Price, O.L.Hooper

Cope,James R.--21   Dec.15,1887   W.M.Rhea   J.P.
    Wilks,Charity E.--21   At Silas Wilks'
       Wit; John Cogdill, Robert Wilks

Cope,Joseph A.--21   Sept.3,1874   M.W.Bryson   J.P.
    Dillard,Edith--20   At A.Cope's
       Wit; Andy Bryson

Cope,L.L.--26   Feb.9,1896   Joseph Hoyle J.P.
    ·Lindsey,Elizabeth--17   At Scotts Creek Ts.
       Wit; S.J.Banner,G.W.Hoyle, M.D.Duncan

Cope.Sebern--22   Dec.31,1898   J.L.Buchanan   B.M.
    Hall,Alice--26   At His Mother's
       Wit; J.W.Morgan, R.J.Morgan
       He From Macon,Co.N.C.

Cpe,Walter--29   Nov.17,1898   J.P.Brendle   J.P.
    Hooper,Amanda--27   At R.L.Watson's
       Wit; A.C.Cope, J.H.Barnes

Cope,Walton--22   Jan.24,1892   H.P.Brendle   J.P.
    Sitton,Maggie--15   At Sylva Ts.
       Wit; E.D.Brendle, C.Cope, John Cope

Cope, W.F.--21   July 6,1890   W.T.Crisp   J.P.
    Higdon,Margarett J.--18   At Savannah Ts.
       Wit; Andrew Cope, D.P.Walker, I.D.Woodard

Cope,Wesley--21   Aug.26,1894   W.C.Buchanan J.P.
    Ridley,Polly--18   At Savannah
       Wit; W.Crawford, J.L.Kinsland

Cope,William--45   Sept.25,1887   S.R.Cook   J.P.
    Baily,Stacy E.--22   At Wm.Cope's
       Wit; R.O.Phillips, Mary J.Cope

Cope,William L.--19   License Issued Dec.24,1886
    Brown,Lilly G.--18   NOT Returned

Cope,W.W.--24   Aug.13,1891   S.R.Cook   J.P.
    Barker,Caroline--23   At Scotts Creek
       Wit; Jno.Baily, Guss McKay, Joe Hooper

Corben,William--   Sept.28,1854   Jacob Wike   J.P.
    Mathes,Prudy An --   At --------

Corn Tassel,Thomas-- (Red)   Dec.25,1871   --------   ----
    Oolscosty,---- (Red)   At --------

Cory,W.O.--60   Mar.14,1890   J.O.Shelley   M.G.
    Hedden,Sallie E.--23   At Webster Ts.
       Wit; Mr.& Mrs. Schreiber, G.N.Emry
       He From Haywood, Co. N.C.

Coulter,James B.--28   May 1,1892   B.N.Queen   B.M.
    Hooper,Callie--18   At River Ts.
       Wit; S.S.Chishom, M.T.Hooper, J.D.Zachery

Cowan,Alfred--42   Jan.3,1886   J.T.Wike   J.P.
    Hooper,Elizabeth--40   At George Rogers'
       Wit; Lewis Rogers, Wilson Rogers

Cowan,Arch--20   Mar.10,1895   A.W.Davis   B.M.
  Brogdon,Arlissa--18   At Savannah
    Wit; R.D.Cowan, J.S.Sellers, A.C.Cawan

Cowan,James--   Jan.17,1866   E.T.Stillwell J.P.
  Stillwell,Elizabeth--   At --------

Cowan,James--25   Dec.23,1894   A.W.Davis   B.M.
  Frady,Manda Allecia--17   At Savannah
    Wit; J.J.Buchanan,J.R.Buchanan,J.S.Frady

Cowan,James F.--30   Dec.27,1881   R.H.Stephen·   J.P.
  Hooper,Mary J.--22   At R.H.Stephen's
    Wit; W.B.Hooper, E.M.Cowan

Cowan,J.H.--21   Mar.26,1879   S.C.Owens   J.P.
  Lovedahl,Julia--19   At A.L.Lovedahl's
    Wit; E.M.Cowan, H.L.Brown

Cowan,M.D.--27   Jan.18,1898   J.J.Gray   M.M.E.C.S.
  Leatherwood,Annie C.--20   At F.H.Leatherwood's
    Wit; L.D.Cowan,W.D.Honeycutt,J.B.Sherrill

Cowan,Roiston D.--21   Feb.3,1879   E.G.Ash   J.P.
  Bradley.Amanda J.--18   At E.C.Ash's
    Wit; P.P.Buchanan, E.Buchanan

Cowan,Samuel A.--24   Jan.12,1887   G.W.Hawkins   J.P.
  Hawkins,Mollie--19   At James Hawkins'
    Wit; James Hawkins, S.C.Painter

Cowan,W.L.--23   Jan.20,1891   A.J.Long Sr.   J.P.
  Wild,Luthena--21   At Webster Ts.
    Wit; M.D.Cowan, L.D.Cowan,S.T.Bryson

Cowen,D.L.--   Feb.26,1869   J.L.Buchanan   M.G.
  Dietz,Nancy--   At --------

Cowen,William R.--32   Sept.14,1873   J.L.Buchanan   B.M.
  Allman,Mary--27   At Mary Allman's
    Wit; W.O.Buchanan, J.S.Stillwell

Coward,Andrew--27 (Col)   Aug.7,1892   J.C.Watkins   J.P.
  Moore,Lou--21   (Col)   At Dillsboro Ts.
    Wit; W.A.Dills, J.C.Fisher, S.S.Enloe

Coward,Charles--22   License Issued   Sept.1,1892
  Henson,Callie--26   NOT Returned

Coward,Javan B.--24   Apr.1,1875   B.N.Queen   B.M.
  Hooper,Jane--20   At E.C.Hooper's
    Wit; J.Davis,M.D.Hooper

Coward,Jonathan D.--23   Mar.4,1875   C.B.Fugate   M.M.
  Norton,Lou--21   At William Norton's
    Wit; Mary A.Fugate, Eliza B.Zachary

Coward,Nathan--67   Oct.18,1885   G.W.Spake   M.M.
  Hadden,----18   At E.D.Davis'
    Wit; W.C.Tompkins, Joseph Davis

Coward,O.B.--   July 1,1885   J.S.Keener   J.P.
  Long,Emma C.--14   At E.R.Hampton's
    Wit; J.M.Watson,E.R.Hampton

Coward,Robert R.--19   Apr.20,1886   C.M.Jones   M.M.
  Allen,Lena E.--16   At P.C.Allen's
    Wit; W.C.Norton, E.C.Headen

```
Coward,Samuel--21            License Issued    Jan.2,1883
    Parker,Martha E.--24     NOT Returned

Coward,Silas--23  (Col)      Sept.31,1886        F.P.Mastin      M.G.
    Saunders,Julia--25  (Col) At Mrs. Saunders'
                             Wit; G.D.Hooper, Ellen Mastin

Coward,Tolvin B.--22         Mar.6,1873          B.N.Queen       B.M.
    Bryson,Rebecca--18       At H.R.Brown's
                             Wit; R.H.Brown, E.C.Chastin

Coward,William--             Dec.27,1868         B.N.Queen       B.M.
    Queen,Elizabeth--        At --------

Coward,William--20  (Col)    Jan.2,1882          G.W.Spake       M.M.
    Allen,Josie--18  (Col)   At Moses Allen's
                             Wit;Will Love, Alfred Coward

Coward,William--22           Mar.11,1886         Bragg Hooper    J.P.
    Long,Dora--18            At Wm.Hooper's
                             Wit; W.C.Long, T.H.Hooper

Coward,William--25  (Col)    Dec.29,1887         A.D.Hooper      J.P.
    Love,Clerrisa--20 (Col)  At A.D.Hooper's
                             Wit; D.H.Rogers, J.M.Hooper

Cox,Thomas--24               Oct.27,1887     D.Hillhouse Buel  Cleg.
    Davis,Cora K.--19        At Cullowhee Church
                             Wit; D.L.Love, Minnie L.Lewis

Crawford,Andrew--18          Sept.1,1889         H.A.Hall        J.P.
    Mills,Zettie Ann--19     At Scotts Creek
                             Wit; J.M.Crawford, R.B.Shular,Blenton ----

Crawford,Ellis W.--19        Apr.22,1878         J.R.Crawford  J.P.
    Parris,Martha--19        At Marth Crawford's
                             Wit; Samuel Parris, Wm.Clayton

Crawford,George C.--18       Aug.23,1888         J.R.McKay       J.P.
    Pannel,Sarah--17         At J.R.McKay's
                             Wit; J.T.Carson, A.C.Bryson

Crawford,George W.--19       Dec.4,1873          S.H.Bryson      J.P.
    Morrow,Nancy--21         At A.J.Morrow's
                             Wit; D.G.Estis

Crawford,Hamilton--25        Jan.1,1896          A.C.Queen       B.M.
    Massengale,Alsey--16     At Canada Ts.
                             Wit; John Ashe, P.H.Brown, G.W.W.Hamilton

Crawford,Henry--16           Aug.5,1900          T.J.Mathis      J.P.
    Massengale,Alusta--17    At T.J.Mathis's House
                             Wit; H.E.Crawford,R.H.Brown,T.M.Galloway

Crawford,H.R.--23            Apr.8,1900          A.B.Henson      B.M.
    Mills,Frances--24        At D.Knight's Store
                             Wit; J.E.Mathis,Ben Saunders,J.H.Phillips

Crawford,James--22           Apr.14,1901         J.C.Owen        M.G.
    Watson,Daisy--16         At Nathan Watson's
                             Wit; H.E.Crawford,T.S.Fortner,E.C.Mathis

Crawford,James E.--20        Sept.30,1880        J.R.Crawford  J.P.
    Henson,Mary M.--20       At Frank Henson's
                             Wit; R.J.Crawford, J.B.Ensley

Crawford,James M.--19        Oct.14,1879         W.Ensley        J.P.
    Ensley,Codella--15       At William Ensley's
                             Wit; T.N.Snider,W.T.Ensley
```

Crawford,John L.--25
Phillips,Rebecca E.--21

Jan.25,1894   J.T.Carson   J.P.
At Cullowhee Ts.
Wit; Judson Corn,W.L.Henson,J.T.Phillips

Crawford,Joseph W.--20
Watson,Martha--19

Dec.6,1887   A.H.Sims   M.G.
At R.L.Watson's
Wit; R.J.Crawford, Walher Potts

Crawford,M.W.--
Snider,Margret E.--

Dec.31,1862   S.Montieth   J.P.
At --------

Crawford,Ramsey--22
Bryson,Julia--19

Mar.6,1898   Wm.Pruitt   M.G.
At Nancy Crawford's
Wit; T.D.Bryson, W.L.Fisher

Crawford,Reece--21
Queen,Rebecca--21

Mar.25,1880   E.D.Brendle   B.M.
At J.S.Queen's
Wit; T.N.Snider, Thos.Montieth

Crawford,Samuel--23
Hoyle,Mollie--25

Jan.14,1894   J.P.Brendle   J.P.
At Sylva Ts.
Wit; R.P.Crawford,A.C.Robinson,J.L.Crawfor

Crawford,S.N.--26
Adams,D.M.--19

Mar.8,1891   Lee Hooper   J.P.
At Cullowhee Ts.
Wit; N.Fox, J.A.Adams

Crawford,William E.--25
Painter,Emma--18

Dec.29,1886   J.R.Crawford   J.P.
At S.M.Painter's
Wit; John Bryson, Sam Henson

Crawford,Wilson B.--20
Dills,Sarah M.--17

Aug.30,1883   R.L.Watson   J.P.
At Marion Dills'
Wit; W.S.Henson, W.E.Crawford

Crisp,Ben--22
Aiken,Lillie--18

Mar.30,1899   J.R.Crawford   J.P.
At J.M.Crawford's
Wit; J.M.Crawford,A.L.Ensley,H.M.Snider

Crisp,Millard--22
Jones,Lizzie--19

Feb.20,1898   Thomas L.Brown   J.P.
At S.B.Jones's
Wit; A.C.Elders, T.S.Brooks

Crisp,Thomas J.--20
Jones,Harriet L.--17

.Nov.17,1872   P.G.Green   B.M.
At --------
Wit; B.H.Jones, Amos Cabe

Crook,Robert T.--25
McElray,Lula--22

July 11,1886   J.T.Wike   J.P.
At L.J.Smith's
Wit; L.J.Smith, Lena Smith

Crow,Sevier--22   (Red)
Maney,Laura--   (Red)

Nov.5,1885   John Conat   M.G.
At John Conat's
Wit; Jane Jutte,Nancy Jutte

Crumley,H.C.--31
Thompson,Mary--19

License Issued   July 24,1901
NOT Returned

Crumpton,Richard--22
Mathis,Mary--17

Oct.27,1881   S.J.Bryson   J.P.
At D.J.Parker's
Wit; A.B.Bryson, R.C.Bryson

Cunningham,Cling--22
Forster,Maggie--17

May 22,1890   A.M.Parker   J.P.
At Sylva Ts.
Wit; J.B.Clayton, Newt Phillips,C.Wood

Cunningham,Cling--32
Fisher,Nannie--19

Mar.25,1900   W.E.Conner   B.M.
At T.J.Fisher's
Wit; Howard Fisher,Claud King, M.J.Panel

Cunningham,D.L.--21 Cagle,Emma--18	License Issued Jan.23,1889 " License returned and not executed and the same cancelled."
Cunningham,E.K.--34 Fulmer,Maggie--20	Dec.25,1889 J.O.Shelley M.G. At Dillsboro Ts. Wit; Sam L.Rogers, T.S.Munday, J.H.Wolff He From Macon,Co. N.C. She From Buncombe, Co.N.C.
Cunningham,Edwin K.--26 Enloe,Ida J.--22	Nov.3,1881 W.C.Carden M.G. At"Church in Webster" Wit. Frank Ray, G.W.Dillard He From Macon, Co.N.C.
Cunningham,John-- Cowan,Margaret--	Oct.10,1869 J.L.Buchanan J.P. At --------
Cunningham,J.F.--20 Stillwell,Mary J.--19	Mar.6,1895 A.H.Sims B.M. At Webster Wit; C.C.Cowan, H.C.Cowan, Wm.Stillwell He From Macon, Co.N.C.
Cunningham,Rufus--22 Deitz,Florence--16	Apr.6,1893 A.W.Davis J.P. At Savannah Ts. Wit; T.L.Deitz, Nelson Deitz, Mary Deitz
Cunningham,Wiley--25 Bumgarner,Rebecca--21	Jan.10,1895 A.W.Jacobs, Min.M.E.C.S. At Sylva Wit; Verta Pharr, T.F.Mashburn,Ella Bumgar He From Macon,Co.N.C. ner.
Curry,George W.--22 Mills,Malinda--18	Nov.24,1899 A.B.Henson B.M. At G.T.Mills' Wit; T.L.Mills, Z.T.Mills, Margaret Raines He From McDowell, Co.N.C.
Curtis,Joshua--49 Arrington,Laura--25	Dec.5,1879 T.K.Welch J.P. At James Arrington's Wit; W.B.Sherrill, C.C.Boone
Dalton,Henry--25 (Col) Freeman,Nannie--16 (Col)	May 28,1895 L.W.Allen J.P. At Sylva Wit; Robt.Fretwell, James Pickens
Daniels,Charles--30 Enloe,Florence--24	Dec.11,1900 J.H.Weaver M.M. At Dillsboro, N.C. Wit;G.S.Ferguson,Jr.T.B.Allison,M.A.Sherril He From Malden, Mass.
Darby,Logan--23 (Col) Bryson,Roxanna--23 (Col)	Dec.24,1884 Jas.R.Crawford J.P. At J.R.Crawford's Wit; G.W.Bryson, John Crawford
Daves,James H.--20 Brown,Sarah--18	Sept.11,1875 B.N.Queen B.M. At Susan Brown's Wit; J.F.Stapp, Mary Stapp
Daves,J.H.--35 Queen,E.C.--26	Mar.19,1896 R.R.Coward J.P. At Caney Fork Ts. Wit; F.B.Price, W.B.Morris, John Stephens
Daves,John--22 Moody,Nine--20	Nov.24,1892 B.N.Queen B.M. At River Ts. Wit; S.A.Wood, J.J.Powell, M.G.Davis

Daves,T.J.-- Allen,Darcus--	Dec.7,1871 At -------	H.H.Gibbs,	J.P.
Davis,A.L.-- Raby,Nancy Jane--	Sept.7,1863 At --------	E.D.Brendle	Elder
Davis,Benjamin W.--27 Potts.Addie--22	Mar.3,1901 At M.J.Henson's House Wit; J.D.Davis, P.C.Henson, John Phillips	W.L.Henson	J.P.
Davis,Charley--24 Phillips,Harriet--18	Sept.8,1896 At Sylva Ts. Wit; A.M.Parker, R.L.Cook, H.M.Sanders	A.M.Parker	J.P.
Davis, E.D.-- Allen,Nancy--	Dec.24,1857 At --------	Allen Fisher	J.P.
Davis,Green B.--27 Gibson,Holcedonia--19	Dec.19,1880 At J.B.Gibson's Wit; Thomas Gibson, J.B.Gibson	E.D.Brendle	B.M.
Davis,Issac-- Chumluski-ta-- (Red)	Nov.13,1869 At --------	I.T.S.Sherrill	M.G.
Davis,Issac C.--21 Dillard,Ellar L.--14	Nov.14,1880 At W.H.T.Dillard's Wit; R.E.Long, Wm.Davis	W.Ensley	M.G.
Davis,James M.--28 Dills,Martha J.--25	Dec.26,1876 At "Home of Wm.Dills" Wit; G.M.Gunter, Thos,Dills	Wm.Bumgarner	J.P.
Davis,Javan--27 Messer,Ella--22	Sept.16,1875 At J.L.Potts' Wit; J.L.Potts, J.M.Hunter	W.A.Brown	J.P.
Davis,Javan--41 Alley,Susan--37	Sept.22,1889 At Cashers Valley Ts. Wit; F.W.Thompson, A.W.Jacobs, Cassie Hill	B.G.Wild	M.G.
Davis,Jeff--21 Ward,Catherine--26	Aug.14,1881 At J.B.Raby's Wit; J.H.House	J.B.Raby	J.P.
Davis,Jeff--26 Brinkley,Mary--23	Feb.27,1888 At R.Davis' Wit; W.D.Hill, R.Davis	Wm.Bumgarner	J.P.
Davis,John--24 Slaton,Dollie--19	Oct.18,1885 At A.Zachary's Wit; A.C.Long, G.M.Cole	J.A.Hooper	J.P.
Davis,John--42 Messer,R.A.--42	------- 1894 At Barker Creek Wit; T.C.Jones, T.L.Davis	J.F.Brown	J.P.
Davis,Joseph Nelson--55 Wilks,Rebecca--36	License Issued June 13,1898 NOT Returned		
Davis,Joseph W.--31 Snider,Lillie E.--20	Sept.13,1896 At Webster Ts. Wit; J.P.Brendle, Geo. E.Boggs	A.M.Parker	J.P.
Davis, J.L.-- Allen,Manda M.--	Sept.3,1862 At --------	J.M.Bryson	J.P.
Davis,J.R.--29 (Col) Love,Mary M.--21 (Col)	Mar.12,1890 At "Near Webster" Wit; George Allen,L.L.Rogers,J.C.Love	B.G.Wild	M.G.

Davis,J.Sherman--24   Jan.101892   W.Ensley   M.G.
    Monteith,Mary--22   At Dillsboro Town
                             Wit; J.N.Parris, Thad Clayton, A.S.Ross

Davis,L.G.--21   Jan.23,1879   B.H.Jones   J.P.
    Collins,Allice--21   At W.H.Buchanan's
                             Wit; W.T.Crisp,M.P.Jones
                             He From Haywood, Co.N.C.

Davis,Monroe--25   Dec.19,1886   John M.Earls   M.G.
    Davis,Callie D.--20   At R.D.Davis'
                             Wit; J.T.Lawson, F.M.Davis
                             He From Swain,Co.N.C.

Davis,Mont G.--20   May 27,1894   B.N.Queen   M.G.
    Webster,Dialpha--18   At River Ts.
                             Wit;Baxter Hooper,T.W.Wood,J.R.Cope,
                                          D.V.Moody,R.A.Brown.

Davis,R.C.--   License Issued Dec.16,1896
    Ward,Sallie L.--   NOT Returned

Davis,Robert M.--22   Dec.26,1889   A.B.Thomas   M.G.
    Hampton,Eugenia May--19 At Sylva Ts.
                             Wit; D.L.Love, A.M.Parker, J.W.McKee

Davis,Silas--52 (Col)   Jan.18,1880   R.G.Watson   J.P.
    Sherrill,Susan--52 (Col) At Silas Davis'
                             Wit; D.H.Phillips, J.D.Moore

Davis,Thomas--21   Dec.18,1893   W.W.Reed   B.M.
    Moody,Artie--19   At Scotts Creek
                             Wit; Jas.Davis, Eston Moody, W.A.Mckay
                             He From Haywood, Co.N.C.

Davis,Thomas--29   Apr.23,1899   A.W.Davis   B.M.
    Frady,Charlotte--19   At"My Home"
                             Wit; Reuben Frady,C.W.Frady, Martha Davis
                             He From Haywood, Co.N.C.

Davis,Thomas S.--28 (Col)   Aug.31,1887   Jessee A.Wild   J.P.
    Whitmin,Mary--18 (Col)   At Webster
                             Wit; Mrs.Juliet Wilde
                             He From Salisbury,N.C.

Davis,William--   Aug.5,1871   T.K.Welch   J.P.
    ----,Mary-- (Red)   At -------

Davis,William G.--26   Aug.10,1880   H.S.Baker   J.P.
    Gibbs,Mary A.--18   At J.F.Gibbs'
                             Wit; J.F.Gibbs, Mattie Davis

Davis,Wm.--   Oct.7,1862   E.D.Brendle   Elder
    Bryson,Caranhuppoc ? -- At -------

Davis,W.V.--23   Oct.23,1884   T.J.Love   J.P.
    Fisher,I.Cumi--17   At A.C.Fisher's
                             Wit; T.B.Farmer, J.C.Fisher

Dawsin,J.C.--   Mar.1,1858   J.B.Sherrill   J.P.
    Harriss,Pricilla--   At --------

Dawson,J.R.--23   July 25,1897   T.J.Mathis   J.P.
    Queen,Laura--22   At Canada Ts.
                             Wit; M.A.Burrell,Casper Brown,Andrew Hend
                                                                  rex

Dean,Adam--24　　　　　　　May 15,1890　　　A.J.Hall　　　J.P.
　Smith,Etta--18　　　　　　At Scotts Creek Ts.
　　　　　　　　　　　　　　Wit; Joseph Hoyle, W.D.Duncan, G.W.Hoyle

Dean,C.R.--20　　　　　　　Dec.12,1878　　　W.R.Crawford　J.P.
　Carson,Haseltine E.--19　At Charlotts Carson's
　　　　　　　　　　　　　　Wit; J.F.Queen, T.G.Bryson

Dean,George--22　　　　　　Nov.1,1894　　　T.L.Jemsen　　J.P.
　McCall,Mattie--18　　　　At Hamburg Ts.
　　　　　　　　　　　　　　Wit; S.R.McCall, E.M.McCall, E.A.Bryson

Dean,James--24　　　　　　 Sept.20,1896　　J.T.Carson　　J.P.
　Smathers,Mary--22　　　　At Scotts Creek Ts.
　　　　　　　　　　　　　　Wit; C.R.Jones, John M.Queen,J.B.Bryson

Dietz,Jacob--　　　　　　　Feb.2,1857　　　John Wilson　　J.P.
　Cabe,Mary--　　　　　　　At -------

Dietz,James N.--21　　　　Aug.13,1878　　　W.H.Buchanan　J.P.
　Buchanan,Lucy A.--22　　At Charles Buchanan's
　　　　　　　　　　　　　　Wit; J.R.Buchanan,Leander Buchanan

Dietz,John J.--　　　　　　Mar.8,1871　　　J.L.Buchanan　J.P.
　Stiles,Harriet--　　　　At -------

Dietz,Julius W.--　　　　　Oct.3,1869　　　J.L.Buchanan　M.G.
　Frady, Margaret--　　　　At -------

Dietz,Marcus C.--21　　　 Apr.5,1883　　　C.S.Buchanan　M.G.
　Green,Nancy--23　　　　　At Joseph Green's
　　　　　　　　　　　　　　Wit; W.H.Sutton, A.B.Ash

Dietz,Martin L.--19　　　 Oct.14,1878　　　J.C.Watkins　　J.P.
　Cope,Josephine--19　　　At J.A.Collins'
　　　　　　　　　　　　　　Wit; A.M.Parker

Deitz,Nathaniel J.--26　　Feb.211889　　　J.L.Buchanan　M.G.
　Green,Eugenia--18　　　　At Savannah Ts.
　　　　　　　　　　　　　　Wit; J.A.Gribble, L.D.Hall, J.N.Buchanan

Deitz,Nelson--21　　　　　 Dec.20,1891　　　T.H.Dietz　　M.G.
　Buchanan,Martha--22　　 At Savannah Ts.
　　　　　　　　　　　　　　Wit; L.D.Hall, J.W.Frady,W.L.Buchanan

Dietz,Thadeus F.--19　　　Jan.22,1886　　　J.G.Ammons　　M.G.
　Cowan,Mollie--18　　　　At B.Cowan's
　　　　　　　　　　　　　　Wit; C.C.Higdon, N.J.Dietz

Dietz,Thomas J.--20　　　 Dec.22,1895　　　A.W.Davis　　B.M.
　Bryson,Lola--19　　　　　At Cullowhee
　　　　　　　　　　　　　　Wit; A.A.Dietz,J.W.Barker, R.N.Dietz

Dietz,Thos.L.--19　　　　　License Issued　Sept.24,1891
　Wilson,Alice--17　　　　NOT Returned

Dietz,Thos.W.--30　　　　　Apr.9,1891　　　B.G.Wild　　　M.G.
　Powell,Mary--18　　　　　At Webster
　　　　　　　　　　　　　　Wit; M.R.Moss, J.L.Reynolds, J.M.Dietz

Dietz,William A.--22　　　Dec.16,1900　　　A.W.Davis　　B.M.
　Stiles,Melvina--18　　　At William Stiles'
　　　　　　　　　　　　　　Wit; N.J.Dietz,R.L.Montieth,Will Buchanan

Dietz,William--35　　　　　Oct.26,1882　　　J.G.Ammons　　M.G.
　Buchanan,Agnus E.--31　 At Margaret Buchanan's
　　　　　　　　　　　　　　Wit; M.Buchanan, J.W.Montieth

Dietz,William H.--38 Monday,Martha M.--25	Aug.9,1885 At Elizabeth Monday's Wit; E.M.Coward, A.J.Jones Sr.	P.M.Frizell	J.P.
Dietz,Wm.H.-- Buchanan,A.Josea--	June 19,1872 At ---------	J.L.Buchanan	M.G.
Dietz,William T.--19 Wilson,Zelphia E.--17	Nov.12,1885 At Brunette Wilson's Wit; Sarah Sutton, Jessee Cockerham	B.F.Brown	J.P.
Dillard,D.Z.--23 Ward,Margaret S.--15	Feb.10,1878 At L.G.Ward's Wit; A.W.Gibson, M.C.Ward	J.E.McLain	J.P.
Dillard,D.Z.--35 Woods,Tabitha--25	Jan.29,1889 At Webster Ts. Wit;Joseph Cope, Eda Cope, Delosur Cope	W.Ensley	B.M.
Dillard,James--21 Rigden,Mary--18	Mar.24,1887 At Cullowhee Wit; John A.Dills, Lee Hooper	A.D.Hooper	J.P.
Dillard,John M.--25 Holland,F.J.--15	Nov.25,1886 At H.P.Holland's Wit; D.Z.Dillard, B.F.Davis	W.H.T.Dillard	J.P.
Dillard,L.M.-- Allison,Sarah Ann--	May 2,1861 At -------	Rev.Edward Gillium	M.G.
Dillard,Thadeus B.--26 Hooper,Maggie--20	June 4,1882 At J.M.Hooper's Wit; Bell Rogers, Lee Hooper	William Wilsn	J.P.
Dillard,Thomas A.--29 Fugate,Susan--21	Dec.27,1896 At Cashier Valley Wit;J.C.Allison,W.G.Allison,J.L.Zachary	T.R.Zachary	J.P.
Dillard,Thos.B.--23 Reid,H.L.--23	June 22,1892 At Sylva Town Wit; C.B.Reid, J.W.Parker He From White,Co.Ga.	A.M.Parker	J.P.
Dillard,W.H.T.-- Gipson,Julia A.--	Sept.27,1865 At ---------	J.M.Harris	Elder
Dillard,Will--29 Hooper,Dora--15	Apr.9,1891 At Hamburg Ts. Wit; T.A.Dillard,F.P.Hooper,I.H.Wilson	T.R.Zachary	J.P.
Dillard,Willaim H.T.--40 Henry,Jane--28	Mar.17,1890 At Sarah Henry's Wit; Mat Smith, J.R.Queen	S.R.Cook	J.P.
Dills,A.B.-- Brendle,C.J.--	Feb.1,1872 At -------	W.Bumgarner	J.P.
Dills,Andrew J.--21 Gibson,Mary--16	Feb.18,1894 At Dillsboro,Town Wit; S.T.Earley,T.N.Hasting, C.W.McDade	E.B.McDade	J.P.
Dills,Arrelius--20 Morgan,Florence--18	Sept.12,1900 At Phil Morgan's Wit; T.F.Morgan,Irwin Tatham,W.H.Green	A.W.Davis	B.M.
Dills,Bartlett-- Parris,Fanny--	Sept.30,1858 At ---------	E.D.Brendle	Elder

```
Dills,Bartlett--           Apr.6,1861          I.T.S.Sherrill  Elder
  Jones,Elizabeth--        At -------
Dills,Cicero L.--21        July 6,1879         E.P.Stillwell   J.P.
  Gribble,Matilda--21      At John Gribble's
                           Wit; M.L.Dills, V.Buchanan
Dills,C.M.--21             Jan.16,1898         R.R.Coward      J.P.
  Wise,Jane--18            At Thomas Hooper's
                           Wit; L.M.Stephens,J.E.Long,W.V.Hooper
Dills,C.W.--20             Dec.20,1891         J.W.Buchanan  J.P.
  Conner,Candas--18        At Dillsboro Ts.
                           Wit; M.M.Benson, J.R.Conner, A.D.Dills
Dills,David--21            Aug.31,1898         J.B.Price       J.P.
  Brown,Tina--19           At J.B.Price's
                           Wit; Russell Painter,J.J.Powell,M.B.Price
Dills,D.C.--22             Apr.18,1892         J.B.Raby        J.P.
  Nations,Bettie--20       At Barker Creek
                           Wit; Ervin Nations,C.L.Jones,Z.V.Nations
                           He From Swain,Co.N.C.
Dills,George P.--22        License Issued   Dec.15,1880
  Mathis,Darcus A.--22     NOT Returned
Dills,H.G.--20             Feb.13,1889         G.W.Spake       M.M.
  Jones,Mary A.--18        At Barker Creek
                           Wit; T.M.Frizell,J.W.Holcomb,John Gibson
                           He From Macon,Co.N.C.
Dills,Jasper A.--27        Jan.7,1886          J.B.Raby        J.P.
  Rogers,Trude--25         At J.R.Messer's
                           Wit; William Dills, J.R.Messer
Dills,John A.--24          Apr.14,1889         A.D.Hooper      J.P.
  Wilson,Laura L.--21      At Cullowhee
                           Wit; J.W.Davis, R.W.Fisher
Dills,John E.--19          Jan.25,1881         Sam H.Bryson  J.P.
  Crawford,M.C.--19        At J.K.Mills'
                           Wit; J.S.Bryson, J.B.Mills
Dills,J.R.--21             Mar.22,1896         W.E.Conner      B.M.
  Fowler,Oct.--20          At Dillsboro, N.C.
                           Wit; J.D.Conner,S.C.Franklin,Auston Dills
Dills,Marcus L.--44        July 12,1885        C.S.Buchanan  M.G.
  Dills,Lyda C.--33        At Phillip Dills'
                           Wit; Isaac Mason,Martha Mason
Dills,Marrian--            Dec.3,1865          L.G.Ward        J.P.
  Hill,Margaret--          At -------
Dills,P.L.--               Feb.25,1872         J.M.Candler     J.P.
  Sutton,L.C.--            At --------
Dills,Ramsey--20           Oct.3,1899     M.M.Bennett  M.M.E.C.S.
  Presley,Callie--18       At H.M.Bennett's Home
                           Wit; C.E.Bennett,Margaret Parker,Sam Fox
                           He From Macon,Co.N.C.
Dills,Samuel--21           Oct.18,1895         D.H.Ashe        J.P.
  Cabe,Laura T.--16        At Webster
                           Wit; A.D.Cabe,C.C.Cagle, A.C.Parris
```

```
Dills,Thomas Henson--20      Mar.28,1875        W.Ensley      J.P.
    Buchanan,Margaret--19     At J.B.Allen's
                              Wit; P.G.Green, A.W.Farmer

Dills,Thomas W.--21          Feb.10,1878        R.L.Watson    J.P.
    Long,Rhoda E.--28         At William Watson's
                              Wit; John Bryson, T.B.Coward

Dills,Wm.--                   Sept.23,1870       J.M.Candler   J.P.
    Rogers,Ann--              At ---------

Divelbiss,J.E.--28           Jan.27,1897        T.E.Wagg      M.G.
    Leatherwood,Florence May--24- At Webster
                              Wit; J.J.Gray,W.W.Rhinhart,Nathan Caward

Dowser,Solomon--40   (Col)   Dec.31,1888        J.A.Wild      J.P.
    Hooper,Harrett--19 (Col)  At Webster
                              Wit; L.C.Hall, M.J.Fisher, Hannah Hall

Dorser,H.D.--19   (Col)      Jan.17,1897        Rev.R.P.Powell  M.G.
    Coward,Melvina--16 (Col)  At Webster
                              Wit; R.G.Wilson, M.C.Fisher, S.R.Coward

Dorser,Solomon--48   (Col)   Mar.2,1892         J.C.Watkins   J.P.
    Love,Delitha--22  (Col)   At Dillsboro
                              Wit; S.R.Davis, F.G.Watkins, Lou Dorsey

Dorsey,Solomon--50   (Col)   Mar.20,1898        R.P.Powell    B.M.
    McDowell,Minta--26 (Col)  At Webster Ts.
                              Wit; C.G.Sylva,John Howell, Rev.R.P.Powell

Dowdle,James M.--23          Oct.2,1887         C.A.Bird      J.P.
    Green,Sarah L.--17        At C.A.Bird's
                              Wit; John Miller, S.E.Bird

Dryman,James--22             Nov.1,1891         W.Ensley      M.G.
    Davis,Ella--20            At Dillsboro
                              Wit; R.P.Potts, S.S.Enloe,J.Jacobs
                              He From Macon, Co.N.C.

Ducket,D.B.--19              Aug.5,1900         A.B.Thomas    B.M.
    Wells,Exie--19            At A.B.Dills'
                              Wit; T.C.Bryson, J.W.Divelbiss
                              BOTH From Buncombe,Co.N.C.

Ducket,Douglas--22           Nov.7,1886         W.P.Jones     J.P.
    Buchanan,Sarah--17        At M.M.Buchanan's
                              Wit; L.N.Allen, E.M.King
                              He From Buncombe, Co.N.C.

Ducan,Whitfield L.--21       Feb.8,1897         J.C.Wood      J.P.
    Shook,Nancy J.--19        At J.D.Hamilton's
                              Wit; W.F.Galloway,David H.Mathis,J.D.Hamil
                              He From Haywood,Co.N.C.               ton.

Duncan,William P.--21        Mar.7,1880         S.H.Bryson    J.P.
    Blanton,Martha A.--20     At J.M.Blenton's
                              Wit; R.J.Crawford, J.A.Blanton

Dunn,J.H.--30                July 10,1894       J.C.Wood      J.P.
    Shelton,Nancy--18         At Cananda Ts.
                              Wit; J.W.Shelton,R.C.Owens,W.E.Slatton
                              He From Transylvania,Co.N.C.

Earley,Sein P.--33           July 8,1885        J.J.Brooks    M.G.
    Enloe,Sarah E.--23        At J.B.Allison's
                              Wit; R.S.Cannon,Lillie Allison
```

Edmonston,Bazil B.--   Jan.21,1869   D.B.Nelson   M.G.
  Brown,Mary E.--   At --------
                                 She the Dau.of Wm.Brown
                                 He the Son of Ninean Edmonston

Edmonston,John--36   Apr.26,1884   James R.Crawford   J.P.
  Woody,Mary--34   At John Smith's
                                 Wit; D.J.Clayton, R.R.Fisher

Edmonston,Z.A.--   Nov.3,1853   Allen Fisher   J.P.
  Bryson,S.Magdaline--   At -------

Edmunds,Jacob--40   Jan.15,1897   J.R.Love   J.P.
  Woodard,Lyda--19   At Sylva Ts.
                                 Wit; Ida E.Love,Ellen Phillips,Smart Carter

Edward,A.E.--54   License Issued   June 6,1895
  Hawkins,Josie--   NOT Returned
                                 He From Haywood, Co.N.C.

EdwardsCharlie--21   License Issued   Apr.28,1898-By M.D.Edwards
  Rice,Bessie--16   At Cashier Ts.   J.P.
                                 Wit;Lena Picklesimer,Arthur A.Miller,L.E.
                                 The date of marriage is   Nicholson.
                                                          blank.

Edwards,James--   July 15,1864   Samuel Conley J.P.
  Gibbs,Margret W.--   At ---------

Edwards,M.D.--30   License Issued   Aug.27,1897
  Neeley,Alice--23   "Never married,license Returned"
                                 She from Union,Co.Ga.

Edwards,Willie I.--23   Nov.15,1897   W.C.Buchanan   J.P.
  Jones,Hattie--22   At John Jones'
                                 Wit; J.J.Wild, Candler, Geo.R.Tatham
                                 He From Graham, Co.N.C.

Ecooih,Buck--34   (Red)   Apr.9,1884   J.O.Wallace   J.P.
  Elarge,Elsie--24 (Red)   At Shoal Creek
                                 Wit; C.C.Martin, Geo.E.Sherrill

Elder,A.E.--21   Dec.28,1874   F.M.Nations   J.P.
  Moody,M.E.--15   At"In Road"
                                 Wit; J.A.Buchanan, S.M.Crawford

Elder,Ira--19   Dec.23,1898   T.C.Jones   J.P.
  Wikle,Brunettie--17   At Ham Wikle's
                                 Wit; L.R.McMehan,F.J.Wikle, J.C.Urst

Elder,John--24   Oct.10,1886   Wm.Bumgarner   J.P.
  Bradley,Sallie--19   At John Bradley's
                                 Wit; Dillard Gribble,Jas.Bradley

Elders,Berry--53   Jan.2,1899   Nathan Coward J.P.
  Morison,Vina--27   At Webster, N.C.
                                 Wit; F.H.Leatherwood,W.W.Rhinehart,J.S.Bla
                                 He From Georgia   ckwell.

Elders,David F.--21   Sept.15,1878   W.M.Bumgarner J.P.
  Jones,Sylvaia B.--16   At Lenord Jones'
                                 Wit; A.Jones, S.B.Jones

Elford,Sidney--26   July 10,1883   J.A.Deal   M.G.
  Foster,Catherine F.--23   At D.D.Davis'
                                 Wit; Carie S.Davis, D.D.Davis
                                 She From TROY, New York
                                 He From Swansea, England

Ellack,Isaac--19
Brown,Ellen--18

Nov.26,1894   N.A.Orr   M.G.
At Canada Ts.
Wit; Refus Brown,John Brown,Rutledge Alex-
                                        ander.

Elliot,Samuel B.--19
Watson,Darcus--16

May 19,1881   George W.Spake   M.M.
At Mrs. Margaret Dills'
Wit; W.W.Rhineheart,Phillip Dills

Elloit,W.T.--20
Jenkins,Mary J.--17

Aug.3,1873   John McLean   J.P.
At School House
Wit; Thomas Ward, J.M.Raby

Elmore,John T.--19
Green,Mary--19

Nov.16,1876   E.C.Ash   J.P.
At Silas Green's
Wit; D.C.Ash, L.Jones
He From Macon,Co.N.C.

English,Thomas--26
Fowler,Varina--18

Dec.26,1900   J.C.Henderson J.P.
At W.A.Fowler's
Wit; Julia Wilson,Bessie Wilson,Jas.Montie

Enloe,A.T.--
Battle,Angeline--

Oct.25,1857   L.G.Ward   J.P. th.
At --------

Enloe,Birum--21
Conley,Clmantin--18

Sept.15,1872   J.L.Buchanan   M.G.
At Wm.Conley's
Wit; -------

Enloe,B.M.--
Stanford,Margaret--

Dec.28,1854   Allen Fisher   J.P.
At --------

Enloe,Ezekiel A.--24
Wilson,Isabells--25

Sept.2,1880   J.A.Marshall   M.G.
At Thompson Wilson's
Wit; C.C.Martin, W.S.Wilson
He From Swain,Co.N.C.

Enloe,John M.--
Sherrill,Issubella--

Oct.30,1869   I.T.S.Sherrill Elder
At --------

Enloe,J.F.--39
Knight,Bettie--24

June 20,1894   R.B.Shelton   M.G.
At Dillsboro Ts.
Wit;Fred Moore, C.T.Chace, E.B.McDade

Enloe,Scoop W.--25
Steadman,Mary E.--25

June 27,1900   J.J.Gray   M.M.
At Sylva, N.C.
Wit; Walter E.Moore,Edward L.Addington,
                                     F.E.Hearn.

Enloe,Scoop--34
Montieth,Sally--24

Oct.17,1878   J.W.Bird   J.P.
At J.W.Bird's
Wit; Sopia Bird,Mary Massie

Enloe,W.A.--
Conner,M.G.--

Aug.27,1869   W.H.Conner,   M.G.
At --------

Enloe,W.H.--24
Hyatt,Elizza--29

Jan.14,1875   J.M.Bird   M.M.
At E.G.Hyatt's
Wit; J.R.Hyatt, Manley Hyatt

Enloe,Wm.--
Allison,M.A.--

Oct.6,1859   W.H.Higdon   J.P.
At -------

Ensley,Abraham L.--19
Sherrill,Laura--15

Sept.10,1885   W.A.Dills   J.P.
At William Sherrill's
Wit; Mary Montieth,Sarah Cunningham

Ensley,Coleman--22
Henson,Rebecca E.--21

Dec.20,1883   J.R.Crawford   J.P.
At Mary Henson's
Wit; J.B.Ensley, D.H.Phillips

Ensley,D.H.--26
Nicols,N.V.--18

Aug.9,1896   John V.Ensley   J.P.
At Sylva Ts.
Wit;J.M.Crawford,J.A.Martin,D.W.Ensley

Ensley,Henry--20
Painter,Belle--19

Apr.28,1890   A.M.Parker   J.P.
At Sylva Ts.
Wit; C.C.Miller,J.D.Sitton,A.C.Robison

Ensley,James--
Cogdle,Elizabeth--

Jan.22,1858   I.T.S.Sherrill   M.G.
At --------

Ensley,James E.--21
Snider,Eva--23

Jan.1,1888   A.B.Henson   J.P.
At Mary Henson's
Wit; R.P.Potts, J.A.Smith

Ensley,James R.--21
Parris,Mary A.--21

Feb.2,1876   S.H.Bryson   J.P.
At J.E.Cogdill's
Wit; J.E.Cogdill; D.J.Clayton

Ensley,John--20
Franklin,Sarah--20

Mar.6,1873   F.M.Nations   J.P.
At William Dills'
Wit; Richard Jones, Wm.Dills

Ensley,John--19
Davis,Amanda--19

June 3,1894   E.B.McDade   J.P.
At Dillsboro Ts.
Wit; C.N.Candler,J.W.Conner,G.J.Davis

Ensley,John--23
Dalton,Vallie--19

Apr.3,1898   E.B.McDade   J.P.
At John Lewis'
Wit; T.J.Bollen, D.H.Shuler
She From Macon,Co.N.C.

Ensley,John B.--20
Queen,Mollie--17

July 30,1882   Wilson Ensley   M.G.
At Wilson Ensley's
Wit; S.B.Ensley,John M.Long

Ensley,John E.--24
Henson,S.Ella--18

Aug.18,1889   A.B.Henson   B.M.
At Scotts Creek
Wit; W.A.Henson,J.R.Henson, R.R.Fisher

Ensley,Joseph--
Watson,Ruth--

Jan.17,1869   A.J.Hall   J.P.
At --------

Ensley,Joseph S.--21
Farmer,Talitha J.--21

Dec.15,1879   W.Ensley   J.P.
At A.W.Farmer's
Wit; Wm.Fisher, Nelson Ensley

Ensley,J.Henry--20
Crawford,Melvina--17

July 2,1899   J.B.Ensley   J.P.
At R.J.Crawford's Res.
Wit; J.M.Crawford,D.A.Clayton,W.R.Crawford

Ensley,J.R.--24
Moody,Sallie--18

Sept.20,1888   W.P.Jones   J.P.
At J.H.Moody's
Wit; W.J.Evans,W.D.Hill

Ensley,Pozy--25
Murdock,Mable--25

Feb.10,1899   H.D.Welch   Bap.Min.
At Mable Murdock's
Wit; Z.B.Bryson,Pearl Jones,James Joyce

Ensley,Robert E.--19
Hall,Martha H.--14

Mar.24,1878   E.D. Brendle   B.M.
At June Hall's
Wit; J.J.Ensley, John Dills

Ensley,Samuel B.--18
Long,Elizabeth L.--16

Jan.31,1875   T.M.Henson   J.P.
At H.M.Cook's
Wit; H.M.Cook, Andrew Cope

Ensley,Sherman--20
Jones,Hattie--16

Feb.25,1885   William Bumgarner   J.P.
At W.P.Jones'
Wit; Wm.Gibson, Mack Bryson

Ensley,Sims W.--22	Oct.1,1882	S.R.Cook	J.P.
Queen,Margaret H.--25	At J.S.Queen's		
	Wit; Robert Snider, T.J.Fisher		
Ensley,Thadeus C.--20	Oct.24,1875	E.D.Brendle	B.M.
Fisher,Nancy T.--16	At Rufus Fisher's		
	Wit' Rufus Fisher, Lafayett Fisher		
Ensley,William H.--22	Feb.14,1878	S.H.Bryson	J.P.
Dills,Ingabo P.--23	At J.M.Parris's		
	Wit; J.M.Parris, David Norman		
Ensley,Wilson--17	Sept.18,1879	James R.Crawford	J.P.
Cogdille,Mary E.--15	At John Cogdille's		
	Wit; T.N.Snider, R.J.Crawford		
Ensley,W.T.--	Nov.28,1871	E.D.Brendle	Elder
Aiken,Sarah E.--	At --------		
Ensley,W.W.--22	Feb.26,1891	A.B.Henson	M.G.
Bryson,M.M.--18	At Scotts Creek		
	Wit; J.B.Queen, B.C.Bryson, T.C.Bryson		
Estes,Andrew--24	June 25,1899	L.B.Queen	J.P.
McMahan,Ellie--20	At Locust Field School House		
	Wit; George Davis,Phillip Sutton,Willie Sutton		
Estis,Jessee--29	July 31,1881	Samuel H.Bryson	J.P.
Blanton,Mary L.--21	At J.W.Blanton's		
	Wit; R.Plott, Lee Queen		
Estis,John--23	Aug.12,1894	J.C.Watkins	J.P.
Cunningham,Eva--21	At Dillsboro		
	Wit; M.Sutton, J.A.Sutton, C.Watkins		
Estis,Thomas--73	Apr.12,1880	W.Ensley	M.G.
Wilks,Sarah--40	At Ensley's Farm		
	Wit;Joseph Cope, George Cope		
Estis,William L.F.--	Sept.26,1869	E.H.Cagle	J.P.
Martin,Mary Katherine--	At ---------		
Estis,William W.--19	Aug.11,1886	E.C.Ashe	J.P.
Brooks,Rhoda C.--18	At A.B.Ashe's		
	Wit; A.B.Ashe, S.M.Brooks		
Extine,George--17	Apr.10,1895	A.M.Parker	J.P.
Stanford,Ella--15	At Sylva		
	Wit; T.M.Frizzel, T.M.Green		
Extine,George--21	May 28,1899	J.R.Love	J.P.
Ashe,Dela--26	At W.I.Ashe's		
	Wit; J.H.Robinson,J.W.Robinson, W.I.Ashe		
Extine,Henry--20	Dec.1,1893	J.P.Brendle	J.P.
Billingly,Altha--21	At Webster Ts.		
	Wit; M.L.Bumgarner, L.L.Brendle,George Bumgarner		
Extine,W.T.--22	Jan.20,1895	J.R.Frizzel	J.P.
Conner,Bell--18	At Sylva		
	Wit; D.B.Franklin, M.J.Frizzel, Geo.Extine		
Evans,F.H.--29	Feb.26,1891	A.J.Long Sr.	J.P.
Bumgarner,Maggie--22	At Webster Ts.		
	Wit; J.W.Bumgarner, W.D.Frizzle		

Evans,Jerry--50　　　　　　Sept.25,1892　　　B.G.Wild　　　M.G.
　Roberson,Bethena--40　　At Webster Ts.
　　　　　　　　　　　　　　Wit; A.J.Long, J.P.Brendle, Geo.Bumgarner

Everett,Daniel--19　　　　Dec.12,1875　　　　S.H.Bryson　　J.P.
　Arrington,Laura M.--18　At Franklin Arrington's
　　　　　　　　　　　　　　Wit; A.B.Henson, Wm. Laney

Everett,James E.--23　　　Oct.19,1876　　　　W.R.Crawford J.P.
　Thompson,Louisa--18　　At S.H.Bryson's
　　　　　　　　　　　　　　Wit; S.H.Bryson, Robert Bryson

Evitt,John--27　　　　　　Nov.3,1881　　　　W.C.Carden　　M.G.
　Simson,Analine--17　　　At Meth.Church in Webster.
　　　　　　　　　　　　　　Wit; L.C.Hall, Hattie Woodfin

Fairbanks,Harry E.--30　　May 29,1889　　　Wm.Bumgarner J.P.
　Wiggins,M.A.--40　　　　At Barker Creek Ts.
　　　　　　　　　　　　　　Wit; J.C.Fisher, E.B.McDade

Farley,Emeless--22　　　　Apr.3,1873　　　　John McClain J.P.
　Allman,Sarah--20　　　　At Peyton Allman's
　　　　　　　　　　　　　　Wit; E.Jones, Luther Farley

Farley,S.James--　　　　　Oct.2,1864　　　　J.L.Buchanan J.P.
　Hall,Ingrebo C.--　　　At -------

Farley,W.H.--19　　　　　　May 2,1889　　　　A.H.Sims　　　B.M.
　Conner,Cordelia--19　　At Webster Ts.
　　　　　　　　　　　　　　Wit; Calvin Conner,J.H.House, Munroe Parris

Farley,W.H.--27　　　　　　Nov.11,1896　　　W.B.Sherrill J.P.
　Whitted,Mary--23　　　　At Qualla Ts.
　　　　　　　　　　　　　　Wit; Lee J.Hall,James B.Farmer,Varden Hippe
　　　　　　　　　　　　　　She From Haywood,Co.N.C.

Farley,W.M.--21　　　　　　Jan.10,1892　　　A.M.Parker　　J.P.
　Cogdill,L.J.--18　　　　At Sylva Town
　　　　　　　　　　　　　　Wit; Jno.Saunders,C.Allen,C.Bryson

Farley,W.T.--28　　　　　　Nov.1,1897　　　J.H.House　　　J.P.
　Nations,Margaret--28　　At Barker Creek Ts.
　　　　　　　　　　　　　　Wit; W.T.Gibson,J.L.Nations,W.E.Nations

Farmer,Ambus M.--27　　　Jan.2,1881　　　　W.Ensley　　　M.G.
　Fisher,Harriet--20　　At"In Public Road"
　　　　　　　　　　　　　　Wit; J.W.Farmer,Samuel Kelley
　　　　　　　　　　　　　　He From Haywood,Co.N.C.

Farmer,James W.--26　　　Aug.18,1886　　　W.Ensley　　　J.P.
　Fisher,M.C.--20　　　　At T.G.Fisher's
　　　　　　　　　　　　　　Wit; Wm.Allen, R.W.Fisher
　　　　　　　　　　　　　　He From Haywood,Co.N.C.

Farmer,Sylvester B.N.--　Apr.23,1871　　　J.L.Buchanan M.G.
　Sherrill,Lew L.--　　　At -------

Farmer,W.P.--20　　　　　　May 16,1892　　　W.P.McGee　　　M.G.
　Sherrill,Lou A.--17　　At Webster
　　　　　　　　　　　　　　Wit; J.B.Sherrill, Maud Cannon,Hattie Allis
　　　　　　　　　　　　　　He From Haywood,Co.N.C.　　　　　　　　　on.

Ferguson,J.D.--23　　　　Oct.28,1894　　　T.B.McCurdy　　M.G.
　Medford,Flora--18　　　At Webster
　　　　　　　　　　　　　　Wit; J.W.Davis, D.Snider, W.T.Fisher
　　　　　　　　　　　　　　He From Haywood,Co.N.C.

Ferguson,John L.--31　　Mar.24,1880　　　R.A.Owens　　　M.G.
　Conley,Emma--26　　　　At J.W.Conley's
　　　　　　　　　　　　　　Wit; D.K.Collins, J.B.Cauley

```
Fincannon,John--24          Nov.18,1897        A.B.Thomas     B.M.
   Nicholson,L.L.--16          At J.Z.Nicholson's
                               Wit; Nellie Smith,R.L.Madison,Ella Madison

Fish,William B.--22          Mar.22,1888        W.P.Jones      J.P.
   Bumgarner,Laura M.--19      At Wm.Bumgarner's
                               Wit; John Bumgarner, G.W.Pangle

Fisher,B.F.--                Mar 30,1861        S.W.Reid       J.P.
   Patterson,Nancy--           At --------

Fisher,B.F.--                Oct.21,1869        I.T.S.Sherrill Elder
   Gibbs,M.A.--                At --------

Fisher,Calhoun--21           Sept.10,1885       John T.Wike    J.P.
   Rogers,Annie--15            At J.W.Wike's
                               Wit; Ella Wike, Sarah Hooper

Fisher,Cilngman--20  (Col)   May 7,1896         T.B.Hackett    M.G.
   Lattimore,Mary--17 (Col)    At Webster's
                               Wit; B.F.Cathey, F.A.Love

Fisher,D.G.--                May 19,1865        H.M.Bennett    Elder
   Harris,E.J.--               At --------

Fisher,Howard--20            Apr.30,1893        A.M.Parker     -----
   Fisher,Maggie--18           At Sylva Town
                               Wit; D.Bryson, T.C.Bryson

Fisher,James A.--19          Jan.13,1888        J.S.Leopard    J.P.
   Leopard,Alice--15           At Thomas Leopard's
                               Wit; M.S.Brown, A.F.Bryson

Fisher,James L.--23          Feb.23,1879        W.Ensley       M.G.
   Queen,Emma--18              At S.H.Queen's
                               Wit; W.J.Fisher, J.L.Snider

Fisher,James M.--20          Sept.25,1889       W.Ensley       M.G.
   Gibson,Julia--21            At Sylva
                               Wit; R.W.Fisher,R.O.Phillips,W.A.Fisher

Fisher,John--27    (Col)     License Issued     Mar.7,1896
   Love,Florence--18 (Col)     License NOT Returned

Fisher,J.C.--35              Jan.15,1893        W.P.Jones      J.P.
   McDade,Susan--25            At Dillsboro  Ts.
                               Wit; C.M.Parks, M.A.Parks, S.R.Jones

Fisher,J.W.--                Oct.11,1866        J.W.Enloe      J.P.
   Hall,M.L.--                 At --------

Fisher,L.L.--                May 16,1861        J.B.Sherrill   J.P.
   Hyatt ,Harriett--           At --------

Fisher,Ellis--24  (Col)      Feb.12,1894        R.M.Worley     B.M.
   Bowman,Della--17 (Col)      At Dillsboro  Ts.
                               Wit; Jo.M.Love, Leudge Thomas,Wade Williams

Fisher,Robert C.--20         May 9,1875         W.H.Conner     B.M.
   Miller,Margaret A.--20      At S.H.Miller's
                               Wit; S.H.Miller, T.K.W.

Fisher,Rufus--19             Aug.6,1875         E.D.Brendle    B.M.
   Brown,Emila C.--21          At John Brown's
                               Wit; L.P.Brown, J.ohn Brown

Fisher,R.W.--27              Feb.5,1893         A.M.Parker     J.P.
   Allen,Minnie--19            At Sylva  Town
                               Wit; R.F.Allison, Thos Moneith,H.Fisher
```

Fisher,Thos.G.-- Crawford,Manervey--	Jan.11,1872 At --------	W.R.Crawford M.G.
Fisher,T.J.-- Allen,M.A.--	Jan.15,1857 At --------	E.D.Brendle B.M.
Fisher,T.J.-- Ray,C.--	Oct.26,1871 At --------	W.Ensley J.P.
Fisher,William--21 Crawford,Alice--19	Nov.29,1896 At Scotts Creek Ts. Wit; H.D.Welch,Golman Bryson,David Green	J.T.Carson J.P.
Fisher,William--28 Gunter,Nancy J.--27	Nov.21,1874 At Mary Gunter's Wit; Thomas J.Love, J.R.McKay	W.R.Crawford B.M.
Fisher,W.A.--22 Snider,Sarah J.--21	Nov.23,1883 At Margaret Snider's Wit; J.B.Queen, T.B.Farmer	W.Ensley B.M.
Fisher,William J.--20 Davis,Sarah E.--20	Dec.4,1882 At E.D.Davis' Wit; J.B.Queen, W.A.Fisher	W.Ensley B.M.
Fisher,William P.--51 Mills,Isabella--24	Aug.4,1888 At Malinda Mills' Wit; J.K.Mills, M.A.Mills	J.R.McKay J.P.
Fisher,W.L.--23 Mills,Rhoda Jane--18	Jan.22,1899 At Bud Mills' Wit; G.L.Cook, E.H.Stephens	J.R.Stephens J.P.
Forley,Emanless Hicks--22 Allman,Sarah--20	Apr.3,1873 At -------	John E.McCain J.P.
Forley,Jacob--50 (Col) Cox,Rosetta--26 (Col)	License Issued Dec.14,1897 NOT Returned He From Haywood, Co.N.C.	
Forster,John--21 Dills,Della--18	Mar.29,1891 At Sylva Ts. Wit; N.S.Phillips, Sam Rhea	A.M.Parker J.P.
Fortner,Alfred-- Brown,Bindy--	Jan.23,1862 At --------	Wm.Wilson J.P.
Fortner,D.W.--26 Long,Caroline--22	Jan.3,1897 At Canada Ts. Wit;T.J.Mathis,Jas.A.Galloway,W.T.Fortner, A.L.Beaver.	T.J.Mathis J.P.
Foster,W.A.--30 Galloway,Cora M.--20	Oct.29,1899 At Rufus Galloway's Res. Wit;W.T.Burgess,R.J.Galloway,Annie Galloway	J.C.Henderson J.P.
Four,Adolphus E.--22 Norman,Mary--21	Aug.27,1873 At Louisa Norman's Wit; G.D.Estes	Wm.Estes J.P.
Fouts,Dr.J.H.--27 Watson,L.Arlesa--18	Aug.17,1893 At Hamburg Ts. Wit; Jno.Henderson,Teliha Watson,A.Woodring He From Macon,Co.N.C.	Thomas V.Henson J.P.
Fowler,B.F.-- Jackson,Mary C.--	Mar.----1862 At ---------	E.C.Chastain J.P.

Fowler,James --22
  Robison,Maggie--17

Oct.8,1898   Thomas Queen J.P.
At Phillips Sutton's
Wit; Phillips Sutton,Lee Pangle,J.K.Keener

Fowler,J.Nelson--23
  Monteith,Otelia--22

License Issued   Aug.21,1901
NOT Returned

Fowler,S.J.--
  Jackson,Nancy A.--

Mar.----1862   E.C.Chastain J.P.
At ---------

Fox,David H.--19
  Burnell,Nellie--17

Dec.24,1876   J.P.Stuart   J.P.
At Joseph Carroll's
Wit; M.G.Watson, J.C.Evett

Fox,John--21
  Adams,Jane--17

Nov.6,1881   J.P.Stuart   J.P.
At B.Adama'
Wit; Joseph Carroll, A.J.Adams

Fox,Nelson--
  Ash,Margaret--

Dec.9,1868   H.M.Bennett M.G.
At -------

Fox,Robert--21
  Adams,Angeline--21

Nov.29,1891   John Bumgarner J.P.
At Cullowhee Ts.
Wit; B.M.Ashe, N.N.Fox, J.A.Adams

Fox,Sam--21
  Presley,Ida--20

Oct.19,1894   Lee Hooper   J.P.
At Cullowhee
Wit; A.M.Dills, Thomas Presley,John Ashe

Foy,James--23
  Hooper,Rebecca--20

Jan.29,1888   John T.Wike   J.P.
At Daniel Bryson's
Wit; Hattie Rogers, James Buchanan

Frady,Albert--
  Frady,Nancy--

June 20,1870   J.L.Buchanan M.G.
At ---------

Frady,A.B.--38
  Buchanan,Sarah--35

Jan.12,1896   J.C.Reed   J.P.
At Savannah
Wit; Lee Buchanan, William Green

Frady,Colman--31
  Mince.Ellen--23

Nov.27,1898   A.W.Davis   B.M.
At Rufus Frady's
Wit; Reuben Frady, Wm.Buchanan,Polk Laney

Frady,James--
  Gennings,Charity J.--

Jan.31,1860   Wm.Wilson   J.P.
At --------

Frady,Jason--23
  McMahan,Nancy--18

June 29,1875   J.G.Ammons   J.P.
At John Frady's
Wit;John S.Frady

Frady,John--20
  Buchanan,May--21

License Issued   Oct.19,1901
NOT Returned

Frady,J.B.--40
  Barker,Martha Elmina--35

Jan.27,1895   W.A.Sutton   J.P.
At Savannah
Wit; Marion Marker,Ann Frady, Alva Frady

Frady,J.W.--18
  Bryson,Sarah--18

License Issued   Apr.8,1886
NOT Returned

Frady,Leander--19
  Brooks,Emila--25

Jan.22,1881   J.B.Allison   J.P.
At Alfred Barker's
Wit; Alfred Barker, Martha Barker

Frady,Loranzie--19
  Buchanan,Della--20

July 27,1890   A.W.Davis   M.G.
At Savannah Ts,
Wit; R.N.Deitz, W.L.Buchanan

Frady,Lynch D.--20
Bryson,Mary--20
Dec.25,1879   E.J.Stillwell   J.P.
At E.S.Stillwell's
Wit; John Stillwell, W.M.Frizzel

Frady,Manley M.--19
Smith,Sarah--20
Dec.9,1876   D.G.Fisher   ----
At Lafayatt Frady's
Wit; J.C.Fisher, Lafayatt Frady

Frady,Marian A.--22
Buchanan,Ida--22
Aug.19,1900   J.L.Buchanan   B.M.
At "At my own house"
Wit; John A.Jones, W.A.Deitz, W.R.Frady

Frady,Napoleon B.--24
Green,Lizzie--21
Oct.7,1900   J.L.Buchanan   B.M.
At J.L.Buchanan,Green's Creek
Wit; T.F.Buchanan,F.M.Ashe, Mrs.Rufus Frady

Frady,Richard--18
Mathis,Martha J.--17
Oct.26,1878   B.H.Jones   J.P.
At "Near Agnus Bryson's"
Wit; N.P.Jones, W.B.Gribble

Frady,Rufus Solomon--21
Green,Addie--18
Apr.7,1895   J.L.Buchanan   B.M.
At Savannah
Wit; Barter Sutton, J.M.Ashe, Belle Ashe

Frady,R.M.--21
Stillwell,Florence--20
Sept.5,1891   A.W.Davis   M.G.
At Webster Ts.
Wit; J.A.Stillwell, S.Buchanan, M.Gribble

Frady,Wilburn--20
Penland,Jane--18
Dec.18,1879   J.S.Keener   J.P.
At Wm.Penland's
Wit; Mary Smith,Elizabeth Lewis

Frady,W.Riley--21
Wilson,Lillie--19
Mar.28,1900   John D.Sitton   B.M.
At "At the Jail"
Wit; W.H.Frasier,S.M.Buchanan,B.Frady

Franklin,E.David--30
Hoyle,N.Virginia--25
Oct.1,1899   J.P.Calhoun   J.P.
At W.H.F.Dillard's
Wit; W.H.F.Dillard,G.E.Bumgarner,C.T.Dillar

Franklin,George--23
Norman,Cansadia--17
Aug.19,1892   A.M.Parker   J.P.
At Webster Ts.
Wit; L.F.Franklin, Jessee Franklin

Franklin,Joseph--21
Parker,Vashti--21
Dec.31,1879   J.N.Cathey   J.P.
At W.T.Parker's
Wit; Thomas Brown, R.J.Brown

Franklin,J.A.--30
Keener,Sallie--22
Aug.23,1896   P.P.McLean   J.P.
At Qualla Ts.
Wit; J.N.Gibbs,John Thompson,Bonnie Keener
He From Swain,Co.N.C.

Franklin,S.C.--26
Bryson,Sina--20
Apr.30,1900   A.B.Smith   B.M.
At Wm.Dills' Res.
Wit; James Robeson,James Fowler,L.T.Jones

Franklin,William--18
Potts,Mary--25
Feb.21,1883   J.O.Shelley   M.G.
At R.P.Potts'
Wit; R.P.Potts,E.B.Cowan

Franks,Emerson A.--19
Webb,Lucinda--20
Nov.22,1885   J.G.Ammons   M.G.
At James Webb's
Wit; S.A.Johnson, N.H.Sassmore

Franks,Isom--30
Moose,Esie--20
Apr.30,1898   James W.Divelbliss Min.
At Phillip Moore's
Wit; Hattie Divelbliss,D.J.Knight,Martha-
                                    Knight

Franks,Jackson--21 Bryson,Lou--21	Oct.11,1888 At John A.Montieth's Wit; J.B.Young, A.S.Parris	A.B.Thomas	M.G.
Franks,James B.-- Webb,Magdolin--	This marriage date not recorded,but in book with others of the fall of 1868,-- By, J.L.Buchanan		M.G.
Franks,James Henry--19 Scott,M.E.--21	Feb.7,1895 At Savannah Wit; P.A.Wilson,N.H.Passmore,Robt.Tatham	W.C.Buchanan	J.P.
Franks,John--24 Owens,Lula--17	Nov.4,1883 At John Owens' Wit; J.M.Wilson, C.L.Woodring	A.B.Clements	M.G.
Franks,John P.--18 Passmore,Eva--20	Dec.27,1898 At Elisha Passmore's Wit;A.A.Johnson,H.G.Crisp,D.C.Higdon	D.C.Jones	J.P.
Franks,Thomas A.--21 Wilson,Martha J.--24	Jan.10,1875 At Alfred Wilson's Wit; J.C.Keener, W.A.Wilson	A.H.Wilson	J.P.
Frazeir,James-- Wadkins,Pollyan--	Nov.2,1856 At -------	N.G.Abram	J.P.
Frizel,James H.-- Buchanan,Rebecca E.--	Nov.21,1855 At --------	Peter King	J.P.
Frizzle,Samuel-- Dietz,Sabina--	Feb.26,1869 At --------	J.L.Buchanan	M.G.
Frizzle,Thomas M.-- Dills,M.M.--	Mar.17,1870 AT --------	G.W.Spake	M.M.
Frizzell,Coleman--24 Cabe,Lucy--20	Aug.15,1892 At Webster Ts. Wit; E.L.Gribble,Floyd Cabe, Jno.Cunningham	B.G.Wild	M.G.
Frizzell,James M.--23 Berry,Annie--17	Aug.6,1893 At Webster Ts. Wit; W.D.Frizzell,Steve Wood	J.A.Wild	J.P.
Frizzell,James R.--28 Baily,Martha J.--21	Mar.19,1884 At James Baily's Wit; W.Bailey, W.Bryson	B.F.Barron	J.P.
Frizzell,Jason--17 Deitz,Lillie--16	Aug.6,1893 At Savannah Ts. Wit; W.T.Deitz, J.W.Beck, A.F.Bryson	T.F.Deitz	M.G.
Frizzell,John--22 Mathas,Fannie--21	Apr.8,1898 At Sapphire Valley Wit;W.A.Parker,Monta Galloway,Ellon Parker	F.R.Huffman	J.P.
Frizzell,John E.--21 Frady,Kansas--19	Feb.5,1898 At Rufus Frady's Wit;Rufus Frady,T.N.Davis,R.L.Cunningham	A.W.Davis	Bap.Min.
Frizzell,J.T.--22 Cabe.Lizzie--17	May 12,1895 At Webster Wit; J.M.Frizzell,J.W.Frizzell,Geo.Land	J.P.Yarborough	B.M.
Frizzell,William--20 Lilley,Mary--19	Sept.20,1896 At Cullowhee Ts. Wit; Wilborn S.Frady, Margaret Lilley	D.D.Davis	J.P.
Frizzell,William D.--24 Long,Hattie E.--18	Dec.21,1875 At A.J.Long's Wit; --------	J.W.Bird	M.M.

Frizzell,W.H.--27   Oct.31,1897 J.J.Gray M.M.
 Moss,Sallie--29   At Webster Ts.
          Wit; W.W.Johnson,J.W.Terrell,D.McAdams

Freeman,John--20 (Col) Nov.3,1889 A.J.Hall J.P.
 Bryson,Candas--19 (Col) At Scotts Creek
          Wit; R.A.Nicholson, J.C.Bryson

Fugate,Frank T.--28 License Issued July 11,1901
 Dunn,Hessie--21   NOT Returned

Fulbright,John--   Dec.17,1868 J.J.Hooper J.P.
 Slatton,L.M.--   At --------

Fullbright,A.B.--21   Dec.5,1889   B.G.Wild M.G.
 York,Bettie--19   At Sylva Ts.
          Wit; M.R.Moss, J.N.York, M.V.York

Fullbright,David M.-- Apr.15,1869 James Mahoney M.G.
 Allison,Martha E.-- At --------
          He son of Eli & Elizabeth Fullbright.
          She Dau.of Agustice & Rebecca Allison.

Fullbright,Miles B.--28 Oct.30,1898 J.A.Marshall B.M.
 Hooper,Alma A.--21 At Mother's Home
          Wit; C.H.Kitchen,P.C.Henson, John Stewart

Fullbright,T.P.--22   Oct.5,1893   B.G.Wilds M.G.
 Cowan,Ellen--18   At Webster Ts.
          Wit; James Ashe, Bragg Cowan, Robt.Cowan

Fullbright,William E.--25 Nov.30,1898 R.L.Phillips J.P.
 Moffit,Alma--17   At Huston Moffit's
          Wit;F.Booth Price,W.B.Morris,J.B.Coward

Gaither,Henry--19   Dec.1,1887   John T.Wike J.P.
 Brown,Sarah--21   At Joe Brown's
          Wit; Wm.Casey,Richard Thomas

Galloway,Alfred J.--24 Jan.3,1876   John H.Mathis J.P.
 Wood,Mary A.--24   At J.H.Parker's
          Wit;John Parker, J.M.Wood

Galloway,Alfred J.--36 Mar.10,1887 C.A.Bird J.P.
 Beck,Josephine--30   At S.J.Beck's
          Wit; S.J.Beck, Samuel Beck

Galloway,Anderson E.--19 Jan.4,1880   J.N.Cathey J.P.
 Brown,Martha--21   At Tho.M.Brown's
          Wit; Edwin Akin, J.H.Mathis

Galloway,Carson C.--23 Mar.1,1877   ,.Mason ----
 Owens,Angeline--22 At Jackson Owens'
          Wit; J.C.Wood, W.W.Hooper

Galloway,Flem--21   Mar.18,1894 J.A.Marshall M.G.
 Rochester,Daisy--19 At Cashiers Valley
          Wit; Elbert Hudson, Vance Alexander

Galloway,James A.--19 May 9,1880 James N.Cathey J.P.
 Brown,Mary--18   At J.N.Cathey's
          Wit; J.M.Brown, M.Brown

Galloway,William--21 Dec.18,1879 J.N.Cathey J.P.
 Davison,Sarah--21   At D.JParker's
          Wit; A.W.Cathey, James Galloway

Garland,C.W.--36   Nov.5,1889   A.B.Thomas M.G.
 Thomas,Rachel E.--16 At Dillsboro
          Wit; J.C.Watkins,G.W.Garland,J.C.Rockwell

Garner,Elias--28 Leopard,Myra--22	Oct.11,1882 At James Leopard's Wit; John Woodring, J.W.Henderson	Elbert Watson	J.P.
Garret,Robert--21 Chastine,Martha A.--19	Dec.3,1879 At Elizabeth Chastain's Wit; -----	R.H.Stephens	J.P.
Garrett,Robert--23 Dills,Spurgeon--21	May 28,1899 At J.W.Divelbliss' Wit; Jas.Holeman, Alice Holeman	James W.Divelbliss	Min.
Gasaway,John H.--21 Paxton,Luisey--18	Aug.25,1883 At James Gasaway's Wit; Sarah J.Wood, George A.Burrell	W.H.Hooper	J.P.
Gasaway,J.N.--19 Burrell,Margaret--22	Oct.8,1889 At River Ts. Wit; D.H.Fox, J.M.Davis, S.N.Burrell	J.L.Owens	B.M.
Gates,Wm.H.--25 Gibson,Margaret--16	Sept.13,1885 At A.H.Ward's Wit; A.H.Ward, S.C.Allison	J.B.Raby	J.P.
Gattis,Davis--26 Watson,Lou--20	July 14,1900 At P.M.----- Wit; John T.Wike	R.A.Painter	J.P.
Geisler,John A.--27 Buchanan,Bessie O.--22	Dec.5,1900 At M.Buchanan's Wit; J.D.Buchanan,C.Buchanan, M.Buchanan	J.J.Gray	M.M.
George,David--20 (Red) Tekinik,Ann--20 (Red)	July 17,1874 At T.K.Welch's R.B.Smith, E.G.Hyatt	T.K.Welch	J.P.
Gibbs,Arthur--24 Knight,Fannie--18	Jan.31,1892 At Cullowhee Ts. Wit; J.B.Farmer, E.Wilson, C.E.Wilson	Lee Hooper	J.P.
Gibbs,Charley--28 Morison,Lula--21	Apr.23,1899 At Bride's Home Wit; H.H.Bryson,D.R.Bryson,L.C.Bryson	B.Norton	J.P.
Gibbs,H.F.-- ------,Elizabeth--	Feb.1,1866 At -------	John N.Harris	Elder
Gibbs,J.A.-- Keener,Sary M.--	Apr.24,1864 At --------	Wm.Hix	Min.
Gibbs,W.A.--22 Bumgarner,Callie--20	Dec.20,1891 At Barker Creek Wit; H.B.Kemlee, C.B.Allison	T.M.Frizzel	J.P.
Gibson,Americus W.--32 Ward,Lemora--22	Mar.20,1892 At Barker Creek Wit; J.E.Gibson, R.N.Gibson	T.M.Frizzel	J.P.
Gibson,Brownlow--18 Queen,Ansa B.--20	Apr.7,1878 At Mrs. Queen's Wit; John Partin, J.W.Stiles	J.W.Bird	J.P.
Gibson,James--22 Elders,Artie--21	July 3,1898 At School house Wit; C.A.Gibson, Jason Wikle, C.A.Calhoun	L.Bumgarner	J.P.
Gibson,J.A.Jr.--26 Hyde,Martha--19	Dec.3,1898 At Mrs.Zachary's Wit; Sam Zachary, James Turpin, John Cope	P.P.McLean	Min.M.E.C.S.
Gibson,J.L.-- Russell,Malvina--	Aug.15,1864 At --------	Wm.Wilson	J.P.

Gibson,Manly--21   Jan.21,1897   J.B.Raby   J.P.
  Ward,Hattie--21   At Qualla Ts.
                          Wit; James Cocherham,L.E.Suttlemyer

Gibson,Pinkney--19   Sept.3,1885   J.W.Bird   M.G.
  Wilks,Rebecca--20   At Mary Enloe's
                          Wit; E.J.Strulin, Allen Ratcliff

Gibson,Robert E.--27   Aug.19,1900   Wiilliam W.Cooper,M.M.E.C.
  Blanton,Fannie B.--21   At S.W.Cooper's
                          Wit; S.F.Cooper,H.V.Hipps,Virgie Hipps,
                                                    Hattie Cooper.

Gibson,Samuel--30   Feb.6,1873   F.N.Nations   J.P.
  Messer,Racheal--24   At David Turpin's
                          Wit; J.A.Gibson, David Turpin

Gibson,Sol--   Jan.16,1858   J.B.Sherrill J.P.
  Gibson,Frankey--   At --------

Gibson,Street--25   Feb.10,1901   Thomas L.Brown J.P.
  Jones,Mary M.--16   At T.C.Jones'
                          Wit; G.G.McMeham, J.M.Gibson

Gibson,Thomas B.--22   Jan.9,1881   W.Ensley   M.G.
  Beck,Sarah A.--22   At J.B.Gibson's
                          Wit; W.L.Gibson, Thos.C.Jones

Gibson,W.T.--38   July 12,1897   J.H.House   J.P.
  Nations,L.M.--35   At John Nation's
                          Wit; J.L.Nations,W.T.Farley,M.E.Nations

Gidney,J.B.--26   Apr.29,1890   B.G.Wild   M.G.
  Warren,Ida--23   At Webster Ts.
                          Wit; W.L.Gidney,T.H.Evans, Sallie Bumgarner

Gidney,W.L.--27   Aug.14,1889   G.W.Spake   M.M.
  Farley,Vicie--22   At Webster Ts.
                          Wit; A.J.Long, J.A.Wild, W.H.H.Hughes

Gillam,E.--   Nov.3,1861   Fletcher Smith Min.
  Portor,Sarah E.--   At -------

Gipson,J.L.--21   Oct.19,1890   T.M.Frizzel   J.P.
  Messer,Francis--18   At Qualla Ts.
                          Wit; J.H.Holcomb,Jas.Messer, H.A.Messer

Gipson,Washington--   Oct.22,1855   J.B.Sherrill J.P.
  Carter,Angeline--   At --------

Golden,David S.--   May 5,1872   B.N.Queen   M.G.
  Huffman,Fannie L.--   At -------

Golden,Harrison--22   July 22,1875   L.W.Hooper   B.M.
  Nicholson,Sarah F.--18 At George Nicholson's
                          Wit; N.J.Hooper, W.H.Hooper

Golden,James A.--19   June 1,1873   B.N.Queen   M.G.
  Huffman,Samanth--18   At Elias Huffman's
                          Wit; James Wilson, A.J.Mathis

Golden,James--25   Aug.18,1880   J.A.Marshall M.G.
  Shook,Margaret--19   At Daniel Shook's
                          Wit; M.H.Golden, J.M.Parker

Golden,John--19   June 3,1880   S.T.C.Shelton J.P.
  Shook,Laura E.--15   At Daniel Shook's
                          Wit; John Ash, W.Ash

Golden,J.B.--27   Nov.24,1889   C.L.Hooper   J.P.
  Wood,Viney--18   At River Ts.
                           Wit; R.H.Wood, J.C.Woodring, S.M.Parker

Golden,J.E.--22   Feb.13,1898   L.W.Hooper   B.M.
  Woods,Lou--16   At John Golden's
                           Wit; G.D.Sherrill, J.O.Price, A.C.Price

Golden,M.H.--48   July 31,1895   L.W.Hooper   M.G.
  Wiggins,Annie Bell--25   At Hamburg Ts.
                           Wit; W.A.Wiggins,M.E.Price,W.L.Young,
                                H.B.Woods,A.M.Henson,N.J.Parker

Golden,Sloan--51   May 7,1898   N.Coward   J.P.
  Wood,Mickey Ann--21   At W.A.Henson's
                           Wit; C.C.Cowan, W.A.Henson, T.B.Cowan

Grant,John--   Nov.5,1868   -------
  Ivens,N.C.--   At -------

Grant,Samuel F.--30   Nov.23,1898   T.D.Watson   B.M.
  Bradley,Callie--21   At Mrs.Bradley's
                           Wit; H.D.Welch,F.M.Ashe, T.F.Deitz

Gray,James J.--30   Nov.15,1897   T.E.Wagg, M.M.E.C.S.
  Buchanan,Gertrude--25   At Webster Ts.
                           Wit; J.H.Bradley,J.W.Terrell,J.W.Diverbliss

Grey,E.D.--22   (Col)   Feb.10,1897   H.W.Walace   M.G.
  McDonal,Ella--21 (Col) At Dillsboro Ts.
                           Wit; T.B.Hasket,Levi Murrey,J.M.Long,
                                Gus Leach, A.C.Bryson

Green,Adolphaus--23   Sept.9,1900   J.P.Calhoun   J.P.
  Ensley,Hannah--21   At R.R.Fisher's House
                           Wit; H.T.Wilbar,R.R.Fisher, B.M.Smith

Green,P.Bryson--28   Apr.28,1901   J.C.Reed   J.P.
  McMehan,Bertha--22   At Dillard Jones'
                           Wit; Thos.L.Brown,C.Sutton,Thad.Gunter

Green,B.N.--18   Nov.15,1884   J.B.Raby   J.P.
  Brown,Mary A.--20   At Wm.Brown's
                           Wit; S.B.Jones, A.D.Jones

Green,Charles--19   July 11,1875   J.L.Buchanan   B.M.
  West,Rebecca--19   At Mrs.Waldroup's
                           Wit; John Lewis, Thomas Brooks

Green,Clingman--22   Jan.24,1892   J.L.Buchanan   M.G.
  Buchanan,Lula--16   At Savannah Ts.
                           Wit; G.Buchanan,W.Green, P.E.Buchanan

Green,David--   Aug.1,1861   W.H.Buchanan   J.P.
  Guilliam,Elisa--   At -------

Green,David--22   Sept.8,1895   W.T.Derrick   J.P.
  Crawford,Candas--18   At Scotts Creek
                           Wit; E.E.Derrick,R.B.Smathers,S.Smathers

Green,George--22   Feb.11,1890   J.L.Buchanan   B.M.
  Ashe,Sultena--22   At Savannah Ts.
                           Wit; A.B.Ashe, J.N.Buchanan, A.Sutton

Green,G.W.--17   Dec.17,1874   E.C.Ash   J.P.
  Estes,Sarah A.--16   At G.W.Queen's
                           Wit; John Lewis, Wm.Cope

Green,Howell--20 Beasley,Delia--18	Dec.29,1895 At Savannah Ts. Wit; W.T.Green, W.F.Green, Lee Buchanan	C.S.Buchanan B.M.
Green,James--25 Jones,Sophia--17	Mar.24,1891 At Barker Creek Wit; A.E.Elders, John Davis, R.J.Justice	J.F.Brown J.P.
Green,Jeremiah-- Briggs,Elmina--	July 10,1870 At ---------	J.L.Buchanan M.G.
Green,Jeremiah A.-- Guilliam,Nancy E.--	Apr.25,1861 At ---------	Eloanat Ash J.P.
Green,Jerry Jr.--21 Buchanan,Sallie--21	Aug.10,1890 At Savannah Ts. Wit; Jas.Green, H.Buchanan, Benj.Buchanan	H.C.Cannon J.P.
Green,John--23 Ensley,Kate--19	Aug.6,1899 At John Johnson's Res. Wit; D.O.Green, B.P.Norman, W.J.Johnson	A.B.Henson B.M.
Green,John A.--53 Hooper,Maggie--19	Sept.6,1896 At Caney Fork Ts. Wit; E.M.Coward,J.B.Coward, J.F.Coward He From Knox,Tenn.	T.F.Arrington M.G.
Green,John R.--22 Morris,Pauline--21	July 30,1894 At Sylva Wit; Lela Potts, Ella Potts	A.M.Parker J.P.
Green,Joseph-- Brooks,Parthena--	Oct.13,1853 At --------	W.H.Higdon J.P.
Green,Judson--20 Brooks,Amanda--18	Sept.12,1889 At Savannah Ts. Wit; A.B.Ashe, J.N.Buchanan, Etc.	C.S.Buchanan M.G.
Green,Judson--30 Hensley,Sarah--18	June19,1898 At "In the Road" Wit; B.B.Green, J.C.Cagle, M.Sutton	C.S.Buchanan B.M.
Green,Marion-- Childers,Emiline--	Oct.12,1869 At --------	E.H.Cagle J.P.
Green,Matthew M.--21 Jones,Synthia--16	Mar.4,1888 At Barker Creek Wit; John Davis, A.Jones, R.L.Elders	J.B.Raby J.P.
Green,Meritt--22 McMahan,Aveline--18	Feb.7,1892 At Savannah Wit; A.B.Ashe, R.W.Green, G.R.Hall	J.L.Buchanan M.G.
Green,Nathen-- Barker,Charity--	Oct.7,1869 At -------	E.H.Cagle J.P.
Green,Powell--21 Moody,Lillie--16	Mar.28,1889 At Barker Creek Wit; John Davis, R.L.Elders, A.E.Elders	Wm.Bumgarner J.P.
Green,R.W.--19 Buchanan,Sallie--18	Aug.25,1892 At Savannah Wit; W.C.Cagle, B.B.Green, J.E.B.	J.L.Buchanan M.G.
Green,Thad.--27 Shook,Matilda--29	July 19,1897 At Sylva Ts. Wit; S.N.Phillips,Ellen Phillips,Laura Bro wn	J.R.Love J.P.

Gribble,E.L.--25   Feb.28,1895   A.W.Davis   B.M.
   Pangle,Martha--22   At Webster
                          Wit; R.T.Gribble, Margaret Buchanan,John -
                                                        gribble.

Gribble,F.L.--28   Oct.13,1898   W.C.Buchanan J.P.
   Stiles,Otelia--18   At Wm.Stiles'
                          Wit; W.B.Gribble,Will Buchanan,John Gribble

Gribble,John--22   Oct.30,1898   W.D.Frizzle   J.P.
   Cathey,Minnie--18   At L.L.Buchanan's
                          Wit; L.E.Gribble,L.L.Buchanan,Thos.Messer

Gribble,J.A.--26   Oct.13,1889   B.N.Queen   B.M.
   Wilson,R.Avey--24   At Hamburg Ts.
                          Wit; J.L.Owen,J.M.Wilson, E.F.Watson

Gribble,Lucius E.--23   Oct.21,1883   C.S.Buchanan M.G.
   Deitz,Jane--23   At Merv J.Deitz's
                          Wit; S.W.Allison, W.B.Gribble

Gribble,L.C.--26   Oct.3,1895   A.B.Thomas   M.G.
   Allen,Modenia L.--24   At Sylva
                          Wit; T.C.Fullbright,T.G.Allen,A.A.Allen

Gribble,L.C.--31   Apr.1,1900   J.R.Crawford J.P.
   Dills,Maggie--21   At Thomas Dills'
                          Wit; Joseph Roberson,Thad Allen,Haywood Yor

Gribble,R.T.--23   Mar.16,1884   B.F.Barron   J.P.
   Tatham,Ann--18   At T.N.Tatham's
                          Wit; D.G.Bigham, Mitchall Cabe

Gribble,William B.--29   Jan.12,1878   B.H.Jones   J.P.
   Deitz,Nancy--14   At N.Deitz's
                          Wit; N.P.Jones, W.P.Crisp

Gribble,William B.--53   Feb.12,1901   W.P.Jones   J.P.
   Tatham,Mary--56   At Mary Tatham's
                          Wit; Henderson Jones,W.T.Crisp, J.C.Jones

Grimshaw,Chrisopher--30   June 2,1880   C.B.Fugate   M.G.
   Graves,Catherine B.--20 At D.M.Wike's
                          Wit; Wm.Norton,David Wike

Grindenstaff,R.V.--27   Nov.19,1897   J.D.Sitton   J.P.
   Painter,Lillie--24   At J.D.Parker's
                          Wit; J.H.Painter,Davis Parker,A.M.Painter

Guiliam,Isaac--   July 5,1855   Wm.R.Buchanan J.P.
   Simons,Lurruner--   At --------

Guilliam,Benjamin--   Feb.26,1863   W.H.Buchanan J.P.
   Stiles,Martha--   At --------

Gunter,Coleman--21   Mar.16,1892   Coleman Gunter J.P.
   Parton,Margaret J.--18 At Barker Creek
                          Wit; J.L.McMahan & at al

Gunter,Enos--   Aug.22,1866   W.A.Enloe   J.P.
   Parris,May-   At --------

Gunter,George--30   Aug.1,1886   S.R.Cook   J.P.
   Cogdill,Talitha M.--30 At Sarah Beard's
                          Wit; A.C.Exine, John Cogdill

Gunter,G.M.--   Apr.3,1857   --------
   Turpin,Sarah--   At -------

```
Gunter,James--20              Apr.27,1879        J.B.Raby       J.P.
York,Jane--19                 At John Bradley's
                              Wit; Mary Wike,M.V.York

Gunter,James R.--19           Jan.14,1877        F.M.Nations    J.P.
Davis,Martha--19              At Alpho Davis'
                              Wit; A.L.Jones, W.L.Jones

Gunter,Marion A.--19          Dec.25,1881        J.E.McLain     J.P.
Messer,Margaret--19           At Barker Creek Church
                              Wit; W.W.Jones, L.P.Brown

Gunter,Robert--20             Nov.25,1888        W.P.J.Jones    J.P.
Gibson,Desimonia--20          At Qualla Town
                              Wit; A.D.Jones, W.T.Gibson, C.B.Davis

Gunter,Robert --22            July 3,1893        J.R.McKay      J.P.
Jones,Lizzie--15              At Scotts Creek
                              Wit; S.L.Crawford, L.B.McKay

Gunter,Samuel--22             May 16,1875        T.M.Henson     J.P.
Gunter,Darcus--20             At T.M.Henson's
                              Wit; M.E.Henson, J.Cogdill

Gunter,Thomas--21             Jan.5,1896         T.C.Brown      J.P.
Brooks,Laura Elizabeth--22- At Barker Creek
                              Wit; Samuel Jones, F.L.Fisher

Gunter,T.B.--21               Apr.13,1881        J.E.McLain     J.P.
Messer,L.J.--22               At Burt Jones'
                              Wit; H.Messer,J.T.Nations

Gunter,W.L.--24               Mar.2,1885         A.J.Hall       J.P.
Mills,Sarah J.--24            At Malinda Mills'
                              Wit; J.K.Mills,J.B.Queen

Guys,Fred--19                 Aug.16,1900        E.F.Pell       J.P.
Bryson,Alma--17               At Preston Bryson's
                              Wit; Javan Long,Riley Hooper, Harlin Mathis
                              He From Macon,Co.N.C.

Hale,E.D.--                   July 17,1855       Wm.Wilson      J.P.
Mathis,Margaret--             At ---------

Hall,Ansel J.--45             License Issued   Nov.1,1888
Jenkins,Marth--32             NOT Returned

Hall,A.J.--                   Oct.18,1863        W.R.Crawford   Elder
Ensley,Elizabeth--            At --------

Hall,Charlie K.--21           Feb.11,1883        C.S.Buchanan   M.G.
Beasley,Palestine--18         At Andrew's Hall's
                              Wit; A.M.Hall, A.B.Cabe
                              She From Macon,Co.N.C.

Hall,Colman--21               Jan.24,1897        Charles Buchanan  M.G.
Buchanan,Mary--19             At Webster  Ts.
                              Wit; Charles Buchanan,James Marshall,
                                   Hannah Hall, Annie Leatherwood.

Hall,Crayton--                Feb.--,1870        P.G.Green      M.G.
Dills,Polly--                 At --------

Hall,George--20               Jan.21,1891        J.W.Buchanan   J.P.
Buchanan,Ella--18             At Webster  Ts.
                              Wit; T.B.Cabe,R.H.Hall, J.N.Deitz
```

Hall,Henry--20
Bradley,Lora--18

Apr.18,1897 D.H.Ashe J.P.
At Savannah Ts.
Wit;A.C.Queen,E.N.Brown,J.O.Price,
       J.V.Lovdohl.

Hall,I.R.--
Buchanan,Margaret--

June 22,1861 W.H.Buchanan J.P.
At --------

Hall,Jemison--60
Cunningham,Margaret--30--

May 29,1879 E.P.Stillwell J.P.
At Margaret Cunningham's
Wit;Rufus Cowan, Cicro Cowan

Hall,J.F.--
Montieth,D.J.--

Feb.13,1862 Wilson Ensley J.P.
At --------

Hall,John B.--20
Henry,Dovy M.--18

Oct.13,1889 J.G.Ammons M.G.
At Scotts Creek
Wit; J.L.Ballard, A.J.Hall

Hall,L.C.--
Allison,M.A.--

------   Wm.Buchanan J.P.
At ----

Hall,L.D.--25
Buchanan,L.A.-18

Sept.12,1889 J.G.Ammons M.G.
At Savannah
Wit; N.Cowan, James Cowan, W.Buchanan

Hall,Lee J.--27
Farmer,Dora M.--19

Apr.20,1890 S.W.Cooper J.P.
At Qualla Ts.
Wit; Lee W.Cooper,J.J.Enloe,J.F.Enloe

Hall,M.C.--18
Green,Darcus--22

Mar.9,1874 P.G.Green B.M.
At Silas Green's
Wit; J.Hall, Josiah Green

Hall,R.F.--25
Battle,Dida--18

Nov.11,1900 Ebenezar Myers M.M.
At J.F.Battle's
Wit; Nellie Smith,Mattie Shelton,C.A.Bird

Hall,Richard H.--21
Buchanan,Belle--21

July 19,1885 C.S.Buchanan M.G.
At J.A.Buchanan's
Wit; J.C.Buchanan, A.T.Buchanan

Hall,Robert--19
Woodring,Catherine--19

Oct.24,1872 J.L.Buchanan B.M.
At A.Woodring's
Wit; -------

Hamilton,David--23
Owen,Margaret--18

Apr.3,1884 J.A.Marshall M.G.
At Tennessee Gap
Wit; A.S.Brown, Z.V.Shelton

Hamilton,Elias--34
Cathey,Bethena--23

Jan.13,1895 James A.Galloway J.P.
At Canada
Wit; H.E.Crawford,J.R.Hamilton,J.M.Massen-
          gale.

Hamilton,Wesley--21
Masengale,Guesa--18

Sept.2,1883 Levi Brown J.P.
At R.Masengale's
Wit; David Hamilton,Daniel Masengale

Hamilton,William S.--24
Tritt,Alace R.--22

Feb.22,1885 L.M.Dillard J.P.
At A.C.Tritt's
Wit; S.T.Tritt,S.A.Dillard

Hamlin,W.S.--29
Fullbright,Belle--18

Oct.6,1889 Thomas Wilson J.P.
At Hamburg Ts.
Wit; H.W.Hooper, L.L.Hooper, H.H.Hooper

Hamlin,John D.--23
Shook,Martha E.--30

Apr.16,1887 John A.Hooper J.P.
At On State Road
Wit; J.C.Moore, John Woodring

Hammit,Pleasant--45 Feb.2,1890 J.A.Galloway M.G.
 Aikins,Martha--50 At Caney Fork Ts.
         Wit; T.H.Queen,H.R.Parker,W.L.Fortner

Hampton,Grinsfield T.--20 Dec.28,1886 J.W.Bird M.G.
 Shelton,Emma J.--16 At P.Shelton's
         Wit; W.T.Shelton, W.J.Miller

Hampton,Wade--21   Nov.1,1899 A.Walker White Pres.Min.
 Profit,Mary--21   At H.F.Ray's Res.
         Wit; H.F.Ray,James McLean, A.C.Ray
         He From Graham, Co.N.C.

Hancock,Leander--21 Mar.12,1893 W.C.Norton J.P.
 Jackson,Alcey Ann--30 At Cashiers Ts.
         Wit; Press Bryson, A.C.Long, J.D.Long

Hancock,William--28 License Issued Apr.3,1888
 Pruit,Mary M.--18 NOT Returned

Hanks,David--   Apr.25,1864 J.Wilson J.P.
 Clark,Elendor--   At --------

Hanner,A.R.--22   Apr.3,1892 S.R.Cook J.P.
 Hoyle,Mary--22   At Scotts Creek
         Wit; David Linsey,H.Hooper, J.L.Ballard

Harkins,William--23 June 7,1883 G.W.Spake M.M.
 Davis,Ivey--17   At J.C.Wakins'
         Wit; Mary J.Long, J.C.Watkins

Harnett,John--64   Dec.10,1888 G.W.Hawkins J.P.
 Aiken,Caroline--53 At Caney Fork
         Wit; James Henson, J.H.Hawkins

Harrell,Robert--51   Oct.13,1899 H.D.Welch Min.
 Conner,Lillie May--22 At H.D.Welch's
         Wit; Thad Conner, Ruf.Jones, Mark Conner

Harris,J.M.--   Sept.18,1864 W.H.Conner Elder
 Wilson,Elizabeth-- At ---------

Harris,J.R.--44   June 2,1895 J.F.Brown J.P.
 Hooper,Frona--32 At Barker Creek
         Wit;N.H.Bumgarner,A.W.Bumgarner,C.B.Conner

Harris,J.W.--21   Dec.25,1895 J.B.Ensley J.P.
 Ward,Katie--22   At Sylva, N.C.
         Wit; J.P.Reid,D.L.Bryson, S.W.Ensley

Harris,L.Charles--28 June 11,1893 A.C.Queen M.G.
 Jemison,Emma--21 At Glenille, N.C.
         Wit; A.T.Hord, D.M.Presley, W.R.Owens

Harris,Lee--18   Jan.21,1894 P.P.McLean M.G.
 Bumgarner,Mary--17 At Wilmont, N.C.
         Wit; M.M.Ashe, J.L.Nation, G.W.Montieth

Harris,Shuford--21 Sept.19,1899 J.M.Thomas J.P.
 Hoxit,Dollie--18   At Eveline Hoxit's
         Wit; D.L.Queen, Estes Hoxit, Virgill Hoxit

Harris,T.H.--35   Sept.11,1898 J.B.Ensley J.P.
 Runnels,Nannie--22 At Wm.Harris'
         Wit; W.C.Reed,R.T.Reynolds,D.L.Bryson

Harris,W.M.--21   Sept.19,1889 W.M.Rhea J.P.
 Reynolds,Alley--18 At Sylva Ts.
         Wit; D.Z.Dillard, Thos.Harris, Wm.Ledford

Harrison,Calvin--24 May 16,1899 D.C.Jones J.P.
 Franks,Josephine--19 At Harrison Franks'
  Wit; W.T.Crisp, W.C.Ridley, C.C.Jones

Hasket,John B.--28 Dec.7,1893 A.W.Davis B.M.
 Buchanan,Laura--20 At Savannah Ts.
  Wit; Matt Deitz,T.C.Monteith,L.P.Buchanan

Hasket,William M.--22 Oct.4,1885 C.S.Buchanan M.G.
 Presley,Mary Ann--20 At Mary A.Presley's
  Wit; J.F.Deitz, W.P.Presley

Hawkins,E.M.--24 Feb.20,1898 J.H.Smith J.P.
 Page,Rena--19 At E.L.Watson's
  Wit; H.L.Wood, E.L.Watson, W.H.Watson

Hawkins,F.E.--26 Oct.2,1898 E.F.Pell J.P.
 Hill,Frances--17 At Bride's Mather
  Wit; J.D.Cole, Rodger Foy

Hawkins,G.W.-- Aug.27,1861 N.Coward J.P.
 Hooper,Ruth-- At --------

Hawkins,Harrison--20 Aug.19,1886 J.T.Wike J.P.
 Hooper,Nancy--23 At T.Hooper's
  Wit; John Middleton,Nathan Middleton

Hawkins,James--28 July 11,1886 G.W.Hawkins J.P.
 Moffit,Hiley L.--16 At D.H.Moffate's
  Wit; W.S.Hyatt, J.H.Hawkins

Hawkins,Samuel--21 July 3,1888 G.W.Hawkins J.P.
 Moffit,Margaret--17 At G.W.Hawkins'
  Wit; J.B.Painter,Jasie Hawkins

Hawkins,William T.--22 Oct.10,1877 C.B.Fugate J.P.
 Bradley,Mary E.--16 At Sarah Bradley's
  Wit; Ellen Coffee,Alfred Zachary

Hedden,D.L.--32 Mar.23,1890 John P.Stewart J.P.
 Parnell,Catherine--19 At Hamburg Ts.
  Wit; J.P.Stewart, W.J.Pearson, J.C.Evitt

Hedden,Elisha C.--20 License Issued July 31,1886
 Parker,Sarah C.--20 NOT Returned

Henderson,James M.--27 License Returned NOT Executed
 ------,Marcella--27 At -----

Henderson,John--19 Oct.10,1878 J.P.Stewart J.P.
 Wilson,Delphia--20 At Alex. Wilson's
  Wit; John Carroll, J.J.Moss

Henderson,John C.--40 Dec.17,1899 Ebenezer Myers,M.M.E.C.S.
 Raby,Maggie--32 At Elizabeth Raby's
  Wit; Minnie M.Bird,J.J.Gibbs,Annie Gibbs.

Henderson,John E.-- Oct.22,1861 -------
 Grimes,Mary-- At --------

Henderson,J.C.--33 Oct.30,1892 Elbert Watson J.P
 Taylor,Jane--21 At Hamburg Ts.
  Wit; J.H.Fouts, J.A.Williams

Henderson,Thomas V.--25 Mar.1,1888 John P Stewart J.P.
 Slaton,Julia--18 At J.M.Zachary's
  Wit; J.M.Zachary, Alex.Zachary

Henderson,William--19 Norton,Octava--22	Nov.2,1875 At Drucilla Norton's Wit; John Carroll, E.Hedden	J.P.Stewart	J.P.
Hendrick,William-- Green,Hanah--	Sept.7,1855 At --------	J.B.Sherrill	J.P.
Hendrix,Samuel--18 Sherrill,Loula--17	Mar.24,1895 At Qualla Town Wit; W.B.Sherrill, G.C.Sherrill,Mary Sherr- ill.	J.B.Raby	J.P.
Herren,Thomas M.--37 Cocheriham,Mary Jane--20	Mar.10,1895 At Barker Creek Wit; John Johnson,J.R.Ensley,Sam Dills He From Swain, Co. N.C.	Wm.Bumgarner	J.P.
Herren,William--26 Gibson,Emily--36	Oct.14,1886 At John Johnson, John Henson She From Swain,Co.N.C.	Wm.Bumgarner	J.P.
Herrin,Robert-- Wilkes,Nancy L.--	Oct.21,1860 At --------	L.G.Ward	J.P.
Henry,Columbus-- Dawsey,Mary--	Jan.3,1872 At -------	E.D.Brendle	Elder
Henry,Columbus--22 Stiles,Polly--21	Dec.31,1899 At A.B.Henson's Wit; T.C.Shular,J.B.Fisher, J.E.Henson	A.B.Henson	B.M.
Henry.Dallas--25 Painter,Violet--20	License Issued July 29,1899 NOT Returned		
Henry,E.Z.-- Hooper,A.E.--	Feb.23,1871 At --------	W.R.Crawford	J.P.
Henry,John-- Johnston,E.A.--	Feb.15,1864 At --------	A.Fisher	J.P.
Henry,Samuel-- Hyett,Catherine--	Sept.22,1870 At ---------	D.W.Wells	Elder
Henry,W.B.--23 Parris,M.E.--25	Feb.26,1891 At Sylva, Ts. Wit; J.A.Smith, T.N.Snider, J.E.Ensley	J.R.McKay	J.P.
Henry,Zeb Vance--22 Jones,Lena--17	Nov.2,1899 At D.C.Jones' Wit; W.P.Collins,W.T.Crisp	D.C.Jones	J.P.
Hensley,James--21 Hensley,Jane--18	Sept.11,1898 At M.W.Hensley's Wit;Dock McMahan,Killie Keener,Wm.Hensley	Thomas Queen	J.P.
Hensley,Jeremiah-- Guilliams,Ingabo--	Oct.29,1868 At --------	E.H.Cagle	J.P.
Hensley,J.B.--19 McMahan,L.--18	Mar.24,1881 At On Savannah River Wit; H.T.Bradley, T.A.McMahan	J.L.Buchanan	B.M.
Hensley,Will--20 Hensley,Norsisa--18	Nov.7,1893 At Savannah Ts. Wit; J.E.Buchanan,B.B.Queen, W.G.Brooks	J.L.Buchanan	B.M.
Henson,Alonzo--23 Coward,Nellie--20	License Issued May 18,1900 NOT Returned		
Henson,Andrew--18 Ensley,Mary A.--15	Nov.26,1878 At James Ensley's Wit; D.L.Robinson,Julius Carson	W.Ensley	J.P.

Henson,Barlett-- Fisher,Margaret--	Feb.24,1856 At --------	Allen Fisher J.P.
Henson,B.B.--35 Cooper,Maybell--25	Aug.6,1891 At Qualla Ts. Wit; J.J.Gibbs, C.A.Wallace, A.D.Raby	W.P.McGee M.M.E.C.S.
Henson,B.R.--21 Calhoun,Nancy A.--17	Feb.28,1891 At Dillsboro Wit; A.B.Henson, J.E.Ensley, D.L.Robison	W.Ensley M.G.
Henson,James--20 Buchanan,Laura B.--17	Sept.25,1883 At J.R.Buchanan's Wit; Dillard Gribble,William Crawford	R.L.Watson J.P.
Henson,James T.--24 Hawkins,Pink--18	Dec.11,1887 At G.W.Hawkins' Wit; John R.Henson, D.B.Painter	L.W.Hooper M.G.
Henson,John R.--22 Long,Hester--21	Dec.20,1885 At A.J.Long's Wit; D.H.Phillips,John Bumgarner	J.R.Crawford J.P.
Henson,Pink--27 Pierson,Fannie--21	Nov.20,1898 At McPierson's Wit;A.C.Norton,J.L.Collins,C.S.Wilson	B.Norton J.P.
Henson,Rufus--18 Crawford,Laura--20	Dec.27,1885 At J.A.Crawford's Wit; W.S.Henson, John Watson	J.R.Crawford J.P.
Henson,Samuel W.--22 Watson,Mila--16	Feb.3,1889 At Cullowhee Ts. Wit; John Henson, John Hooper	W.C.Norton J.P.
Henson,S.L.--19 Childers,Emma--16	July 25,1897 At Mounain Ts. Wit; Wm.Moss, Mabell Peek, J.M.Moss	J.J.Moss J.P.
Henson,Thomas M.--50 Cunningham,Elizabeth A.--44-	Nov.24,1878 At C.A.Bryson's Wit; C.A.Bryson,J.T.Carson	S.R.Cook J.P.
Henson,Thos.W.--28 Edwards,Mary Ann--22	Apr.30,1900 At Dillsboro Ts. Wit; J.W.Keener, W.J.Miller, J.S.Keener He From Macon, Co.N.C.	E.B.McDade J.P.
Henson,Wesley--21 Collins,Hattie A.--16	Dec.26,1886 At C.G.Wilson's Wit; Julius Collins	J.C.Wilson M.G.
Henson,William A.--19 Shular,Ellen--15	Sept.23,1883 At W.L.Shular's Wit; Thomas Shular,J.C.Shular,Wilson Crawford.	James R.Crawford J.P.
Henson,W.T.-- Snider,Mary E.--	Feb.22,1872 At --------	W.Ensley M.G.
Henson,W.T.--22 Bryson,Mollie--19	Nov.30,1890 At Cullowhee Ts. Wit; S.E.McGuire,W.A.Henson,J.C.Stewart	John Bumgarner J.P.
Higdon,Americus V.--20 Ash,Ida R.--19	Mar.9,1881 At Malinda Ash's Wit; Columbus Higdon,James Buchanan	E.P.Stillwell J.P.

Higdon,A.L.--44   Oct.10,1889   W.P.Crisp   J.P.
  Bishop,Louisa J.--33   At Cullowhee Ts.
                         Wit;D.F.Bishop, M.E.Gribble

Higdon,Columbus--26   Jan.8,1883   J.G.Ammons   M.G.
  Buchanan,Violet--25   At V.Buchanan's
                         Wit; J.W.Montieth, R.D.Cowan

Higdon,Grade--21   License Issued   Dec.13,1883
  Wobd,Pressella--18   NOT Returned

Higdon,John--26   Mar.16,1873   Sydney Ash   J.P.
  Baily,Darcus M.--26   At Lee Baily's
                         Wit; James Woodard, J.L.Baily

Higdon,Leander--30   May 14,1882   W.W.Reed   M.G.
  Higdon,Saphroney--30   At W.W.Reed's
                         Wit; E.J.Reed, C.Higdon

Higdon,William H.--26   Aug.21,1879   W.H.Buchanan J.P.
  Woodard,Harriet--22   At --------
                         Wit; ------

Hill,Charles S.--   Feb.5,1870   T.W.Jamson   J.P.
  Pearson,Larurah A.--   At -------

Hill,George--21 (Col)   Apr.11,1897   W.J.Fisher   J.P.
  Bryson,Delia--22 (Col) At Sylva Ts.
                         Wit; J.P.Reed, T.J.Fisher, W.V.Davis

Hill,R.T.--   June 26,1861   Wm.Wilson   J.P.
  Potts,Margret--   At ---------

Hill,William--41   Feb.3,1895   P.P.McLean,Elder of the
  King,Ida--25   At Qualla--   Congregational Church.
                         Wit; Geo.Montieth,J.A.Parks,Mrs Parks

Hill,W.E.--   Aug.24,1869   Thos. Wilson J.P.
  Mathis,Laura--   At --------

Hipps,C.J.--23   Aug.2,1891   J.P.Painter   M.G.
  Beck,Laura--23   At Qualla Ts.
                         Wit; S.A.Beck,W.C.Patterson,W.E.Carver

Hipps,J.R.--20   Oct.8,1893   J.W.Bird   M.G.
  Miller,Belle--18   At Qualla Ts.
                         Wit; J.E.Bird, C.T.Hipps, J.B.Farmer

Hipps,Varder--23   Oct.17,1897   J.W.Bowman M.M.E.C.S.
  Cooper,Virginia--22   At Qualla Ts.
                         Wit; J.B.Farmer,Mattie May Shelton,
                                         Wade McGaughlin.

Hix,Henry--   May 29,1859   Peter King   J.P.
  Buchanan,R.--   At --------

Hix,Sampson--22   Oct.21,1877   R.H.Stephens J.P.
  Smith,Susan--17   At A,E,Smith's
                         Wit; E.E.Chastain, J.V.Stephens
                         He From Rabun, Co.Ga.

Hoge,John--   Nov.2,1856   L.G.Ward   J.P.
  Walker,Lucinda--   At -------

Hoil,Jacob--   Dec.21,1862   Wm.Ensley   J.P.
  Blanton,Sarah An--   At --------

Hoile,A.J.--28   Feb.11,1897   John H.Smith J.P.
  Paxton,Sarrah Jane--23 At Caney Fork Ts.
                         Wit; R.J.Crawford,James C.Shular,B.L.Parker

Hoile,Joseph-- Hix,J.Elizabeth--	Aug.9,1864 At -------	A.Fisher	J.P.
Holcomb,George--22 Jones,Rachel--22	Nov.9,1894 At Cashiers Wit;M.Nicholson,T.A.Kinsey, John Hooper	John A.Hooper	J.P.
Holden,John--22 Cunningham,Coldona--17	Aug.23,1885 At Cullowhee Wit; J.H.Brendle	J.H.Weaver	M.G.
Holder,John C.--40 Long,Rebecca--53	"NOT executed on account of my being dissatisfied" Sgn. John C.Holden.		
Holden,Miles--25 Bumgarner,Sula--18	Nov.20,1887 At Lucinda Bumgarner's Wit; E,M.Bumgarner,John Holden	Elbert Watson	J.P.
Holden,Taylor--32 Taylor,Della--19	License Issued Aug.14,1901 NOT Returned		
Holden,W.F.--26 Moss,Bessie--16	License Issued Aug.29,1901 NOT Returned		
Holland,A.M.--22 Bennett,Josaphene--16	Feb.8,1885 At H.M.Bennett's Wit; --------	H.M.Bennett	M.G.
Holland,John--23 Bennett,Lena--19	Mar.29,1890 At Cullowhee Ts. Wit; S.N.Crawford, R.N.Fox, N.Fox He From Macon, Co.N.C.	James E.Moss	J.P.
Holland,J.T.--21 Jennings,Martha--20	Jan.15,1893 At Hamburg Ts. Wit;G.W.Stiwinter,J.H.Peek,J.C.Evitt He From Macon,Co.N.C.	J.M.Keener	M.G.
Holland,Sedney--25 Crawford,Sarah S.--21	Sept.30,1883 At M.Bennett's Wit; William Crawford, Sam Crawford He From Macon, Co.N.C.	R.L.Watson	J.P.
Hollifield,Fons--21 Morris,Lou--18	Feb.23,1901 At Joseph Sutton's Wit; Alice Dasey Sutton, J.M.Sutton	J.P.Calhoun	J.P.
Holt,Calvin-- Stratten,Caroline--	Oct.25,1854 At --------	Allen Fisher	J.P.
Hooper,Aaron-- Parker,Arilla-	NO date of license.		
Hooper,Aaron--27 Zachary,Mary Jane--22	Sept.9,1900 At John's Creek Wit; F.B.Price, Dillard Hooper	J.R.Stephens	J.P.
Hooper,A.H.--28 Brown,Arilla--21	Nov.25,1892 At Caney Fork Ts. Wit;J.H.Hawkins, Belle Painter	G.W.Hawkins	J.P.
Hooper,Bragg--26 Coward,Sylintha--16	Dec.25,1882 At R.H.Stephens' Wit; E.E.Chastain,T.H.Hooper	R.H.Stephens	J.P.
Hooper,C.C. Tilly,M.A.--	Aug.7,1870 At -------	Tho.Wilson	J.P.
Hooper,Charles L.--26 Wike,Annie--18	Mar.14,1878 At John Wike's Wit; J.B.Elmore, W.H.Ammons	J.S.Woodan	J.P.

Hooper,D.Y.--30 Hooper,S.M.--14	Nov.26,1893 A.C.Queen B.M. At River Ts. Wit; D.L.Hooper, J.B.Golden, O.L.Hooper	
Hooper,E.M.--22 Bryson,Lathia--18¾	Oct.30,1890 V.F.Brown J.P. At Hamburg Ts. Wit; T.N.Hammitt, S.J.Hoxit	
Hooper,E.M.--33 Woodring,Belle--23	Mar.27,1890 R.H.Stephens J.P. At River Ts. Wit; Robt. Chastain, John Woodring	
Hooper,Ephraim M.--29 Stephens,Varina--24	License Issued Dec.29,1885 NOT Returned	
Hooper,Frank Jr.--23 Watson,Bessie--18	Feb.27,1901 N.J.Fox J.P. At Speedwell School House Wit; B.B.Keener, Loronso Tilley	
Hooper,Franklin P.--18 Wilson,Julia--18	Mar.11,1875 M.M.Brown B.M. At Thomas Wilson's Wit; Thomas Wilson, A.D.Hooper	
Hooper,F.P.--46 Carroll,Sarah--26	Mar.20,1898 Elbert Watson J.P. At Elbert Watson's Wit; C.G.Wilson, W.A.Wilson	
Hooper,Gabrial D.--25 (Col) Addington,Laura--17(Col)	Dec.1,1877 G.W.Spake M.M. At Dol Addington's Wit; Franklin Addington, Frances Addington	
Hooper,George C.--22 Presly,Nellie--20	Mar.31,1901 H.M.Bennett M.M.E.C.S. At W.A.Hooper's Wit; Jero O.Hooper, B.W.Hooper	
Hooper,G.W.-- Golden,Elizor--	Aug.21,1868 B.N.Queen Elder At --------	
Hooper,Henry--18 Massey,Mary--17	Dec.4,1883 W.H.Hooper J.P. At Benj.Jenkins' Wit; Baxter Hooper, Samuel Hooper Jr.	
Hooper,Henry B.--29 Hooper,Margaret-J.--17	July 15,1883 W.H.Hooper J.P. At L.W.Hooper's Wit; J.M.Wilson, John A.Hooper	
Hooper,James--27 Moses,Gather--20	Oct.13,1899 James H.Wike J.P. At River Ts. Wit; J.W.Hooper, D.J.Moses, Hermie King	
Hooper,Jefferson R.--26 Watson,Julia--18	Sept.18,1887 C.L.Hooper J.P. At "In Public Road" Wit; Virgil Brown, R.L.Wike	
Hooper,John--30 Queen,Mary J.--18	Jan.21,1897 L.W.Hooper M.G. At River Ts. Wit; Lila Price, M.Galloway, John A.Hooper	
Hooper,John A.--24 Hooper,Rutha A.--22	Dec.3,1874 B.N.Queen B.M. At A.D.Hooper's Wit; M.B.Hooper, Mary Rogers	
Hooper,John A.--24 Wike,Mary--20	Dec.6,1885 L.W.Hooper M.G. At John Wike's Wit; Barter Hooper, Docie Hooper	
Hooper,Joseph--21 (Col) McDonald,Violet--14(Col)	Sept.25,1892 J.P.Petet M.G. At Cullowhee Ts. Wit; V.M.Bryson, Bowman Davis, G.D.Hooper	

```
Hooper,Joseph--24  (Col)      Dec.26,1895        T.B.Haskett       M.E.Min.
  Love,Sallie--18  (Col)      At Cullowhee Ts.
                              Wit; W.C.Norton, John Casey

Hooper,Joseph C.--23          Mar.6,1881         W.M.Hooper        J.P.
  Brooks,Sarah J.--17         At Van Brooks'
                              Wit; H.B.Hooper, T.M.Woodring

Hooper,J.--                   Sept.15,1866       W.Zachary         J.P.
  Brown,C.--                  At ---------

Hooper,J.H.--48               Nov.11,1894        Javan Davis       J.P.
  Brown,Susan--44             At River  Ts.
                              Wit; N.M.Long, Pauline Davis, Bessie Davis

Hooper,J.J.--                 Sept.28,1856       Wm.R.Crawford     J.P.
  Brown,Racheal--             At ---------

Hooper,J.J.--25               Feb.5,1890         J.O.Shelley       M.G.
  Enloe,Maggie M.--21         At Webster  Ts.
                              Wit; J.W.McKee, B.H.Sherrill

Hooper,J.L.--25               Oct.25,1893        Javan Davis       J.P.
  Watson,Amanda--22           At Cullowhee  Ts.
                              Wit; R.B.Shuler, J.M.Watson, R.L.Phillips

Hooper,Judson--21             Apr.1,1898         A.C.Queen         B.M.
  Wiggins,Amanda--18          At  L.W.Hooper's
                              Wit; M.H.Golden,O.L.Hooper,L.W.Hooper

Hooper,Lawrence--20           Dec.29,1898        Elbert Watson     J.P.
  Wilson,Daisy--18            At Henry Wilson's
                              Wit; W.M.Fowler, M.T.Wilson

Hooper,L.B.--41               Apr.24,1895        A.M.Parker        J.P.
  Young,Laura--18             At Webster
                              Wit; R.F.Allison, Kit Robison

Hooper,Lee--27                Apr.15,1890        B.G.Wild          M.G.
  Madison,Margueritte B.--24- At Cullowhee
                              Wit; John Clayton, L.J.Smith

Hooper,L.E.--21               Mar.28,1897        R.R.Coward        J.P.
  Stephens,Clara H.--20       At Caney Fork  Ts.
                              Wit; R.R.Coward, W.C.Brown, W.B.Morris,J.R.Step
                                                                        hen
Hooper,Mike B.--22            Nov.12,1876        R.L.Watson        J.P.
  Wilson,Minta--18            At E.D.Davis'
                              Wit; E.D.Davis, J.B.Long

Hooper,Newel J.--19           Aug.26,1875        L.W.Hooper        B.M.
  Stephens,Sabra--15          At D.M.Stephens'
                              Wit; J.C.Wood, G.W.Hawkins

Hooper,O.L.--22               May 13,1897        A.C.Queen         M.G.
  Bradley,Jane--19            At Hamburg  Ts.
                              Wit; E.L.Barrus,R.L.Hooper, A.Bumgarner

Hooper,Pinkney--23            Aug.1,1885         L.W.Hooper        M.G.
  Hawkins,Dora--21            At Jacob Woodring's
                              Wit; J.C.Woodring

Hooper,Ruthage--20            Sept.5,1889        A.C.Queen         M.G.
  Watson,Laura--18            At River  Ts.
                              Wit; John Milston,J.D.Middleton,D.E.Golden

Hooper,Samuel--               June 16,1853       Jacob Wike        J.P.
  Watson,Nancy J.--           At ---------
```

Hooper,Samuel Jr.--24 Coggins,Lizzie--20	July 28,1886 At J.A.Hooper's Wit; Frank Coggins, P.Hooper	John A.Hooper	J.P.
Hooper,Thomas-- Shelton,Mary	Oct.9,1853 At -------	L.C.Hooper	J.P.
Hooper,Thomas H.--23 Stephens,Lousena--18	July 25,1880 At --------- Wit; Bragg Hooper, Robert Chastian	R.H.Stephens	J.P.
Hooper,Thos. L.--42 Price,T.L.--22	Feb.16,1893 At River Ts. Wit; Susie Hooper, M.S.Queen, L.Price	U.F.Brown	J.P.
Hooper,Thomas W.--18 Parker,Elmina--18	Apr.11,1886 At Wm.Hooper's Wit; W.C.Long, T.H.Hooper	Bragg Hooper	J.P.
Hooper,T.W.--30 Wood,Mary J.--15	Feb.23,1894 At River Ts. Wit; C.L.Hooper, W.P.Wood, J.C.Woodring	A.J.Galloway	J.P.
Hooper,T.W.--26 Wood,Fannie--21	Nov.14,1899 At John Prince's Wit; D.L.Hooper, John C.Woodring, John Price.	A.C.Queen	B.M.
Hooper,Vance--21 Woods,Ellen--19	Sept.11,1898 At Brides Father's Wit; W.B.Morris, E.M.Coward, M.M.Wike	R.R.Coward	J.P.
Hooper,Western H.--18 Parker,Catherine--18	Sept.21,1876 At P.M.Parker's Wit; G.W.Hawkins, J.C.Wood	L.W.Hooper	M.G.
Hooper,William--26 (Col) Sanders,Millie-- (Col)	Apr.1,1894 At Cullowhee Wit; G.D.Hooper,W.R.McDaniels,S.R.Coward	J.E.Moss	J.P.
Hooper,William A.--19 Wood,Mary E.--20	Oct.14,1880 At James Wood's Wit; T.D.Wood, Thomas Hooper	S.C.Owens	M.G.
Hooper,William A.--26 Presley,Etta--23	Oct.6,1900 At Brides Father's Wit; Geo.Hooper, Robt.Presley,John Hooper	H.M.Bennett	M.M.
Hooper,William B.-- Staten,Susan--	May 8,1853 At -------	Jacob Wike	J.P.
Hooper,William M.--44 Cogdins,Mary T.--29	Oct.18,1883 At M.Church at Cashiers. Wit; Lizie Zachary, John O.Hicks	B.N.Queen	B.M.
Hooper,Wm.--20 Melton,Hester--20	Jan.26,1899 At Granvill Melton's Wit; L.E.Hooper, Vance Hooper,M.F.Henson	R.R.Coward	J.P.
Hooper,Wm.M.-- Wilson,Emmy--	Feb.18,1870 At---------	M.M.Brown	J.P.
Hooper,Wm.R.-- Hooper,M.A.--	Mar.1,1866 At -------	J.J.Hooper	J.P.
Hooper,Wm.W.-- Long,Mary A.--	Sept.11,1864 At ---------	E.D.Brendle	Elder

```
Horn,B.M.--28                  Dec.22,1889        J.M.Keener     M.G.
  Jennings,Addie L.--21        At Hamburg  Ts.
                               Wit; J.C.Evitt, J.M.Rogers, etal
                               He From Macon,Co.N.C.

Hornbuckle,George--21          Mar.23,1898        Lee J.Hall     J.P.
  Maney,Lilly Adeline--20      At Qualla  Ts.
                               Wit; V.Bradley,R.Hornbuckle,Lou Hornbuckle

Hornbuckle,Leander--20         Apr.19,1874        J.R.Long       M.M.
  Oocuma,Anna--18  (Red)       At Echata
                               Wit; ------

Hornbuckle,Lewis--27           Nov.24,1885        JohnJackson    M.G.
  Oocumimer,Caroline--26 (Red) At Qualla
                               Wit; Jessee Reed, Wm.Locust

Hornbuckle,Rans--25  (Red)     Feb.7,1895         A.H.Sims       B.M.
  Tucker,Louise--19 (Red)      At Qualla
                               Wit; E.G.Hyatt,R.L.Hyatt, Mandy Gibson

Hornbuckle,William--21         Mar.6,1890         Suate Owle (Ind) M.G.
  Maney ,Margaret T.--18       At Qualla
                               Wit; Going Snake,M.Maney,J.Maney

Houston,James T.--23           Nov.29,1883        J.P.Stuart     J.P.
  Potts,May--18                At Allen Potts'
                               Wit; J.R.Owens, M.C.Pierson

Howel,Christenberry--19(Col)   Oct.26,1879        Mitchall Worley
  Powell,Sarah--18   (Col)     At Clark Turk's
                               Wit; V.M.Bryson, Joe M.Love

Howell,Henry--66  (Col)        May 17,1899        N.P.Powell     Min.
  Gather,Adeline--38  (Col)    At Dillsboro,  Ts.
                               Wit; Major Wells,Martin Hyatt

Howell,Kansas--21              License Issued,Aug.21,1886-NOT Returned
  Turpin,Tennessee--20         At David Turpin's
                               Wit; James Messer,J.E.Turpin
                               He From Haywood, Co.N.C.

Howell,Leander--21  (Col)      Dec.25,1894        A.W.Jacobs,M.E.C.S.Min.
  Dorsey,Laura--19 (Col)       At Webster
                               Wit; R.E.Love, W.H.Williams,L.H.Alston

Howell,R.C.--21                July 14,1897       R.C.Powell     B.M.
  Moody,Laura A.--24           At Qualla
                               Wit; C.A.Wallace,W.P.Shelton,E.G.Hyatt
                               He From Haywood,Co.N.C.

Howell,Thomas--21  (Col)       May 16,1880        J.R.Crawford   J.P.
  Love,Chloe E.--20 (Col)      At Thomas Love's
                               Wit; James Love,L.F.Fisher

Hoxet,G.W.--22                 Dec.18,1890        John P.Stewart J.P.
  Pierson,Connie--18           At Hamburg  Ts.
                               Wit; P.N.Price, W.S.Person,W.S.Brown

Hoxit,James--20                June 5,1873        J.A.Galloway J.P.
  Owens,Evaline--17            At Jackson Owens'
                               Wit; J.M.Owens, C.C.Galloway

Hoxit,J.C.--18                 Jan.17,1895        Javan Davis    J.P.
  Watson,R.C.--13              At Cullowhee
                               Wit; A.J.Watson,P.C.Watson, S.D.Hoxit
```

Hoxit,Stonewell--28 Smith,Abersine--25	Dec.20,1891 At Hamburg Ts. Wit; B.F.H.Owens, C.P.Hoxit	J.P.Stewart J.P.
Hoxit,Thomas--21 Wilson,Katherine--18	Dec.27,1883 At James Wilson's Wit; Emma Walker, J.B.Hooper	Wm.M.Hooper J.P.
Hoxit,Walter--22 Case,Alace--23	Feb.23,1885 At C.Dean's Wit; C.B.Zachary,George Hoxit	J.L.Wike J.P.
Hoxit,William--25 Bryson,Jane--25	Jan.22,1885 At Joe A.Woodring's Wit; J.H.Shelton, Reed White	W.H.Hooper J.P.
Hoxit,William I.--23 Sorrells,Louisa--18	License Issued Sept.28,1883 NOT Returned	
Hoyle,Asbury--21 Shular,Tine--21	July 21,1889 At Scotts Creek Wit; J.L.Ballard, J.B.Hall, W.B.Henry	A.J.Hall J.P.
Hoyle,George--34 Gunter,Elmina--19	May 14,1873 At Joseph Hoyle's Wit; G.D.Estis	Wm.Estis J.P.
Hoyle,G.W.--19 Lindsey,Lillie G.--17	May 22,1892 At Scotts Creek Wit; W.G.Snider,J.L.Ballard,J.L.Moore	J.R.McKay J.P.
Hoyle,Martin--21 Blanton,Alice--19	Mar.7,1888 At W.R.Blanton's Wit; Joseph Hoyle,J.M.Crawford He From Swain,Co.N.C.	A.J.Hall J.P.
Hoyle,Wesley--20 Henry,Mary J.--20	Oct.24,1897 At A.E.Henry's Wit; W.D.Henry,R.V.Norman, A.C.Calhoun	J.P.Calhoun J.P.
Huffman,G.M.-- Watson,Sallie--26	July 1,1892 At Canada Ts. Wit; F.R.Huffman,John Shelton,T.M.Mathis	M.C.Warlick M.G.
Huffman,H.M.--19 Alexander,Sarah--19	Sept.1,1881 At T.J.Bryson's Wit; A.S.Queen,R.C.Bryson	T.J.Bryson J.P.
Huffman,John--20 Parker,Cora--18	June 30,1884 At Nancy Parker's Wit; W.T.Coward,W.H.Price	J.B.Coward J.P.
Huffman,Ramsour-- Seret,Clarantine--	Oct.4,1855 At -------	J.Wike J.P.
Huffman,Riley--20 Mathis,Melvina--20	Sept.5,1890 At Canada Ts. Wit; W.S.F.Wood, R.H.Brown, J.C.Moore	M.C.Warlick M.G.
Hughes,Benjamin H.--26 Tatham,Callie--20	Mar.4,1900 At James Tatham's Wit; L.D.Hall,C.C.Higdon,Burton Buchanan	Thadius F.Deitz B.M.
Hughes,C.M.--23 Snider,Carrie--19	June 23,1898 At G.W.Moody's Wit;Lena Moody,Manley Moody, George Moody	G.W.Moody J.P.

Hughes,Horace--22 Cooper,Mary--24	Jan.11,1900 At "At home of Berry Cooper" Wit; C.E.Miller,James Cocherham,B.A.Ayers	J.B.Raby	J.P.
Hughes,H.B.--24 Phillips,Betty Jane--25	Mar.18,1900 At D.H.Phillips' Home Wit; Nannie Smith, Claralus Norton, Bessie Davis	W.L.Henson	J.P.
Hughes,J.C.--25 Rochester,Pennie--14	Dec.16,1894 At Cashier Wit;J.W.Rochester,H.E.Childers,W.H.Fowler	J.A.Mashburn	B.M.
Hughes,Talor-- Conner,Elizabeth--	Feb.11,1869 At --------	W.H.Conner	M.G.
Hughes,William H.--32 Rogers,Polly P.--19	July 28,1878 At Hugh Roger's Wit; Sarah Davis,David Davis	J.S.Woodard	
Humphrey,John--21 Wood,Susan--19	May 18,1898 At J.M.Humphrey's Wit; J.F.Shelton, J.B.Shelton She From Transyvania,Co.N.C.	J.C.Wood	J.P.
Humphrey,J.M.--17 Mathis,Rachel--21	Sept.22,1889 At Canada Ts. Wit; E.J.Huffman,J.M.More, D.H.Warlick	W.C.Warlick	M.G.
Humphrey,William David--19 Cabe,Margaret J.E.--18	July 15,1891 At Cullowhee Ts. Witl Sophia Brown,Martha & Jane Hamilton	H.M.Bennett	M.G.
Humphrey,W.E.--26 Reece,Alcester--15	Apr.2,1897 At Canada Ts. Wit; J.M.Thomas,T.S.Farther,T.C.Cook	T.J.Mathis	J.P.
Hunnicutt,Lee--24 Montieth,Mary A.--25	Aug.11,1881 At Mary A.Queen's Wit; B.Harris,C.C.Reed	J.L.Buchanan	B.M.
Hunnicutt,Thos,N.--24 Monday,Bettie--24	Nov.1,1884 At J.W.Holland's Wit; Jerry Evans,M.J.Hunnicutt	Thos.J.Love	J.P.
Hunnicutt,Thomas--36 William,Saphronia--21	Aug.26,1896 At Webster Ts. Wit; D.H.Montieth,M.J.Frizzle,J.A.Williams	J.R.Frizzle	J.P.
Hunter,John N.--32 Brown,Manerva--18	Dec.3,1872 At Phiniah Brown's Wit; B.Edmonston, J.R.Bigham	B.N.Queen	B.M.
Hunter,J.N.--53 Edmonston,Emily--53	Dec.31,1893 At Caney Fork Wit; Miles Parker, Avilla Hooper,Clora Par- ker.	Javan Davis	J.P.
Hurst,John--20 Green,Laura--19	Mar.21,1877 At Joseph Green's Wit; D.H.Ash, John Lewis	E.C.Ash	J.P.
Hurst,J.G.--19 Franks,Annie--17	Aug.14,1894 At Savannah Wit; W.C.Ridley,J.W.Roberts,G.W.Franks	W.C.Buchanan	J.P.
Huskins,Williams--19 Parker,Elizabeth--20	License Issued Nov.9,1876 NOT Returned		

Hyatt Andrew-- Murry,Nancy--	Spet.4,1872 At --------	H.M.Bennett	M.G.
Hyatt,Love--24 Herske,Haseltine--22	Dec.18,1884 At Reueuies Bryson's Wit; J.W.Mathis, J.R.Bryson	J.G.Ammons	B.M.
Hyatt,J.G.--22 (Col) Murry,(Casey) Della--17	Apr.25,1891 (Col) At Sylva Ts. Wit; P.F.Hyatt, et al	A.M.Parker	J.P.
Hyatt,O.Willis--23 Sherrill,May L.--19	License Issued Aug.25,1900 NOT Returned		
Hyatt,R.L.--23 Cooper,Dora--20	July 21,1889 At Qualla Town Wit; W.H.Cooper,A.M.Bennett, J.U.Gibbs	P.P.McLean	M.G.
Hyatt,------ --26 Allison,Mary--20	Feb.24,1897 At Barker Creek Ts. Wit; J.E.Tedwell, H.G.Crisp He From Swain,Co.N.C.	J.J.Gray	M.G.
Hyde,W.P.--31 Battle,Sarah C.--30	Nov.3,1875 At Qualla Town Wit; E.G.Hyatt, B.Price	T.K.Welch	J.P.
Ina-ka-la-ku--19 (Red) Ol-nih--18 (Red)	July 18,1874 At T.K.Welch's Wit J.Blythe, Elizabeth Blythe	T.K.Welch	J.P.
Inman,Joseph P.--24 Franklin,Susan--18	Dec.28,1875 At David Franklin's Wit; ----------	E.D.Brendle	B.M.
Jackson,James T.--26 Hooper,Varina--20	Feb.3,1880 At W.B.Bryson's Wit; D.T.Slaton, W.A.Fowler	W.H.Hooper	J.P.
Jackson,John--26 Shelton,Sarah--19	Apr.23,1874 At "In the road" Wit; A.Brown, Samuel Jackson	J.A.Moore	J.P.
Jackson,Samuel--28 Nicholson,A.A.--21	July 24,1879 At Meeting House Wit; H.Lusk, J.T.Watson	J.H.Alley	
Jackson,Thomas--32 Wike,Amanda--30	License Issued Nov.6,1888 NOT Returned		
Jacobs,P.S.--20 Tritt,Florence--14	Dec.29,1889 At Cashier Ts. Wit; W.B.Wike, Carl Wike	T.R.Zachary	J.P.
Jacob,Samuel--23 Messer,Cora Belle--17	July 4,1895 At Dillsboro Wit; R.F.Allison, M.E.Jarrett,T.M.Messer	E.B.McDade	J.P.
Jacob,Sam A.--24 Gibson,Emma--19	July 9,1898 At Dillsboro Wit; J.H.Lewis, --- Lewis	B.McDade	J.P.
Jamison,T.W.-- Williams,Catherine--	July 29,1857 At ---------	Wm.Wilson	J.P.
Jamison,William Montraville--22- Fox,Sallie--18	Nov.23,1899 At D.H.Fox's Wit; J.D.Mitchel,R.A.Passmore,R.A.Painter	R.A.Painter	J.P.

```
Jemison,Louren--21        Mar.18,1883        J.P.Stuart    J.P.
   Moss,M.J.--18          At Wm.Moss's
                          Wit; J.C.Henderson,J.M.Peek

Jenkins,Abram--20         May 27,1874        J.C.Watkins   J.P.
   Cope,Sarah J.--14      At John Cope's
                          Wit; James M.Candler

Jenkins,D.W.--21          July 30,1880       E.P.Stillwell J.P.
   Gribble,Martha--23     At John Gribble's
                          Wit; James Cowan,Dillard Gribble

Jenkins,John D.--         Nov.8,1868         A.A.Justice   Cleg.
   Cline,Nancy--          At -------

Jenkins,Thomas--22        Apr.23,1883        G.W.Spake     M.M.
   Burnett,Jane--20       At Thos. Burnett's
                          Wit; Thos.Burnett,Polly Burnett
                          He From Swain,Co.N.C.

Jenkins,W.G.--            May 13,1866        W.R.Grant     J.P.
   Millsap,J.A.--         At --------

Johnson,A.A.--30          License Issued  Apr.7,1890
   Buchanan,Della--19     NOT Executed

Johnnson,Daniel--58       Apr.30,1884        H.M.Bennett   M.G.
   Kirkindall,Mary E.--40 At Woodring's House
                          Wit; Mrs.R.N.Long,Mrs.Maggie Bryson

Johnson,Joseph--45        Nov.7,1898         D.C.Jones     J.P.
   Bishop,Jennet--20      At Hence Bishop's
                          Wit; R.B.Stiles,D.C.Higdon,A.L.Higdon

Johnson,Steve--           Apr.3,1871         W.H.Conner    M.G.
   Junie -- (Red)         At -------

Johnston,Alfred A.--29    Jan.17,1886        B.H.Jones     J.P.
   Stiles,Sarah--20       At Wm.Stiles'
                          Wit;W.T.Crisp, W.T.Stile

Johnston,A.W.--           July --1862        Wm.Wilson     J.P.
   Phillips,Rebecca--     At --------

Johnston,Jason--          Jan.--1863         N.S.Abram     J.P.
   Wiggins,Matilda--      At -------

Johnston,Joel A.--21      Aug.21,1887        A.H.Sims      M.G.
   Mills,Eliza M.--16     At B.N.Watson's
                          Wit;W.H.Queen,B.N.Watson

Johnston,Joseph--22 (Col) Sept.2,1888        J.A.Wilde     J.P.
   Freeman,Belle--18 (Col) At Webster
                          Wit; A.J.Long, G.W.McConnell

Johnston,Samuel--24 (Col) Aug.24,1895        Jas.M.Bristol B.M.
   Hancock,Margaret--20 (Col) At Cashiers
                          Wit; Pres Bryson, J.H.Price,B.A.S.Collins

Jones,Andrew--21          Mar.13,1873        F.M.Nations   J.P.
   Killpatric,Sarah--18   At Washington Green's
                          Wit; M.R.Buchanan,W.W.Jones

Jones,Andrew D.--20       Jan.9,1881         W.Ensley      M.G.
   Gibson,Palestine M.--22 At J.B.Gibson's
                          Wit; W.L.Gibson, Thos. C.Jones
```

Jones,A.D.--28   Jan.8,1889   E.C.Ashe   J.P.
  Buchanan,Laura E.--18   At Savannah Ts.
                         Wit; R.L.Elders, J.F.Gibson, J.W.Green

Jones,A.L.--22   Jan.26,1880   Wm.Bumgarner J.P.
  Gibson,Nancy L.--21   At Finley Gibson's
                         Wit;J.F.Gibson,Finley Gibson

Jones,Charles L.--20   Aug.6,1882   J.E.McLain   J.P.
  Nations,Harriet--18   At F.M.Nations'
                         Wit; J.T.Nations, Sam Jones

Jones,Charles R.--25   June 17,1875   S,H.Bryson   J.P.
  Crawford,Cynthia--19   At James R.Crawford's
                         Wit; C.A.Jones, S.C.Bryson

Jones,Charles R.--38   Jan.19,1888   A.B.Henson   M.G.
  Smathers,Martha--31   At Alfred Smathers'
                         Wit; T.L.Snider, J.R.Davis

Jones,Coleman--21   Dec.8,1881   D.H.Ash   J.P.
  Woodard,Theodacia--19   At J.T.Woodard's
                         Wit; O.M.Allison, C.A.Webb

Jones,Henderson--23   May 4,1899   D.C.Jones   J.P.
  Buchanan,Dora--18   At R.G.Buchanan's
                         Wit; Coll Sutton, N.G.Crisp,John C.Jones

Jones,James--20   Mar.4,1897   J.B.Raby   J.P.
  Roawland,Lizzie--21   At Barker Creek Ts.
                         Wit; L.M.Jones, A.I.Roawland,J.F.Jones

Jones,Jessee--43   Jan.14,1875   E.C.Ash   J.P.
  Barron,Lousia--22   At Wilson Barron's
                         Wit; James Woodard, W.B.Gribble

Jones,Jessee--45   Sept.21,1876   E.C.Ash   J.P.
  Buchanan,Eva--21   At W.H.Buchanan's
                         Wit; James Collins, Joshus Cole

Jones,John--   Oct.27,1859   E.D.Brendle   Elder
  Dillard,Rutha--   At --------

Jones,John C.--20   Jan.6,1901   JohnSutton   J.P.
  Buchanan,Tina--18   At Savannah Ts.
                         Wit; R.O.Brown, W.H.Jones, Robt.Tatham

Jones,John H.--   Dec.19,1871   J.M.Candler   J.P.
  Cabe,S.T.--   At --------

Jones,Jno.L.--22   Sept.17,1893   W.E.Bryson   J.P.
  Brooks,Donie--17   At Scotts Creek
                         Wit; W.A.McKay, T.C.Clayton,R.H.McKay

Jones,Joseph--   July 1,1869   H.M.Bennett   M.G.
  Carson,Rhody--   At --------

Jones,Julius P.--21   Oct.22,1884   S.H.Bryson   J.P.
  Sanford,Polly--21   At Schulhoffer Store
                         Wit; Wm.S.Snider, R.C.Smathers
                         He From Haywood,Co.N.C.

Jones,Lucius B.--16   May 21,1874   M.W.Bryson   J.P.
  Garrison,Sarah--16   At A.Cope's
                         Wit; ------

Jones,L.J.--25   License Issued   June 9,1899
  Gibson,Pearl--18   NOT Returned

Jones,Lee--22   Jan.17,1895 JohnW.Terry J.P.
 Waycaster,Alice--18 At Scotts Creek
          Wit; C.C.Boone,Y.W.Reed, J.M.Terry

Jones,Regene--20   Aug.22,1887 C.S.Buchanan M.G.
 Green,Lavada--20   At Lee Green's
          Wit; R.L.Elders, A.D.Jones

Jones,Samuel--21   Feb.22,1883 B.Hawkins J.P.
 Watson,Rhoda C.--21 At George Watson's
          Wit; D.Parker,Robert Sitton

Jones Samuel--20   License Issued Oct.10,1888
 Montieth,Talitha C.--20 NOT Returned

Jones,Samuel A.--23   Aug.31,1883 W.P.Jones J.P.
 Parris,Rhoda--24   At A.J.Parris'
          Wit; F.L.Parris,A.C.Parris

Jones,Samuel C.--20   Feb.13,1876 S.H.Bryson J.P.
 Crawford,Manervia E.--15 At Martha Crawford's
          Wit; C.A.Bryson, Wm.Laney

Jones,Stanbury--20   May 3.1877 G.W.Spake M.M.
 Brown,Mary E.--18   At"In.Register Office"
          Wit; A.J.Long, T.L.Brown

Jones,Stanford B.--26 Feb.18,1875 E.D.Brendle M.G.
 Dills,Elamona--20   At P.L.Dills'
          Wit; Wm.Jones, P.Dills

Jones,Thomas--20   Mar.16,1882 J.E.Martin J.P.
 Moody,Dovie O.--13   At J.H.Moody's
          Wit; Lebo Parris, S.W.Cooper

Jones,Thomas--28   Dec.28,1890 J.F.Brown J.P.
 Gunter,Josephine--28 At Barker Creek
          Wit; W.W.Jones,R.N.Fisher,J.H.Bradley

Jones,Thomas--33   Apr.14,1895 Thomas Queen J.P.
 Sutton,Martha C.--32 At Dillsboro
          Wit; R.L.Pangle, H.A.Messer,Phillip Sutton

Jones,Welse--22   Feb.21,1875 J.L.Buchanan B.M.
 Woodard,Stacie--21   At William Woodard's
          Wit; James Woodard, E.Baily

Jones,William--19   Dec.25,1873 M.W.Bryson J.P.
 Jenkins,Margaret--19 At George Cope's
          Wit; -------

Jones,William--21   July 26,1896 J.B.Raby J.P.
 Bumgarner,Iola--18   At Barker Creek Ts.
          Wit; E.G.Watkins,L.M.Ashe, Sam Bradley

Jones,William--28   License Issued July 4,1901
 Jones,Guta--18   NOT Returned

Jones,William W.--36   Dec.21,1879 E.D.Brendle B.M.
 Brown,Rebecca E.--36 At John Brown's
          Wir;L.PBrown, J.F.Brown

Jones,Wm.R.--   Dec.9,1855 Peter King J.P.
 Wilson,Mary J.--   At -------

Jorden,Coldwell--25   Dec.29,1885 J.A.Wild J.P.
 Roberts,Mary J.--25   At J.A.Wild's
          Wit; Jason Messer, Annie C.Leatherwood
          She From Haywood,Co.N.C.

Justice,J.W.--30
  Childers,Sudie--18

License Issued   Oct.31,1888
NOT Returned

Justice,Randolph--19
  Jones,Mary C.--18

Mar.8,1883   L.P.Brown   J.P.
At Leonard Jones's
Wit; A.D.Jones, John Davis

Justice,Samuel--24
  Hyatt,Laura--25

June 20,1896   A.H.Sims   B.M.
At Qualla Ts.
Wit; E.G.Hyatt, J.L.Walker, C.H.Moody

Keener,Elbert S.--
  Battles,Mary--

Jan.21,1869   J.Mahoney   Cleg.
At --------

Keener,J.B.--22
  Gibbs,Verlinda--19

Sept.30,1872   H.F.Gibbs   J.P.
At H.F.Gibbs'
Wit; Sarah Parks

Keener,J.S.--
  Hicks,Francis C.--

Sept.3,1865   Wm.H.Howell   Elder
At --------

Keener,Joseph W.--22
  Wilson,Ida--14

Aug.23,1888   B.G.Wilds   M.G.
At Hix Wilson's
Wit; T.B.Allison, G.W.McConnell

Keener,Robt.--27
  Cooper,Estella--24

Nov.27,1895   E.H.Hampton   M.G.
At Qualla
Wit; A,H,Hayes,S.W.Cooper,Mattie May Shelt
                                             on.

Keener,Thomas J.--33
  Montieth,Mary A.--25

Oct.23,1881   J.L.Owens   M.G.
At B.Montieth's
Wit; Zeb V.Watson,William Maontieth

Keener,Thomas W.--26
  Parks,Sarah J.--20

Feb.18,1875   H.F.Gibbs   J.P.
At H.F.Gibbs'
Wit; S.S.Enloe,John Parks

Keener,Thomas W.--37
  Holden,Martha--28

Mar.25,1886   J.O.Wallace   J.P.
At John Holden's
Wit; C.C.Boone

Keller,W.H.--36
  Bryson,M.L.--26

Jan.29,1884   William Bumgarner J.P.
At Wm.Bumgarner's
Wit; Monroe Bumgarner Joseph Bumgarner

Kelsay,Robin C.--22
  Sutton,Jane--21

License Issued   Mar.17,1879
NOT Returned
He From Tennessee

Kerr,Jessee--26
  Gibbs,Mary--22

Dec.7,1872   H.F.Gibbs   J.P.
At H.F.Gibbs'
Wit; ------

Kerr,Jessee--26
  Gipson,Mary--20

Dec.20,1873   H.F.Gibbs   J.P.
At --------

Kever,J.K.--25
  Queen,Allie May--17

Dec.21,1898   A.B.Smith   B.M.
At Thos.Queen's
Wit; Henry Lawing,W.A.Sutton,J.M.Forrster

Killpaterick,Luther--29
  Owen,Martha--17

Dec.25,1898   J.H.Owen   Bap.Min.
At --------
Wit;M.W.Mason,Dillard Owen,M.M.Galloway

Kimsey,James--27
  Carver,Margaret--20

July 25,1897   G.W.Moody   J.P.
At Qualla
Wit; S.T.Moody,S.J.Beck,E.S.Keener
He From Swain,Co.N.C.

King,Arthur--22
  Montieth,Callie--22

June 11,1899   J.R.Crawford J.P.
At D.G.Bryson's
Wit; T.M.Frizzell,D.G.Bryson,P.W.Michell

King,Claud--19
  Cunningham,Sallie--19

May 26,1900   W.E.Conner M.G.
At Cling Cunningham's
Wit; D.L.Bryson,Tho.G.Allen, Howard Fisher

King,C.B.--21
  Hill,R.I.--19

May 5,1895   Wm.Bumgarner J.P.
At Barker Creek
Wit;C.A.Bumgarner,Gordon Bumgarner,
                     Polly Fisher.

King,W.A.--30
  Gibbs,E.--19

Dec.7,1884   J.O.King   J.P.
At H.F.Gibbs'
Wit; S.S.Enloe,W.M.Conley

Kinsland,L.H.--
  Hall,M.A.--

Nov.1,1866   J.L.Buchanan J.P.
At -------

Kitchen,C.H.--25
  Hooper,Laura--20

Aug.22,1894   B.N.Queen   B.M.
At Hamburg
Wit; J.H.Mathis, M.H.Wilke, W.A.Wiggins
He From Transylvinia,Co.

Knight,William--23
  Pierson,Ettie--16

Dec.24,1899   B.Norton   J.P.
At Rodrick Pierson's
Wit; E.M.Moss, J.B.Wilson, Pearl Zachary

Lance,J.C.--
  Cooper,T.J.--

Oct.22,1866   W.H.Hicks   J.P.
At --------

Landers,John--23
  Estes,Sarrah--16

Dec.15,1895   W.C.Buchanan J.P.
At Savannah
Wit; W.T.Stiles, J.S.Buchanan,J.A.Wilks

Landon,W.G.--22
  Wilson,Martha A.--21

Oct.12,1890   J.T.Woodard J.P.
At Savannah Ts.
Wit; Noah Wilson, N.Browning, W.Wilson

Laney,William--22
  Morrow,Nicy--26

Jan.31,1878   W.R.Crawford J.P.
At G.W.Crawford's
Wit; J.T.Carson, E.W.Crawford

Lang,A.J.--
  Ensley,Melvina--

Aug.20,1865   Wm.Wilson
At --------

Lany,Polk--20
  Ensley,Mellie--19

July 22,1894   R.L.Hyatt   J.P.
At Qualla
Wit; J.L.Cooper, C.C.Cooper, L.M.Hyatt

Lattimer,William--48 (Col)
  Cox,Amanda--28 (Col)

Sept.30,1897   R.P.Powell M.G.
At Webster Ts.
Wit; Henry Alston,R.G.Wilson,M.S.Casey

Law,Gideon--
  Miller,Naomi--

Oct.15,1855   N.G.Abram   J.P.
At --------

Lawen,John Q.--21
  Franklin,Martha J.--24

May 22,1878   E.D.Brendle B.M.
At Geo.Cunningham's
Wit; A.L.Jones, Geo.Cunningham

Lawrence,F.E.L.--26
  Fox.Laura--23

May 23,1897   Fred"k W.Wey, M.M.E.C.S.
At Cullowhee
Wit; D.D.Davis, Otelia Davis, Dasey Davis

Leach,W.L.--24 Rogers,Fannie E.--24	Feb.17,1897 J.J.Gray M.G. At Cullowhee Ts. Wit; F.B.Price, J.H.Parker He From Macon, Co.N.C.	
Leadford,William--21 (Col) Watson,Mary--18 (Col)	Oct.21,1899 Rev.T.B.Hasket Pres. Min. At Eliza Watson's Res. Wit; W.S.McDonnell,W.H.Williams, Lanlee Davis.	
Leatherwood,Thomas B.--26 Sutton,Mary C.--17	Mar.6,1884 S.R.Cook J.P. At J.M.Sutton's Wit; G.W.Crawford,Robert Snider	
Ledford,Dan--25 Fore,Maggie--16	May 4,1899 A.W.Davis Bap.Min. At "My Home" Wit; J.R.Buchanan,Will Cabe, D.V.Moore	
Ledford,James B.--24 Hooper,Dosia--25	Dec.29,1891 V.F.Brown J.P. At River Ts. Wit; D.R.Bryson, P.N.Price, T.L.Hooper	
Leming,G---- -- Burchfield,Eliz.--	Jan.20,1856 N.B.Thompson J.P. At --------	
Lemmon,James--19 Estes,Mary J.--18	Feb.16,1880 J.R.Crawford J.P. At James Norman's Wit; James Norman, J.E.Crawford	
Lemmon,William--23 Grant,Jane--21	June 1,1883 J.B.Raby J.P. At J.B.Raby's Wit;-------	
Leopard,Jessee--21 Owens,Haseltine C.--18	May 18,1882 Elbert Watson J.P. At Lila Owens' Wit; M.T.Owens, N.C.Brown	
Leopard,John M.--22 Owens,Airy J.--15	Dec.20,1885 John P.Stuart J.P. At John Owens' Wit; J.S.Leopard, J.R.Owens	
Leopard,J.H.--22 McCall,Mily--22	Apr.1,1886 Elbert Watson J.P. At J.M.Brown's Wit; H.O.Smith,J.H.Mathis	
Lepard,Whit F.--22 Moore,Josephine--18	Sept.26,1880 S.P.C.Shelton J.P. At --------- Wit; J.H.Alley, T.N.Lepard	
Lewis,Benjamin-- Kerkland,Carolina--	Sept.17,1864 M.Coleman J.P. At ---------	
Lewis,George--24 Bishop,Ticia--20	Sept.9,1900 J.D.Sitton B.M. At J.B.Bishop's Wit; W.D.Bishop, J.T.Woodard, Hue Bishop	
Lewis,Henry C.--47 Ryefield,Charity A.--20	Dec.28,1880 J.W.Bird M.G. At J.W.Bird's Wit; Nellie Jones, A.H.Knight	
Lewis,John-- Green,Lucy Ann--	May 28,1871 J.L.Buchanan M.G. At --------	
Lewis,John--35 Estes,Margaret--30	Apr.18,1892 J.W.Buchanan J.P. At Savannah Ts. Wit; W.A.McMahan, N.B.Wilson	

Lewis,John H.--21   Jan.2,1887   Wm.Bumgarner J.P.
 Messer,Manervia E.--18 At"Tunnel"
             Wit; W.J.Messer, Robert Parten

Lewis,William--21   Feb.24,1895   W.A.Sutton J.P.
 Frady,Alma--18   At Savannah
             Wit; Richard Hall,Felix Ashe,Mincher Hall

Lindsey,David--20   Aug.9,1873   Wm.Estes   J.P.
 Duncan,Ellen--18   At M.B.Duncan's
             Wit; G.D.Estes

Lindsey,James--26   Aug.1,1897   Joseph Hoyle J.P.
 Lindsey,Maggie--17   At Scotts Creek Ts.
             Wit; L.L.Pope, C.M.Cope, G.W.Hoyle

Linsey,John--21 (Col) Feb.20,1886   G.W.Spake   M.M.
 Howell,Jane--18 (Col) At Webster
             Wit; Nathan Coward, Will Tompkins

Littrel,G.W.--22   Oct.16,1897   T.C.Jones   J.P.
 Elder,Jane--18   At J.B.Elder's
             Wit; A.D.Jones, W.A.Chastain, John McMahan

Littleton,W.H.--36   Oct.5,1882   L.M.Dillard J.P.
 Rochester,Caroline--22 At A.M.Hooper's
             Wit; Nettie Rogers, A.M.Hooper

Lombard,Hi I.--30   Jan.14,1880   H.M.Bennett M.M.
 Edwards,Bell--24   At G.Edwards'
             Wit; James Zachary, G.Edwards

Lompkins,Fred M.--23 July 6,1886   B.G.Wild   M.G.
 Conner,Laura--22   At R.H.Conner's
             Wit; W.T.Lompkins, A.M.Parker

Loney,W.H.--   Apr.6,1861   Wm.Wilson   J.P.
 Bryson,M.L.--   At -------

Long,Andrew C.--24   Jan.13,1875   A.H.Wilson   J.P.
 Hooper,Rhoda--23   At Flex Wilson's
             Wit; Laura Wilson, Sarah Wilson

Long,Charley--23 (Red) Aug.23,1894   J.W.Bird Meth. Min.
 Sampson,Sallie--17 (Red) At Qualla
             Wit; Lizzie Brown,Levi Queen,Sophia Bird

Long,G.M.--   Oct.21,1865   S.P.C.Shelton J.P.
 Long,Elizabeth--   At --------

Long,H.B.--   License Issued May 4,1891
 Morris,L.D.--   NOT Returned

Long,James--   Dec.25,1865   N.H.Bennett Rev. --
 Bryson,Rebacca--   At --------

Long,James--22   Jan.5,1896   J.M.Keener B.M.
 Woods,Hester--20   At Caney Fork
             Wit; E.M.Coward, E.H.Stephens,N.M.Long

Long,John B.--25   Apr.13,1876   M.M.Brown   B.M.
 Hooper,Lou--19   At Catherin Hooper's
             Wit; H.A.Brown

Long,John M.--19   Jan.22,1874   S.P.C.Shelton J.P.
 Stephens,Alis--16   At Marion Long's
             Wit; -------

Long,John M.--18   Oct.8,1884   A.D.Hooper J.P.
 Hall,Florence I.--17 At River Hill
             Wit; John B.Long

Long,John R.--24   Nov.13,1892   W.P.McGhee   M.G.
  Brown,Sadie J.--19   At Cullowhee Ts.
                          Wit; A.J.Long, M.A.Bennett, L.B.McGhee

Long,J.--   (Red)   Apr.6,1871   T.K.Welch   J.P.
  ------,Mary -- (Red)   At -------

Long,J.H.--45   Nov.12,1896   A.C.Queen   M.G.
  Moore,Delia--15   At Mountain Ts.
                          Wit; A.C.Queen, T.J.Mathis, T.J.Powell,
                                                    S.C.Wood.

Long,J.Robert--24   Feb.11,1900   Robt. S.Howe   M.M.
  Smith,Ethel--18   At Bride's Res.
                          Wit; M.H.Morris, J.N.Wilson, A.J.Dills

Long,J.R.--   Aug.23,1866   E.D.Brendle   Elder
  Ensly,M.A.--   At --------

Long,Nathan M.--35   License Issued   Sept.12,1901
  Watson,Lela--23   NOT Returned

Long,R.E.--25   Dec.6,1884   G.W.Spake   M.M.
  Henson,Maggie S.--22   At M.J.Henson's
                          Wit; John Bumgarner, W.T.Henson

Long,S.M.--   June 14,1860   Wm.Wilson   J.P.
  Parker,Vilet L.--   At ---------

Long,Thos.F.--22   July 1,1889   B.G.Wild   M.G.
  King,Mollie V.--22   At Webster Ts.
                          Wit; W.D.Frizell, Sallie E.Long, A.J.Long

Long,William C.--26   Mar.1,1888   G.W.Hawkins   J.P.
  Chastain,Callie--21   At R.A.Nicholson's
                          Wit; R.A.Nicholson, G.W.Nicholson

Lonns,John L.--   May 28,1862   E.D.Brendle   Elder
  Maghee,Sary M.--   At --------

Loury,Andrew--50   (Col) Dec.15,1887   W.P.Jones   J.P.
  Saunders,Liza--50 (Col) At A.Lowery's
                          Wit; W.D.Hill, T.D.Beasly

Love,Charley--19   June 17,1876   G.W.Spake   M.M.
  Cockerham,Eva--18   At G.W.Spake's
                          Wit; W.P.Allman, J.M.Candler

Love,David M.--64   (Col) License Issued   June 7,1901
  Bolt,Hattie--50   (Col) NOT Returned
                          He From Macon, Co.N.C.

Love,Edward F.--24 (Col) Dec.16,1900   David M.Franklin M.M.
  Lowery,Hattie--24 (Col) At Henderson Love's House
                          Wit; Delly Casey,Sallie Casey,Hyman Davis

Love,Felex--21   (Col) Oct.7,1899   R.A.Painter   J.P.
  Hyatt,Addie--20   (Col) At Lawrence Hyatt's
                          Wit; W.H.Williams,W.H.Hyatt, W.M.Watson

Love,Frank--24   (Col) June 18,1896   W.T.Fisher   J.P.
  Mills,Jennie--19 (Col) At Webster Ts.
                          Wit; Wm.Lattiemer,Wm.C.Fisher

Love,George--   (Col) Sept.10,1893   J.E.Moss
  Underwood,Rebecca--17 (Col) At Cullowhee Ts.
                          Wit; L.L.Rogers, Geo.Rogers, W.H.Coward

```
Love,Grantisan--            Jan.7,1872        J.M.Candler    J.P.
  Thomas,Magdalien--        At -------
Love,Henry--50              Aug.18,1895       J.B.Ensley     J.P.
  Bryson,Laura--30          At Sylva
                            Wit; James Pickens,W.T.Mills, M.L.Ensley
Love,Henry--22    (Col)     Aug.26,1897       J.C.Reed       J.P.
  Gibbs,Martha--22 (Col)    At Sylva Ts.
                            Wit; D.G.Bryson, W.J.Fiaher, T.M.Frizell
Love,Hix--25      (Col)     Aug.12,1894       L.W.Allen      J.P.
  Bryson,Emiline--22  (Col) At Sylva
                            Wit; F.Love, W.G.McDaniel, G.W.Franks
Love,I.Z.--21     (Col)     Aug.9,1896        W.C.Norton     J.P.
  Sanders,Josephine--22 (Col) At Cullowhee Ts.
                            Wit; J.R.Hooper, Gabe Hooper, John Cassey
Love,Jack--21     (Col)     Nov.22,1891       R.R.Fisher     J.P.
  Rogers,Mellie--18 (Col)   At Scotts Creek
                            Wit; Cal.Fisher, T.L.Howell
Love,James E.--19           Dec.25,1886       Wilson Ensley  M.G.
  Love,Sarah M.--19         At J.M.Love's
                            Wit; Lafayte Love, Thomas Davis
                            He From Haywood,Co.N.C.
Love,Jerry--23              Sept.7,1899       Nathan Coward  J.P.
  Phillips,Julia--28        At Rufus Cunningham's
                            Wit; A.R.Stillwell, C.J.Love, A.Stillwell
Love,John--18     (Col)     Sept.6,1897       J.W.Cowan      J.P.
  Dorsey,Lula--18  (Col)    At Webster Ts.
                            Wit; Frank Love, Allen McDowell,Bale Moore
Love,J.Rufus--25  (Col)     Dec.21,1891       L.W.Allen      J.P.
  Hix,Mary--23    (Col)     At Sylva Ts.
                            Wit; J.Pickens, E.Smith
Love,Monroe--               Jan.28,1870       J.M.Candler    J.P.
  Wilson,Lavina--           At --------
Love,Monroe--35   (Col)     Jan.24,1886       G.W.Spake      M.M.
  Howell,Fannie--20 (Col)   At G.W.Spake's
                            Wit; J.W.Terrell, J.A.Wild
Love,Nelson--25   (Col)     License Issued    Dec.22,1881
  Love,Martha--25  (Col)    NOT Returned
Love,Phidelia--21 (Col)     July 5,1891       S.R.Cook       J.P.
  Gibbs,Mary--18  (Col)     At Sylva Ts.
                            Wit; Henry Love, Thos. Pickens,Harrison Love.
Love,Richard--28  (Col)     Apr.25,1880       J.R.Crawford J.P.
  Bryson,Caroline--23 (Col) At Richard Love's
                            Wit; D.W.Love,Joseph Johnston
Love,Sambo--51    (Col)     Apr.26,1897       R.P.Powell     B.M.
  Howell,Annie--30 (Col)    At Webster Ts.
                            Wit; Clary Howell, Jane Lindsey,A.E.Brown
Love,William--18  (Col)     Mar.14,1881       G.W.Spake      M.M.
  Love,Mary--14   (Col)     At Charlie Love's
                            Wit; Geo.W.Dillard,Charlie Love
Love.Wm.A.--28    (Col)     Dec.2,1880        J.R.Crawford   J.P.
  Bryson,Mary J.--16 (Col)  At Stephen Bryson's
                            Wit;Simeon Bryson, Adam Bryson
```

```
Lovedahl,Lawrence G.--20        Jan.15,1880        G.W.Hooper      B.M.
   Smith,Marthey--20            At J.H.Smith's
                                Wit; J.C.Wood, J.M.Wood

Lovedahl,J.V.--21               Dec.3,1893         G.W.Hawkins     J.P.
   Hooper,M.L.--20              At Caney Fork
                                Wit; R.L.Mehaffey,J.H.Hawkins,J.F.Shelton

Lovedahl,W.A.--21               Feb.17,1889        A.C.Green       B.M.
   Coward,Azela--18             At Caney Fork
                                Wit; E.M.Coward, W.T.Coward

Low,A.J.--                      Feb.1,1872         R.H.Stephen     J.P.
   Queen,W.E.--                 At -------

Low,William.M.--                Aug.28,1871        B.N.Queen       Elder
   Redley,Sousan R.--           At --------

Lowdermilk,Irons--23            Oct.26,1879        C.E.Buchanan
   Browning,Sina--23            At James Browning's
                                Wit; N.B.Wilson, N.C.Browning

Lowe,Charley E.--26    (Col)    June 3,1899        Rev.Moses H.Craig  B.M.
   Knox,Lizzie--18     (Col)    At N.E.Knox's Res.
                                Wit; Lillie Love, Relious Bryson

Lowery,George--22      (Col)    Nov.22,1891        R.R.Fisher      J.P.
   Casey,Hattie--19    (Col)    At Scotts Creek
                                Wit; Cal.Fisher, T.L.Howell, J.T.Pickens

Lowry,Wilson--23                Sept.23,1888       S.R.Cook        J.P.
   Casey,Caroline--19           At Henderson Love's
                                Wit; Thomas Howell, John Freeman

Luker,Charles--21               May 28,1893        J.A.Galloway    M.G.
   McCall,Elizabeth--18         At Cananda Ts.
                                Wit; W.S.Brown, W.U.Mathis, J.H.O.

Macerrory,J.R.--29              Oct.3,1897     J.W.Bowman, M.M.E.C.S.
   Kerkindoll,Julia--19         At Qualla  Ts.
                                Wit; Lee J.Hall, T.D.Self,J.J.Kerkinkoll

Madford,J.B.--40                Nov.11,1900        Robt.S.Howell   M.M.
   Long,Sallie--30              At Bride's Father Res.
                                Wit; W.E.Tustin,W.D.Frizzell, C.C.Love
                                He From Haywood, Co. N.C.

Madison,Boleon--21              License Issued     Feb.21,1889
   Jarrett,Mamie--              NOT Executed

Madison,R.L.--25                Nov.25,1891     William S.Barrows  M.G.
   Richards,Ella V.--25         At Cullowhee
                                Wit; T.A.Cox, Cora K.Cox, M.E.Cox
                                She From Elizabeth,N.J.-- Now Jackson,Co.

Marion,W.A.--                   Jan.8,1871         W.B.Garrett     J.P.
   Chambers,Nancy A.--          At -------

Marr,John--23                   Dec.16,1894        W.W.Reed        B.M.
   Bryson,Fannie--16            At Scotts Creek
                                Wit; A.C.Bryson, S.S.Cook, L.W.Crawford
                                He From Swain, Co. N.C.

Martin,C.S.W.--22               Aug.16,1891        J.W.Bird        M.G.
   Hampton,Eddie N.--19         At Qualla  Ts.
                                Wit; J.L.Farley,F.W.Battle,R.L.McLaughlin

Martin,D.A.--25                 Jan.17,1892        J.W.Bird        M.G.
   Edwards,America--21          At Qualla  Ts.
                                Wit; W.H.Enloe, C.C.Martin, C.S.W.Martin
```

Martin,H.Z.--18   Dec.8,1897   C.S.Buchanan B.M.
  Green,Maggie--16   At Luther Green's
                                 Wit; J.R.Pickens,Lee Green,Griffin ----
Martin,J.E.--28   Feb.7,1892   J.W.Bird   M.G.
  Laney,Mary--19   At Qualla Ts.
                                 Wit; J.M.Martin, J.E.Bird, W.Laney
Martin,John H.--   July 12,1860   J.L.Buchanan J.P.
  Barker,Hette E.--   At ---------
Martin,John M.--29   Aug.14,1881   W.A.Brown   J.P.
  Brown,Mary L.--19   At Ervin Brown's
                                 Wit; John Ash, James Davis
Martin,William--21   (Col)   License Issued   Sept.12,1900
  Bolt,Queen Victoria--18 (Col)   NOT Returned
Marshall,John A.--   Dec.---,1869   J.L.Buchanan M.G.
  Wilson,S.J.--   At ---------
Mashburn,Mathaw--   Feb.4,1863   E.D.Brendle   Elder
  Wilson,Elizabeth--   At -------
Masengale,J.C.--20   Apr.24,1898   B.N.Queen   B.M.
  Crawford,Crecia Ellen--19   At Canada Ts.
                                 Wit; L.W.Hooper, W.L.Foriner, H.R.Queen
Masengale,Nick--24   Apr.10,1898   T.J.Mathis   J.P.
  Mathis,Arlena--19   At Canada Ts.
                                 Wit; S.A.Hamilton, Mary A.Mathis,D.J.Mull
Mashburne,Thomas H.--29   May 15,1895   A.W.Jacobs   M.G.
  Sherrill,P.Mellie--28   At Dillsboro
                                 Wit; J.B.Sherrill, C.T.Chace, Ella Potts
                                 He From Macon,Co.N.C.
Masingale,Daniel--21   Dec.24,1877   Thos.J.Bryson
  Adams,Sarah--18   At E.W.Fortner's
                                 Wit; Thos.Brown, John Queen
Mason,J.M.--22   Apr.8,1894   W.A.Sutton   J.P.
  Frady,Martha C.--18   At Savannah
                                 Wit; W.G.Brooks, W.Barker, M.Barker
Mason,William--   Aug.12,1869   W.M.Roberts   M.G.
  Smallwood,Sarah--   At --------
Mason,Wm.P.--50   May 14,1899   J.L.Buchanan B.M.
  Waldroup,Florence--25   At "My own house"
                                 Wit; T.F.Buchanan,W.C.Buchanan,Will Lewis
Massey,William--20   June 3,1894   A.C.Queen   M.G.
  Daves,Cloe--21   At River Ts.
                                 Wit; J.B.Wood
Massengill,John--21   July 28,1891   M.C.Warlick   M.G.
  Hamilton,Drucilla--18   At Canada Ts.
                                 Wit; J.Huffman, S.A.Hamilton,D.W.Massengill
Massingill,David--   Dec.5,1856   B.N.Queen   B.M.
  Parker,Jane--   At -------
Massingell,Dred--20   Jan.11,1889 M.C.Warlick,Min.Free Will Bap.
  Hughes,Mary--18   At Caney Fork
                                 Wit; Elie Watson,John Massingell,D.E.Ham-
                                                                   ilton.
Massingal,Robert--   Oct.24,1861   Wm.Wilson   J.P.
  Willson,Milly--   At --------

Mathis,Aaron-- Cope,Sarah--	July 3,1864 At --------	W.H.Conner	Elder
Mathis,Andrew J.-- Turner,Susan--	June 2,1869 He son of James & Arty Mathis She Dau.of Pick Turner,Mother not known	Thos.Wilson	J.P.
Mathis,A.J.-- Huffman,Mary S.--	Feb.14,1869 At --------	Levi Brown	J.P.
Mathis,Benjamin--18 Broom,Kate--18	Oct.27,1884 At E.W.Fortner's Wit; E.W.Fortner, S.H.Parker	B.N.Queen	B.M.
Mathis,Coleman--20 Parker,Juda--18	Jan.9,1898 At T.J.Mathis' Wit; R.B.Mathis, L.J.Mathis, Mary A.Mathis	T.J.Mathis	J.P.
Mathis,D.A.--22 Norman,Belle--18	Dec.19,1896 At Scotts Creek Wit; J.W.Mathis, I.H.Terry, Sam Cogdill	W.E.Bryson	J.P.
Mathis,George--26 Fox,Elizabeth--22	Oct.27,1872 At "On highway" Wit; Jerry Wike, Mary Wike	D.D.Davis	J.P.
Mathis,Hardie--21 Spencer,Lola--18	July 31,1898 At "School House" Wit;Baxter Nations,G.T.Owenby, R.L.Nations	T.C.Jones	J.P.
Mathis,Hugh-- Crawford,Melinda--	Oct.10,1863 At --------	Wm.Wilson	J.P.
Mathis,Jackson-- Crawford,Lucinda--	Jan.31,1855 At --------	J.Wike	J.P.
Mathis,James-- Mathis,Rebecca--	Feb.8,1871 At -------	W.C.Berry	Min.
Mathis,James--70 Chapman,Sarah--30	Feb.21,1881 At Hasltine Mathis' Wit; Phillip Dills, Sarah Mathis	Wm.Wilson	J.P.
Mathis,James--21 Hall,Mary--22	Jan.15,1888 At Wm.Hall's Wit; J.B.Miller, Wm.Mathis	S.R.Cook	J.P.
Mathis, James A.-- Graham,Lucinda--	Feb.23,1862 At --------	Wm.Wilson	J.P.
Mathis,James W.--31 Baley,Mary J.--35	Sept.24,1899 At Mary J.Baley's Res. Wit; M.D.Terry, A.C.Calhoun, Alie Cope	J.P.Calhoun	J.P.
Mathis,Jeff--35 Brown,Lizzie--	Oct.29,1892 At River Ts. Wit; R.L.Cabe, A.B.Snider,J.O.Brown	A.C.Queen	M.G.
Mathis,Jessee-- Mathis,Margret--	Feb.27,1861 At --------	Wm.Wilson	J.P.
Mathis,John E.--20 Fisher,Susan E.--18	Feb.2,1890 At Scotts Creek Wit; W.E.Bryson,A.C.Bryson, W.A.McKay	J.R.McKay	J.P.
Mathis,Joseph F.--20 Ashe,Rebecca--24	Feb.20,1887 At E.J.Huffman's Wit; S.M.Parker, H.R.Queen	W.A.Queen	J.P.

Mathis,J.D.--22   Mar.20,1881   D.D.Davie   J.P.
  Daves,Sallie--22   At D.D.Davis'
                           Wit;R.L.Davis, M.D.Grible

Mathis,J.Hardy--22   License Issued   June 26,1901
  Webb,Annie--20   NOT Returned

Mathis,J.H.--21   Oct.8,1893   J.C.Wood   J.P.
  Bryson,Callie--16   At Canada Ts.
                           Wit; J.P.Boon, D.H.Mathis, H.M.Parker

Mathis,Mat--48   Oct.25,1896   I.S.Leopard   J.P.
  Coggins,Lish--19   At Mountain Ts.
                           Wit; M.L.Coggins, I.M.Brown, A.F.Bryson

Mathis,Merrit R.--24   June 30,1895   J.J.Owen   B.M.
  Philips,Victory M.--21   At Canada Ts.
                           Wit; A.H.Queen, W.L.Fortner, W.V.Mathis

Mathis,Patrick--30   Sept.6,1883   W.P.Allman
  Garret,Elizabeth--18   At Reg Office
                           Wit; A.J.Long,Jr., W.P.Allman
                           He From Sevier,Co. Tenn.
                           She From Macon,Co.N.C.

Mathis,Peter--   Nov.---,1871   A.D.Hooper   J.P.
  Morton,Nancy--   At ---------

Mathis,R.B.--22   Sept.13,1896   F.R.Huffman   J.P.
  Parker,Hester--18   At Caney Fork
                           Wit; H.B.Wood, G.C.Mathis

Mathis,Rufus M.--24   Jan.15,1876   D.D.Davis   J.P.
  Deitz,Rachel L.--22   At James Mathis'
                           Wit; R.Bryson, Ben D.Davies

Mathis,Thomas--19   Apr.6,1884   S.R.Cook   J.P.
  Miller,Sarah E.--18   At W.P.Mills'
                           Wit; R.L.Cook, L.D.Queen

Mathis,Thomas J.--60   Nov.24,1895   J.C.Wood   J.P.
  Dawson,Mary Ann--30   At Canada Ts.
                           Wit; T.S.Fortner, W.L.Fortner, H.M.Parker

Mathis,T.J.--   Aug.9,1860   J.Wike   J.P.
  Parker,M.T.--   At -------

Mathis,T.M.--25   Nov.22,1895   J.C.Wood   J.P.
  Sutton,Pollie Ann--23   At Canada
                           Wit; S.E.Shelton, F.S.Jones

Mathis,William L.--19   Jan.23,1887   John H.Mathis J.P.
  Brown,Emmer--18   At Ed.Dills'
                           Wit; D.H.Mathis, T.M.Brown

Mathis,William T.--21   May 19,1882   T.J.Bryson   J.P.
  Russell,Lucy C.--24   At T.J.Bryson's
                           Wit; M.O.Brown, H.S.Cope

Mathis,W.M.--23   June 26,1892   J.C.Wood   J.P.
  Owen,Jane--19   At Canada Ts.
                           Wit; M.R.Mathis, W.L.Fortner, R.C.Owen

Mauna,W.A.--23   Mar.17,1889   J.C.Watkins   J.P.
  West,Eliza Jane--24   At Webster Ts.
                           Wit; Sam Bryson, J.H.House
                           He From Buncombe, Co.N.C.

Maw,Joseph A.--36   Apr.6,1884   C.B.Fugate   M.G.
  Zachary,Ida--19   At A.W.Zachary's
                       Wit; W.D.Adams, T.M.Holms
                       He From Pickens,Co.S.C.

McBride,Ed.--32   Aug.15,1895   J.R.Crawford J.P.
  Parker,Nancy--21   At Sylva
                       Wit; C.B.Jones
                       He From Haywood, Co. N.C.

McCall,Daniel M.--38   Apr.29,1900   J.R.Stephens J.P.
  Chastain,Mary--23   At James Chastain's
                       Wit; J.H.Morris, J.B.Coward, E.Coward
                       He From Transylvania, Co.N.C.

McCall,James--   Nov.18,1866   J.Wike   J.P.
  Jackson,Margaret--   At --------

McCall,James--29   Apr.6,1899   J.C.Henderson J.P.
  Moody,Rosana--23   At B.J.Moody's
                       Wit; J.M.Moss, Will Nicholson, Arlesa--

McCall,Silas--21   July 1,1888   J.L.Owens,M.G.Bryson
  Buchanan,Emma--19   At J.R.Buchanan's
                       Wit; A.J.Montieth, W.R.Owens

McCall,W.M.--21   Oct.27,1895   J.H.Owens   M.G.
  Owens,S.M.--18   At Canada
                       Wit; James R.Pylande,W.E.McCall,W.S.Brown
                       He From Transylvania, Co.N.C.

McClendone,A.L.--   Dec.25,18--   W.H.Conner
  Enloe,Lora B.--   At -------- (Reg.in year 1868)

McClure,James--20   Nov.30,1890   H.M.Bright   J.P.
  Moody,Mary--18   At Scotts Creek
                       Wit; J.P.Davis, J.S.Mehaffee,J.S.McClure
                       Both From Haywood,Co.N.C.

McClure,Rolen--   Nov.31,1855   Wm.R.Crawford J.P.
  Brown,Maegaret M.-- At --------

McClure,Rolen--57   May 2,1889   A.B.Henson   B.M.
  Barker,Mrs.Sarah J.--33 At Webster
                       Wit; Wm.Bumgarner,L.W.Cogdill,A.B.Henson
                       He From Haywood, Co.N.C.

McConnell,George W.--28 Dec.24,1889   J.O.Shelley M.G.
  Keener,Sallie--19   At Webster Ts.
                       Wit; J.J.Hooper, M.Buchanan,J.N.Worley

McCoy,John L.--   Mar.2,1869   L.G.Ward   J.P.
  Gipson,----- --   At -------
                       He son of John & Nancy McCoy.
                       She Dau. of Henry & Elizabeth Gipson.

McDade,Clark W.--24   Oct.20,1877   J.E.McLean
  Potts,Callie H.--23   At Margaret Potts'
                       Wit; J.L.Potts, G.P.Brown

McDade,E.B.--23   Mar.24,1889   J.C.Watkins J.P.
  Slatton,Maud M.--14   At Dillsboro Ts.
                       Wit; C.M.McDade,J.W.Philips,Callie McDade

McDade,W.H.--22   June 18,1887.   J.C.Watkins J.P.
  Farley,Mary--19   At "In Tunnell"
                       Wit; W.A.Dills, C.W.McDade

McDaniel,H.B.--19   July 6,1890   P.P.McLain   M.G.
  Bryson,Elvira--17   At Qualla Ts.
                             Wit; G.W.Montieth, Fate Bryson,Thos.Gibson

McDaniel,W.R.--27   (Col)   Apr.26,1896   A.B.Thomas   B.M.
  Brown,Julia--25   (Col)   At Cullowhee Ts.
                             Wit; A.W.Davis, J.R.Bryson, S.R.Edwards

McDonald,W.R.--24   (Col)   Oct.15,1891   D.D.Davis   J.P.
  Brown,M.C.--17   (Col)   At Cullowhee Ts.
                             Wit; T.W.Davis, M.L.Senasbaugh,Marie E.Dav

McDonnell,Hesikiah--23   Nov.11,1900   Thomas H.Queen, B.M.[18.]
  Parton,Minnie--18   At "In State Road"
                             Wit;W.I.Bishop,Elizabeth Isrel,John Warren

McDowel,James--   Mar.9,1862   J.B.Sherrill J.P.
  Stillwell,Dovey--   At -------

McDowell,Louallen--   Aug.11,1872   J.M.Candler   J.P.
  Allison,Rachel--   At --------

McDowell,J.R.S.--21 (Col) July 25,1897   J.W.Cowan   J.P.
  Hooper,Maggie--19 (Col)   At Webster
                             Wit; Coleman Cowan,L.D.Cowan,H.D.Dorsey

McFalls,G.A.--25   License Issued--- Aug.26,1901
  Sutton,Alice--25   NOT Returned

McFalls,Green Lee--21   Sept.26,1900   Nathan Coward J.P.
  Church,Emma--19   At Webster, N.C.
                             Wit; Jess Bryson, A.W.Davis

McFalls,G.A.--19   May 5,1895   R.L.Hyatt   J.P.
  Carver,Mary--16   At Qualla Town
                             Wit; D.W.Carver,David McFalls,Delice Seller

McFalls,W.L.--21   June 24,1898   J.W.Cowan   J.P.
  Angel,Emma--22   At Mr. Mashburn's
                             Wit; A.M.Frady,S.E.Grant,E.H.Loudermilk

McFee,William M.--23   Dec.27,1896   J.E.Sitton   J.P.
  Bryson,Flora--19   At Cullowhee Ts.
                             Wit; J.Z.Nicholson,C.V.Bryson

McGruter,Martin--   Oct.20,1854   Allen Fisher   J.P.
  McFalls,Malissa--   At --------

McGuire,Samuel L.--28   Feb.1,1881   C.B.Fugate   M.G.
  Norton,Mercella--26   At Drucilla Norton's
                             Wit; R.A.Jacobs, David Norton

McKay,Jessee R.--46   Apr.17,1888   G.W.Crawford   M.G.
  Crawford,Laura B.--22   At P.J.Crawford's
                             Wit; H.J.Barnes, J.B.Hall

McKay,J.R.--   July 23,1870   A.J.Hall   J.P.
  Gunter,Mary--   At ---------

McKay,R.H.--20   June 13,1891   S.R.Cook   J.P.
  Cogdill,N.M.--16   At Scotts Creek
                             Wit; J.B.Cogdill, G.W.Gunter,S.L.Cook

McKee,Ernest Lyndon--25   Sept.7,1897   J.J.Gray   M.M.
  Moody,Mattie--25   At Dillsboro
                             Wit; J.W.McKee, W.A.Enloe, Lillie Enloe

McKee,H.C.--27
McLain,Mattie--18

July 19,1891   B.G.Wilds, Min.M.E.C.S.
At Webster Ts.
Wit; J.M.Worley,T.B.X.Cowan, R.B.Cowan

McKee,J.W.--29
Bryson,Carrie--20

Mar.23,1899   W.V.Honeycutt, M.M.E.C.S.
At Sylva
Wit;J.W.Divebliss,Mrs.Buchanan, Mrs.F.Long

McLain,John E.--
Allison,Ann C.--

Feb.14,1866   G.W.Spake   Rev.
At --------

McLaughlin,Wade A.--25
Hipps,Edith--24

June 30,1900   E.H.Hampton M.M.E.C.S.
At ---------
Wit; Ony Hyatt, Lee Hall, Robert Hall

McLean,William H.--21
Cooper,Maggie--18

July 20,1890   P.P.McLean   M.G.
At Qualla Ts.
Wit; G.W.Montieth, J.U.Gibbs, S.W.Allison
Both from Swain, Co. N.C.

McLean,W.S.--33
Bracken,Nellie--22

June6,1897   J.H.Owens   M.G.
At J.H.Owens'
Wit; J.H.Owen- J.D.Hamilton, E.W.Owen

McMahan,Alfred M.--19
McMahan,Blanch L.--18

Sept.17,1879   E.C.Ash
At Stephen McMahan's
Wit; M.L.Frady, Jasper A.Dills

McMahan,Arch--21
Beasley,Docia--18

Dec.20,1895   C.S.Buchanan   B.M.
At Savannah
Wit; W.F.Green, P.H.Green, M.A.Green

McMahan,Curtis--21
Morgan,Emma J.--22

Jan.5,1890   J.L.Buchanan   M.G.
At Savannah Ts.
Wit; J.C.Buchanan, Jo. Allison

McMahan,Curtis--34
Thompson,Laura--36

License Issued   Aug.17,1901
NOT Returned

McMahan,Gates--
McGee,Laura--18

Sept.11,1892   J.W.Bird   M.G.
At Qualla Ts.
Wit; I.L.McGee, Sarah McGee, M.T.Stanford

McMahan,G.N.--
Trantham,Clora--

July 29,1866   E.C.Ash   J.P.
At ---------

McMahan,G.N.--
Trantham,Sarah--

July 29,1866   E.C.Ash   J.P.
At ---------

McMahan,John--
Jones,Rutha--

Apr.5,1866   Sol.Messer   J.P.
At -------

McMahan,Rutha--

Apr.3,1866   Sol.Messer   J.P.

McMahan,Levi--57
Sutton,Lucy Ann--38

Sept.22,1890   A.B.Thomas   M.G.
At Dillsboro Ts.
Wit; J.M.Phillips, E.B.McDade, S.R.Davis

McMahan,Levi M.--21
Parton,Rebecca--18

Aug.6,1887   W.P.Jones   J.P.
At "R.R.Crossing"
Wit;J.B.Raby, C.L.Jones

McMahan,L.M.--30
Turpin,Collie--25

July 25,1897   T.C.Jones   J.P.
At Barker Creek
Wit; J.B.Elders, Samuel Jones, M.C.Jones

McMahan,L.R.--24
Wilke,Allie F.--18

Feb.29,1894   J.F.Brown   J.P.
At Barker Creek
Wit; S.C.Franklin, J.A.Messer, R.L.Elders

McMahan,Riley--21
Partin,Mary--19
Mar.29,1881   J.E.McLain   J.P.
At "No top of Mack Mt."
Wit; Russell Sutton, H.Partin

McMahan,Robert--21
Burgess,Della--18
Mar.3,1890   H.C.Cannon   J.P.
At Savannah Ts.
Wit; Thos.McMahan, Thos.Bradley

McMahan,Thomas--21
McMahan,Margaret--18
Feb.15,1882   D.H.Ash   J.P.
At D.H.Ash's
Wit; Nathan M.Ash, L.M.Ash

McMahan,Warren--22
Green,Josephine--28
Feb.17,1892   C.S.Buchanan   M.G.
At Savannah
Wit; A.B.Ashe, W.A.Green

McMahan,William C.--20
Sutton,Clerisa--20
Aug.7,1874   J.L.Buchanan   M.G.
At J.L.Buchanan's
Wit; John Bradley, Mitchell Sutton

McMahan,W.A.--24
Sutton,Menervia--24
Feb.19,1877   E.C.Ash   J.P.
At Alfred McMahan's
Wit; A.Sutton, Wm.Sutton

Medford,Ansel--26
Melton,Diana--19
Jan.23,1896   W.A.Brown   J.P.
At Caney Fork
Wit; L.Mull, A.Henson, M.J.Zachary

Medford,H.C.--22
King,Josie--27
Dec.24,1891   T.M.Frizzell   J.P.
At Barker Creek Ts.
Wit; J.M.Worley, W.D.Hill
He From Haywood, Co. N.C.

Medford,Samuel--25
Robinson,May Bell--17
Nov.25,1900   J.R.Crawford   J.P.
At Ellen Robinson's
Wit; Samuel Franklin, Joseph Robinson,
                    W.D.Robinson.

Meek,David--
Shular,Margret--
Feb.9,1864   I.T.S.Sherrill Elder
At -------

Mehaffie,James--
Moffit,Mary Jane--
Oct.10,1870   Levi Brown   J.P.
At --------

Melton,Granvill--21
Mills,Synthia--18
Mar.9,1876   L.W.Hooper   B.M.
At S.N.Wood's
Wit; G.W.Hawkins, John Lowe

Melton,Houston--20
Shelton,Sarah E.--17
Dec.20,1883   B.N.Queen   B.M.
At J.W.Shelton's
Wit; J.N.Ash, W.J.Mills

Melton,Sylvester--20
Hawkins,Belle--27
Nov.10,1898   R.L.Phillips   J.P.
At R.M.Hawkins'
Wit; James Henson,Vance Hooper,Wm.Hooper

Melton,Sylvester--21
Mull,Mary E.--19
Nov.3,1881   B.N.Queen   B.M.
At B.Mull's
Wit; R.E.Medford,W.D.Parker
She From Haywood,Co.N.C.

Merrick,W.K.--29
Allen,Mamie--22
Sept.7,1898   A.Walker White, Pres. Min.
At Pres. Church
Wit; W.L.DeWitt, S.W.Enloe, W.J.Kinkaid

Messer,Coleman--20   May 29,1897   Wm.Bumgarner J.P.
  Shuler,Melvina--20   At G.W.Shuler's
                             Wit; Hershel Candler, Will Ward,Thos.Messer

Messer,Dock--21   Aug.20,1900   R.A.Painter J.P.
  Snider,Etta--18   At Sylva Ts.
                             Wit; S.C.Russell,Russell Painter,Jake Pain-
                                                                    ter.
Messer,Graham--21   Feb.8,1881   D.H.Ash   J.P.
  McMahan,Matilda--21   At Mitchell Sutton's
                             Wit; Russell Sutton, Anderson Sutton

Messer,Harrison--30   Oct.13,1887   J.C.Watkins J.P.
  Gunter,Laura--21   At " H.P.Bugpole's Sawmill"
                             Wit; T.A.Carpenter

Messer,James--20   Feb.3,1889   S.J.Beck   J.P.
  Ward,Elizabeth--18   At Qualla Town
                             Wit; G.B.Davis, A.L.Beck, L.L.Reid

Messer,John--21   Nov.23,1884   Wilson Ensley M.G.
  Sutton,Dollie--18   At Wilson Ensley's
                             Wit; R.A.McMahan,W.S.McMahan

Messer,John--22   Dec.24,1889   A.B.Thomas   M.G.
  Kimsey,Emma--23   At Dillsboro Ts.
                             Wit; M.H.Morris,Mary Long

Messer,J.F.--21   Apr.6,1893   J.F.Brown   J.P.
  Wikle,Neely E.--18   At Barker Creek
                             Wit; A.P.Jones, W.W.Jones, R.L.Elders

Messer,Levi--22   Sept.14,1873   J.L.Buchanan B.M.
  Cunningham,Margaret--18   At Jamison Hall's
                             Wit; M.Buchanan, Jamison Hall

Messer,Robert--22   Mar.3,1881   J.E.McLain   J.P.
  Parton,Nancy--18   At Burton Jones'
                             Wit; Henry Parton, Russell,Sutton

Messer,Solomon--   May 31,1869   E.H.Cagle   J.P.
  Guillioms,Sarah--   At --------

Messer,William--18   Feb.20,1890   W.P.Jones   J.P.
  Bradley,Ella--18   At Barker Creek
                             Wit; J.H.Bradley, J.A.Nations

Messer,W.R.--29   Dec.8,1898   W.V.Honeycutt,Meth.Min.
  Rogers,Lula--29   At Miss Rebecca Rogers'
                             Wit; W.F.Berry, W.F.Holden, T.B.Dillard
                             He From Buncombe, Co. N.C.

Middleton,James--22   Apr.22,1880   S.C.Owens   M.G.
  Ash,G.J.--15   At C.A.Ash's
                             Wit; John Middleton,David Middleton

Middleton,James--23   Sept.20,1873   A.C.Queen   B.M.
  Shook,Arleasa--   At James S.Shook's
                             Wit; J.H.Middleton,F.M.Ashe, T.W.Hooper

Middleton,John--   Sept.1,1873   Lewis Queen M.G.
  Chastain,Cloe--   At --------

Middleton,R.L.--23   License Issued   Sept.4,1900
  Ashe,Lula--18   NOT Returned

Middleton,W.N.--20   Apr.30,1891   A.C.Queen   M.G.
  Long,N.A.--18   At Caney Fork
                   Wit; Aron Hooper, H.Stephens,R.Phillips

Middleton,W.W.--   License Issued   Oct.16,1899
  Shook,Cordelia--18   NOT Returned

Miller,Charles H.--23   Sept.12,1895   J.B.Raby   J.P.
  Jones,Hattie--21   At Barker Creek
                   Wit; W.E.Benjamin, Mrs.W.E.Benjamin,
                         R.L.Jerris.

Miller,C.E.--21   Apr.28,1898   W.E.Conner   B.M.
  Moody,Fannie--18   At J.J.Moody's
                   Wit; S.T.Moody,D.H.Snider, W.J.Fisher

Miller,David T.--   Jan.20,1862   Willson Ensley J.P.
  Mills,Ruthy--   At --------

Miller,Jacob--25   (Col)   Oct.16,1879   E.P.Stillwell J.P.
  Coleman,Ann--22   (Col)   At Virgie Bryson's
                   Wit; Samuel Hix, Wm.Messer

Miller,John--21   Oct.3,1880   J.B.Raby   J.P.
  Jemson,Kittie--20   At J.B.Raby's
                   Wit; J.E.Angel

Miller,John B.--29   Apr.12,1891   S.T.Ensley   J.P.
  Parris,A.E.--20   At Dillsboro Ts.
                   Wit; J.P.Calhoun, V.R.Henson

Miller,J.R.--35   Nov.12,1891   J.M.Wilson   J.P.
  Miller,S.E.--19   At Hamburg Ts.
                   Wit; R.D.Morgan,D.A.Watson,Mary Watson
                   He From Transylvania,Co. N.C.
                   She From Macon,Co. N.C.

Miller,Wesley W.--20   Mar.2,1880   J.W.Bird   M.G.
  Morris,Mary W.--20   At J.W.Bird's
                   Wit; J.F.Enloe, B.C.Fisher

Miller,W.J.--23   Dec.1,1889   J.A.Wild   J.P.
  Rogers,Sallie Viola--19   At Cullowhee Ts.
                   Wit; J.H.Bryson,Sadie Brown

Miller,W.L.--   Aug.16,1860   A.Fisher   J.P.
  Clayton,Martha Ann--   At --------

Mills,Allen--22   May 2,1874   J.C.Watkins   J.P.
  Sparks,Martha--18   At A.Montieth's
                   Wit; John Cope, J.C.Fisher

Mills,Clingman--22   Dec.25,1887   A.J.Hall   J.P.
  Sutton,Ida--19   At J.M.Sutton's
                   Wit; J.E.Ensley,W.E.Bryson

Mills,Davis--21   Jan.21,1900   A.B.Henson   B.M.
  Mills,Carisus--18   At A.B.Henson's
                   Wit; J.W.Henry, C.M.Henry, E.Watkins

Mills,George--19   Aug.18,1899   A.B.Henson   B.M.
  Gunter,Ida--21   At " In Road"
                   Wit; W.D.Mills, J.W.Mills, H.R.Crawford

Mills,Isaac J.--38   Dec.4,1879   R.H.Stephens   ---
  Wood,Syntha--21   At Mary Wood's
                   Wit; James Beard, S.N.Wood

Mills,I.J.-- Wyatt,Jane--	Aug.30,1865 At --------	W.R.Crawford Elder
Mills,James-- Crawford,Racheal--	Mar.6,1870 At -------	J.H.Hall J.P.
Mills,J.B.--22 Farley,Virginia--16	Sept.20,1883 At W.V.Farley's Wit; D.J.Clayton, T.B.Leatherwood.	S.R.Cook J.P.
Mills,J.W.--21 Bryson,Maggie J.--20	Aug.15,1889 At Cullowhee Wit; D.D.Davis, Kate E.Davis, H.J.Reece	Rev.Chas.L.Hoffman
Mills,Liston--24 Crawford,Mattie--19	Nov.27,1900 At J.P.Calhoun's House Wit; J.C.Mills, Davis Mills, M.J.Calhoun	J.P.Calhoun J.P.
Mills,Reuben--20 Woodruff,Mary--20	May 5,1881 At S.R.Cook's Wit; Hanry Robison, John Robison	S.R.Cook J.P.
Mills,Robert--21 Ensley,Cora--19	Dec.24,1899 At Henry Ensley's Wit; D.L.Ensley, E.W.Watson,S.R.Brooks	R.A.Painter J.P.
Mills,Ruben--21 Woodruff,Jane--20	Nov.30,1879 At S.H.Bryson's Wit; W.P.Gunter,W.P.Duncan	S.H.Bryson ---
Mills,Rufus--22 Henry,Ellen--17	Jan.18,1900 At Cornelius Henry's Wit; J.W.Henry, C.M.Henry, J.E.Henson	A.B.Henson B.M.
Mills,Samuel--25 Bryson,Ida--17	License Issued Apr.27,1899 NOT Returned	
Mills,Samuel--47 Crawford,M.M.--26	Jan.28,1891 At Sylva Ts. Wit; Allen Mills,John Warren,Samuel Parris	S.R.Cook J.P.
Mills,Samuel--20 Wood,Julia S.--22	Nov.28,1883 At M.B.Wood'd Wit; S.N.Wood, L.M.Wood	A.J.Hall J.P.
Mills,Samuel S.-- Darosey,Sarah C.--	Nov.6,1870 At -------	E.D.Brendle Elder
Mills,Thadous B.--20 Miller,Artic C.--18	Sept.19,1880 At W.Y.Mills' Wit; John Dills, J.B.Miller	S.H.Bryson J.P.
Mills,Wilburn--19 Brooks,Nancy--22	Apr.3,1873 At John Cope's Wit; -------	W.Ensley B.M.
Mills,Wilburn--45 Henry,Melaine--26	Oct.12,1898 At Scotts Creek Wit; S.B.Mills, R.R.Sutton, J.A.Melton	J.P.Calhoun J.P.
Mills,William T.--22 Pruitt,Sarah--21	Oct.1,1876 At W.B.Love's Wit; W.B.Love, R.J.Bryson	D.G.Fisher ---
Mills,W.A.--22 Montieth,Juda--17	Oct.21,1897 At Sam Montieeh's Wit;Miles Parker,Daniel Bryson,Dillard- Bryson.	J.B.Ensley J.P.

```
Mills,W.T.--37              Aug.8,1893      John A.Hooper      J.P.
   Watkins,Abigil--26       At Cashier Valley
                            Wit; T.L.Mills, S.L.Mills, Geo Pruitt
Mills,Z.T.--                Jan.6,186-         A.J.Hall        J.P.
   Norris,Rebecca--         At --  (Entered in book 1 in year 1868)
Millsaps,F.M.--             Sept.18,1853       M.Coleman       J.P.
   Hyde,F.M.--              At ---------
Mincy,J.H.--                Nov.8,1894         T.B.McCurdy     M.G.
   Bryson,Sallie M.--       At Webster
                            Wit; J.W.Fisher,Jas.D.Bryson,David Hall
                            He From Macon, Co. N.C.
Mingus,Charles--21  (Col)   Sept.25,1898       J.C.Love      Bap.Min.
   Turk,Alice--21   (Col)   At Clark Turk's
                            Wit; Mirah Love,T.B.Hobkett,Henry L.Alston
                            He From Macon, Co. N.C.
Mingus,Daniel--             Oct.1870           W.H.Conner     Elder
   Pinion,Sarah--           At -----
Mitchell,L.F.--24           License Issued   July 9,1901
   Clayton,Maggie--25       NOT Returned
Mitchell,P.W.--48           June 12,1898       J.B.Ensley      J.P.
   Taylor,Mattie M.--24     At James Taylor's
                            Wit; A.S.Bryson,Paula Fowler,C.D.Mitchell
Mitchell,W.M.--24           Dec.25,1895        J.B.Ensley      J.P.
   Harris,Ida--16           At Sylva Ts.
                            Wit; T.C.Fullbright,D.G.Bryson,L.W.Ward
Moffit,Baxton--24           July 3,1884        J.B.Coward      J.P.
   Queen,Jane--18           At Martha Akin's
                            Wit; H.R.Parker,Martha Akin
Moffit,D.C.--               Sept.24,1879       Levi Brown      J.P.
   Mahaffie,Margaret--      At ---------
Moffit,Freeman--21          Mar.4,1900         A.B.Henson      B.M.
   Sanders,Lona--17         At Ben Sanders'
                            Wit; Jacob Davis,J.L.Ballard,S.H.McNealy
Moffit,Houston--24          Jan.28,1883        R.H.Stephens   J.P.
   Coward,Mary--24          At Benj.Coward's
                            Wit; Thomas Hooper, Elihu Coward
Moffit,H.B.--30             Oct.3,1891         G.W.Hawkins     J.P.
   Thompson,S.L.E.--16      At Caney Fork
                            Wit; J.E.Hawkins, J.T.Henson,D.H.Wood
Moffit,Robert M.--19        Sept.27,1875       John H.Mathis  J.P.
   Huffman,Mardinia--16     At A.J.Mathis'
                            Wit; A.W.Cathey,A.J.Mathis
Monday,Pleasant M.--26      Oct.5,1879         John S.Keener   ---
   Mann,Nancy E.--26        At Wm.B.Morris'
                            Wit; W.N.Baker, James Parris
Mongomery,Spence--20 (Col)  May 20,1877        D.G.Fisher      J.P.
   Bobo,,Lula E.--22 (Col)  At D.G.Fisher's
                            Wit; E.Fisher
```

Montieth,A.J.--26 Taylor,Mary--19	Dec.23,1888 At Hamburg Wit; Wm.R.Owens,Dora L.Taylor,Z.W.Campbell	J.L.Owens	M.G.
Montieth,David H.--22 Ensley,Arry--20	Sept.13,1877 At Thadeus Beard's Wit; T.Beard, Samuel Montieth	E.D.Brendle	B.M.
Montieth,George--30 Allen,Roxie--24	Nov.9,1876 At Nathan Allen's Wit; T.B.Allison	J.B.Allison	J.P.
Montieth,Heron-- Wilson,Elimna--	Mar.30,1856 At --------	Peter King	J.P.
Montieth,Hiram-- Deitz,Talitha--	Oct.28,1875 At Laborn Deitz's Wit; L.F.Deitz, Ninian Bryson He From Haywood, Co. N.C.	G.W.Spake	M.M.
Montieth,James A.-- Gipson,M.M.--	Sept.27,1865 At ---------	J.H.Harris	Elder
Montieth,John--31 Frizzell,Sarah--22	Dec.17,1893 At Webster Wit; W.E.Moore, Jeob Wild, J.C.Buchanan	J.E.Moss	J.P.
Montieth,John A.-- Brendle,S.A.--	Mar.22,1864 At --------	A.Mingus	J.P.
Montieth,Lucius--19 Pressly,S.A.--30	Apr.13,1889 At Cullowhee Wit; R.A.Painter	W.C.Norton	J.P.
Montieth,N.E.--22 Buchanan,Thurisa C.--22	Mar.1,1883 At J.K.Hall's Wit; Oat Allison, G.D.Hall	J.G.Ammons	M.G.
Montieth,Samuel H.--23 Fisher,Ida C.--18	Nov.14,1897 At T.J.Fisher's Wit; Howard Fisher,W.D.Montieth, E.B.Montieth	W.J.Fisher	J.P.
Montieth,Samuel L.--27 Smith,Catherine--27	Feb.20,1881 At W.B.Allen's Wit; H.A.Long, W.B.Allen	W.Ensley	M.G.
Montieth,Samuel W.--23 Ensley,Fannie C.--17	Oct.7,1878 At Thadeus Beard's Wit; Thadeus Beard,Benjamin Harris	E.D.Brendle	B.M.
Montieth,Thomas--28 Queen,Maranda P.--19	Oct.26,1875 At J.S.Queen's Wit; W.H.T.Dillard, Hicks Montieth	W.Ensley	B.M.
Montieth,Thomas S.--27 Burris,Mary E.--20	Mar.19,1876 At M.E.Love's Wit; C.C.Love, Wm. Love	G.W.Spake	M.M.
Montieth,William--25 Jemison,Sarah--18	Jan.15,1885 At T.W.Jemison's Wit;A.H.Wilson, D.B.Jemison	W.H.Hooper	J.P.
Montieth,W.T.-- Queen,M.A.--	Sept.14,1871 At ---------	E.D.Brendle	Elder

Moody,Clarence--20   Apr.22,1894   J.P.Painter M.G.
 Fisher,Martha--19   At Barker Creek
              Wit; ----

Moody,Daniel--   NO Dates--(License was issued between
 Slatton,Nancy A.--   July and Oct. 1862)

Moody,Frances--   NO Dates-- (License was issued between
 Zachary,Emmy--   July and Oct. 1862)

Moody,Francis--24   Jan.--1889   John P.Stewart J.P.
 Leopard,Mary--22   At Hamburg Ts.
              Wit; J.L.Leopard, John Bumgarner,
                      J.W.Leopard.

Moody,H.L.--   Dec.17,1868   W.H.Conner Elder
 Hyatt,Cordelia--   At --------

Moody,J.Martain--25   Dec.10,1899   J.C.Henderson J.P.
 Jennings,Ellen B.--19   At N.M.Jennings'
              Wit; J.A.Moody, H.R.Queen, J.F.McCall

Moody,John H.--   Jan.12,1869   G.W.Spake M.M.
 Davis,Manda M.--   At --------

Moody,John H.--59   Nov.26,1895   S.C.Allison J.P.
 Enloe,R.A.--57   At Barker Creek
              Wit; C.W.Allison, John Martin

Moody,John T.--22   Sept.28,1885 A.D.Hooper J.P.
 Wike,Emma--24   At "In the Road"
              Wit; J.R.Stewart, T.V.Henderson

Moody,Joseph H.--45   Nov.13,1884   Wilson Brown's---
 Brown,Sarah--38   At John Brown's
              Wit; Rufus Fisher, Joseph House

Moody,Vest--21   Jan.16,1898   V.F.Brown J.P.
 Conner,Bessie--18   At River Ts.
              Wit; Baxter Hooper,P.F.Webster,J.M.Davis

Moody,W.R.--21   Jan.8,1891   John P.Stewart J.P.
 Leopard,Josephine--16   At Hamburg Ts.
              Wit; W.F.Moody, J.S.Leopard

Moon,C.G.--35   Aug.28,1890   A.J.Hall J.P.
 Henry,Matilda--16   At Scotts Creek
              Wit; J.B.Hall, D.C.Henry, D.M.Hall

Moon,J.A.--   Jan.21,1858   J.Wike   J.P.
 Parker,E.P.--   At --------

Moore,Andrew J.--24   Jan.28,1874   G.W.Hawkins J.P.
 Miller,Milley M.--19   At --------
              Wit; ------

Moore,Bale--23 (Col)   Nov.25,1879   R.M.Worley ----
 Allen,Millie--20 (Col)   At M.Worley's
              Wit; Cudge Thomas, James Thomas

Moore,Bale--37 (Col)   Jan.8,1891   B.G.Wild M.G.
 McDowell,Hattie--18 (Col) At Webster Ts.
              Wit; Andy Coward, Frank Love, Wm.Casey

Moore,David V.--24   Sept.19,1880 Wm.Wilson J.P.
 Buchanan,Mary--18   At R.Bryson's
              Wit; N.J.Adams, Artie Tatham

Moore,Fred--26
Enloe,Lela--24

Nov.27,1895   D.H.Coman,Min.M.E.C.S.
At Dillsboro
Wit;Charles A.Moore,Minnie Dills,F.L.Siler.
He From Buncombe, Co. N.C.

Moore,James--42
Shular,Ruth A.--35

Jan.11,1888   James T.Cathey   J.P.
At Ruth A.Shular's
Wit; W.A.Queen, A.W.Parker

Moore,Jerry--32
Crumpton,Maggie--26

Feb.5,1888   L.W.Hooper   M.G.
At Caney Fork Church
Wit; T.L.Hooper, J.C.More

Moore,Jorden--34
Hawkins,Julia--18

May 4,1888   E.A.Cook   J.P.
At Joseph Hughes'
Wit; E.L.Watson, S.V.Jones

Moore,J.L.--31
Hoyle,Emma--20

Feb.12,1893   Joseph Hoyle J.P.
At Scotts Creek
Wit; J.L.Ballard, W.H.T.dillard

Moore,Lon--19
Pannell,Maggie--24

Dec.24,1899   J.R.Crawford J.P.
At M.G.Pannell's
Wit; R.L.Cook, John Clayton, Estis Bryson
He From Macon, Co. N.C.

Moore,L.A.--26
Styles,Rebecca--20

May 23,1897   J.D.Sitton   J.P.
At Webster Ts.
Wit; W.M.Atkin, J.H.Robison
He From Macon, Co.N.C.

Moore,Rufus--21
Enloe,Belle--21

May 28,1882   G.W.Spake   M.M.
At R.A.Enloe's
Wit; J.S.Keener, G.B.Cooper
He From Macon, Co. N.C.

Moore,Walter E.--26
Enloe,Laura R.--17

Jan.10,1883   R.A.Owens   M.G.
At W.A.Enloe's
Wit; A.B.Allison, J.W.Terrell

Moore,William--
Wood,Emila--

Nov.16,1873   R.A.Stephens J.P.
At M.B.Wood's
Wit; --------

Moore,William--30
Cordelle,Mary--26

Apr.19,1896   William H.Thomas J.P.
At Qualla Ts.
Wit; Mary Wright,R.J.Reed, Hattie Cordell

More,Sam--
Wilson,Margaret--

Oct.9,1863   W,H.Buchanan J.P.
At -------

Morgan,John S.--20
Deitz,Myrah--18

Dec.17,1899   W.C.Buchanan J.P.
At John Dietz's
Wit; R.L.Cunningham,R.J.Morgan, T.M.Deitz

Morgan,Philip--18
Green,Jane--18

Sept.8,1881   D.H.Ash   J.P.
At Silas Green's
Wit; G.W.Green, Wm.Trantham

Morgan,Robert--21
Cope,Laura--19

Nov.22,1888   E.C.Ash   J.P.
At Savannah Ts.
Wit; A.B.Ash, R.L.Pangle, Andrew Sutton

Morgan,William--23
Barnes,Annah--18

Dec.18,1898   J.L.Buchanan B.M.
At "My Own House"
Wit; John Allison,Candler Sutton,Thos.Carso n.

Morris,James--24
Chastine,Sarah--18

Jan.5,1873   R.H.Stephens   J.P.
At Elizabeth Chastine's
Wit;-------

Morris,M.H.--27   Jan.1,1890   J.O.Shelley M.G.
  Long,Mary J.--20   At Dillsboro Ts.
           Wit; O.B.Coward, C.Buchanan

Morris,W.B.--23   Dec.27,1899 J.R.Stephens J.P.
  Parker,Arrilla--25   At W.J.Parker's
           Wit; L.N.Stephens,J.E.Long, J.H.Middlrton

Morrison,George W.--36 Jan.6,1876   Wm.Bumgarner J.P.
  Davis,Malovina--21   At Jonathan Herren's
           Wit; J.Herren,G.C.Davis

Morrison,John--21   July 14,1883 W.H.Hooper J.P.
  Hooper,Eva--22   At Samuel Hooper's
           Wit; Henry Hooper, Pinkney Hooper

Morrow,A.B.--22   Mar.2,1889   G.W.Crawford B.M.
  Smathers,Mary A.H.--19 At Scotts Creek
           Wit; B.R.Henson, T.C.Bryson, N.Bryson

Morson,A.J.--   Mar.22,1871 Wm.R.Crawford --
  Stiles,Elmira--   At --------

Morton,John--31 (Col) Apr.5,1885   W.A.Dills J.P.
  Clayton,Ellen--25 (Col) At W.Ensley's
           Wit; H.R.Snider, J.M.Scott

Moses,O.D.--21   Nov.3,1895   J.N.Wilson J.P.
  Parker,Isabella--19 At River Ts.
           Wit; J.W.Hooper, Viola Brown,S.B.Parker

Moses,Hosea--   Dec.25,1863 E.D.Brendle Elder
  Jones,Mary E.--   At --------

Moses,Larkin J.--21   June 27,1886 B.N.Queen B.M.
  Brown,Laura L.--20   At M.M.Brown's
           Wit; V.F.Brown, H.A.Brown
           He From Macon, Co.N.C.

Moss,Albert S.--25   Oct.17,1889 B.G.Wild M.G.
  Bryson,Jennie--18   At Webster Ts.
           Wit; H.C.McKee, L.L.Leatherwood,
                  May Leatherwood.

Moss,E.M.--21   Apr.14,1895 R.H.Stewart J.P.
  Pierson,S.T.--19   At Mountain Ts.
           Wit; B.M.Peek, G.B.Bumgarner,T.B.Bumgarner

Moss,James E.--32   Apr.29,1875 J.A.Moore J.P.
  Rogers,Addie--18   At Hugh Rogers'
           Wit; J.M.Hooper, Hix Wike

Moss,John J.--21   Nov.21,1878 J.P.Stuart ---
  Stuart,L.J.--17   At M.M.Stuart's
           Wit; A.S.Bryson, G.S.Bowman

Moss,John M.--36   License Issued May 9,1901
  Moody,Nassie--18   NOT Returned

Moss,Julius M.--21   Dec.6,1899   J.C.Evitt J.P.
  Stewart,Rutha J.--17 At Wm.Stewart's
           Wit; John Stewart,Dick Henderson,
                  Mandie Stewart.

Moss,Matt R.--23   Oct.10,1889 B.G.Wild M.G.
  York,Cora--21   At Webster Ts.
            Wit; J.M.Long,Jr. James Ashe, J.B.Wild

Moss,Milton-- Montieth,Mary Ann--	May 28,1863 At --------	Wm.Wilson	J.P.
Moss,Milton W.-- Wilson,Margaret C.--	Sept.12,1863 At ---------	Wm.Wilson	J.P.
Moss,Thomas L.--23 Butler,H.E.--19	Jan.5,1873 At Levi Butler's Wit; -------	David Wike	J.P.
Moss,Wilburn R.--17 Stuart,Sarah--20	Dec.17,1884 At Wm.Moss' Wit; B.F.Owens, W.D.Childers	John Owens	M.G.
Moss,William--67 Shelton,Caroline--67	Jan.4,1900 At "Bride's Res." Wit; V.F.Brown, J.O.Price, D.A.Watson	A.C.Queen	B.M.
Moss,W.R.--18 Pierson,Saddie--17	Sept.6,1896 At Hamburg Ts. Wit; W.R.Stewart, J.M.Moss, B.Norton	R.H.Stewart	J.P.
Mull,David N.--21 Buchanan,Synthia--20	Dec.12,1885 At Jeff Hooper's Wit; N.J.Hooper, E.M.Hooper	A.B.Henson	M.G.
Mull,Jerry B.--20 Huffman,Hiley--18	License Issued Dec.16,1886 NOT Returned		
Mull,John A.--21 Melton,Vianna--21	Sept.29,1881 At Gilbert Melton's Wit; W.A.Queen, G.B.Queen	B.N.Queen	B.M.
Mull,J.A.--31 Watson,Lena--31	June 27,1891 J.M.Keener,Min.Free Bapt. At Caney Fork Wit; E.Watson, M.C.Warlick, W.J.Mull		
Mull,L.N.--21 Massangale,Deby--21	Aug.21,1891 At Canada Ts. Wit; J.M.Keener, M.C.Warlick, E.J.Rader	W.T.Campbell	M.G.
Mull,Willaim--20 Melton,Artie--20	Dec.25,1881 At Gilbert Melton's Wit; Allen Mull, George Queen	R.H.Stephens	J.P.
Murry,L.--22 Clayton,Sarah--21	Mar.11,1885 At G.W.Clayton's Wit; J.P.Calhoun, J.B.Clayton He From "Alabama,U.S.A."	J.R.Crawford	J.P.
Naff,William C.--24 McCambell,Mary V.--18	Feb.9,1879 At D.G.Bryson's Wit; D.G.Bryson, S.A.Montieth Both From Haywood, Co. N.C.	W.Ensley	B.M.
Naly,Dier-- Bumgarner,Rachal--	Feb.23,1865 At --------	J.B.Sherrill	J.P.
Naly,John-- Sherrill,M.D.--	Nov.1,1866 At -------	W.A.Enloe	---
Nations,Albert--19 Wike,Rebecca--19	May 22,1898 At "Near V.W.Jones'" Wit; Lee Fisher, A.C.Elders, B.A.McMahan	T.C.Jones	J.P.
Nations,Allen--22 Ward,J.U.--16	Apr.6,1890 At Qualla Ts. Wit; J.T.Nations, J.B.Gibson, R.C.Parris	S.W.Cooper	J.P.

Nations,Asaph-- Cocherham,C.P.--	Feb.4,1866 At -------	John M.Harris	Elder
Nations,Baxter--21 Harris,Sallie--21	License Issued NOT Returned	June 16,1901	
Nations,James E.--22 Amburs,Mary--18	July 1,1877 At Wm.Bumgarner's Wit; Aseph Nations, R.D.Davis	W.M.Bumgarner	J.P.
Nations,James T.--19 Franklin,Mary--21	Feb.5,1882 At J.E.McLain's Wit; S.G.Ensley, S.C.Nations	J.E.McLain	J.P.
Nations,Jessie--24 Bridges,Josie--19	Jan.1,1899 At " In Public Road" Wit;W.A.Cunningham,W.J.Miller,W.P.McLain	D.S.Coley	B.M.
Nations,John S.--19 Turpin,Lily--18	July 17,1898 At Wm.Holcombe's Wit; Mack Buchanan, A.W.Bumgarner	Wm.Bumgarner	J.P.
Nations,Marion-- Gibson,Polly--	Apr.10,1853 At --------	J.B.Sherrill	J.P.
Nations,Robert V.--21 Farley,Laura C.--17	July 9,1882 At James Farley's Wit; J.H.House, S.H.Hughes He from Swain, Co. N.C.	J.B.Raby	J.P.
Nations,Reb.V.--20 Franklin,Emila--20	Feb.5,1882 At J.E.McLain's Wit; S.G?Ensley, S.C.Allison	J.E.McLain	J.P.
Nations,R.L.--22 Dillard,Jane--18	Sept.2,1877 At -------- Wit; Thad.Dillard, Thad. Harris	J.S.Keener	---
Nations,W.E.--22 Gipson,Alma--10	Dec.11,1897 At Wilmont,N.C. Wit; W.L.Farley,Mattie R.House,J.H.House	J.H.House	J.P.
Nelson,E.W.--27 Shaw,Mary E.--23	Nov.29,1885 At T.J.Shaw's Wit; R.N.Fisher, B.F.Shaw	A.B.Clements	M.G.
Nelson,Joseph--24 Browman,Frances--18	Apr.2,1873 At -------	Sidney Ash	J.P.
Nichols,A.A.--25 Cole,Kidder--20	June 4,1899 At George Cole's Res. Wit;Lillie Sisk,W.R.Hooper,Martha Huck- leby.	J.C.Henderson	J.P.
Nichols,J.F.--20 Brooks,Emma--18	Aug.19,1898 At "Home of Bride's" Wit;Hattie E.Divilbliss,Pearl Swearinger, Dillard Brooks.	James E.Divilbliss	M.G.
Nichols,Robert--22 Parker,Cornellie--19	June 24,1900 At Henry Nichols' Wit;H.C.Crumly,H.Nichols,T.M.Frizzell	J.B.Ensley	J.P.
Nicholson,Andrew-- Hooper,Elizabeth--	Mar.26,1871 At --------	R.H.Stephens	J.P.

Nicholson,David--31 Rochester,Emma--28	May 6,1894 At Cashiers Valley Wit; F.Rochester,J.B.Rochester,Maud H.	J.A.Hooper	J.P.
Nicholson,Davis--39 Mull,Debby--29	June 25,1900 At Andrew Nicholson's Wit; Steve Shelton, G.W.Nicholson	W.A.Brown	J.P.
Nicholson,E.Oscar--21 Walker,Alice--18	License Issued NOT Returned	July 6,1901	
Nicholson,George--19 Hooper,Maranda--17	Dec.19,1878 At Thomas Hooper's Wit; T.W.Leopard, G.R.Murphree	G.W.Hooper	---
Nicholson,John D.A.--20 Dillard,Mattie E.--23	License Issued NOT Returned	Sept.2,1887	
Nicholson,John E.--21 Watson,Margaret--35	Jan.23,1890 At Sylva, N.C. Wit;W.Nicholson,E.Nicholson,M.Nicholson	A.M.Parker	J.P.
Nicholson,John W.--50 Price,M.E.--30	May 1,1898 At L.W.Hooper's Wit;A.E.Hooper,O.L.Hooper,S.B.Golden	L.W.Hooper	B.M.
Nicholson,Lemuel--18 Ash,Mary--16	Nov.25,1883 At Harriet Sitton's Wit; G.E.Painter, J.D.Zachary	O.B.Coward	J.P.
Nicholson,Marion--20 Wood,Ellen--23	Oct.21,1894 At Caney Fork Wit;Nelse Henson,Miles Revies,Booth Price.	M.C.Warlick	M.G.
Nicholson,M.F.--21 Dillard,Nannie L.--19	May 5,1895 At Cashiers Wit;W.L.Dillard,Will Nicholson,J.C.Wike	J.A.Hooper	J.P.
Nicholson,Nathan--23 Fox,Emeline--22	License Issued Returned-- NOT EXECUTED	Oct.31,1900	
Nicholson,Nathan--22 Alexander,Belle--22	Apr.2,1901 At Robert Dills' Wit;Robt.Dills,Mag Dills,Gill Philips	J.M.Watson	J.P.
Nicholson,Thomas--24 Page,Bethena--17	Apr.18,1897 At Caney Fork Wit; R.P.Powell, Julia Wells	A.C.Queen	B.M.
Nicholson,Will--25 Pruitt,Florence--20	Oct.7,1894 At Cashier Valley Wit; J.C.Wike, F.P.Zachary	L.M.Dillard	J.P.
Nicholson,William--21 Wikle,Adline--30	Sept.16,1888 At Robt.Watson's Wit; Clingman Ashe, Robt.Watson	John T.Wike	J.P.
Noblett,Ed.E.--24 Anderson,L.L.--26	July 25,1886 At Wm.Bumgarner's Wit; G.E.Nations, D.Davis	Wm.Bumgarner	J.P.
Noland,Masengale--26 Berry,Minnie G.--20	Sept.17,1885 At Emila Davis' Wit; M.Bumgarner, D.A.Davis	W.H.H.Hughes	J.P.
Norman,Benjamin-- Parris,Lucinda--	Oct.13,1869 At --------	A.J.Hall	J.P.

Norman,B.P.--20   License Issued   Oct.12,1901
  Cabe,Mary C.--18   NOT Returned

Norman,D.S.--   Nov.31,1871   W.R.Crawford   M.G.
  Brooks,Elizabeth--   At --------

Norman,James--21   Oct.24,1897   J.E.Cogdille   J.P.
  Hooper,Zola--18   At Joseph Hooper's
                          Wit; Ida Nichols

Norman,M.A.--22   Jan.2,1881   S.R.Cook   J.P.
  Wilson,Sarah--14   At Wm.Cogdill's
                          Wit; Samuel Queen, J.I.Norman

Norman,Robt.V.--19   Sept.4,1892   R.R.Fisher   J.P.
  McKay,Mary J.--17   At Scotts Creek
                          Wit; S.D.McKay, W.H.Blanton, S.E.Blan---?

Norris,L.D.--19   Mar.10,1901   J.P.Stewart   J.P.
  Stewart,Sarah--18   At "Home of Bride"
                          Wit; Jno.Stewart,Ella Carrol, M.M.Pierson

Norton,Barrach P.--   Dec.25,1855   N.G.Abram   J.P.
  Hill,Levina--   At --------

Norton,Burris--23   License Issued   Jan.27,1880
  Wilson,Sarah--20   NOT Returned

Norton,Griffin--19   Oct.13,1887   John P.Stuart J.P.
  Robinson,Fannie--18   At M.D.Adams'
                          Wit; D.Adams, Ellen Bennett

Norton,E.P.--42   Oct.23,1889   B.N.Queen   M.G.
  McGuire,Sally--26   At Hamburg Ts.
                          Wit; J.N.Bumgarner, S.L.McGuire
                          He From Macon, Co. N.C.

Norton,J.E.--28   Jan.16,1887   J.H.Brendle   J.P.
  Davis,Sallie--28   At Emily Davis'
                          Wit; J.D.Zachary, W.C.Norton

Norton,William--66   May 3,1886   G.W.Spake   M.M.
  Floody,Sarah E.--50   At Mrs.Floody's
                          Wit; W.L.Dillard, W.R.Hooper

Norton,William C.--22   May 6,1880   R.S.Owens   M.S.
  Coward,Sallie J.--18   At N.Coward's
                          Wit; J.E.Norton, J.R.Zachary

Norwood,Stephens--21 (Col) May 14,1874   T.K.Welch   J.P.
  Knox,Caroline--18   (Col) At Jackson Hyatt's
                          Wit; Jackson Hyatt, Mary Hyatt

Ogle,Isaac--   Oct.26,1857   Eli Robert   ----
  Collens,Sarah E.--   At --------

Owens,James--19   Feb.14,1884   W.A.Queen   J.P.
  Mathis,Dove E.--16   At D.E.Bryson's
                          Wit; D.E.Bryson, J.Owen

Owen,James--22   Aug.13,1900   A.B.Thomas   B.M.
  Saunders,Belle--21   At A.B.Thomas'
                          Wit; J.E.Henson, C.M.Henry, C.W.Owen

Owen,J.D.--29   Oct.28,1894   J.C.Wood   J.P.
  Brown,Laura--33   At Canada Ts.
                          Wit; G.W.Banthes, G.W.Shook
                          He From Transylvania,Co.N.C.

Owen,Luther--22   Mar.26,1893   J.A.Galloway M.G.
  Brown,Varina--19   At Canada Ts.
                          Wit; J.B.McCall, A.E.Galloway, T.H.Owen

Owen,W.R.--23   Aug.4,1892   A.C.Queen   M.G.
  Sims,Stacy--20   At Hamburg Ts.
                          Wit; H.R.Queen,Thomas Franks,Geo.Bryson

Owenby,G.T.--26   Nov.5,1893   W.P.Jones   J.P.
  Brown,Florence I.--19   At Barker Creek
                          Wit; T.B.Gunter, W.H.Gates, A.D.Jones

Owens,Benjamin F.H.--21   Aug.26,1888   John P.Stuart J.P.
  Smith,Maletha A.J.--25 At R.H.Smith's
                          Wit; W.J.Stuart, M.S.Brown

Owens,Charles--21   June 12,1898   J.A.Galloway M.G.
  Galloway,Paralee--22   At Clifford Galloway's
                          Wit; A.H.Owens, E.P.Galloway, S.R.Owens
                          He From Transyania, Co. N.C.

Owens,Dock--   June 10,1870   Jas. Hooper   J.P.
  Long,Sary Jane--   At ---------

Owens,Elijah--22   Jan.27,1901   J.H.Owens   M.G.
  Brown,Mattie Jane--18   At Geo.Owens'
                          Wit; W.S.McLain, Thos.Owens, Delly Queen

Owens,Jasper--18   Aug.17,1887   J.A.Galloway M.G.
  Shular,Novella J.--15   At Ruth Shular's
                          Wit; R.H.Brown, H.R.Queen

Owens,Jessee--28   Sept.20,1888   John P.Stuart J.P.
  Carroll,Rhoda A.--26   At James Carroll's
                          Wit; Zeb V.Watson, A.C.Watson

Owens,John--77   Oct.25,1872   W.C.Berry   B.M.
  Blackburn,Frances--35   At Hugh Rogers'
                          Wit; --------

Owens,J.W.--27   Feb.28,1889   A.C.Queen   B.M.
  Slatton,Clarissa I--18 At Hamburg Ts.
                          Wit; W.A.Ashe, R.C.Owens, G.H.Slatton
                          He From Transylvania,Co. N.C.

Owens,L.M.--21   Dec.24,1896   J.A.Galloway M.G.
  Woods,V.J.--17   At Canada Ts.
                          Wit; J.H.Owens, H.B.Woods, Mat Woods

Owens,Marion--46   Mar.13,1884   G.W.Spake   M.M.
  Brown,Elizabeth--36   At A.J.Long's
                          Wit; W.E.Moore, F.H.Leatherwood

Owens,Marion--50   Nov.18,1886   B.H.Queen   M.G.
  Middleton,Nelly Ann--34 At Mary Middleton's
                          Wit; J.M.Brown, J.M.Shook

Owens,Mills T.--22   Dec.23,1880   S.P.C.Shelton J.P.
  Leopard,Sarah A.--16   At T.N.Leopard's
                          Wit; Nathan Coward, A.N.Bumgarner

Owens,Pulaski E.--20   License Issued   July 18,1895
  Hoxit,Tinie--16   "NO MARRIAGE"

Owens,Robert A.--27   Nov.17,1881   George D.French M.G.
  Sherrill,Elizzie--23   At "Church in Webster"
                          Wit; A.J.Long Jr. J.M.Candler

Owens,Tillman--22 Parker,Sarah L.--19	Jan.6,1874 At A.W.Parker's Wit; ------	J.H.Mathis	J.P.
Owens,William E.--27 Tally,Elizabeth J.--19	Mar.14,1879 At Wm.Moss' Wit; Wm.Moss, J.M.Henderson	J.P.Stuart	----
Owens,William J.--22 Parker,Maggie M.--22	Mar.10,1886 At B.N.Queen's Wit;Lilly O.Brown, M.C.Queen	B.N.Queen	B.M.
Oxineer,Wm.M.--22 Queen, Mary E.--22	Mar.26,1899 At T.H.Queen, J.L.Snider, T.F.Grear He From Haywood,Co. N.C.	A.B.Queen	B.M.
Oxner,Lewis--23 Watson,Rebecca--21	Mar.31,1889 At Cullowhee Wit; S.W.Henson,J.F.York, John Crawford He From Haywood, Co. N.C.	A.B.Thomas	B.M.
Oxner,William--28 Messer,Laura--20	Apr.10,1892 At Webster, N.C. Wit; Alice Snider,R.L.Snider, M.E.Snider	B.G.Wild	M.G.
Painter,Andrew C.--20 Hawkins,Demogna B.--16	Oct.18,1885 At G.W.Hawkins' Wit; R.Coward, W.C.Long	Bragg Hooper	J.P.
Painter,Elbert M.--36 Bryson,Mary A.--18	Nov.11,1878 At "Near Cullowhee Church" Wit; ------	R.L.Watson	----
Painter,Ellis--24 Ensley,Julia--18	May 11,1890 At Sylva Ts. Wit; A.C.Robison,R.J.Crawford,J.M.Crawford	A.M.Parker	J.P.
Painter,H.H.--27 Allison,Hattie--22	Nov.22,1899 At Meth. Church Wit; H.E.Johnson,A.B.Brown,Joseph J.Hooper	J.E.Abernathy	M.M.
Painter,Julius H.--20 King,Laura--19	Apr.27,1888 At Love's Church Wit; J.D.Parker, Thos.F.Long	A.H.Sims	M.G.
Painter,R.A.--52 Watson,Sallie--19	Apr.17,1892 At Sylva, N.C. Wit; J.D.Sitton, J.W.Cope, J.L.Ashe	J.A.Wild	J.P.
Painter,William--24 Crawford,Cumire--22	Aug.2,1885 At Mathew Crawford's Wit; R.A.Painter, J.M.Sutton	A.J.Hall	J.P.
Page,John H.--50 Jones,Saronias--45	Jan.2,1891 At Caney Fork Wit; James E.Hawkins	G.W.Haekins	J.P.
Pangle,Geo.W.--27 Sutton,Lula--18	Feb.26,1888 At Solomon Sutton's Wit; N.C.Dills, J.W.Buchanan	W.A.Dills	J.P.
Pangle,Robert L.--26 Sutton,Catherine--26	May 12,1895 At Dillsboro Wit; P.H.Sutton,Martha Fowler, N.E.Pangle	W.C.Conner	B.M.

Pangle,William--26   Aug.26,1888   J.C.Watkins   J.P.
  Sutton,Mary--22   At "Bogg's & Loe saw mill"
                             Wit; Flora Watkins, J.B.Young

Pannel,John--22   Jan.15,1882   J.B.Raby   J.P.
  Gunter,Sallie--18   At J.B.Raby's
                             Wit; W.A.Raby

Pannel,John--21   Jan.22,1899   J.R.Crawford   J.P.
  Clayton,Alma--15   At D.Clayton's
                             Wit; Wiley Conner,R.L.Cook,S.R.Cook

Panter,R.A.--   Sept.27,1863   W.A.Enloe   J.P.
  Hall,Amanda--   At ---------

Panter,S.C.--   Dec.15,1868   A.J.Hall   ----
  Smith,J.E.C.--   At --------

Parker,Albert N.--23   Sept.4,1872   A.D.Hooper   J.P.
  Bryson,Margaret C.--18   At "In Road"
                             Wit; -------

Parker,Alfred--21   May 6,1900   E.M.Coward   J.P.
  Phillips,Lavada--19   At Moses Creek
                             Wit;D.H.Stephens,W.B.Morris,E.H.Stephens

Parker,Alfred M.--29   Nov.9,1880   R.A.Owens   M.G.
  Cannon,Lula A.--18   At E.R.Hampton's
                             Wit; E.R.Hampton, A.D.Allen

Parker,Anderson--46   July 29,1888   G.W.Hawkins   J.P.
  Parker,Ann--27   At Caney Fork
                             Wit; James E.Hawkins

Parker,A.F.--20   Mar.15,1898   R.L.Phillips   J.P.
  Stephens,Etta--18   At J.N.Arrington's
                             Wit;L.E.Hooper,A.Hooper,D.H.Stephens

Parker,A.J.--22   Oct.27,1892   A.C.Queen   M.G.
  Crawford,Mary--18   At Canada Ts.
                             Wit;J.G.Parker,Henry Ashe,H.Crawford

Parker,A.Jerome--22   Mar.5,1899   Hardy M.Bennett, M.M.
  Presley,Margaret--16   At M.H.Bennett's
                             Wit; Haynes Bennett,Wm.Rigdon,J.W.Benett

Parker,Charlie W.--26   Dec.18,1881   G.W.Spake   M.M.
  Morris,Sarah E.--18   At M. Church in Webster
                             Wit; A.J.Long, W.A.Enloe

Parker,C.B.--20   Feb.27,1898   J.M.Keener   B.M.
  Shuler,Lora--20   At Caney Fork
                             Wit; J.C.Shuler,J.H.Smith,D.L.Parker

Parker,David--22   Feb.24,1881   L.W.Hooper   M.G.
  Parker,Allice--21   At M.M.Brown's
                             Wit; G.W.Hawkins, O.B.Coward

Parker,E.S.--21   Dec.7,1897   R.L.Phillips   J.P.
  Stephens,Teola--19   At R.H.Stephens'
                             Wit; J.E.Long

Parker,George M.--20   Aug.21,1883   J.M.Smith   J.P.
  Wood,Elsie--16   At J.M.Wood's
                             Wit; J.H.Parker, Martha Parker

Parker,Henry--19 Leadford,Elvira--19	June 12,1881 At T.J.Bryson's Wit; Nathan Queen, R.C.Bryson	T.J.Bryson	J.P.
Parker,Henry--28 Mills,Cyntha--29	License Issued NOT Returned	Oct.18,1890	
Parker,Hugh A.-- Hawkins,Mary--	Sept.29,1855 At ---------	B.N.Queen	B.M.
Parker,Hugh A.--40 Parker,Martha J.--40	Oct.3,1872 At R.L.Watson's Wit; R.L.Watson She From Georgia	Lewis Queen	B.M.
Parker,Hugh Robert--27 Davis,Sally--18	June 14,1890 At Webster Ts. Wit; J.M.Wearley,D.G.Bigham,Scott Brown	B.G.Wild	M.G.
Parker,James--60 Bumgarner,Rebecca--30	Sept.2,1873 At James Parker's Wit;A.Nations, R.Jones	F.M.Nations	J.P.
Parker,James--21 Coward,Candall--16	Feb.6,1894 At Caney Fork Wit; D.H.Moffit, Jno. Aiken	G.W.Hawkins	J.P.
Parker,James A.--24 Parker,Viola--18	Sept.1,1896 At River Ts. Wit; John Woodring,F.S.Jones, J.H.Wood	A.C.Queen	B.M.
Parker,James M.-- Low,Sarah--	Feb.20,1872 At --------	R.H.Stephens	J.P.
Parker,Jason A.--22 Brown,Elmira--18	Dec.6,1873 At Levi Brown's Wit; ---------	G.W.Hawkins	J.P.
Parker,John--35 Jenkins,Bettie--25	July 16,1891 At --------- Wit; S.Hadley,Mrs.S.Hadley,J.A.Williams He From Swain, Co. N.C.	P.P.McLean	M.G.
Parker,John--22 Parker,Martha--18	Nov.19,1873 At P.M.Parker's Wit; ----------	G.W.Hawkins	J.P.
Parker,John--28 Wood,Joice S.--22	May 6,1894 At Caney Fork Wit; H.G.Cook,W.A.Hooper, L.E.Hooper	R.R.Coward	J.P.
Parker,J.A.--22 Woodring,Millie--18	Dec.3,1893 At River Ts. Wit; J.R.Queen,John Middleton, A.M.Parker	A.C.Queen	B.M.
Parker,J.D.--28 Painter,Ellen--19	Nov.10,1889 At Webster Ts. Wit; J.H.Painter, E.D.Franklin, J.W.B..	A.J.Long	J.P.
Parker,J.M.-- Brown,W.C.--	Dec.27,1870 At --------	B.N.Queen	Elder
Parker,Levi-- Queen,Mary M.--	Mar.16,1871 At --------	John H.Mathis	J.P.
Parker,Loamer--19 Hooper,Dillard--14	License Issued NOT Returned	Jan.12,1901	

Parker,M.Arlander--22 Nov.29,1900 James Cook J.P.
Hooper,Fannie--18   At Aaron Hooper's
           Wit; S.P.Parker, Garlan Wood, W.A.Hooper

Parker,O.Augustus--25 Dec.25,1900 W.F.Cook B.M.
Aiken,Anner--20   At "At home of Bride"
           Wit; J.H.Phillips, P.L.Parker, W.F.Wood

Parker,Perry D.--20   Nov.11,1875 W.A.Brown J.P.
Brown,Mary A.--   At D.M.Brown's
           Wit; A.M.Parker, H.A.Phillips

Parker,Robert L.--20   Jan.22,1878 Lewis Queen ----
Brown,Rebecca--18   At D.M.Brown's
           Wit; Ellen Brown, S.J.Queen

Parker,Samuel--   Mar.8,1864 Nathan Coward ---
Carson,Jane--   At -------

Parker,Samuel--21   Sept.30,1890 G.W.Hawkins J.P.
Brown,Georgiann--18   At Caney Fork
           Wit; J.E.Hawkins, W.H.Hooper, E.L.Watson

Parker,Solomon H.--30 Dec.24,1879 J.N.Cathey J.P.
Barker,Lydia--30   At Lydia Parker's
           Wit; S.J.Parker, Thomas Brown

Parker,S.M.--23   June 12,1892 B.N.Queen M.G.
Woodring,Laura--19   At River Ts.
           Wit; Victoria Queen, A.J.Parker, A.R.Queen

Parker,S.M.--28   Sept.20,1896 J.P.Calhoun J.P.
Henry,Sarah--23   At Scotts Creek
           Wit; W.H.T.Dillard, B.Hooper, C.K.Ensley

Parker,S.V.--22   Jan.28,1897 W.H.T.Dillard J.P.
Henry,Mila--19   At Scott Creek
           Wit; J.O.Price, A.E.Henry, E.L.Henry

Parker,Thos.Jr.--21   Oct.22,1891 A.C.Queen M.G.
Nicholson,Sarah E.--19 At Caney Fork
           Wit; E.M.Coward, C.H.Coward

Parker,Thos.--22   Aug.13,1891 G.W.Hawkins J.P.
Woods,Altha--19   At Caney Fork
           Wit; N.J.Hooper, Arilla Parker

Parker,Weston--21   Jan.31,1894 A.V.P.Bryson J.P.
Brendle,Hattie--18   At "Harness shop, Webster,N.C."
           Wit; H.C.McKee, N.Coward, W.W.Rhinehart

Parker,Wilburn--21   Feb.17,1895 A.C.Queen B.M.
Parker,Ida--16   At Caney Fork
           Wit; J.H.Painter, D.W.Massingale,Boon Ward

Parker,William M.--2- Sept.1,1882 L.W.Hooper M.G.
Hooper,Mary J.--17   At "In the Road"
           Wit; James Cook, Thad Wood

Parker,Willie--21   Sept.4,1885 Bragg Hooper J.P.
Hooper,Leah--15   At "In the Road"
           Wit; H.Hooper, W.C.Long

Parks,J.D.--23   Dec.21,1892 L.W.Allen J.P.
York,Callie--16   At Sylva,Town.
           Wit; M.N.Moss, S.J.York, J.M.York
           He From McDowell, Co.N.C.

Parks,Thomas--24   Jan.10,1883   J.W.Bird   B.M.
  Baker,Julettie--19   At J.W.Bird's
                              Wit; Sopha Bird, Nellie Jones

Parmel,Andrew G.--   Mar.16,1857   E.D.Brendle   M.G.
  Gibson,Marthy--   At --------

Parnell,James--20   Oct.10,1899   Jas.W.Terrell J.P.
  Mills,Mary--22   At Webster,N.C.
                              Wit; W.W.Rhinehart,J.Robert Long
                              He From Swain,Co. N.C.

Parris,Andrew C.--20   Sept.4,1884   William Bumgarner J.P.
  Jones,Caddo--20   At Samuel Jones'
                              Wit; J.E.Nations, David Nations

Parris,A.C.--28   Aug.15,1897   A.B.Thomas   M.G.
  Frizzell,Laura--23   At Savannah Ts.
                              Wit; A.B.Thomas, Joseph J.Hooper,
                                    D.H.Ashe, Maggie Raby.

Parris,A.S.--27   Sept.12,1897   D.H.Ashe   J.P.
  Green,Lavisa--26   At Green's Creek
                              Wit; J.W.Cabe, Belle Ashe

Parris,Ed.--22   Oct.3,1897   J.B.Ensley   J.P.
  Reed,Mary--16   At C.C.Reed's
                              Wit; A.C.Barnes,S.W.Ensley, W.A.Mills

Parris,Fidells--21   Aug.27,1899   A.B.Henson   B.M.
  Cogdille,Lela--19   At W.J.Cogdille's Res.
                              Wit; J.B.Cogdille,J.W.Blanton,W.J.Cogdille

Parris,Isaac D.--21   Sept.30,1877   J.E.McLain   J.P.
  Davis,Mary Jane--22   At A.J.Davis'
                              Wit; A.J.Parris, J.E.Davis

Parris,James--25   Apr.14,1889   A.J.Hall   J.P.
  Wilson,Florance--17   At Scotts Creek
                              Wit; Pursell Parris,J.C.Ensley, A.C.Henry

Parris,John A.--21   June 5,1895   W.H.H.Hughes   J.P.
  Frizzell,Maggie C.--23   At Webster
                              Wit; Belle Allison,Love Keener,W.P.Allman

Parris,J.M.--   Aug.27,1865   E.D.Brendle   Elder
  Hall,D.E.--   July 20,1865 (Both dates marked through)
                              (Mr.E.D.Brendle was clerk of Court.)

Parris,Manly--23   Oct.6,1895   A.B.Thomas   M.G.
  Bryson,Lettie E.--19   At Scotts Creek
                              Wit; Samuel Cogdille,J.T.Carson,J.A.Smith

Parris,Monroe--21   Jan.29,1895   A.W.Jacobs, Min.M.E.C.S.
  Collins,Dora--19   At Webster
                              Wit; Hannah Hall,Lou Jacobs,James Marshall

Parris,Nelson--24   Nov.28,1894   Joseph Hoyle   J.P.
  Jones,Alma P.--16   At Sylva, N.C.
                              Wit; W.B.Henry, James Parris,D.E.Henry

Parris,R.C.--23   Apr.28,1896   L.L.Brown   J.P.
  Cunningham,Malissa--21   At Barker Creek
                              Wit; T.S.Brooks, Julius Jones

Parris,Samuel--21   Jan.29,1874   W.Ensley   B.M.
  Bryson,Sarah J.--21   At James Queen's
                           Wit; ----------

Parris,Wm.C.--   Jan.1,1854   Allen Fisher   J.P.
  Duts,Louina--   At -------

Parris,William L.--21   Aug.19,1877   W.Bumgarner   J.P.
  Nations,Mary--19   At James Parker's
                           Wit; Elias Jones, James Parker

Parton,Harry--25   Mar.3,1889   William Bumgarner J.P.
  Jones,Ella--20   At Savannah Ts.
                           Wit; Fuller Elder, Riley McMahan

Parton,Mon--21   Jan.16,1894   J.F.Brown   J.P.
  Gunter,Dona--21   At Barker Creek
                           Wit; S.Jones, J.A.Messer, W.W.Jones

Paterson,J.M.--   Oct.29,1869   L.G.Ward   J.P.
  Carr,Julianan--   At --------

Patterson,Lon--20   Nov.26,1893   Wiley E.Conner B.M.
  Jones,Sallie--21   At Barker Creek
                           Wit; J.L.Nations, S.A.Bradley

Patterson,Wisdom E.--19   July 18,1900   J.B.Ensley   J.P.
  Williams,Josie--19   At Beta, N.C.
                           Wit;T.M.Frizzell,B.G.Spearman,John A.Will-
                                                                iams.
Patton,Andrew J.--   Mar.29,1866   A.Mingus   J.P.
  Enloe,Sarah E.--   At --------

Paxton,W.M.--19   Aug.19,1894   Joseph Hoyle   J.P.
  Walker,S.J.--20   At Scotts Creek
                           Wit; W.H.T.Dillard,R.J.Mills,A.C.Robinson

Payton,John--30   Dec.25,1898   E.Myers   Meth.Min.
  Cogdill,Lizzie--23   At L.J.Hall's
                           Wit; F.R.Enloe, Lee J.Hall, W.R.Hyatt

Pearson,Jeremiah--25   Jan.10,1875   J.H.Alley   J.P.
  Adams,Ema--19   At David Norton's
                           Wit; David Norton, Octa Norton

Pearson,Lee W.--19   June 4,1881   J.P.Stuart   J.P.
  Watson,Laura--18   At William Watson's
                           Wit; Jehu P.Stuart, J.R.Owens

Pearson,Mack M.--20   Dec.2,1875   J.P.Stuart   J.P.
  Potts,Martha--18   At Allen Potts'
                           Wit; John Carroll, E.Hedden

Pearson,Rodrick--20   May 6,1875   J.L.Corbin   J.P.
  White,Susan--16   At J.J.Jennings'
                           Wit; J.J.Jennings, M.M.Jennings

Peek,Beaufort M.--20   Mar.7,1878   J.P.Stuart   J.P.
  Moss,Harriet M.--18   At Wm.Moss'
                           Wit; W.E.Owens, J.T.Peek

Peeler,J.A.--24   Sept.24,1894   T.B.McCundy   M.G.
  McLain,M.E.--24   At Webster
                           Wit; W.E.Moore, J.W.Terrell, Fred Moore

Pell,E.F.--38 Allison,E.H.--42	Oct.15,1890 At Cashiers Valley Wit; Eva S.Bryson, M.A.Bennett	C.P.Bryson	J.P.
Pickens,J.M.--22 (Col) Freeman,Martha--19 (Col)	Aug.16,1892 At Sylva Town Wit; R.A.Tretwell, John Casey	A.P.Parker	J.P.
Pickens,Robert--21 (Col) Gibbs.Ida--18 (Col)	July 28,1894 At Sylva Wit; Tom Pickens, W.M.Smith, P.L.Hyatt	L.W.Allen	J.P.
Pickens,Thomas--21 (Col) Gibbs,Sarah--21 (Col)	Apr.1,1893 At Sylva,N.C. Wit; A.Bryson, Fidelia Love	L.W.Allen	J.P.
Picklesimer,Henry B.--28 Alley,Effie M.--27	Dec.25,1897 At White Side Cove Wit; Cora Alley, H.J.Bumgarner, T.G.Picklesimer.	M.D.Edwards	J.P.
Pinion,James--20 Frady,Sarah--15	Apr.9,1882 At Baxter Rogers' Wit; J.S.Stillwell, G.B.Rogers	E.P.Stillwell	J.P.
Pitts,Clifton--30 Tilley,Modenia--34	License Issued Aug.9,1901 NOT Returned		
Phillips,A.L.--22 Moore,Oda(Ida)--18	Oct.15,1897 At Sylva Ts. Wit; B.W.Thomas, J.F.Phillips	R.A.Painter	J.P.
Phillips,Daniel H.-- Crawford,Iffa--	Feb.27,1871 At --------	A.W.Vaughn	---
Phillips,D.A.--26 Woods,Nora--18	Nov.27,1898 At Jerry Woods' Wit; A.J.Woods, F.J.Hooper, W.A.Hooper	J.M.Keener	Bap. Min.
Phillips,Houston--18 Hooper,Callie--16	July 27,1884 At R.H.Stephens' Wit; W.C.Wood, R.C.Moffit	R.H.Stephens	J.P.
Phillips,James M.--57 Davis,Lena--27	June 18,1887 At In Tunnel Wit; Winnie Slaton,S.R.Davis	J.C.Watkins	J.P.
Phillips,James M.--57 Slaton,Minnie--17	Jan.1,1888 At J.C.Watkins' Wit; T.A.Carpenter, G.W.Spake	J.C.Watkins	---
Phillips,John G.--26 Barron,Maggie--20	Dec.10,1885 At P.W.Barron's Wit; D.F.Wilbar, Sydney Ashe	P.P.McLain	M.G.
Phillips,John F.--21 Watson,Casie--18	Feb.27,1895 At Sylva Ts. Wit; L.A.Holland, J.M.Crawford, H.M.Shuler	J.P.Brendle	J.P.
Phillips,J.M.--57 Seay,Jenette--20	Dec.3,1895 At Dillsboro, N.C. Wit; G.W.Spake, T.M.Honeycutt; J.H.Lewis	J.C.Watkins	J.P.
Phillips,J.M.--58 Patterson,Nannie--18	Nov.24,1889 At Dillsboro Ts. Wit; A.J.Long, N.N.Thomas, Flora Watkins	J.C.Watkins	J.P.

Phillips,J.O.--18   Oct.29,1899   Rev.J.H.Owen   M.G.
  Shook,Mary E.--20   At James Shook's
                           Wit; C.L.Hooper, J.H.Dunn, J.D.Hamilton

Phillips,J.W.--23   Mar.16,1890   M.C.Warlick   M.G.
  Crawford,Artie--22   At Canada Ts.
                           Wit; D.H.Mathis, A.J.Parker, A.L.Owen

Phillips,Lee--20   Oct.29,1899   J.C.Wood   J.P.
  Mathis,D.M.--18   At Wolf Creek Church
                           Wit; M.F.Galloway, R.J.Shelton

Phillips,M.R.--   Oct.3,1869   A.J.Hall   J.P.
  Blanton,M.M.--   At -------

Phillips,Robert--24   Feb.21,1897   R.R.Coward   J.P.
  Parker,Clara--20   At Caney Fork
                           Wit; L.K.Phillips, J.B.Sherrell,
                                A.S.Patterson, Virgie Cooper.

Phillips,R.A.--   Oct.13,1853   W.H.Higdon   J.P.
  Tatham,Clurinda--   At --------

Phillips,R.O.--42   Mar.17,1895   A.M.Parker   J.P.
  Brinkly,Dellie--41   At Sylva
                           Wit; J.L.Fisher, A.C.Cope, D.J.Bryson

Phiney,Joseph--   Sept.26,1869   Thos. Wilson   J.P.
  Mathis,Elizabeth--   At ---------

Plott,Hebron F.--   May 15,1862   Wm.Ensley   J.P.
  Hall,G.Lavada--   At -------(He son of David Plott Sr.)
                           He From Haywood, Co. N.C.

Plott,Robert H.--22   License Issued   Oct.20,1888
  Crawford,Margaret L.--   NOT Returned

Pope,Thomas--24   (Col)   Nov.17,1895   H.D.Welck   M.G.
  Love,Hattie--19 (Col)   At Scotts Creek
                           Wit; Samuel Cogdill, L.C.Welch, Goleman-
                                                            Bryson.
Potts,Calvin--   Dec.1,1870   Wm.C.Berry M.G.
  Woodard,Sarah--   At -------

Potts,D.H.--22   Dec.18,1890   H.C.Cannon   J.P.
  Cagle,Canadas E.--18   At Webster
                           Wit; S.B.Buchanan, John Cagle, A.D.Cagle

Potts,E.M.--34   Apr.24,1890   W.T.Crisp   J.P.
  Webb,Rutha--17   At Savannah
                           Wit; D.W.Buchanan, E.G.Franks

Potts,Hampton G.--23   June 4,1882   J.P.Stuart   J.P.
  Watson,Margaret--18   At William Watson's
                           Wit; J.R.Owens, John P.Stuart

Potts,Jerry--18   Dec.15,1878   J.P.Stuart   J.P.
  Evitt,Sarah J.--18   At O.M.Evitt's
                           Wit; J.C.Potts, J.D.Evitt

Potts,John B.--20   Sept.29,1881   J.P.Stuart   J.P.
  Stuart,Allis--18   At John Stuart's
                           Wit; J.R.Owens, H.G.Potts

Potts,Rufus P.--26   Oct.18,1877   G.W.Spake   M.M.
  Monday,Ellen--18   At P.M.Monday's
                           Wit; D.D.Davis, P.M.Monday

```
Potts,R.P.--41              May 22,1895        G.W.Spake      M.M.
  Conners,Laura Belle--32   At  Dillsboro, N.C.
                            Wit; A.C.Curtis, Jane Potts,Mary Franklin

Potts,Walker--19            Aug.24,1873        B.H.Jones      J.P.
  Woodard,Rachel--18        At  David Woodard's
                            Wit; James Woodard, Nelse Jones

Potts,William H.--24        Dec.15,1899        W.L.Henson     J.P.
  Deitz,Annie--15           At  Martin Deitz's
                            Wit; John Phillips, Phillips Henson,
                                                    E.J.Watson.

Powell,Jefferson O.--26     Mar.25,1888        C.L.Hooper     J.P.
  Webster,Laura J.--18      At  John Webster's
                            Wit; J.J.Powell, James Pruitt

Powell,Joseph--21           Nov.20,1887        L.W.Hooper     J.P.
  Moore,Emily--19           At  James Moore's
                            Wit; John Green

Powell,Thomas--20           Feb.28,1886        L.W.Hooper     M.G.
  Slaton,Haseltine--18      At  Dick Slaton's
                            Wit; Gurley Nations, F.L.Moody

Prather,J.B.--20    (Col)   Mar.3,1886         Wm.Bumgarner   J.P.
  Loury,Virrdie Q.--18 (Col) At  W.D.Hill's
                            Wit; W.D.Hill, Luther Farley

Presley,A.M.--24            Nov,21,1898        N.J.Fore       J.P.
  Burrell,Agnes--16         At  N.E.Fox's
                            Wit; W.J.Fox, W.S.Fox

Presley,D.L.--              Aug.16,1860        Wm.Wilson      J.P.
  Bennet,Vinna--            At --------

Presley,F.M.--20            July 1,1888        A.D.Hooper     J.P.
  Painter,Mary J.--19       At  Cullowhee
                            Wit; Milas Ashe, Mack Presley

Presley,H.D.--21            May 21,1893        J.W.Davis      J.P.
  Bennett,Bettie J.--20     At  Cullowhee
                            Wit; N.Fox, H.H.Bennett, S.T.Fox

Presley,James--30           Aug.21,1898        V.F.Brown      J.P.
  Presley,Pink--24          At  V.F.Brown's
                            Wit; Sussie Hooper, Dora Brown,Gertie Brown

Presley,L.C.--              Apr.20,1864        E.D.Brendle    J.P.
  Mathis,Matilda--          At  -------

Presley,Robert D.--21       Mar.25,1900        A.C.Queen      B.M.
  Ashe,Iva--16              At  N.J.Fox's
                            Wit; R.C.Ashe, N.J.Fox

Presley,Thomas C.--26       Jan.17,1900        W.L.Henson     J.P.
  Franklin,Bessie--17       At  Cullowhee
                            Wit; W.N.Coward, J.G.Phillips,P.C.Henson

Presley,W.P.--25            Feb.15,1886        J.O.Wallace    J.P.
  Dyers,Maggie--22          At  James Henry's
                            Wit; C.A.Bumgarner, D.C.Wheeler

Prewit,George W.--          Oct.17,1869        E.P.Stillwell
  Buchanan,Martha--         At --------
```

Prince,Cornelius--18
Watson,Elizabeth--18
Aug.9,1895   J.E.Moss   J.P.
At River Ts.
Wit; R.M.Thompson, J.U.Prince

Prince,James--20
Nicholson,Clara--18
Dec.26,1897   W.A.Brown   J.P.
At Bud Nicholson's
Wit; J.M.Nicholson,R.V.Brown,T.T.Nicholson.

Price,James M.--19
Monday,Baty S.--19
Aug.7,1878   D.D.Davis   M.G.
At R.H.Brown's
Wit; A.W.Bryson, David Coward

Price,John B.--19
Stapp,Mary R.--18
Oct.10,1875   L.W.Hooper   B.M.
At Jessee F.Stapp's
Wit; J.M.Price, W.E.Brown

Price,J.N.--25
Wood,Mary--26
Jan.24,1897   Javan Davis, Magistrate
At River Ts.
Wit; D.S.Golden, John Golden, James Parker

Price,M.--
Jones,M.J.--
Dec.31,1865   J.M.Harris,   Rev.--
At --------

Price,P.N.--22
Hooper,Lizzie--27
License Issued   Sept.16,1892
"License Returned NOT Executed no Marriage"

Price,P.N.--24
Hooper,Lizzie--29
May 27,1894   Javan Davis   J.P.
At Cullowhee
Wit; Mary Rogers,Susie Hooper, John Rogers

Price,William H.--21
Watson,Mary E.--18
Sept.28,1882   J.L.Owens   M.G.
At J.M.Parker's
Wit; S.L.Price, J.D.Parker

Price,W.P.--23
Brown,Victoria--23
Mar.26,1899   L.W.Hooper   B.M.
At River Ts.
Wit; John Wike, J.H.Painter, V.F.Brown

Pruit,Elijah--21
Inman,Mattie--21
Sept.18,1881   J.C.Watkins   J.P.
At J.P.Inman's
Wit; James Pruit, T.B.Dillard

Pruett,G.W.--21
Church,Alice V.--16
Apr.10,1898   E.F.Pell   J.P.
At George Pruitt's
Wit; M.Nicholson, John Buchanan, W.C.Buchanan.

Pruit,John--24
King,Emma--16
Dec.24,1884   Thos.J.Love   J.P.
At W.D.King's
Wit; A.M.King, W.Frizzell

Queen,Askew C.--18
Wood,Darcus C.--20
Oct.31,1878   J.W.Galloway   ---
At B.N.Queen's
Wit; J.C.Wood, W.A.Queen

Queen,B.N.--
Carson,Mary--
Nov.8,1855   Wm.R.Crawford   J.P.
At -------

Queen,Ellis W.--24
Ensley,Amy P.--18
Jan.30,1887   J.R.Crawford   J.P.
At T.N.Crawford's
Wit; J.T.Carson, Clingman Bryson

Queen,George W.--20
West,Louisa R.--15
July 12,1878   T.J.Bryson   ---
At --------
Wit; Jeptha Queen, Manley Reece

Queen,Hampton--18   July 15,1882   B.N.Queen   B.M.
 Dawson,Martha J.--18   At Caney Fork
                           Wit; Sylvester Melton, H.R.Queen

Queen,Henry--   Oct.17,1870   A.J.Hall   J.P.
 Ray,Rebecca--   At --------

Queen,H.R.--23   Sept.25,1892   J.L.Owen   M.G.
 Franks,Sallie--18   At Hamburg Ts.
                           Wit; C.L.Harris,Luanna Wilson, J.O.Price

Queen,James--19   Mar.10,1874   G.W.Hawkins   J.P.
 Morris,Margaret--18   At Benjamin Coward's
                           Wit; ------

Queen,James--19   Oct.4,1892   Henry D.Welch M.G.
 Parris,Alice--17   At Scotts Creek
                           Wit; Z.V.Watson, R.J.Crawford

Queen,Jeptha--34   Dec.20,1881   Levi Brown   J.P.
 Shelton,Lucinda--34   At Cinda Shelton's
                           Wit; ------

Queen,John--77   Oct.25,1872   William C.Berry   M.G.
 Blackburn,Frances--35   At --------

Queen,John--30   Apr.20,1879   Tho. Bryson   ----
 Leopard,Feba--25   At John Queen's
                           Wit; Nathan Queen, M.M.Queen

Queen,John--31   Apr.5,1885   R.H.Stephens J.P.
 Woods,V.--30   At R.H.Stephens'
                           Wit; C.T.Woods, D.H.Stephens

Queen,John B.--29   Aug.11,1881   S.R.Cook   J.P.
 Gunter,Margaret--29   At Mary Gunter's
                           Wit; J.R.McKay, T.J.Love

Queen,Joseph--20   Mar.4,1873   W.R.Crawford B.M.
 Carson,Jane--17   At Charlotte Carson's
                           Wit; W.T.Carson, G.W.Crawford

Queen,J.B.--25   Dec.5,1899   S.R.Cook   J.P.
 Bryson,Mary J.--16   At Scotts Creek
                           Wit; R.R.Fisher, Estice Bryson, J.S.Bryson

Queen,J.L.--21   Nov.7,1886   B.N.Queen   B.M.
 Fortner,Mary Ann--18   At E.(M)W.Fortner's
                           Wit; T.H.Fortner, S.N.Coward

Queen,J.M.--   Dec.12,1871   ----   ---
 Manous,M.M.--   At --------

Queen,Levi--23   (Ind) Oct.8,1893   J.W.Bird   M.G.
 Washington,Mary--15 (Ind) At Qualla Ts.
                           Wit; W.T.Crook, C.P.Hipps, J.E.Bird

Queen,Lewis--   May 1,1854   William Hooper J.P.
 Brown,Lucinda--   At -------

Queen,L.D.--29   June 2,1890   S.R.Cook   J.P.
 Harris,M.E.--23   At Scotts Creek
                           Wit; J.R.McKay, S.D.McKay

Queen,L.R.--22   Nov.28,1897   R.R.Coward   J.P.
 Wood,M.M.--19   At J.A.Melton's
                           Wit; S.C.Wood, H.M.Parker, Jim Belt

Queen,Marvin--22   May 25,1883   T.J.Bryson   J.P.
  Wood,Synthia S.--18   At --------
                          Wit; Miles Wood, Robert Queen

Queen,Nathan--33   Jan.8,1874   B.N.Queen   B.M.
  Bryson,Artie A.--33   At F.J.Bryson's
                          Wit; S.L.Parker, T.J.Mathis

Queen,R.R.--22   Feb.13,1898   T.J.Mathis   J.P.
  Parker,Fannie--18   At T.H.Queen's
                          Wit; J.R.Dawson,J.H.Green,Andrew Herden

Queen,Samuel--19   Aug.27,1878   Tho.J.Bryson ----
  Fortner,Sarah--19   At --------
                          Wit; E.W.Fortner, Geo. Parker

Queen,Samuel--22   June 25,1881   J.W.Bird   M.M.
  Warren,Mattie--22   At J.W.Bird's
                          Wit; J.E.Rall, J.W.Stiles

Queen,Samuel--21   Aug.11,1880   S.R.Cook   J.P.
  Cogdill,Matilda--14   At John Cogdill's
                          Wit; J.R.Queen,T.J.Fisher

Queen,S.I.M.--45   Jan.18,1894   A.V.P.Bryson J.P.
  Craigg,Jane--23   At Webster
                          Wit; H.C.McKee, J.E.McLain, N.Phillips

Queen,Thomas--24   Jan.11,1880   J.S.Keener   J.P.
  Sutton,Jane--22   At John Lain's
                          Wit; James Robison, Wm.Dills

Queen,Thomas--34   Dec.22,1887   A.H.Sims   M.G.
  Parris,Margaret--26   At Clayton Church
                          Wit; T.N.Snider, J.R.Ensley

Queen,Thomas H.--22   Sept.16,1874   W.Ensley   B.M.
  Ensley,Elizabeth J.--16 At Wm.Ensley's
                          Wit; Wm. Ensley

Queen,T.C.--20   Nov.1,1890   W.Ensley   M.G.
  McCoy,Harriett--23   At Dillsboro Town
                          Wit; J.B.Clayton, G.Cunningham,L.S.Jones

Queen,Wilks--18   Mar.19,1899   John Stephens J.P.
  Parker,Sarah--18   At Henry Parker's
                          Wit; E.H.Stephens, G.L.Cook, W.D.Mills

Queen,William--30   Jan.1,1878   W.Ensley   B.M.
  Fisher,Sarah A.--19   At T.G.Fisher's
                          Wit; S.W.Farmer, Thomas Montieth

Queen,William A.--23   Nov.3,1881   S.C.Owens   M.G.
  Price,Viney--21   At A.N.Price's
                          Wit; James Wike, T.D.Wood

Queen,William S.--   May 15,1869   James Mahoney M.G.
  Hornbuckle,Lucinda--   At --------
                          He "Son of Sim & Nicy Queen"
                          She "Dau.of Jefferson & Jane Hornbuckle"

Queen,Wilson E.--21   Aug.5,1883   J.R.Crawford J.P.
  Queen,Amanda C.--18   At John B.Queen's
                          Wit; Wilson Snider, John B.Queen

Quilliam,Silas--25   Feb.12,1893   J.C.Reed   J.P.
  Mason,Drusey--19   At Savannah Ts.
                          Wit; D.B.Green, S.Cunningham, Jno.Lewis

Raby,Bedford--18
Chambers,Hester--27

Feb.11,1884   A.B.Clemanett M.G.
At Samuel Beck's
Wit; C.L.Gibson, W.M.Massay

Raby,D.M.--
Cathey,Elivabeth--

(Reg.in the year 1866--no other inf.)

Raby,Henry L.--16
Watts,Syntha--28

Oct.22,1882   W.P.Jones   J.P.
At Henry Raby's
Wit; W.H.Bumgarner, W.S.Wike

Raby,J.B.Jr.--26
Bradburn,Lillie--16

Nov.8,1896   J.B.Raby   J.P.
At Qualla Ts.
Wit; A.B.Watts, B.V.Martin, J.M.Raby

Raby,Rodo--21
Gibson,Cordelia--19

Apr.21,1889   S.J.Beck   J.P.
At Qualla Town
Wit; S.A.Beck, A.E.Beck, L.J.Beck

Radford,Ellick--49
Reed,Pollie--48

May --,1898   C.W.Allen   J.P.
At B.F.Dillard's
Wit; Belle Dillard, M.E.Farley,Lula Blanken-
                                        ship.

Randolph,Nelson--32
Shephard,Mary--26

Jan.16,1892   J.F.Brown   J.P.
At Barker Creek
Wit; W.L.Shephard, B.N.Shephard

Ratcliff,James--20
Buff,Mary--18

Nov.15,1874   J.R.Long   M.M.
At "Meeting House"
Wit; Joe Lawn, John Dobson

Ratcliff,Manson--48
Buff,Rosanah--21

Dec.6,1874   J.R.Long   M.M.
At "Meeting House"
Wit; Joe Lawn, Alex Hornbuckle

Rathbone,J.D.--
Harris,Fannie--

Nov.6,1870   E.D.Brendle   Elder
At -------

Ray,Roy R.--29
Potts,Maggie E.--16

Sept.18,1898 A.Walker White, Pres. Min.
At Dillsboro
Wit; R.F.Jarrett, Bessie Franklin

Rayfield,William B.--21
Rogers,Arena--15

Aug.1,1886   J.B.Raby   J.P.
At J.B.Raby's
Wit; J.B.Raby

Reagan,Frady--26
Watson,Sallie--22

Jan.27,1885   G.W.Spake   M.M.
At G.W.Spake's
Wit; C.D.Shepard, W.W.Rinehart

Reece,Bryson--24
Queen,Mary--18

Mar.4,1878   T.J.Bryson   ----
At Canada Ts.
Wit; A.Bryson

Reece,Bryson--23
Queen,Malinda M.--21

June 15,1878   T.J.Bryson   J.P.
At David Reece's
Wit; David Reece, S.Bryson

Reece,Elcana--19
Luker,Francis E.--14

Aug.28,1884   Levi Brown   J.P.
At Alfred Luker's
Wit;James Hoxit, William Hoxit

Reece,Lewis--26
Fortner,C.A.--18

May 1,1898   T.J.Mathis   J.P.
At E.W.Fortner's
Wit; R.A.Nicholson,J.S.Fortner,I.L.West

Reed,Charles--24   Dec.18,1879   E.D.Brendle B.M.
 Montieth,Sarah H.--19 At W.B.Montieth's
            Wit; Benjamin Harris, Hicks Montieth

Reed,George--19   License Issued Dec.20,1895
 Cantrell,Lou--20   NOT Returned

Reed,George--21   License Issued Aug.6,1895
 Jones,Jane--21   NOT Returned

Reed,George--22   License Issued May 14,1885--(No date
 Bailey,Florence M.--19 or place of marriage given.)
            By-John S.Keener J.P.
            Wit; Wm.Bailey, Wm. Young

Reed,J.P.--22   Nov.2,1882   W.Ensley M.G.
 Farmer,M.T.--20   At A.W.Farmer's
            Wit; Judson Allen, Joseph Ensley

Reed,Samuel W.--75   Nov.12,1899   Elbert Watson J.P.
 Stewart,Lucinda E.--64 At Lucinda E.Stewart's
            Wit; R.D.Morgan, J.M.Alexander, B.B.Morgan
            He From Transylvania, Co. N.C.

Reed,William E.--40   Sept.5,1883'   T.J.Bryson J.P.
 West,Eliza J.--37   At E.Dills'
            Wit; A.H.Queen, E.Dills

Reed,William W.--59   Aug.3,1879   S.H.Bryson J.P.
 Jones,Elizabeth J.--30 At B.P.Jones'
            Wit; G.W.Crawford, P.J.Crawford

Reed,Willie--21   June 15,1900   J.M.Thomas J.P.
 Blanton,Lillie--19   At "In public road"
            Wit; R.E.Thomas,Horrace Thomas,M.J.Thomas

Reid,John C.--24   Nov.15,1888   J.L.Buchanan B.M.
 Buchanan,Callie--20   At Savannah Ts.
            Wit; J.P.Reid, D.S.Reynolds, L.D.Hall

Reid,J.T.--28   Nov.2,1890   Wm.H.Thomas,Jr. J.P.
 Styles,Mollie--20   At Qualla Ts.
            Wit; Pierce Allen, D.A.Martin, G.W.Montieth

Reid,William M.--21   Sept.16,1886   S.W.Cooper J.P.
 Cordell,Roxie--18   At T.A.Reece's
            Wit; J.O.Wallace, J.W.Stiles

Revis,George W.--20   Feb.27,1885   J.B.Raby J.P.
 Nations,Cordelia--20   At John Nations'
            Wit; R.L.Nations, I.L.Nations

Reynolds,David S.--25   Sept. 8,1887   W.Ensley M.G.
 Reed,Sarah J.--28   At Cosly Reed's
            Wit; B.F.Dillard, J.C.Reid

Reynolds,T.B.--30 (Col) Nov.13,1891   J.A.Wild J.P.
 Porter,Mollie--21 (Col) At Webster Ts.
            Wit; W.E.Moore, D.G.Bigham,et al.
            He From Union, Co. S.C.

Rhea,Sam--28   Aug.6,1899   J.B.Raby J.P.
 Hill,Mary--21   At Wilmont, N.C.
            Wit; A.W.Bumgarner, R.C.Bumgarner

Rhea,T.Z.H.--23   Oct.7,1890   A.M.Parker J.P.
 Wilson,Lora--21   At Sylva, Ts.
            Wit; Pierce Allen,Ed.Divelbliss,J.H.Rhea

Rhea,William--18 Strutton,Roda--24	Feb.29,1876 At Christina Strutton's Wit; Mary Shular	G.W.Spake	M.M.
Rhinehart,J.W.--25 Reece,Altha--22	Apr.28,1900 At J.M.Thomas' House Wit; J.C.Reece, S.J.Reece, D.A.Reece	J.M.Thomas	J.P.
Rhodarmer,Jessee O.--25 Haynes,Mattie E.--19	Sept.30,1899 At Whitter, N.C. Wit; A.H.Haynes, B.A.Ayers,C.G.Enloe Both From Haywood, Co. N.C.	J.W.Bird	M.M.
Rhodarmer,S.B.--24 Henson,Lida--20	Nov.12,1899 At Wiley Henson's House Wit; J.E.Norton, F.B.Price, T.V.Shope He From Haywood, Co. N.C.	W.J.Evans, M.M.E.C.S.	
Rice,Isaac-- Norton,Vinetta--	Dec.18,1862 At --------	N.S.Abram	J.P.
Rice,W.R.--30 Jones,C.R.--15	June 8,1892 At Wolf Knob Wit; D.W.Chastain, G.M.Gunter, M.N.Parton He From Swain, Co. N.C.	J.F.Brown	J.P.
Richey,James--22 (Col) Coward,Lula--24 (Col)	Sept.1,1895 At Dillsboro, N.C. Wit; Annie Howel,Flora Watkins,Charles-Watkins.	J.C.Watkins	J.P.
Rickman,M.--22 Tompson,Mary--24	Dec.22,1897 At John Tompson's Wit; T.G.Allen, A.L.King	W.J.Fisher	J.P.
Riddle,Lee--21 Pressley,Louisa Jane--22	Dec.2,1894 At Cullowhee Wit; H.S.Sanders,J.A.Adams, J.E.Buchanan He From Macon, Co. N.C.	J.M.Bennett,Min.M.E.C.S.	
Riddle,William C.--20 Franks,M.A.--22	July 1,1894 At Savannah Wit; W.D.Bishop, J.H.Franks,G.D.Franks	W.C.Buchanan	J.P.
Ridley,Will--26 Buchanan,Alva--18	Apr.6,1901 At W.T.Crisp's Wit; W.T.Crisp, B.M.Brown, John Bishop	John Sutton	J.P.
Ridley,William-- Franks,Loucinda--	Aug.22,1872 At --------	J.L.Buchanan	M.G.
Rigdon,Mitchel--25 Owen,Charlotte--18	June 5,1892 At Canada Ts. Wit; Jas.A.Galloway,W.F.Queen,J.H.Dunn	J.A.Galloway	M.G.
Rigdon,William T.--29 Baird,Laura--19	Jan.14,1900 At"Home of Bride's Parents" Wit; G.O.Coward,A.E.Galloway,R.J.Shelton	B.N.Queen	B.M.
Right,R.R.-- Wilson,M.I.--	Mar.18,1866 At --------	W.H.Cooper	Rev.
Rineheart,Elias--24 Mull,Mary--	License Issued Nov.11,1888 At -- NOT Returned		
Rineheart,James--20 Watson,Margaret--16	Feb.16,1887 At G.W.Watson's Wit; A.J.Wood, J.B.Mull He From Haywood, Co.N.C.	R.A.Sitton	J.P.

Rineheart,William W.--23 Dills,Ida E.--18	July 2,1878 At Margaret Dills' Wit; Geo.W.Dillard, J.A.Dills	J.A.Wiggins	---
Roberts,Aron-- Self,Martha--	July 15,1869 At ---------	W.H.Conner	M.G.
Robertson,James O.--35 Woodfin,Laura M.--26	Apr.9,1873 At H.G.Woodfin's Wit; D.Davis, Eliza Woodfin	G.W.Bowman	M.M.
Roberson,Pleasant--23 Queen,Laura--19	License Issued Nov.9,1895 NOT Returned		
Robeson,H.T.-- Robeson,Margaret--	Aug.23,1856 At --------	Peter King	J.P.
Robins,Andrew-- Mathis,Nancy--	Oct.26,1861 At --------	Wm.Willson	J.P.
Robison,Dillard G.--23 Henson,Mary M.--15	Dec.14,1879 At T.M.Henson's Wit; J.L.Snider, S.J.Hall	S.R.Cook	----
Robison,Cit--24 Wike,Julia--18	Jan.24,1892 At River Ts. Wit; J.T.Jackson, M.M.Wike, C.L.Harris	B.N.Queen	Elder
Robison ,David--20 Gipson,Laura--18	Apr.11,1897 At Dillsboro Ts. Wit; J.W.Conner, J.B.Ensley, J.K.Keener	T.B.Keener	J.P.
Robison,Ephraim--30 Davis,Meriah--16	Mar.6,1882 At John Dills' Wit; Geo. Davis, John Dills	J.E.McLain	J.P.
Robison,Isreal H..--22 Parris,Lucinda E.--15	License Issued Dec.17,1881 NOT Returned		
Robison,James--25 Ensley,Sarah--28	Jan.20,1884 At Sarah Ensley's Wit; R.Wike, J.F.Robison	W.A.Dills	J.P.
Robison,Joseph P.--26 Presnell,Mary--19	Sept.14,1876 At John Wike's Wit; A.M.Hooper, M.M.Wike	B.N.Queen	B.M.
Robison,J.T.--27 Brown,Lizzie--21	Dec.30,1894 At Barker Creek Wit; R.H.Harper, J.H.Bailey	J.F.Brown	J.P.
Robison,J.W.--29 Ashe,Loranda--17	Nov.10,1889 At Webster Wit; M.W.Bryson, J.D.Parker, J.H.Painter	A.J.Long,Sr.	J.P.
Robison,N.P.--25 Queen,Laura--20	Aug.7,1897 At William Queen's Wit; V.F.Brown,Javan Davis, Florence Queen He From Transylvania,Co. N.C.	A.C.Queen	J.P.
Robinson,Pink--21 Davis,Emma--27	License Issued Nov.29,1895 Returned "NOT filled out"		
Robinson,Sam--22 Love,Mary--18	Jan.15,1899 At John Lanning's Wit; James Robinson,J.K.Keener, John Ensley	Thomas Queen	J.P.

```
Rochester,Daniel--20          Sept.18,1880        H.M.Bennett   M.G.
  Hancock,Rebacca--18         At ---------
                              Wit; Daniel Rochester

Rochester,John D.--26         Sept.4,1879         Wm.Bumgarner  ---
  Watson,Theadocia--19        At  Wm.Bumagrner's
                              Wit; John Sutton, Aery Wike

Rochester,JohnF.--22          Dec.29,1872         H.M.Bennett   M.M.
  Dunwoody,Roda--20           At --------

Rochester,Joseph B.--33       June 13,1886        G.W.Wild      M.G.
  Tilly,Rebecca--19           At L.H.Tilly's
                              Wit; J.B.Robison, J.R.Carver

Rogers,George--22             Sept.30,1899        J.W.Bird M.M.E.C.S.
  Fish,Hattie M.--19          At  Whittier Bridge
                              Wit; A.H.Hayes, B.A.Ayers, C.G.Enloe

Rogers,George--               No Date given-- Reg.in year 1872
  Love,Sarah--                               by W.D.Wells.

Rogers,George B.--            Sept.14,1876        G.W.Spake     M.M.
  Stillwell,Roxie--16         At  J.F.Stillwell's
                              Wit; J.C.Watkins, George Cole
                              He From Haywood,Co. N.C.

Rogers,Geo.W.--58       (Col)Mar.29,1891          W.C.Norton    J.P.
  Gibbs,Josephine C.A.--(Col) At  Cullowhee
                              Wit; S.J.Nicholson, Addie Love

Rogers,James--21              Oct.30,1881         J.P.Stuart    J.P.
  Jenning,Elizabeth--16       At  J.J.Jennings'
                              Wit; J.C.Henderson, E.C.Hedden

Rogers,James--23              Sept.9,1877         J.P.Stuart    J.P.
  Jennings,Margaret--19       At --------
                              Wit; J.J.Rogers, J.B.Jennings

Rogers,John--22               Sept.22,1889        B.N.Queen     B.M.
  Jennings,Mary--21           At  Hamburg Ts.
                              Wit; J.C.Stiwinter, J.M.Rogers, B.M.H.?

Rogers,John--21               Sept.22,1888        C.L.Hooper    J.P.
  Hooper,Mary--19             At  Susan Hooper's
                              Wit; V.F.Brown, E.M.Hooper

Rogers,Lewis L.--39     (Col) Dec.25,1890         R.Powell      M.G.
  Gibbs,Catherine M.--21(Col) At  Cullowhee Ts.
                              Wit; Addie Love, C.Fisher, M.C.Casey

Rogers,Thomas--26             Nov.9,1899      J.M.Keener,Min.Free Bap
  Bolick,Lodusky--21          At  Ed.Bryson's Res.
                              Wit; M.D.Edwards,Dick Henderson,L.C.Bryson
                              He From Macon, Co. N.C.

Rogers,Western B.--24         Dec.12,1877         R.L.Watson    ---
  Wike,Rebacca--22            At  Salinda Wike's
                              Wit; A.W.Parker, James Ammons

Rogers,William D.--25         Feb.12,1881         E.P.Stillwell J.P.
  Buchanan,Martha E.--22      At  J.L.Buchanan's
                              Wit; Wm.Dills, L.M.Dills

Rogers,Wilson--22       (Col) Sept.12,1899        James H.Wike  J.P.
  Coward,Lucy--18       (Col) At  Cullowhee
                              Wit; Marion Hamby, Will T.Wike, C.B.Wike
```

Runians,J.E.--   Sept.10,1865   W.L.Norris   J.P.
  Grant,Sarah--   At ---------

Russell,Robert--23   License Issued   Jan.10,1885
  Smathers,Olive--   NOT Returned
                              He From Haywood, Co. N.C.

Russell,Seth C.--30   Sept.19,1900   Robt.S.Howe   M.M.E.C.S.
  Messer,Ida--18   At Meth. Parsiage
                              Wit; Wallie E.Moore, S.A.Jacobs

Ryhard,Robert H.--   Aug.17,1861   J.Wike   J.P.
  Alexander,Mary   At --------

Sanders,John--19   July 16,1892   H.P.Brendle   J.P.
  Brooks,Alth--19   At Sylva Ts.
                              Wit; T.D.Brooks, N.A.P., E.D.B.

Sanders,Robert--21   Apr.19,1875   G.W.Hawkins   J.P.
  Huskins,Catherine--21   At Gabriel Jackson's
                              Wit; A.B.Jackson

Saunders,Benjamin--32   Nov.7,1900   A.B.Henson   B.M.
  Warren,Zona--26   At Benjamin Saunders'
                              Wit; J.L.Balard, T.H.Mofit, J.H.Phillips

Saunders,William--21   Sept.1,1899   H.M.Bennett   M.M.E.C.S.
  Presley,Hester--17   At D.H.Presley's
                              Wit; W.B.Hooper,Jno.R.Hooper,Julia Saunders
                              He From Macon,Co.N.C.

Saunooke,Nicodemus--   (Ind) Apr.8,1871   T.K.Welch   J.P.
  -----,Sallie--   (Ind) At -------

Sawyers,Joel L.--26   Dec.5,1894   T.B.McCurdy   M.G.
  McDade,Carrie--18   At Barker Creek
                              Wit; J.F.Brown, J.H.Moody, S.C.Allison
                              He From Graham,Co. N.C.

Sawyers,William--24   (Ind) Nov.24,1875   T.K.Welch   J.P.
  -----,Charlotte--25 (Ind) At Qualla Town
                              Wit; B.B.Smith, Ruth Cambel

Sayngin,Samuel--57   Oct.30,1873   H.J.Morgan   M.M.
  Montieth,Elizabeth M.--40   At E.M.Montieth's
                              Wit; ------

Schriber,William A.H.--49   License Issued   Aug.17,1886
  Metz,Halena--18   NOT Returned
                              She From Philadelphia,Pa.

Segle,T.M.--24   Jan.17,1897   J.H.House   J.P.
  Bradley,M.E.--21   At Barker Creek
                              Wit; J.L.Nations, E.L.Mathis, G.W.Revis

Self,R.O.--   Dec.24,1857   J.Wike   J.P.
  Hughes,Martha--   At --------

Self,William--29   Nov.23,1881   G.W.Spake   M.M.
  Cowan,Octa--20   At Joseph Cowan's
                              Wit; R.E.Long, John Sutton

Sellers,James--21   Jan.10,1897   S.W.Cooper   J.P.
  Watts,Tennie--17   At Qualla Ts.
                              Wit; G.W.Snider, W.G.Bridges, B.G.Rogers
                                   M.E.Rogers, G.C.Cooper.

```
Sellers,Joseph--            Feb.18,1855         J.B.Sherrell   J.P.
  Frady,Catherine--         At --------

Sellers,Merit--20           License Issued      Mar.15,1876
  Ward,Jane--20             NOT Returned

Sellers,W.H.--24            Sept.24,1890        A.W.Davis      J.P.
  Smith,Dollie--16          At   Savannah Ts.
                            Wit; J.H.Watson, J.Buchanan

Sextan,Alfred C.--26        Nov.21,1886         S.R.Cook       J.P.
  Pannel,Harriet--18        At  M.J.Pannel's
                            Wit; S.L.Cook, J.E.Ensley

Shark,James--22    (Col)    Feb.4,1894          L.W.Allen      J.P.
  Love,Ella--19    (Col)    At  Sylva,Town
                            Wit; R.N.Pickens, Jas.Underwood,Charville

Shaw,A.N.--18               Feb.17,1884         S.J.Beck  J.P.   Cobb.
  Gibbs,M.A.--18            At  Sarah Keener's
                            Wit; R.M.Fishers, H.L.Baker

Shaw,Henry--45     (Col)    Feb.1,1885          J.R.Crawford   J.P.
  Bryson,Lucinda--40 (Col)  At  J.R.Crawford's
                            Wit; Jacob Bolt, M.C.Whitenburg

Shaw,Joseph N.--            Sept.28,1860        E.D.Brendle    Elder
  Fisher,Elizabeth--        At ---------

Shed,Columbus--24           Oct.10,1880         S.C.Owens      M.G.
  Woodring,Roxie--28        At  James Nicholson's
                            Wit; M.M.Brown, John Price

Shelton,David V.--20        Dec.9,1877          J.N.Cathey     J.P.
  Long,Nancy J.--15         At  Pleasant Parker's
                            Wit; J.C.Wood, D.H.Mathis

Shelton,David W.--20        May 16,1883         Levi Brown     J.P.
  Galloway,Lyda C.--18      At  Josiah Galloway's
                            Wit; James Owen, W.T.Brown

Shelton,Elias--21           Oct.16,1892         J.C.Wood       J.P.
  Brown,Ellen--16           At  Canada Ts.
                            Wit; Nancy Shelton, T.L.Shelton,L.C.Shelton

Shelton,Hanry E.--21        May 9,1894          Javan Davis    J.P.
  Crawford,Laura E.--15     At  Cullowhee
                            Wit; Nellie Smith, Lena Smith,Aurie Leather-

Shelton,John--27            Oct.2,1896          J.A.Galloway,M.G.wood.
  Slatten,Anna--22          At  Canada Ts.
                            Wit; A.E.Galloway, J.H.Dunn, N.E.Brachin

Shelton,John--19            Mar.9,1889          John A.Mathis  J.P.
  Mathis,Alice--16          At  Canada Ts.
                            Wit; D.E.Bryson, J.T.Cathey, J.J.Brown

Shelton,John--28            Dec.1,1899          W.C.Henson     J.P.
  Blackwell,Mary K.--27     At  John Woodall's
                            Wit; L.J.Smith, G.L.Shelton, C.C.Coward

Shelton,John F.--21         Jan.7,1886          L.W.Hooper     M.G.
  Lovedahl,Sarah A.--20     At  A.L.Lovedahl's
                            Witl A.M.Brown, T.H.Parker

Shelton,M.M.--              Mar.7,1861          Wm.Wilson      J.P.
  Lewis,Martha E.--         At -------
```

-128-

Shelton,Stephens--19 Brown,Lilly--18	Dec.18,1887 At John R.Brown's Wit; John Brown, M.O.Brown	John H.Martin J.P.
Shelton,Stephens J.-- Conley,Mahala C.--	Oct.26,1865 At --------	Wm.Hicks Elder
Shelton,William M.--26 Rogers,Belle--19	Feb.15,1885 At Robert Rogers' Wit; D.H.Rogers, R.H.Moore	W.H.H.Hughes J.P.
Shelton,W.Perry-- Conley--D.J.--	Apr.1,1869 At ------ He son of Wm.& Racheal Shelton She Dau.of J.W. & Aveline Conl	Jas. Mahoney M.G.
Sheperd,Lafayett--21 Jones,Sarah A.--18	Dec.24,1885 At Leonard Jones' Wit; A.D.Jones, J.W.Elder	J.B.Raby J.P.
Sherrill,Edward--23 King,Josephine--22	License Issued Dec.6,1884 NOT Returned	
Sherrill,George C.--24 Knight,Mary E.--22	May 4,1883 At G.C.Sherrill's Wit; J.B.Raby, S.S.Williams	J.B.Raby J.P.
Sherrill,J.K.-- Allison,Sarah A.--	Mar.22,1856 At --------	J.B.Sherrill J.P.
Sherrill,P.B.--20 Fisher,Emma--18	Aug.23,1896 At Sylva Ts. Wit; Oscar Fisher, Annie Thomas, A.B.Thomas Theo.G.Allen.	A.B.Thomas M.G.
Sherrill,R.E.-- Cooper,Nancy--	Apr.15,1871 At --------	A.Mingus J.P.
Sherrill,William B.--30 Holden,Mollie J.--24	Oct.10,1880 At J.B.Raby's Wit; J.B.Sherrill	J.B.Raby J.P.
Shook,David W.--19 Brown,Manley C.--17	Sept.16,1894 At Canada Ts. Wit; J.B.Coward, W.U.Mathis, T.M.Brown	J.A.Galloway J.P.
Shook,D.L.--23 Middleton,Julia--21	Dec.--,1896 At Caney Fork Wit; J.E.Norton,W.B.Morris, F.B.Price	Javan Davis J.P.
Shook,James--19 Shelton,Nellie--23	Dec.1,1874 At J.F.Shelton's Wit; J.C.Wood, C.C.Galloway	J.A.Galloway J.P.
Shook,James--19 Brown,Hulda C.--20	Mar.30,1878 At J.S.Woodan's Wit; Jemima Hooper, D.E.Woodring	J.S.Woodan ----
Shook,Joseph M.--22 Middleton,Jamima--21	Nov.13,1872 At Allison Watson's Wit; -----	John A.Hooper J.P.
Shook,J.S.--37 Hooper,Mary Ann--36	June 10,1894 At River Ts. Wit; B.N.Queen, J.D.Middleton	L.W.Hooper M.G.
Shular,Epp--30 Cook,Margaret--30	Feb.24,1900 At E.A.Cook's Wit; John H.Smith, James M.Wood, J.C.Shular	J.M.Keener B.M.

```
Shular,James D.--20        License Issued      Aug.21,1901
  Mills,Ellen--20          NOT Returned

Shular,R.B.--19            Mar.19,1890         W.C.Norton        ---
  Watson,Emily--14         At Cullowhee Ts.
                           Wit;J.M.Watson,W.L.Henson,A.J.Watson

Shular,Thomas--19          Jan.31,1884         S.R.Cook          J.P.
  Buchanan,Candis--19      At J.R.Buchanan's
                           Wit; R.P.Henson, J.T.Henson

Shular,William--23         Mar.3,1901       David W.Franklin  M.M.
  Franklin,Ider--21        At Riley Franklin's
                           Wit;Eli Cook,H.Robinson,G.E.Bumgarner

Shuler,Alfred--            Aug.25,1853         E.C.Norton        J.P.
  Newton,Lurana--          At --------

Shuler,D.M.--              Dec.12,1867         Wm.B.Garrett      J.P.
  Evereth,Susan--          At --------

Shuler,H.E.--21            Jan.6,1898          T.F.Arrington     B.M.
  Dillard,Anna--18         At W.H.T.Dillard's
                           Wit;W.A.Clayton,R.J.Crawford,R.L.Cook

Shuler,James--24           Dec.25,1898    Jas.M.Keener,Min.Free-
  Wood,Sallie--16          At A.J.Wood's                  Will Bap.
                           Wit;W.A.Watson,J.H.Wood,J.T.Smith

Shuler,John--              Nov.16,1871         H.M.Cook          J.P.
  Naimon,Rutha--           At---------

Shuler,Joseph--            Jan.14,1866    I.T.S.Sherrill     Elder
  Morris,Margret--         At --------

Sigman,Jeff--21            Dec.11,1900         W.A.McMehan       J.P.
  Chastain,Lizzie--19      At Safona McMehan's
                           Wit;L.L.Sutton,G.F.Keener,L.R.McMehan

Sims,W.B.--23              Oct.6,1898          Geo.A.Hughes      ---
  Smith,Laura--21          At Robt.Smith's
                           Wit; B.F.H.Owens,C.G.Hughes

Sisk,Richard T.--19        Nov.26,1874         C.B.Fugate        M.M.
  Hooper,Lura L.--21       At Sarah Hooper's
                           Wit;Eliza Zachary,Sally Zachary

Sivley,John--18 (Sibley)   Apr.26,1892         H.P.Brendle       J.P.
  Frady,Samantha--21       At Webster, N.C.
                           Wit;W.H.H.Hughes,B.M.Smith,C.C.Love

Slagle,William Woodfin--26 Mar.28,1897         A.H.Sims          M.G.
  Ward,Maggie--16          At Barker Creek
                           Wit;A.A.Marshall,S.C.Allison,D.F.Jarret

Slatten,Dyre--             Nov.5,1865          S.P.C.Shelton     ---
  Hooper,Sarah J.--        At -------

Slatton,D.T.--52           June 5,1894         L.W.Hooper        M.G.
  Barens,Norah--20         At River Ts.
                           Wit; O.L.Hooer

Slatton,John--51           Nov.26,1891         C.L.Hooper        J.P.
  Wood,Jemima--35          At River Ts.
                           Wit; J.A.Wike, C.L.Wike

Slatton,Lee--21            Oct.22,1893         U.F.Brown         J.P.
  Barnes,Lavada--18        At Hamburg Ts.
                           Wit; L.Price, P.N.Price,W.J.Hunncutt
```

Smathers,D.G.--30 Ensley,M.C.--21	Dec.26,1897 W.E.Conner B.M. At Catherine Fisher's Wit; W.V.Davis, T.G.Alley, J.O.Fisher He From Haywood, Co. N.C.
Smathers,George--20 Crawford,Emma--20	Feb.8,1899 H.D.Welch Bap.Min. At Adalaid Crawford's Wit; Shoat Crawford, Wm.Crawford
Smathers,Geo.--48 Buchanan,Cordellia--24	Oct.1,1893 G.W.Hawkins J.P. At Caney Fork Wit; W.F.Arrington,J.U.Long, J.M.Nichols He From Haywood, Co. N.C.
Smathers,J.D.--24 Moody,Dellie--18	Oct.5,1897 W.E.Conner B.M. At J.J.moody's Wit; S.T.Moody, G.W.Moody, C.E.Miller He From Haywood, Co. N.C.
Smathers,William A.--21 Queen,Harret H.--18	Nov.14,1897 H.D.Welch B.M. At John M.Queen's Wit; D.A.Haynes, W.T.Derrick, James Queen
Smith,A.B.--20 Cope,Artie--17	May 1,1898 W.J.Evans M.M.E.C.S. At Joseph Cope's Wit; W.D.Cope, N.M.Fullbright, J.W.Smith
Smith,Benjamin M.--35 Fisher,C.Belle--20	Apr.22,1883 W.Ensley M.G. At L.E.Fisher's Wit; J.R.Crawford, W.C.Clayton
Smith,Elbert S.-- Allen,A.C.--	Sept.11,1870 J.A.Wiggins M.G. At --------
Smith,George--31 Turpin,Jane--26	Jan.2,1881 J.W.Bird M.G. At J.W.Bird's Wit; Nellie Jones, C.A.Bird
Smith,John--20 Wood,Francis M.--24	Aug.3,1876 W.A.Brown --- At J.B.Wood's Wit; E.E.Chastain, H.Hooper
Smith,John T.-- Sanders,Susan--	June 1,1856 N.B.Abram J.P. At -------
Smith,John W.--21 Cope,Daisy G.--17	Oct.15,1896 A.M.Parker J.P. At Sylva, Ts. Wit; Joseph Cook, M.M.Po---?,P.F.Dillard
Smith,Joseph--59 (Col) Maton,Ella--40 (Col)	June 21,1891 R.P.Powell M.G. At Sylva Ts. Wit; J.C.Bryson, J.T.Pickens, M.C.Whitnburg He From Buncombe, Co. N.C.
Smith,Joseph--25 Johnston,Mattie--22	Jan.6,1881 T.M.Frizzell J.P. At G.W.Spake's Wit; R.E.Long, J.B.Sherrill
Smith,J.M.--23 Long,Mary A.--27	June 11,1880 W.Ensley M.G. At John Ensley's Wit; James Crawford, J.B.Ensley
Smith,Ross D.--23 (Ind) Sneed,Mary A.--19 (Ind)	July 20,1874 T.K.Welch J.P. At J.Blythe's Wit; W.M.West
Smith,R.L.--18 Owens,S.E.--18	Nov.24,1889 J.C.Wood J.P. At Canada Ts. Wit; L.S.Shelton,S.A.Queen,M.M.Queen

Smith,T.D.--60 Adams,Sousan--38	Sept.16,1888 John P.Stewart J.P. At T.D.Smith's Wit; J.Pierson, Belle Zachary
Smith,William A.--27 Herrell,Missouri--27	Oct.27,1881 S.R.Cook J.P. At Luisa Norman's Wit; John Henry, J.R.Smith
Smith,William T.--21 Muchel,Sallie--20	Jan.13,1880 S.R.Cook J.P. At M.D.Duncan's Wit; Samuel Queen, Julius Carson
Snider,Geo.W.--29 Ensley,Dicey J.--20	Oct.15,1893 A.B.Henson B.M. At Barker Creek Wit; T.N.Snider, J.E.Ensley, D.S.Snider
Snider,Humphrey R.--23 Ensley,Ellen--19	Apr.13,1876 E.D.Brendle B.M. At W.Ensley's Wit; John Snider, Thadeus Ensley
Snider,H.M.--23 Phillips,L.H.--17	Feb.5,1895 A.M.Parker J.P. At Sylva Wit; J.P.Brendle, A.J.Long,Sr.,D.S.Snider
Snider,James L.--27 Robison,Harriet--17	Sept.20,1876 W.Ensley B.M. At Elbert Hall's Wit; Thomas Love, W.S.Snider
Snider,John L.--24 Queen,Mary J.--16	Oct.31,1875 W.Ensley B.M. At S.H.Queen's Wit; John Bryson, J.H.Queen
Snider,Julius P.--21 King,Fannie C.--19	June 29,1889 B.G.Wild M.G. At Webster Ts. Wit; A.Bumgarner,J.P.Brendle,J.V.Ashe
Snider,L.Dave--22 Fisher,Minnie--20	Oct.16,1898 W.E.Conner Bap.Min. At "In the Road" Wit; G.B.Cooper, B.A.Ayers, J.L.Miller
Snider,Marion E.--20 Messer,Allace--19	Sept.15,1889 J.A.Wild J.P. At Webster Ts. Wit; T.M.Barker, H.R.Snider, J.W.Jones He From Haywood,Co. N.C.
Snider,Robert G.--24 Robison,Melvina M.--24	Jan.29,1885 J.R.Crawford J.P. At Elbert Hall's Wit; W.T.Henson, John B.Queen
Snider,Thomas N.--24 Parris,Julia--22	Mar.27,1881. W.Ensley B.M. At John Parris' Wit; F.M.Bryson, Wm.Henson
Snider,Ulyssis G.--19 Ensley,Martha--16	Dec.23,1886 W.T.Henson M.G. At James Ensley's Wit; J.S.Calhoun, R.P.Potts
Smoke,Walking-- (Ind) ----,Selah-- (Ind)	Apr.24,1871 N.W.Vaughn M.G. At --------
Snipes,T.E.--25 Bryson,Mary V.--17	Dec.22,1888 G.W.Crawford B.M. At Scotts Creek Wit; J.T.Carson, W.E.Bryson, James Foy
Sorrels,Thomas--21 Cope,Julia--18	Jan.17,1890 J.R.McKay J.P. At Scotts Creek Wit; Tate Cope, A.J.Young He From Buncombe, Co. N.C.

```
Sorrells,William--27        June 4,1876          B.Cowen        J.P.
  Browning,Charlotte--20     At  W.W.Woodard's
                             Wit; W.W.Woodard,W.Walker
                             He From Macon, Co. N.C.

Spake,G.W.--                 Mar.19,1876          ------        ---
  Love,Mrs.M.E.--            At --------
                             Wit; C.C.Love, Wm.Love
                             This Marriage is in front of book # 2.

Spearman,B.G.--36            Oct.21,1901          -----         ----
  Rogers,Annie--32           At --------

Spriman,B.G.--25             Apr.16,1893          B.G.Wild       M.G.
  Harris,Florence--18        At  Webster Ts.
                             Wit; W.Self, J.S.Calhoun, J.E.Stillwell

Stanford,Gorden--21          Mar.6,1899           J.R.Love       J.P.
  Elders,Richy--18           At  Joicy Queen's
                             Wit; George Extine,Henry Moore, Joice Queer

Stanford,John--70            License Issued      July 27,1876
  Woodruff,Ann--25           NOT Returned

Standing Wolf,Andrew--21 (Ind) July 20,1874       T.K.Welch      J.P.
  Owee,Margaret--19      (Ind)  At  T.K.Welch's
                             Wit; R.B.Smith, E.G.Hyatt

Statlcup,Robert C.--24       Oct.13,1874          H.F.Gibbs      J.P.
  Conly,Haseltine A.--22     At  W.H.Thomas'
                             Wit; Sarah J.Thomas, Finley Gipson

Stallcup,Seth Jr.--25        Dec.22,1881          J.C.Watkins    J.P.
  Zachary,Sarah M.--22       At  M.Zachary's
                             Wit; Flora Watkins, Lizzie Zachary

Stephens,Adolphus--20        License Issued      July 27,1892
  Parker,Addie--18           NOT Returned

Stephens,Douglas--18         Nov.3,1889           E.A.Cook       J.P.
  Parker,Altena--            At  Caney Fork
                             Wit; J.H.Morris, E.Coward, W.A.Hooper

Stephens,D.M.--              June 16,1855          J.Wike         J.P.
  Brown,Louisa--             At ---------

Stephens,J.R.--19            Oct.20,1892          Bragg Hooper   ----
  Coward,Savina--17          At  Caney Fork
                             Wit; Huff Stephens, Lillie Coward

Stephens,L.M.--20            Aug.29,1897          R.L.Phillips  J.P.
  Parker,Lula--22            At  W.J.Parker's
                             Wit; E.M.Coward,T.H.Hooper, W.A.Long

Stephens,R.Huston--18        Jan.13,1900          John R.Stephens  J.P.
  Nicholson,Varina--18       At  A.Nicholson's
                             Wit; D.H.Stephens, L.E.Hooper, H.W.Hooper

Stephens,Ruben H.--          Apr.24,1870          B.N.Queen      M.G.
  Brown,Mary C.--            At --------

Stephens,Vance--19           Mar.4,1880           R.H.Stephens  J.P.
  Hooper,Varina--19          At  D.M.Stephens'
                             Wit; J.M.Long

Stewart,David--23            License Issued      Aug.1,1901
  Moss,Addie--17             NOT Returned
```

Stewart,Jack--18
Brown,Narlecia--19

Dec.20,1894   G.B.Bumgarner   J.P.
At Mountain Ts.
Wit; Wm.Moss, D.A.Watson, E.M.Moss

Stewart,John--
Gipson,Mary--

Oct.23,1863   I.T.S.Sherrill Elder
At --------

Stewart,Jno.M.--22
Moss,A.D.--21

Feb.15,1894   R.H.Stewart   J.P.
At Mountain Ts.
Wit; B.M.Peek, W.J.Henderson, E.M.Moss

Stewart,J.N.--23
Taylor,Mary--22

Sept.26,1899   Jas.W.Terrell   J.P.
At "My Resident"
Wit; Lula Terrell, W.A.H.Sheriber,
                              W.W.Rhinehart.

Stewart,J.T.--25
Leopard,Palestine--19

Aug.26,1892   John P.Stewart J.P.
At Hamburg Ts.
Wit; W.J.Henderson, R.H.Stewart, W.J.S.

Stewart,W.R.--27
Henderson,Macsie--18

Apr.29,1897   J.N.Bumgarner   J.P.
At Mountain Ts.
Wit; T.V.Anderson, J.M.Moss

Street,Edward S.--30
Enloe,Melvina--35

Mar.4,1875   J.M.Bird   M.M.
At J.B.Allison's
Wit; L.C.Hall, Hix Wilson

Stiles,Benjamin B.--19
Bailey,Mary O.--14

Feb.19,1887   C.S.Buchanan M.G.
At Mary Woodard's
Wit; W.T.Crisp, W.T.Stiles

Stiles,C.J.--
Hicks,Rebecca--

Sept.11,1865   J.D.Buchanan Elder
At ---------

Stiles,George--20
Stallcup,Grace--18

Sept.29,1900   Ebenezer Myers M.M.E.C.S.
At R.W.Stiles'
Wit; R.W.Stiles, J.S.Stiles, Maggie Cooper

Stiles,Isaac C.--20
Queen,Martha J.--22

Mar.31,1874   W.R.Crawford B.M.
At Mary Queen's
Wit; J.H.Queen, W.T.Carson

Stiles,J.W.--33
Ballard, Lula H.--

License Issued   May 14,1901
NOT Returned

Stiles,J.W.--
Seller,Nancy--

Reg. in the year 1868

Stiles,M.B.--18
Ensley,Mary--16

Feb.19,1891   A.J.Long Sr. J.P.
At Sylva Ts.
Wit; R.J.Crawford, G.E.Painter, W.Cope

Stiles,Robert--21
Wallace,Cannie--18

Nov.17,1892   J.W.Bird   M.G.
At Qualla Ts.
Wit; R.D.Shelton, Lee Cooper, W.P.Shelton

Stiles,William--21
Pressley,Belle--21

Nov.2,1893   John Bumgarner   J.P.
At Cullowhee Ts.
Wit; Jas.Pressley, Riley Morison,Andy Pressl
ey.

Stiles,William P.--22
Barron,Sarah--18

Oct.28,1873   E.C.Ash   J.P.
At Sydney Ash's
Wit; Sydney Ash, W.T.Crisp

Stillwell,------   (Ind)
Casy,------   (Ind)

Apr.14,1871   T.K.Welch   J.P.
At --------

```
Stillwell,Alfred--22  (Col) Feb.1,1886        J.A.Wild         J.P.
  Howell,Tennessee--18(Col)At Webster
                          Wit; E.R.Hampton, A.S.Bryson
Stillwell,A.R.--22          Apr.15,1897       T.B.Queen        J.P.
  Buchanan,Estella--19      At Dillsboro  Ts.
                          Wit; J.C.Estes, L.D.Bradley, W.H.Hall
Stillwell,John--22          Feb.7,1878        E.D.Brendle      B.M.
  Ash,Amanda J.--19         At Amos Ash's
                          Wit; L.Bumgarner, Amos Ash
Stillwell,John A.--30       Sept.9,1894       G.N.Cowan        M.G.
  Calhoun,Sarah E.--        At Scotts Creek
                          Wit; H.C.Cowan, J.S.Calhoun
Sitllwell,John C.--         July 24,1864      J.B.Sherrill     J.P.
  Harris,Sarah Jane--       At ---------
Stillwell,John F.--57       Dec.25,1887       A.H.Sims         M.G.
  Rickman,Sarah--38         At Mrs.Jane Stillwell's
                          Wit; J.C.Stillwell, J.A.Stillwell
Stillwell,J.H.--            May 8,1870        J.L.Buchanan     M.G.
  Buchanan,Mandy--          At -------
Stillwell,Polk--26  (Ind)   Oct.6,1900        G.W.Moody        J.P.
  Reed,Anne--22     (Ind)   At G.W.Moody's
                          Wit; J.L.Shook, Caroline Shook, L.Moody
Stillwell,Posey J.--25      June 8,1873       J.L.Buchanan     B.M.
  Messer,Sarah--19          At J.L.Buchanan's
                          Wit; M.R.Buchanan, A.Sutton
Stillwell,Ranson--24        Aug.4,1899        Nathan Coward    J.P.
  Gribble,Fannie--19        At Webster, N.C.
                          Wit; S.B.Rogers, J.R.Bell
Stillwell,William--20       Mar.26,1880       E.P.Stillwell    J.P.
  Quinn,Mary--18            At John Stillwell's
                          Wit; C.M.Stillwell,Lynch Frady
Stillwell,Willie A.--27     Apr.10,1894       G.N.Cowan        M.G.
  Holden,Octie--22          At Cullowhee
                          Wit; H.C.Cowan, Jno.Bumgarner, H.H.Bryson
Stiwenter,John--            July 10,1856      N.B.Abram        J.P.
  Miller,Mandy--            At ---------
Strain,Floyd--24            Dec.27,1894       J.M.Keener       M.G.
  Jennings,Docia--18        At Hamburg  ̄s
                          Wit; Jas.L.Higdon, G.W.Stiwenter,I.H.Peek
Street,Edward S.--30        Mar.4,1875        J.M.Bird         M.M.
  Enloe,Melvine--35         At J.B.Allison's
                          Wit; L.C.Hall, Hix Wilson
Stuart,Jehue P.--29         Jan.1,1888        John P.Stuart    J.P.
  Jemison,Delphia--24       At L.W.Jemision's
                          Wit; Dallas Jemision, E.F.Watson
Stuart,John--36             May 16,1875       T.M.Henson       J.P.
  Wyatt,Synthia--38         At T.M.Henson's
                          Wit; P.E.Henson,A.D.Henson
Stuart,John B.--26          Feb.9,1888        John P.Stuart    J.P.
  Evitt,Mary J.--21         At D.M.Evitt's
                          Wit; Alfred E.Carroll, John P.Stuart
```

Stuart,Joseph--22 Smith,Mary--19	Jan.12,1888 At Robert Smith's Wit; J.B.Stewart, M.S.Brown	John P.Stuart	J.P.
Stuart,J.P.-- Carroll,S.L.--	Dec.30,1869 At --------	L.C.Hooper	J.P.
Styles,H.C.--26 Rogers,Alice--16	Mar.27,1898 At Lizzie Roger's Wit; J.A.Gibson, W.H.Gates, W.A.Brown	L.Bumgarner	J.P.
Styles,J.D.--26 Shuler,S.M.--22	Aug.28,1893 At Sylva Ts. Wit; Wm.Ensley, J.R.Ensley, G.L.Crawford	A.B.Henson	M.G.
Styles,L.J.--17 Smith,H.L.--16	Jan.2,1890 At Scotts Creek Wit; W.E.Bryson, J.M.Justice	A.B.Henson	M.G.
Styles,Mark--24 Rogers,Candas--15	July 25,1897 At Barker Creek Wit; James Henderson,J.H.York, W.J.Robison	W.T.Carson	J.P.
Suab,----- (Ind) Jiney,----- (Ind)	May 7,1871 At --------	J.R.Long	Min.
Suttlemyer,John W.--23 Raby,Love E.--13	July 7,1889 At Barker Creek Wit; F.M.Nations, J.C.Fisher, J.B.Raby He From McDowell, Co. N.C.	W.P.Jones	J.P.
Sutton,Andrew--21 Green,Cordelia--18	Apr.3,1890 At Savannah Ts. Wit; A.B.Ashe, J.A.Buchanan, D.B.Buchanan	C.S.Buchanan	M.G.
Sutton,Austin--37 Jones,Emma--36	Oct.19,1890 At Caney Fork Ts. Wit; E.L.Watson, G.W.Watson, J.W.Wood	G.W.Hawkins	J.P.
Sutton,Baxter--22 Ashe,Belle--20	Jan.23,1898 At D.H.Ashe's Wit; Allen Parris, Oscar Dills, D.H.Ashe	T.F.Dietz	B.M.
Sutton,Bud--26 McMahan,Alice--19	Sept.15,1884 At Thos. Jones' Wit; John Davis John McLain	W.A.Dills	J.P.
Sutton,Candler--20 Allison,Effie--21	Jan.1,1899 At Montvill Allison's Wit; T.B.Allison, John Wilson, Wm.Margan	T.F.Dietz	Bap.Min.
Sutton,Coleman--21 Bryson,Lou Etta--22	Dec.20,1896 At Savannah Ts. Wit; Mitchel Cabe, John Carson, Lewis Tatham	W.C.Buchanan	J.P.
Sutton,Daniel G.--23 Green,Palestine--18	Mar.3,1883 At G.W.Green's Wit; A.B.Ash, W.D.Rogers	D.H.Ash	J.P.
Sutton,David--26 Cocherham,Elmina M.--	July 16,1876 At A.N.Cocherham's Wit; J.H.Moody, Harrison Messer	J.E.McLain	J.P.
Sutton,James--23 Green,Nancy--19	Nov.28,1890 At Savannah Ts. Wit; N.J.Deitz, A.B.Ashe, A.T.Buchanan	J.L.Buchanan	M.G.
Sutton,Jerome-- Ash,Sarah--	Feb.2,1871 At -------	E.C.Ash	J.P.

Sutton,John-- Ash,Harret--	Nov.2,1871 At -------	W.C.Berry	B.M.
Sutton,John-- Cocherham,Mary E.--	Feb.23,1869 At --------	E.H.Cagle	J.P.
Sutton,John--20 Bryson,Leah--18	Dec.3,1893 At Savannah Ts. Wit; Mitchel Cabe,Pink Tatham,Cole Sutton	W.C.Buchanan	J.P.
Sutton,John--21 Mason,Smir--19	Aug.19,1899 At Green's Creek Wit; G.F.Crisp, J.C.Jones	D.H.Ash	J.P.
Sutton,Julius--20 Leadford,Laura--19	License Issued June 30,1900 NOT Returned		
Sutton,J.C.--18 Fowler,Bugenie--19	Aug.7,1898 At Dillsboro Ts. Wit; F.W.Bumgarner, A.J.Dills, S.W.Conner	E.B.McDade	J.P.
Sutton,Michael--40 Buchanan,Cordelia--30	Aug.21,1898 At Harvey Cagle's Wit; Coleman Cagle,James Sutton, John Cagle	Thomas Queen	J.P.
Sutton,Mitchall--23 Messer,Mary--19	Dec.21,1879 At Ruben Messer's Wit; A.J.Parris, Rissea Sutton	W.Bumgarner	---
Sutton,Nelson--23 Childers,Ella--20	Feb.19,1891 At Dillsboro Wit; J.J.Mason, E.P.McDade	J.C.Walker	J.P.
Sutton,Phillip--24 Fowler,Cordelia--22	Dec.22,1895 At Dillsboro Ts. Wit; G.W.Pangle, W.T.Queen, Charley Pangle	W.E.Conner	B.M.
Sutton,Russell--36 Pangle,Mary E.--21	July 15,1887 At "In Tunnell" Wit; S.H.Gossett, J.B.Young	W.A.Dills	J.P.
Sutton,R.R.--22 Henry,Emma--18	Oct.24,1897 At A.E.Henry's Wit; W.D.Henry, R.V.Norman, A.C.Calhan	J.P.Calhoun	J.P.
Sutton,William-- Sutton,Margaret--	Nov.30,1854 At --------	Peter King	J.P.
Sutton,William A.--21 Keever,Linnie--21	May 12,1889 At Savannah Ts. Wit; J.W.Buchanan, G.W.Pangle, N.L.S.?	W.P.Jones	J.P.
Sutton,Wilson,--23 Franklin,Elizabeth--23	Mar.3,1881 At B.Trantham's Wit; B.Trantham	J.E.McLain	J.P.
Sutton,Wm.A.--21 Allison,Lula--23	Jan.4,1893 At Savannah Ts. Wit; H.C.Cannon, O.W.Allison, Robt.Tatham	T.F.Deitz	M.G.
Ta-Cha-Lah-Nat-- (Ind) Slucy-- (Ind)	May 15,1871 At --------	T.K.Welch	J.P.
Tatham,David-- Pilky,May--	Mar.22,1866 At --------	W.H.Buchanan	J.P.
Tatham,Frank--22 Jones,Bethie--18	Dec.23,1900 At Savannah Wit; C.D.Sutton, P.C.Tatham	John Sutton	J.P.

Tatham,Irvin--23   Jan.27,1879   ------   ---
  Conner,Lena--19   At Savannah Ts,
                              Wit; L.D.Cowan, C.B.Allison, W.L.Cowan

Tatham,James--36   Apr.25,1877   Coleman Campbell --
  Cabe,Arminda--30   At Thos.B.Cabe's
                              Wit; N.B.Cabe, M.C.Webb

Tatham,James L.--   June 9,1861   W.H.Buchanan J.P.
  Boyd,Catherine--   At --------

Tatham,J.Robert--23   Nov.11,1893   Wm.A.Sutton   J.P.
  Cabe,Adeline--19   At Savannah Ts.
                              Wit; G.R.Tatham, N.B.Cabe, R.C.Sutton

Tatham,Thomas--   Feb.15,1865   I.T.Buchanan M.G.
  Bynum,Arty--   At --------

Tatham,W.C.--21   Nov.5,1899   W.C.Buchanan J.P.
  Gribble,Lola--16   At W.R.Gribble's
                              Wit; John Jones, Henderson Jones, C.D.Sutton

Taylor,Amos E.--30   May 9,1880   C.B.Fugate   M.G.
  Norton,Delzmo--19   At David Norton's
                              Wit; David Norton, Perry Adams

Taylor,Cling T.--37   Dec.18,1898   N.J.Fox   J.P.
  Tilley,Bell--26   At William Frizzle's
                              Wit; William Frizzle, Mary Frizzle

Taylor,Henry H.--23   Dec.9,1875   D.D.Davis   J.P.
  Wilson,Martha--17   At Emma Wilson's
                              Wit; Daniel Bryson, Cally Taylor

Taylor,Julius--22   (Ind) Oct.5,1900   E.H.Hampton   M.M.
  Johnson,Stacia--24 (Ind)   At "My Home"
                              Wit; W.T.Lewis, C.K.Roberts, W.N.Randolph

Taylor,William M.--30   Aug.9,1883   S.H.Bryson   J.P.
  Crawford,Mary E.--21   At G.W.Crawford's
                              Wit; P.J.Crawford, Thomas Estis

Teague,Silar L.--21   Oct.3,1876   J.W.Bird   ---
  Terrell,Mollie J.--16   At J.W.Terrell's
                              Wit; L.C.Hall, H.T.Coldwell
                              He From Haywood, Co. N.C.

Tennant,William V.--29   Dec.22,1892   S.H.Harrison M.G.
  McCoy,Nannie E.--   At Dillsboro Ts.
                              Wit; J.C.Watkins, W.A.McCay

Terrell,G.W.--   Sept.28,1853   J.B.Sherrill J.P.
  Farley,Elmina--   At ---------

Terrell,James W.--   Aug.9,1858   Wm.Hicks   M.G.
  Keener,Ann Eliza--   At -------

Terrell,James W.--46   Jan.4,1876   J.W.Bird   M.M.
  Woodfin,Lula N.--33   At H.G.Woodfin's
                              Wit; G.W.Spake, C.A.Bird

Terrell,Joel K.--28   Aug.15,1897   J.J.Gray   M.G.
  Cooper,L.Viola--24   At Qualla Ts.
                              Wit; Henry G.Robertson,James W.Terrell,
Terrell,John L.--   Sept.24,1868   James Mahoney;C.A.Bird
  Staltcup,L.--   At ---------   M.G.

```
Terry,M.D.--20            Apr.16,1893      S.R.Cook        J.P.
  Mathis,Josephine--15    At Scotts Creek
                          Wit;James Mathis,Thos.Mathis,Jas.Terry

Terry,J.M.--21            June 11,1896     W.E.Bryson      J.P.
  Perkins,J.P.--17        At Scotts Creek
                          Wit;J.H.Terry,W.T.Mathis,A.C.Cope

Tilly,George A.--24       Dec.17,1882      R.L.Watson      J.P.
  Presley,Sarah--17       At David Presley's
                          Wit;W.J.Haynes, J.F.Wilson

Tilly,Hamilton H.--22     Sept.2,1872      A.D.Hooper      J.P.
  Frizzell,Ingabo M.--19  At M.L.Frizzell's
                          Wit;--------

Thomas,B.Walter--22       Oct.30,1898      W.Ensley        M.G.
  Dills,Isola--23         At A.B.Thomas'
                          Wit; Mary A.Nichols,Annie J.Thomas,=
                                                  Asa Thomas

Thomas,Cudge--24    (Col) Oct.22,1874      T.M.Henson      J.P.
  Bryson,Mary--24   (Col) At Stephen Bryson's
                          Wit; L.D.Bryson

Thomas,Hugh--             Nov.11,1856      N.G.Abram       J.P.
  Morton,Elizabeth--      At --------

Thomas,James--24    (Col) Feb.27,1881      G.W.Spake       M.M.
  Allen,Violet--20  (Col) At G.W.Spake's
                          Wit; W.P.Allman, J.B.Sherrill

Thomas,J.C.--26     (Col) Dec.25,1890      R.Powell        M.G.
  Gray,Callie--17   (Col) At Webster
                          Wit; J.C.Howell, A.P.Stillwell, John=
                                                  Lattimore.

Thomas,Johnson,--30       Sept.12,1897     T.C.Jones       J.P.
  Jones,Sallie--22        At W.W.Jones'
                          Wit;Samuel Jones,Ida Jones,John Jones

Thomas,Johnson--23        Nov.8,1891       W.Ensley        M.G.
  Jones,Ida--19           At Dillsboro Ts.
                          Wit; S.Jones, J.P.McMehan

Thomas,Newton--27         Oct.3,1899       A.B.Thomas      B.M.
  Siler,Nellie--18        At A.B.Thomas'
                          Wit; O.H.A.Love,B.W.Thomas, A.D.N.?

Thomas,Richard--    (Col) Apr.4,1876       G.W.Spake       M.M.
  Love,Amanda--     (Col) At Eliza Lone's
                          Wit; J.M.Candler, J.W.Terrell

Thomas,William--56  (Col) Oct.27,1887      J.A.Wilde       J.P.
  Bobs,Lissie--44   (Col) At Webster
                          Wit; Bessie Buchanan

Thompson,Coleman--22      Nov.24,1900   James W.Terrell    J.P.
  Wilson,Rebecca--18      At James W.Terrell's
                          Wit; Geo.T.Love, L.C.Gribbel

Thompson,Edwin T.--       June 26,1870     A.J.Hall        J.P.
  Hemphill,Nancy--        At ---------

Thompson,J.--             Aug.19,1866      W.H.Buchanan     J.P.
  Ashe,E.M.--             At --------
```

Thompson,Rickmon--52   License Issued   Aug.1,1901
  Wilson,Mary--45   NOT Returned
Thompson,R.M.--23   Dec.20,1896   J.P.Calhoun   J.P.
  Cope,L.C.--18   At Scotts Creek
                              Wit; W.C.Brown, L.L.Cope, J.M.Lindsey
Thompson,W.R.--   Jan.6,1871   G.W.Spake   M.M.
  Judson,Melvina--   At -------
Thompson,W.W.--20   Feb.7,1892   E.A.Cook   J.P.
  Watson,H.A.--21   At Caney Fork
                              Wit; J.H.Painter, E.L.Watson, H.S.Cook
Thompson,W.W.--25   Oct.29,1896   R.R.Coward   J.P.
  Cook,Talitha Jane--17   At Caney Fork
                              Wit; W.H.Smith, D.M.Shular, G.L.Cook
Thurber,W.L.--53   Apr.16,1897   Henry D.Welch M.G.
  Queen,M.J.--31   At Scotts Creek
                              Wit; Jennie Persons, J.W.Cagle, G.R.Hall,
                              He From Haywood,Co. N.C.   C.K.Hall.
Tompkins,William F.--25   June 27,1886   B.G.Wild   M.G.
  Luck,Anna H.--19   At F.A.Luck's
                              Wit; F.M.Tompkins, J.C.Luck Jr.
Trantham,B.--32   May 11,1893   J.C.Reed   J.P.
  Bradley,Mariah--20   At Savannah Ts.
                              Wit; M.C.Hall, T.L.Hall, H.Lewis
Trantham,David--   Jan.10,1860   W.H.Buchanan J.P.
  Green,Cielcie Ann--   At ---------
Trantham,Isaac--   Dec.28,1859   R.Evans   Elder
  Bradley,Mary Jane--   At --------
Trantham,William--19   Jan.27,1881   J.L.Buchanan M.G.
  Pangle,Nancy M.--19   At J.L.Buchanan's
                              Wit; John Lewis, W.T.Green
Tritt,A.C.--   Aug.30,1860   E.C.Chastain J.P.
  Wike,Margaret--   At --------
Tritt,A.W.--   July 8,1858   W.H.Higdon   J.P.
  Bryson,E.S.--   At --------
Tritt,John--21   Jan.2,1887   J.P.Stuart   J.P.
  Zachary,Cora--18   At S.W.Zachary's
                              Wit; Z.R.Alley, T.V.Henderson
Trotter,John S.--   Jan.9,1855   J.B.Sherrill I.P.
  Coleman,Eliza A.--   At -------
Troutman,David--   Sept.11,1856   Peter King   J.P.
  Dills,Elizabeth--   At ---------
Truiet,James--21   Apr.5,1879   W.Ensley   ---
  Dillard,Aresa--18   At Eda Dillard's
                              Wit; C.C.Love, W.H.T.Dillard
Tumlin,George W.--26   Feb.3,1885   W.H.H.Hughes J.P.
  Coward,Samantha--26   At W.H.H.Hughes'
                              Wit; C.B.Zachary, Florance Smith
Turpin,David--   July 23,1865   L.G.Ward   J.P.
  Messer,Mary-   At ---------

Turpin,James--20   Aug.22,1882 John H.Reed J.P.
 Messer,Emma--22   At David Turpin's
           Wit; Susan Reed, David Turpin
           He From Haywood, Co. N.C.

Turpin,James--70   Nov.15,1876 F.N.Nations ---
 Raby,Jane--25   At James Turpin's
           Wit; J.L.Davis, G.M.Gunter

Turpin,Robert E.--19   Jan.24,1886 W.A.Dills J.P.
 Messer,Callie--18   At John Messer's
           Wit; K.A.Howell, J.J.Enloe, James Turpin
           He From Haywood, Co. N.C.

Turpin,Wm.T.--   Dec.24,1869 E.D.Brendle Elder
 Herrin,Martha--   At --------

Twilley,Frank M.--23   Mar.19,1893 V.F.Brown J.P.
 Shelton,Belle--16   At River Ts.
           Wit; A.M.Brown, Ida Brown, Isola Brown
           He From Clay, Co. N.C.

Underwood,Jessee--21 (Col) Sept.10,1885 J.R.Crawford J.P.
 Rogers,Harriet--20(Col) At Elender Clayton's
           Wit; James Fisher, Dillard Bryson

Underwood,John I.--   June 18,1861 N.G.Abram J.P.
 Bolex,Salina C.--   At ---------

Underwood,William C.--21 (Col) Apr.12,1891 Rev.Ramsey Powell
 Love,Addie--17 (Col) At Cullowhee Ts.
           Wit; L.L.Rogers, John Casey, M.S.Casey

Vanhook,William C.--29 (Col) Oct.18,1885 J.A.Wild J.P.
 Love,Belle--24 (Col)   At Vanhook's
           Wit; J.E.Ensley, J.M.Crawford

Vess,D.M.--   Feb.10,1860 E.D.Brendle Elder
 Hyatt,Mary--   At --------

Vinson,James--21   Mar.4,1883 J.L.Owens M.G.
 Montieth,Ardella K.--17 At Barbara Montieth's
           Wit; F.S.Burris, T.S.Montieth

Wadkins,John--   Apr.20,1853 M.Coleman J.P.
 Pressly,Katarin--   At --------

Wagoner,John--28   Dec.18,1898 I.B.White J.P.
 Zachary,Mamie--18   At Cashiers, N.C.
           Wit; Jessee Wagner, Hidden Cole,Rema Zachar
           He From Henderson,Co. N.C.

Waldroup,Joseph--30   Dec.23,1885 B.H.Jones J.P.
 Waldroup,Martha A.--16 At A.Waldroup's
           Wit; R.Waldroup, I.Woodard

Waldroup,Namon--47   Mar.15,1898 J.R.Love J.P.
 Michael,Lula--33   At George Michell's
           Wit; Ellen Phillips, Martha E Knight,George

Waldroup,William--21   Jan.10,1892 W.T.Crisp J.P.Micheal
 Buchanan,Tiney--21   At Savannah Ts.
           Wit; J.R.Crasp, D.C.Jones, J.C.Woodard

Walker,Powel--21   Sept.7,1879 B.H.Jones ---
 Browning,Carolina--17 At James Browning's
           Wit; A.L.Higdon, W.T.Stiles

Walker,Thomas--20   June 3,1874   J.L.Woodard   J.P.
  Brooks,Malinda C.--20   At Lucinda Brooks'
                            Wit; A.G.Baily, A.S.Higdon

Walker,William--   May 4,1853   William Higdon   J.P.
  Higdon,Margaret--   At -------

Wallace,C.A.--25   Aug.26,1896   J.W.Bowman   M.G.
  Smith,Lena R.--25   At Cullowhee Ts.
                            Wit; O.B.Coward, W.E.Wike, W.L.Henson,
                                                          J.W.Bowman.
Wallace,James--18   (Ind)   Apr.14,1892   Suate Owl,M.G.:
  Thompson,Mary--17 (Ind)   At Qualla Ts.
                            Wit;David Axe, Anna Axe, Uriah

Wallace,Jno.O.--53   Mar.5,1897   J.C.Watkins   J.P.
  Zachary,Josaphine--43   At Dillsboro Ts.
                            Wit; J.C.Watkins, Mrs.S.R.Davis,
                                     Mrs. Laura Hunnicut, Charlie Watkins.

Ward,J.Baxter--20   Feb.28,1892   S.J.Beck   J.P.
  Gibson,Nannie S.--22   At Qualla Town
                            Wit; A.J.Beck, S.A.Beck

Ward,Charles E.--23   June 6,1877   E.D.Brendle   B.M.
  Wilks,Manervia--18   At E.D.Brendle's
                            Wit; Allen Wolks,T.Brendle

Ward,Columbus--   Aug.5,1869   E.D.Brendle   Elder
  Farler,Fanny--   At -------

Ward,H.W.--24   Mar.12,1899   C.W.Allen   J.P.
  Montieth,Mary--20   At "Bride's Home"
                            Wit; J.A.Dills, Nora Allen, J.W.Ensley

Ward,J.E.--23   Apr.26,1896   J.B.Raby   J.P.
  Bumgarner,Martha--19   At Barker Creek
                            Wit; Sam Bradley, J.W.Suttlemer, J.H.Bradley

Ward,J.W.--   June 2,1872   F.R.Welch   J.P.
  Shehan,Elizabeth--   At --------

Ward,Kirk--20   Sept.4,1881   J.B.Raby   J.P.
  Ward,Belzuen--19   At J.B.Raby's
                            Wit; C.C.Boon, S.A.Wike

Ward,R.B.--22   Oct.4,1896   W.B.Sherrill   J.P.
  Bumgarner,Cordelia--17   At Qualla Ts.
                            Wit; Charlie Bumgarner, Kissie Conley,
                                                    Mary Sherrill.

Ward,Thomas,--   Dec.16,1869   E.D.Brendle   Elder
  Bradley,Margaret--   At --------

Ward,William E.--20   License Issued   Apr.1,1891
  Harris,Sallie--18   NOT Returned

Ward,William T.--19   Feb.12,1876   J.C.McLain   J.P.
  Nations,Mary A.--18   At John Nations'
                            Wit; Thomas Ward, Merit Sellers

Ward,W.A.--28   Apr.27,1889   S.J.Beck   J.P.
  Taylor,Mary N.--23   At Qualla Town
                            Wit; J.D.Bridges,J.D.Parris, T.D.Gibson

Warlick,Emmaneuel C.--23   May 14,1888   John H.Mathis   J.P.
  Huffman,Hiley--18   At Bride's Father Home
                            Wit; S.E.Hamilton, D.W.Chastain
                            He From Swain, Co. N.C.

Warren,John Henry--22 Hooper,Mary A.--22	Apr.12,1883 At A.D.Hooper's Wit; Dillard Gribble, D.H.Rogers,	D.D.Davis	J.P.
Warren,L.G.--24 Davis,Martha--17	Feb.21,1892 At Wilmont, N.C. Wit; Frank David(Davis), W.J.Sharp	T.M.Frizzell	J.P.
Warren,Robert--21 Moffit,Zona--19	Nov.26,1896 At Scotts Creek Wit; Arthur Osborne,Joshue Inman,W.H.Inman	A.C.Bryson	J.P.
Warren,Thomas--20 Hooper,Annie--21	May 3,1896 At River Ts. Wit; J.W.Hooper, J.O.Price, W.E.Hooper	A.C.Queen	M.G.
Warren,W.L.--22 Bumgarner,Sallie--18	Aug.10,1890 At Webster Ts. Wit; F.H.Evans, J.B.Gidney, J.W.Bumgarner	B.G.Wild	M.G.
Washington,James--25 (Ind) ----,Lizza--20 (Ind)	July 24,1874 At T.K.Welch's Wit; -------	T.K.Welch	J.P.
Watkins,E.G.--24 King,Effie Jane--18	Apr.28,1896 At Barker Creek Wit; S.C.Allison, D.A.Bailey, C.C.Allison	S.C.Allison	J.P.
Watkins,John C.--34 Zachary,Flora J.--23	Oct.14,1880 At Mary Coggins' Wit; G.W.Spake, A.J.Long	B.N.Queen	B.M.
Wath,-------- -- (Ind) Ailsey,----- -- (Ind)	Apr.24,1871 At --------	A.Mingus	J.P.
Watson,Adolphus J.--21 Mathis,Taxas--17	Nov.4,1894 At Cullowhee Ts. Wit; N.J.Wilson, J.C.Hoxit,Jno. Hoxit	Javan Davis	J.P.
Watson,Alfred--19 Jones,Angelin--19	July 27,1873 At B.Dills' Wit; David Swetman, Charles Ward	John E.McClain	J.P.
Watson,A.M.--23 Melton,Mollie A.--18	Mar.12,1889 At River Ts. Wit; V.F.Brown, J.C.Keva	L.W.Hooper	B.M.
Watson,Barney C.--18 Middleton,Sereptha P.--18	Mar.20,1873 At Mary Middleton's Wit; Allison Watson, John Middleton	B.N.Queen	B.M.
Watson,David--24 Shook,Docia--19	Dec.9,1896 At River Ts. Wit; R.J.Owens, William Davis, John W.Davis	Javan Davis	J.P.
Watson,Elbert J.--25 Deitz,Alice--20	Oct.31,1901 At --------	-------	---
Watson,E.L.--25 Page,Elizabeth--17	Aug.21,1891 At Caney Fork Wit; Thos. Parker, S.Jones, Wm.Page	M.C.Warlick	M.G.
Watson,E.Nathan--19 Hooper,Mollie--18	Apr.10,1890 At River Ts. Wit; J.D.Middleton, O.L.Hooper	A.C.Queen	M.G.
Watson,Henry--29 Brown,Margaret--23	Oct.19,1890 At Hamburg Ts. Wit; M.H.Golden, J.L.Hooper, R.A.Brown	F.P.Hooper	J.P.

Watson,James--22 Love,Mary--16	Jan.2,1873 At James Wilson's Wit; Thomas Moss, J.A.Wiggins	John Hooper	J.P.
Watson,Jasper-- Freeman,Mary--	Mar.15,1863 At --------	H.M.Bennett	J.P.
Watson,John B.-- Parker,Roda--	June 26,1870 At ---------	Levi Brown	J.P.
Watson,John M.--25 Fisher,Theodocia--16	Jan.28,1886 At A.C.Fisher's Wit; Joseph Davis, Lee Hooper	J.S.Keener	J.P.
Watson,J.H.--34 Edwards,Lula--25	Nov.8,1894 At Cashiers Wit;M.D.Edwards,T.G.Picklesimer,E.E.- Lambard.	Felix E.Alley	J.P.
Watson,J.M.--33 Hoxed(Hoxit),Nancy--34	Dec.17,1893 At Cullowhee Ts. Wit; Wilson Crawford,J.Hoxit,J.R.Dills	Javan Davis	J.P.
Watson,L.D.--37 Bumgarner,Bertha--20	July 2,1894 At Cashiers Valley Wit; J.F.Alley,Effie M.Alley,L.Edwards	T.L.Jemison	J.P.
Watson,L.M.--25 Garrett,Estell--18	Jan.17,1897 At Caney Fork Ts. Wit; J.E.Long,J.G.Hooper, H.B.Wood	R.L.Phillips	J.P.
Watson,Moses L.-- Stewart,Elizabeth--	Mar.9,1871 At -------	T.W.Jemison	J.P.
Watson,Nathan--23 Crawford,L.J.--19	Sept.2,1899 At Bride Father's Home Wit;A.J.Parker,W.L.Brown,H.C.Crawford	A.C.Queen	B.M.
Watson,Robert--22 Stanford,Samantha--17	Sept.19,1890 At Sylva Ts. Wit; R.O.Philips,C.C.Love, G.W.Capps	J.A.Wild	J.P.
Watson,Robert W.--55 Morison,Ludia--35	Apr.16,1901 At Webster, N.C. Wit; H.C.Cowan,W.W.Rhinehart,J.C.Cowan	James W.Terrell	J.P.
Watson,R.W.--46 Morrison,Magaline--24	Jan.21,1892 At Cullowhee Ts. Wit; M.Painter,Allen Potts,E.J.Bennett	H.M.Bennett	M.G.
Watson,Smith--21 McFalls,George Anna--19	Jan.20,1899 At -------- Wit;W.W.Rhinehart,W.C.Thompkins,J.B. Watson.	Nathan Coward	J.P.
Watson,Thomas-- Parker,Angeline--	July 20,1861 At ---------	W.A.Enloe	J.P.
Watson,William--19 Henson,Darcus--16	Oct.5,1885 At Margaret Henson's Wit; J.R.Queen, W.E.Crawford	J.R.Crawford	J.P.
Watson,William T.--23 Jamison,Laura L.--20	Apr.3,1879 At T.W.Jamison's Wit;A.S.Bryson, Zeb V.Watson	J.P.Stuart	---
Watson,W.A.--21 Wood,Mary--22	Mar.19,1899 At J.M.Wood's Wit;A.A.Lovedahl,L.J.Mathis,G.C.Mathis	W.F.Cook	B.M.

Watson,Wm.C.--   Feb.13,1855   Jacob Wike   J.P.
  Henderson,Caroline--   At --------

Watson,Wm.H.--23   Aug.26,1897   J.N.Bumgarner   J.P.
  Taylor,Hix--16   At Martha Taylor's
                              Wit;J.A.Stewart,J.B.Bumgarner,W.J.Hend-
                                                             erson.

Watson,Z.V.--27   (Col)   Mar.23,1890   W.W.Ensley   M.G.
  Long,Kansa M.--19 (Col)   At Sylva Ts.
                              Wit; J.H.House, A.C.Watson, W.W.Ensley

Watt,Ashton.B.--23   License Issued   Dec.19,1884
  Coward,Martha--23   NOT Returned

Watt,A.B.--23   License Issued   Dec.6,1884
  King,Mollie--19   NOT Returned

Watts,Wm.--24   Oct.21,1877   W.H.Cooper   ---
  Estis,Synthia--20   At S.M.Gibson's
                              Wit; S.W.Cooper, S.M.Gibson

Webb,Carson E.--21   Feb.7,1882   J.B.Allison   J.P.
  Jones,Ellen--   At Jessee Jones'
                              Wit; S.W.Allison, Lillie Allison

Webb,G.B.--21   Jan.18,1890   W.T.Crisp   J.P.
  Cocherham,Delpha--18   At Savannah Ts.
                              Wit; Love Bailey,G.W.Reid,W.W.Ridley
Webb,John F.--19   Nov.11,1900   W.J.Fox   J.P.
  Bennett,Tabitha--19   At J.M.Bennett's
                              Wit; J.P.Webb, J.M.Bennett

Webb,J.P.--44   Aug.19,1889   J.T.Woodard   J.P.
  Bishop,Louisa--17   At Savannah
                              Wit; Wm.Ridley,Al.Higdon, J.C.Woodard

Webb,Marcus C.--22   Jan.20,1878   W.H.Buchanan   ---
  Jones,Ida--17   At --------
                              Wit; R.A.Buchanan, S.J.Buchanan

Webster,Thomas--19   Jan.15,1899   Hosea Messer   J.P.
  Wilson,Ellen--18   At John Webster's
                              Wit;Cathie Moses,J.A.Hooper,Allie Moses

Welch,Henry D.--25   Oct.20,1878   S.H.Bryson   ---
  Crawford;Charlotte--16   At W.B.Crawford's
                              Wit; W.T.Henson, F.M.Bryson

Welch,T.R.--   Jan.5,1862   J.B.Sherrill   J.P.
  Hyatt,Mary--   At -------

Welch,Zeb V.--24   License Issued   Oct.19,1883
  Cogdill,Candas--15   NOT Returned

Well,Charles M.--34   Jan.2,1895   G.N.Cowan   B.M.
  Cowan,Mary Ellen--20   At Webster
                              Wit;H.C.Cowan,J.S.Stillwell,C.C.Cowan

Wesley,George--19   (Ind)   July 17,1874   T.K.Welch   J.P.
  Tekirih,Mary--18   (Ind)   At T.K.Welch's
                              Wit; ---------

West,A.N.--35   Feb.16,1888   H.C.Cannon   J.P.
  Lakey,Texas--20   At H.W.Lakey's
                              Wit; W.A.Lakey, E.C.Lakey

West,C.C.--22   Dec.26,1895   G.W.Spake   M.M.
  Holland,Lizzie--22   At Dillsboro
                       Wit; Magley Mason, Abram Hyatt, Eva Bryson
                       He From Macon, Co. N.C.

West,David--   Dec.10,1868   E.H.Cagle   J.P.
  Guiliams,Sinthy--   At --------

West,Horace M.--21   Mar.13,1894   A.B.Henson   M.G.
  Bryson,Martha J.--17 At Scotts Creek
                       Wit; T.D.Bryson, A.C.Bryson, R.S.Bryson
                       He From Madison, Co. N.C.

West,Joel--20   Mar.1,1896   J.A.Galloway B.M.
  Owens,Canna--18   At Cananda Ts..
                       Wit; J.B.Woods, Geo.Queen, W.B.Queen

West,T.M.--   Nov.6,1866   J.L.Buchanan J.P.
  Barker,H.R.--   At -------

West,J.W.--29   Feb.6,1898   L.W.Hooper   B.M.
  Slatton,Arvie--18   At Richard Slatton's
                       Wit; John A.Hooper,Wm.Hawkins, O.L.Hooper

West,William P.--40   Jan.2,1888   W.A.Dills   J.P.
  Brinkley,Milley--20 At Wm.Smith's
                       Wit; Thomas Rogers, J.B.Young

Whitehead,Peter--28 (Col) Dec.24,1889   A.M.Parker   J.P.
  Hyatt,Mariah--14   (Col) At Sylva Ts.
                            Wit; John Underwood, W.R.Hooper

White,Ward--22   Aug.26,1882   W.H.Hooper   J.P.
  Davis,Martha--18   At Henry Hooper's
                       Wit; John Shelton, Henry Hooper

White,Wm.--12 ?   June 23,1881   J.P.Stuart   J.P.
  Pearson,R.Berry--15 At "At Church"
                       Wit; W.L.Pearson, C.Evitt

Whitler,William--   Aug.11,1872   B.N.Queen   M.G.
  Wood,Isabella--   At --------

Whitmin,Hal--68   (Col) July 7,1888   R.P.Powell   M.G.
  Martin,Eliza--35   (Col) At Harry Norman's
                            Wit; Harry Norman, Patric Moore

Whitmire,M.W.--28   License Issued   July 19,1901
  Shelton,Mattie May--27 NOT Returned
                       He From Commanche, Texas

Whitmire,N.B.--30   License Issued   Oct.8,1901
  Pearson,Susie--18   NOT Returned

Whitmire,Robert--21   Oct.2,1880   G.W.Spake   M.G.
  Worley,Mollie--20   At Mitchell Worley's
                       Wit; Wm.Love, M.W.Wells

Whitmire,William--23 (Col) Oct.1,1893   F.W.Wallace   M.G.
  Love,Julia--16   (Col) At Scotts Creek
                            Wit; Hattie Pickens,Robert Pickens,Rhoda Love

Whittenburg,Mack--21 (Col) License Issued Nov.25,1886
  Bryson,Margaret--20 (Col) NOT Returned

Wiggins,Ramsour--26   Nov.13,1898   L.W.Hooper   Bap.Min.
  Nicholson,Naoma--22 At Andrew Nicholson's
                       Wit; Wiley Henson, H.C.Baird

Wiggins,R.R.--22   Oct.22,1901   ------   --
   Smith,Elmina--21   At --------
Wiggins,Williams--19   July 24.1897   E.H.Hampton   M.M.E.C.S.
   Monis,Minnie--18   At Qualla Ts.
                            Wit; T.A.Wiggins, Dura Wiggins, Geo.Green
Wike,Cornelius W.--20   Apr.16,1899   L.W.Hooper   B.M.
   Hooper,Winnie--19   At Nell Hooper's
                            Wit; J.H.Painter, P.N.Price, W.E.Price
Wike,James H.--22   Oct.18,1875   M.M.Brown   B.M.
   Moore,Eller J.--14   At J.A.Moore's
                            Wit; H.A.Brown
Wike,Jeremiah--29   Dec.29,1874   Thomas Wilson J.P.
   Zachary,Tennessee T.--22 At W.Zachary's
                            Wit; A.Brown, E.Davis
Wike,John--24   Mar.13,1873   B.N.Queen   B.M.
   Hooper,Laura--21   At J.A.Hooper's
                            Wit; James E.Moore, John A.Hooper
Wike,R.L.--23   May 10,1891   C.L.Hooper   J.P.
   Fincannon,Florance--19   At Cullowhee
                            Wit; W.T.Wike, M.M.Wike, C.B.Wike
Wike,William--19   Dec.19,1886   B.F.Barron   J.P.
   Williams,Matilda--19   At J.Williams'
                            Wit; Mincher Cabe, J.T.Phipps
Wike,W.D.--28   Mar.8,1896   J.W.Bowman   M.G.
   Hampton,Erma--25   At Qualla Ts.
                            Wit; Viola Cooper, Lee W.Cooper,Maggie Rab
Wikle,A.--   Oct.10,1858   A.Dills   M.G.
   Breedlove,Sary--   At --------
Wikle,H.--   Dec.10,1871   Sol Messer   J.P.
   Beasley,A.J.--   At --------
Wikle,Jason--21   Sept.30,1898   T.C.Jones   J.P.
   Wilkens,Laura--21   At John Wikle's
                            Wit; L.R.McMahan, J.B.Wills, W.T.Hust
Wikle,William--18   Mar.10,1901   W.A.McMahan   J.P.
   Messer,Emma--18   At Rufus Messer's
                            Wit; S.R.McMahan, W.W.Davis, T.J.Wykle
Wilke,James R.--26   License Issued   Aug.16,1888
   Montieth,Mary T.--14   NOT Returned
Wilke,Peter--24   June 15,1876   E.D.Brendle   B.M.
   Thompson,Mary--22   At W.B.Love's
                            Wit; W.B.Love, Wm.Burris
Wilke,William A.--26   Mar.31,1878   Wm.Wilson   ---
   Coggins,Mary--17   At M.L.Coggins'
                            Wit; E.Wilson, Daniel Williams
Wilbar,James N.--33   Sept.26,1897   Joseph Hoyle J.P.
   Cogdille,H.E.--19   At George Gunter's
                            Wit; J.E.Cogdille, L.B.Wilbar, H.T.Wilbar
Wilds,Jessee A.--27   Sept.3,1885   G.W.Stephen   M.G.
   Buchanan,Julia--19   At "M.E.Church, Webster, N.C."
                            Wit; Hattie Allison,W.E.Moon

Wilkey,William--30 Messer,Nancy E.--17	Dec.22,1882 At R.C.Conner's Wit;P.Conner, R.C.Conner	G.W.Spake	M.M.
Williams,Daniel--65 Coggins,Sallie--64	Nov.20,1898 At Mrs.Coggin's Wit; W.T.Coggin, W.J.Hughes	Geo.A.Hughes	J.P.
William,Hilliard--23 (Col) Bryson,Melvina--16 (Col)	Feb.3,1885 At Stephen Bryson's Wit; Thomas Howell, J.C.Bryson	J.R.Crawford	J.P.
William,James E.--20 McClain,Robenia--18	Mar.31,1887 At J.E.McLain's Wit; A.W.Jacobs, F.M.Cathey	J.W.Bird	M.G.
Williams,J.K.--60 Waldroup,Artie--27	Apr.2,1891 At Savannah Ts, Wit; D.C.Janes, J.J.Frady, A.L.Higdon	W.T.Crisp	J.P.
Williams,J.L.--21 Walker,Docia--18	Dec.17,1897 At J.I.Franks' Wit; W.T.Crisp, H.G.Crisp, James Franks	D.C.Jones	J.P.
Williams,Martian--21 Raburn,Savannah--18	License Issued Oct.13,1889 NOT Returned		
Williams,Peyton--23 (Col) Love,Josephine--21 (Col)	Aug.15,1889 At Sylva Wit; J.Mat Love, Dave Love, J.Underwood	H.P.Brendle	J.P.
Williams,R.L.--22 Cockeram,Lela--20	Feb.26,1897 At Savannah Ts. Wit; D.P.Walker, P.C.Higdon	D.C.Jones	J.P.
William,Thomas J.--65 Browning,Linie--25	Dec.8,1882 At Charity Browning's Wit; A.L.Higdon, W.T.Reed He From Macon, N.C.	W.W.Reed	M.G.
Williams,T.J.-- Hasket,Mary--	July --,1862 At ---------	Wm.Wilson	J.P.
Williams,W.H.--28 (Col) Thomas,Indianna--28 (Col)	Apr.21,1895 At Webster Wit; J.C.Thomas, Frank Love, Ambros Bobo	R.P.Powell	M.G.
Wilson,Alfred--22 (Col) Wood,Eva--21 (Col)	Apr.6,1893 At Webster Ts. Wit; Tweed Moore, Sol.Dorsey, Ras.Bobo	J.A.Wild	J.P.
Wilson,Algarine-- Collins,Lucy Ann--	Aug.10,1870 At --------	P.G.Green	M.G.
Wilson,A.J.-- Bryson,Martha--	Jan.24,1858 At --------	W.Wilson	J.P.
Wilson,A.L.--20 Wiggins,Dollie--19	Dec.29,1892 At Hamburg Ts. Wit; J.W.Webster, A.B.Wiggins, J.R.Wiggins	J.L.Owen	M.G.
Wilson,Benson-- Golden,W.E.--	June 20,1861 At ---------	E.C.Chastian	J.P.
Wilson,Benton--26 Wilson,Etta--25	Oct.10,1896 At Hamburg Ts. Wit; J.L.Collins,J.C.Collins, P.L.Henson	T.B.Johnson	M.G.

Wilson,Columbus G.--21   Aug.8,1880   C.B.Fugate   M.G.
Wilson,Sallie--17   At Thomas Wilson's
                            Wit; Burres Norton, T.L.Jameson

Wilson,Enos--   Feb.21,1869   E.P.Stillwell
Bennett,S.E.--   At --------

Wilson,E.C.--21   Oct.28,1897   J.L.Owen   B.M.
Wilson,Lillie--18   At W.A.Wilson's
                            Wit; I.L.Collins,Julia Wilson, P.L.Henson

Wilson,Grant--21   (Col)   Dec.4,1890   R.M.Worley   Clg.
Gibson,Taxanna--21 (Col)   At Webster
                            Wit; Joe Smith, Thad Allen, Virge Bryson

Wilson,Henry T.--22   Sept.19,1880   J.A.Marshall M.G.
Bryson,Canses R.--19   At A.M.Hooper's
                            Wit; A.C.Long, S.M.Hooper

Wilson,James--19   Sept.11,1893   John Bumgarner J.P.
Pressley,Florence--16   At Cullowhee Ts.
                            Wit; Julius Cabe, Thornton Jones,Mack Presl

Wilson,James--   Jan.11,1863   J.Wike   J.P.
Hooper,Martha--   At --------

Wilson,James C.--25   July 15,1877   J.P.Stuart   ---
Hooper,Addie--19   At Thos Wilson's
                            Wit; H.M.Hooper, Thos Wilson

Wilson,James N.--22   May 14,1885   John S.Keener J.P.
Painter,Emma--16   At J.T.Painter's
                            Wit; O.B.Coward, M.M.Monday

Wilson,John C.--   Oct.12,1871   W.Zachary   J.P.
Woodring,M.M.--   At --------

Wilson,Joseph--24   Apr.2,1873   Sydney Ash   J.P.
Browning,Francis--18   At James Browning's
                            Wit; David Tatham, Jeron Sutton

Wilson,Mathen E.--20   Aug.13,1882   J.P.Stuart   J.P.
Woodring,Laura--14   At Wm.Henderson's
                            Wit; Lee Hooper, Witcher Wike

Wilson,Noah--   Dec.21,1856   John Wilson   J.P.
Chambers,Livina--   At --------

Wilson,R.W.--   Sept.15,1868   G.W.Spake   Cleg.
Allison,Hick--   At ---------

Wilson,Thos.--   Mar.21,1872   John A.Hooper
Love,N.L.--   At --------

Wilson,Thomas--   Nov.29,1855   B.N.Queen   B.M.
Hooper,Jamima--   At --------

Wilson,T.B.--29   Nov.28,1894   T.R.Zachary   J.P.
Russell,Ida--21   At Hamburg Ts.
                            Wit; C.G.Wilson, J.R.Wilson, Thos. Wilson

Wilson,Wm.--   July 12,1866   A.Fisher   J.P.
Edmonston,Sarah M.--   At ---------

Wilson,William--21   Nov.9,1873   E.C.Ash   J.P.
Collins,Sarah--17   At Daniel Collin's
                            Wit; M.Wilson, H.P.Cabe

-149-

Wilson,W.A.-- Brown,H.S.--	Jan.27,1870 At --------	Thos. Wilson	J.P.
Witt,Rufus M.-- Sorrels,C.A.--	Aug.26,1871 At --------	E.D.Brendle	Elder
Wood,Andrew J.-- Mills,Miley M.--19	Jan.28,1874 At S.N.Wood's Wit; --------	G.W.Hawkins	J.P.
Wood,Andrew J.--35 Huffman,Mary P.--19	Mar.11,1886 At S.Jones' Wit; W.C.Long, J.H.Smith	Bragg Hooper	J.P.
Wood,A.J.-- Queen,S.A.--	Jan.8,1869 At ------	B.N.Queen	Elder
Wood,Brady--21 Jones,Fannie--21	May 1,1898 At A.J.Wood's Wit; G.F.Wood, D.A.Phillips	J.M.Wood	M.G.
Wood,Clayton--24 Hooper,Rebecca--27	May 22,1886 At Terreseci Hooper's Wit; J.B.Hooper, L.H.Wood	Bragg Hooper	J.P.
Wobd,D.H.-- Hooper,Ibin--	Sept.16,1866 At ---------	W.Zachy	----
Wood,Garland--20 Parker,Bettie--21	May 6,1898 At L.M.Parker's Wit; Sam Cook, D.M.Parker, H.L.Wood	J.H.Smith	J.P.
Wood,George W.--35 Burell,Georgia S.--21	June 22,1884 At Mary Barnes' Wit; Jeff Powell, James Wike	J.B.Coward	J.P.
Wood,Goleman--20 Brown,Jane--20	Apr.15,1877 At Jacob Woodring's Wit; Dan Moody	W.H.Hooper	---
Wood,Govan D.--21 Hooper,Jemimia--21	Sept.16,1883 At Wm.Hooper's Wit; V.F.Brown, W.S.Rochester	L.W.Hooper	M.G.
Wood,Hamilton--23 Gazaway,Margarett--23	Dec.15,1892 At River Ts. Wit; C.L.Herris, J.E.Hawkins, Jorden Moore	A.C.Queen	Bap.Min.
Wood,Hamp--22 Davis,Emily--21	Nov.3,1889 At Caney Fork Wit; J.H.Morris, E.Coward, W.A.Hooper	E.A.Cook	J.P.
Wood,Henry B.--23 Long,Sarah R.--16	May 27,1877 At Pleasant Parker's Wit; J.H.Parker, D.H.Mathis	J.H.Mathis	---
Wood,H.L.--25 Page,Emma--18	Aug.27,1899 At Nelson Henson's Wit; R.H.Stephaes, James B.Coward	E.M.Coward	J.P.
Wood,Houstan H.-- Wike,Sousan J.--	Dec.20,1870 At --------	M.M.Brown	J.P.
Wood,Jack--35 Queen,Artie--30	Dec.10,1885 At James Henry's Wit; James Henry, John B.Queen	A.J.Hall	J.P.

Wood,James C.--33 Queen,S.A.--17	Feb.19,1880 L.W.Hooper M.G. At B.N.Queen's Wit; W.A.Queen,J.W.Phillips
Wood,John--20 Watson,Jane#-18	May 21,1886 R.A.Sitton J.P. At G.W.Watson's Wit; R.C.Wood, G.Watson
Wood,John W.--20 Parker,Mindie--18	May 6,1894 J.M.Keener--Min.Free Will Ba At Caney Fork Wit; Boon Wood, H.G.Cook, G.L.Wood
Wood,J.E.--24 Walker,Maggie--18	Nov.20,1898 R.L.Phillips J.P. At A.J.Wood's Wit; E.H.Stephens, J.R.Stephens,L.M.Stephen
Wood,J.R.--20 Gazaway,S.I.D.--19	Jan.28,1894 A.T.Hood-- Miss.Bap. Min. At Hamburg Ts. Wit; E.L.Watson, Jno.A.Hooper, B.J.Moody
Wood,Mikel--48 Arrington,.Martha --24	Oct.11,1885 Bragg Hooper J.P. At S.Melton's Wit; E.E.Chastain, J.B.Hooper
Wood,Rufus--18 Parker,Samantha--18	License Issued Nov.28,1884 NOT Returned
Wood,Rufus C.--20 Parker,Samantha--18	Sept.11,1887 G.W.Hawkins J.P. At Balsam Grove Wit; A.J.Wood, Mary Mull
Wood,Samuel N.-- Mills,Lizy M.--	Feb.11,1870 A.J.Hall J.P. At --------
Wood,S.C.--21 Mills,Hattie--17	Nov.20,1898 R.L.Phillips J.P. At A.J.Wood's Wit; E.H.Stephens, J.R.Stephens,L.M.Stephen
Wood,Stephen--21 Davis,Mary--22	Nov.6,1881 W.A.Brown J.P. At William Davis' Wit; S.A.Davis, Dumont Hooper
Wood,Thadeus D.--24 Parker,Tebitha--20	Sept.1,1882 G.W.Hooper M.G. At "In the Road" Wit; James Cook, Mat Parker
Wood,Thomas C.--26 Mills,Rebecca--26	Jan.26,1874 W.M.Estes J.P. At R.S.Mills' Wit; W.P.Allman, John Cope
Wood,Thomas--21 Hoxit,Belle--19	Oct.27,1894 J.A.Galloway M.G. At Canada Wit; Elias Galloway, M.S.Brown, Jim Hoxit He From Transylvinia,Co.N.C.
Wood,Vance--22 Long,Sarah J.--22	Mar.23,1879 D.D.Davis M.G. At Taylor Wood's Wit; E.E.Chastain, R.H.Brown
Wood,W.P.--75 Mathis,Emma C.--28	Feb.12,1898 James W.Terrell J.P. At Webster Ts. Wit;S.L.Kelley, E.L.Addington,M.W.Bryson
Woodall,John--37 Alexander,Annie--24	Apr.16,1900 W.L.Henson J.P. At John Woodall's House Wit; John R.Henson,JohnW.Shelton,John Phill:

Woodard,Henry--21 Ridley,Nannie--19	Nov.3,1900 At At Wesley Cope's Wit; G.F.Crisp, H.G.Crisp, John R.Jones	D.C.Jones	J.P.
Woodard,I.D.--19 Cope,Maryann-I.--17	Oct.15,1889 At Savannah Ts. Wit; G.B.Webb, A.A.Johnson	W.T.Crisp	J.P.
Woodard,J.C.--25 Buchanan,Victoria--21	Dec.4,1892 At Savannah Ts. Wit; V.Cowan, A.W.Davis, W.T.Deitz	T.F.Deitz	M.G.
Woodard,John--21 Williams,Amanda C.--19	Feb.5,1882 At Jessee Williams' Wit; J.P.Webb, J.O.Franks	W.W.Reed	M.G.
Woodard,John--64 Knight,Elender--40	Dec.19,1872 At John Woodard's Wit; John Woodard, James Woodard	P.G.Green	B.M.
Woodard,Matison--19 Baily,Elizabeth--20	Apr.17,1875 At Wm.Woodard's Wit; A.C.Baily,W.P.Baily	P.G.Green	B.M.
Woodard,Thomas--23 Potts,Rebecca--15	Oct.1,1882 At Allen Potts' Wit; M.C.Owens, J.C.Potts	J.P.Stuart	J.P.
Wooding,J.C.-- Hooper,M.A.--	Jan.7,1872 At -------	John A.Hooper	
Woodring,Avery--21 Shook,Rachel--18	Jan.29,1885 At Rufus Woodring's Wit; J.C.Wilson, H.B.Watson	W.M.Hooper	J.P.
Woodring,Avery--32 Wilson,Mary M.--18	Apr.12,1899 At James Golden's Wit; John Golden, James Golden, R.M.Warring	L.W.Hooper	B.M.
Woodring,Avery--32 Middleton,Maggie--21	License Issued Feb.1,1899 Returned-- "NOT EXECUTED"		
Woodring,Woodring,Carbo--26 Wilson,Margaret--21	Sept.18,1879 At Alfred Wilson's Wit; J.M.Wilson, C.L.Woodring	W.M.Hooper	J.P.
Woodring,Charles L.--25 Wilson,Salina A.--15	Sept.30,1875 At Alfred Wilson's Wit; H.A.Brown, J.L.Owens	M.M.Brown	B.M.
Woodring,Joe A.--24 Slaton,Catherine--21	Nov.26,1874 At "In Road" Wit; Richard Slaton	S.P.C.Shelton	J.P.
Woodring,JohnA.--38 Hooper,Margaret A.--28	Mar.6,1885 At Wm.Hooper's Wit; J.B.Hooper, F.L.Moody	L.W.Hooper	M.G.
Woodring,John A.--28 White,Martha J.--24	Jan.24,1875 At J.A.Woodring's Wit; Thomas Montieth, J.A.Fulbright	M.W.Bryson	J.P.
Woodring,William--21 Hoxit,Mary B.--18	Feb.17,1878 At "On bank of river" Wit; John Webster, Baxter Hooper	J.S.Woodan	---

```
Woodring,Rufus--21          Mar.18,1880        W.H.Hooper      J.P.
   Middleton,Mollie--18     At Mary Middleton's
                            Wit; J.L.Hooper, W.F.Wood

Word,Elias--23              Feb.7,1875         F.N.Nations     J.P.
   Bradley,Mary--20         At F.N.Nations'
                            Wit; Decater Ward, Arron Nations

Worley,Frank--21 (Col)      Aug.26,1897        J.C.Reed        J.P.
   Bryson,Josephine--19 (Col) At Sylva Ts.
                            Wit;D.G.Bryson,W.J.Fisher,T.M.Frizzell

Worley,James E.--23         Sept.25,1889       John C.Orr      M.G.
   Bigham,Nora C.--17       At Webster Ts.
                            Wit;J.W.Terrell,W.W.Stringfield,W.H.H.-
                            He from Buncombe,Co. N.C.         Hughes

Worley,John J.--29          Mar.11,1901        R.R.Coward      J.P.
   Shular,Sallie A.--27     At Susan Shular's
                            Wit;Chas.Cook,James Shular,Dora Cook
                            He from Swain, Co. N.C.

Worley,Marion--21           Feb.23,1887        J.S.Leopard     J.P.
   Leopard,Cary--18         At J.H.Leopard's
                            Wit; W.F.Moore, J.M.Leopard
                            He from Clay,Co. N.C.

Worley,Zebulon--20 (Col)    Oct.14,1877        J.S.Keener      ---
   Love,Josephen--18 (Col)  At J.S.Keener's
                            Wit; W.Bryson, Nancy Cadison

Wright,Barok--              Feb.22,1872        J.Queen         J.P.
   Green,V.A.--             At --------

Wyke,John--24              Mar.13,1873        B.N.Queen       M.G.
   Hooper,Laura--21         At --------

Wyke,Samuel--22            Feb.17,1901        W.A.McMahan     J.P.
   Messer,Lavadia--18       At Graham Messer's
                            Wit; WM.Sutton, L.R.McMahan

Wyke,R.P.--                June 22,1871       P.G.Green       M.G.
   Cocherham,C.C.--         At --------

Wykle,William--18          May 2,1901         W.A.McMahan     J.P.
   Elders,Provy--18         At Ham Wykle's
                            Wit; L.R.McMahan,C.W.Allen,T.J.Wikle

Yeargan,Lawrence D.--30    Nov.1,1899     A.W.White, Pres.Min.
   Yeargan,Catherine P.--18 At W.K.Merrick's
                            Wit;W.K.Merrick,Mrs.J.H.McCoy,F.Merrick
                            He from Murfryboro,Tenn.

York,John--21              June 17,1891       B.G.Wild        M.M.
   Bryson,Jane--18          At Webster
                            Wit; C.C.Cowan,M.W.Bryson,H.C.Cowan

York,J.H.--18              Feb.12,1893        B.G.Wilds       M.G.
   Dills,M.A.--15           At Sylva Ts.
                            Wit; J.M.York, C.M.Parks, H.Fisher

Young,Mack--25             Nov.12,1899    Jas.W.Divelbliss    M.M.
   Williams,Mary--24        At Sylva Ts.
                            Wit;J.Knight,Bob Garret,Gudger Foster
                            He from Mitchell,Co. N.C.
```

Young,Thomas--21   Nov.19,1892   A.C.Queen   M.G.
Wilson,Salena--21   At Hamburg Ts.
Wit;D.L.Shook,M.Shook,M.E.Price,J.Golden

Zachary,Andrew--67   Mar.25,1875   G.W.Spake   M.M.
Cole,Verlinda--40   At Elizabeth Stillwell's
Wit; J.W.Fisher, A.V.P.Bryson

Zachary,Christopher B.--21 Oct.3,1877   R.H.Stephens ---
Coward,Mary--21   At Nathan Coward's
Wit; David Davis, David Rogers

Zachary,Claud--25   Jan.26,1901   G.W.Mating   M.M.
Sisk,Lillie--22   At Riley Hooper's
Wit; A.C.Long, Riley Hooper, H.A.Pell

Zachary,David W.--19   May 13,1883   L.M.Dillard   J.P.
Hooper,Mollie V.--15   At A.M.Hooper's
Wit; O.B.Crawford,J.D.Zachary

Zachary,Ed.--22   Feb.7,1897   B.Norton   J.P.
Pierson,Mary--19   At Hamburg Ts.
Wit;John Stuart,Daisy Zachary,W.R.Rose

Zachary,Grant--21   Sept.19,1886   J.P.Stuart   J.P.
Evitt,Althea--18   At D.M.Evitt's
Wit; J.H.Brendle, R.J.Philips

Zachary,Jefferson D.--23   Dec.14,1884   O.B.Coward   J.P.
Wilson,Lizzie--23   At W.H.Hooper's
Wit; W.H.Hooper, S.A.Davis

Zachary,J.D.--34   Jan.27,1895   A.B.Thomas   B.M.
Potts,Susie Jane--22   At Cullowhee
Wit; Alice Deen,Lula Wike,J.B.Buchanan

Zachsry,William K.--24   Dec.27,1882   J.W.Bird   M.G.
Montieth,Martha--24   At J.E.Angel's
Wit; J.E.Angel, M.M.Angel

Zachary,W.R.--30   May 3,1891   L.M.Dillard   J.P.
Allison,N.A.--37   At Cashier Ts.

Wit;T.R.Zachary,W.T.Hawkins,J.A.Zachary

INDEX OF BRIDES WITH ONE NAME

Ailsey,	160	Lizza	160
Annie, (Aisley)	12	Lucy	12
Anna	38	Marcella	75
Casly	151	Mary	48--97
Charlotte	142	Ol-nih	88
Chumluski-ta	46	Oolscosty	41
Elizabeth	1--66	Sallie	142
Jiney	152	Selah	148
Junie	89	Slucy	154

****
****

INDEX OF BRIDES

Adam,(Adams)	Angeline	55	Allen,	Millie	101
	D.M.	40		Minnie	53
	Ema	114		Modenia	63
	Jane	55		Nancy	42
	Sarah	89		Pattie	5
	Sarah J.	10		Roxie	100
	Sousan	131		Sarah J.	8
Addington,	Laura	72		S.J.	27
Aiken,	Anner	112		Violet	138
	Lillie	40	Alley,	Effie	115
	Sarah E.	51		M.J.	26
Aikin,	Caroline	66		Sarah E.	29
Aikins,	Martha	66		Susan	42
Alexander,	Annie	150	Allison,	Ann C.	94
	Belle	106		Effie	135
	Sarah	17-76		E.H.	115
Alexandria,	Mary	126		Hattie	109
Allen,	A.C.	130		Lillie R.	19
	Darcus	42		Lula	135
	Harriet C.	25		Martha E.	58
	Joaie	39		Mary	78
	Lena E.	38		M.A.	49-65
	Mamie	95		N.A.	152
	Manda M.	42		Sarah A.	128
	M.A.	54		Sarah Ann	45

Allison,	Sallie	45	Ashe,	Lula	96
	Rachel	93		Rebecca	90
	R.A.	30		Sarah	27
Allman,	Lula	33		Sultena	61
	Maggie	32	Babb,	Jane	21
	Mary	38	Baily,	Darcus M.	70
	Sarah	52-54		Elizabeth	151
Allson,	Hick	148		Jane	33
Alman,	Mary	33		Martha J.	57
Amburs,	Mary	105		Mary J.	26
Anderson,	L.L.	106		Stacy E.	37
	Mary	13	Bailey,	Florence M.	122
Angel,	Emma	93		Mary O.	133
Angil,	Ann	3	Baird,	Laura	123
Arington,	Elmira	12	Baker,	Julettie	113
	Polly	5	Baley,	Mary J.	90
Arrington,	Martha	150		N.E.	33
	Laura	41	Ballard,	Lula H.	133
	Laura M.	52		Sallie L.	112
Ash,	Amanda J.	134	Barnes,	Noah	129
	Allow C.	9	Barker,	Caroline	37
	Callie	28		Charity	62
	G.J.	96		Hett E.	89
	Harret	136		H.R.	145
	Ida R.	69		Lucinda	8
	Katherine	2		Lydia	112
	Margaret	55		Margaret M.	8
	Martha	3		Martha Elmina	55
	Mary	106		Mary	
	Melvina	2		Rachel	29
	Rue E.	25		Mrs.Sarah J.	92
	Sarah	5-135		Virginia	12
Ashe,	Belle	135	Barnes,	Annah	102
	Dela	51		F.I.	36
	E.M.	138		Lavada	129
	Ida	15	Barn,	Lydia	14
	Iva	117	Barron,	Lousia	80
	Jane	14		Maggie	115
	Laura	16		Perthinia	28
	Loranda	124			

Barron,	Sarah	133	Blanton,		Catherine	5
Barton,	J.B.	1			Fannie B.	60
Battle,	Angeline	49			Lillie	122
	Bida	65			Martha A.	47
	Mary	82			Mary L.	51
	Sarah C.	78			M.M.	116
Beard,	Lydia M.	31			Sarah An	70
Beasley,	A.J.	146			Vilantie	25
	Caldonia	24	Bobo,		Lula E.	99
	Delia	62	Bobs,		Lissie	138
	Docia	94	Boid,		Sarah	10
	Palestine	64	Bolex,		Salina C.	140
Beck,	Clarinda A.	35	Bolick,		Lodusky	125
	Josephine	58	Bolt,		Hattie	86
	Laura	70			Queen Victoria	89
	Roxie B.	30	Boon,		E.E.	31
	Sarah A.	60	Bowlick,		Lon ?	3
	S.J.	23	Bowman,		Della	53
Bennett,	Bettie J.	117	Boyd,		Catherine	137
	Josaphene	71	Brackens,		Nellie	94
	Lena	71	Bradburn,		Lillie	121
	M.E.	22	Bradley,		Amanda J.	38
	N.R.	36			Callie	61
	S.E.	148			Ella	96
	Tabitha	144			Fannie	37
	Vinna	117			Jane	73
Berry,	Annie	57			Lora	65
	Minnie G.	106			Mandy	15
Bigham,	Nora C.	152			Margaret	141
Billingsly,	Altha	51			Mary	152
Bishop,	Jennet	79			Mary E.	67
	Louisa	144			Mary Jane	139
	Louisa J.	70			M.E.	126
	Octa	11			Sallie	48
	P.L.	17	Bradshaw,		Maggie	33
	Ticia	84	Breedlove,		Sary	146
Blackburn,	Frances	119-108	Brendle,		Hattie	112
Blackwell,	Anna	29			C.J.(Josephine)	45
	Mary K.	127			S.A.(Sarah A.)	100
Blanton,	Alice	76	Bridges,		Josie	105

157-

Briggs,	Elmine	62	Brown,	Georgiann	112
	Elminy	23		Haseltine	9
Bright,	Belle	32		Hulda C.	128
Brinkly,	Dellie	116		H.S.	149
	Mary	42		Jane	149
	Milley	145		Julia	93
Brogdon,	Arlissa	38		Laura	17-107
	Cora	24		Laura L.	103
Browman,	Francis	105		Lilly	128
Brooks,	Alth	126		Lilly G.	37
	Amanda	62		Lizzie	90-124
	Donie	80		Louisa	132
	Dorkie	23		Lucinda	119
	Elizabeth	107		L.I.	18
	Emila	55		Mahala	18
	Emiline	25		Manerva	77
	Emma	105		Manley C.	128
	E.E.	25		Margaret	20
	Laura Elizabeth	64		Margarett	142
	Malinda C.	141		Margaret M.	92
	Mary	8		Martha	58
	Mary J.	5		Martha E.	6
	Nancy	98		Mary	58
	Parthena	62		Mary A.	61-112
	Pattie	33		Mary C.	132
	Rhoda C.	51		Mary E.	81-48
	Sarah J.	73		Mary L.	89
Broom,	Kate	90		Mattie	36
	Sarah	27		Mattie Jane	108
Brown,	Annie	2		Mollie	12
	Arilla	71		M.C.	93
	Bindy	54		Narlecia	133
	Carrie	31		Nelia	1
	C.	73		Racheal	73
	Elizabeth	108		Rebecca	112
	Ellen	49-127		Rebecca E.	81
	Elmina	111		Sadie J.	86
	Emila	53		Sarah	41-58-101
	Emmer	91		Susan	73
	Florence I.	108		Tina	46

Buchanan,	Gertrude	61	Bumgarner,	Leona	23
	Ida	56		Maggie	51
	Jane	8		Martha	141
	Julia	146		Mary	66
	Laura	67		Melvina	22
	Laura B.	69		Rachal	104
	Laura E.	80		Rebecca	41-111
	Louisa	24		Sallie	142
	Lucy A.	44		Sula	71
	L.A.	65		Tennessee	7
	Mandy	134	Burchfield,	Eliz.	84
	Margaret	15-23-28	Burgess,	Della	95
	Margaret	47-65	Burrell,	Agnes	117
	Martha	44-117		Georgia S.	149
	Martha C.	15		Margaret	59
	Martha E.	125	Burnell,	Nellie	55
	Mary	14-64	Burris,	Mary E.	100
	May	55	Buff,	Mary	121
	Mira	21		Rosanah	121
	Rebecca E.	57	Butler,	H.E.	104
	R.	70	Bynum,	Arty	137
	Sallie	62-62	Cabe,	Adeline	137
	Sarah	47-55		Arminda	137
	Sarah J.	28		Cordelia	23
	Synthia	104		Elimina	24
	Thurisa C.	100		Hester	24
	Tina	80		Laura T.	46
	Tiney	140		Lizzie	57
	Victoria	151		Lucy	57
	Violet	70		Margaret	77
Buckner,	Hanner	28		Mary	17-44
Bumgarner,	Annie	59		Mary C.	107
	Bertha	143		Rachel M.E.	25
	Callie	59		Sarinda	25
	Cordelia	141		Susan B.	2
	C.A.	3		S.T.	80
	Ellen	6	Cagle,	Candas E.	116
	Francis	27		Cordelia	23
	Iola	81		Emma	41
	Laura M.	53	Caler,	Maggie	31

Coggins,	Belle	10	Conner,	Oma C.	8
	Lish	91	Cook,	Dora M.	33
	Lizzie	74		Julia	29
	Mary	146		Laura	16-16
	Sallie	147		Margaret	128
Cole,	Kidder	105		Mary A.	33
	Verlinda	153		S.G.	33
Coleman,	Ann	97		Talitha Jane	139
	Eliza A.	139	Cooper,	Dora	78
Collens,	Sarah E.	107		Florence	11
Collins,	Allice	43		Estella	82
	Dora	113		Lucinda	9
	Hattie A.	69		L.Viola	137
	Julia L.	19		Maggie	94
	Lucy Ann	147		Mary	77
	Sarah	148		Maybell	69
Conly,	Clmantin	49		Nancy	128
	Elmina	4		T.J.	83
	Haseltine A.	132		Virgina	70
Conley,	Canney	19	Cope,	Artie	130
	D.J.	128		Daisy G.	130
	Emma	52		Josephine	44
	Mahala C.	128		Julia	131
	Mary E.	21		Laura	102
	M.C.	31		L.C.	139
	R.J.	36		Margaret C.	35
Conner,	Bell	51		Maryann I.	151
	Bessie	101		Mary J.	7
	Dovey	7		Sarah	90
	Candas	46		Sarah J.	79
	Cordelia	52	Cordell,	Roxie	122
	C.P.	10	Coward,	Arlesie	18
	Elizabeth	77		Azela	88
	Julia E.	31		Candall	111
	Laura	85		Fannie M.	23
	Laura Bell	117		Folba M.	16
	Lena	137		Hattie	3
	Lillie May	66		Melvine	47
	Manervia	13		Lucy	125
	M.C.	49		Lula	123

Coward,	Martha	144	Crawford,	Martha	11-23
	Mary	99-153		Mary	12-110
	Nellie	68		Mary E.	137
	Rachel	2		Mattie	98
	Sallie J.	107		Melinda	90
	Samantha	139		Melvina	50
	Savina	132		M.C.	46
	Stella	21		M.M.	98
	Sylntha	71		O.C.	20
Cowart,	Rutha	18		Racheal	98
Cowan,	Ellen	58		Sarah S.	71
	Jane	6		Sina	22
	Laura	4	Crumpton,	Maggie	102
	Lillie	6	Cunningham,	Coldona	71
	Margaret	41		Dovey	35
	Mary Ellen	144		Elizabeth A.	69
	Mollie	44		Eva	51
	Nancy	1		Malissa	113
	Octa	126		Margaret	28-65-96
Cox,	Amanda	83		Peggy	15
	Rosetta	54		Sallie	83
Craigg,	Jane	120	Dalton,	Elmena	13
Crawford,	Alice	54		Vallie	50
	Artie	116	Darcus,	-------	33
	Candas	61	Daves,	Cloe	89
	Charlotte	144		Sallie	91
	Crecia Ellen	89	Davis,	Amanda	50
	Cumire	109		Allie	1
	Cynthia	80		Callie D.	43
	Emma	130		Carrie S.	8
	H.C.	19		Cora K.	39
	I.B.	18		Ella	47
	Iffa	115		Ella Maia	35
	Laura	69		Emily	149
	Laura E.	127		Emma	124
	Laura B.	93		Hattie	29
	Lucinda	90		Ivey	66
	L.J.	143		Lena	115
	Margaret L.	116		Malovina	103
	Manervey	54		Manda	101
	Manervia E.	81		Martha	142-145

Davis,	Martha	14-64	Dillard,	Rutha	80
	Martha Jane	35	Dills,	Almer	23
	Mary	150		Candas	35
	Mary Ann	16		Della	54
	Mary E.	9		Elamona	81
	Mary Jane	113		Elizabeth	139
	Meriah	124		Ida E.	124
	Nancy A.	23		Ingabo P.	51
	Pauline	21		Isola	138
	Sallie	31-107		Laura L.	4
	Sally	111		Lydia C.	46
	Sarah A.	14		Maggie	63
	Sarah E.	54		Martha	25
Davison,	Sarah	58		Martha J.	42
Dawsey,	Mary	68		M.A.	152
Dawson,	Eliza	10		M.M.	57
	Martha J.	119		Pollie	15
	Mary Ann	91		Polly	64
Deen,	Sarah	35		Sarah M.	40
Deitz,	Alice	142		Spurgeon	59
	Annie	117		Susanah	24
	Florence	41		Tiney	22
	Hattie	15	Dorsey,	Laura	75
	Jane	63		Lula	87
	Lillie	57		Sarah C.	98
	Martha T.	25	Dotson,	Eliza	29
	Mary	28	Duncon,	Ellen	85
	Myrah	102		Nancy E.	9
	Nancy	38-63	Dunn,	Hessie	58
	Rachel L.	91	Dunwoody,	Roda	125
	Sabina	57	Duts,	Louina	114
	Talitha	100	Dyers,	Maggie	117
Dillard,	Anna	129	Ecua,	Dina E.	4
	Aresa	139	Edmonston,	Sarah M.	148
	Bessie	26		Emily	77
	Edith	37	Edwards,	America	88
	Ellar L.	42		Bell	85
	Jane	105		Lula	143
	Mattie E.	106		Mary Ann	69
	Nannie L.	106	Elarge,	Elsie	48

Elders,	Artie	59	Ensley,	T.P.	12
	Jane	85	Estes,	Mary J.	84
	Provy	152		Sarrah	83
	Richy	132		Sarah A.	61
Elmore,	Josie L.	23	Estis,	Margaret	84
Enloe,	A.J.	5		Samantha A.	14
	Belle	102		Synthia	144
	Florence	41	Evitt,	Althea	153
	Ida J.	41		Cleninda	1
	Laura R.	102		Mary J.	134
	Lela	102		Sarah J.	116
	Lora B.	92	Evereth,	Susan	129
	Maggie M.	73	Extine,	Amanda J.	7
	Melvina	134	Falen,	Margaret	7
	R.A.	34-101	Farler,	Fanny	141
	Sarah E.	47-114	Farly,	Elmina	137
Ensley,	Amy P.	118		M.B.	11
	Arry	100	Farley,	Emeline	26
	Candis	17		Laura C.	105
	Codelle	39		Lula E.	11
	Cora	98		Mary	92
	Dicey J.	131		Vicie	60
	Elizabeth	64		Virginia	98
	Elizabeth J.	15-120	Farmer,	Dora M.	65
	Ellen	131		M.T.	122
	Fannie C.	100		Talitha J.	50
	F.C.	20	Fincannon,	Florance	146
	Hannah	22-61	Fish,	Hattie M.	125
	Josephine	1	Fisher,	Alice	2
	Kate	62		C.Belle	130
	Juda	21		Elizabeth	127
	Julia	109		Emma	128
	Martha	131		Harriet	52
	Mary	133		Ida C.	100
	Mary J.	68		I.Cumi	43
	Mellie	83		Maggie	19-53
	Melvina	83		Margaret	69
	M.A.	86		Martha	101
	M.C.	130		Mary C.	12
	Sarah	21-124		Minnie	131

Fisher,	M.C.	52	Frady,	Rebecca	28
	Nancy T.	51		Rebecca M.	24
	Nannie	40		Samantha	129
	Pollie	26		Sarah	115
	Sarah A.	120	Franks,	Annie	77
	Susan E.	90		Josephine	67
	Theodocia	143		Loucinda	123
Floody,	Sarah E.	107		Mary	11
Floyd,	Jain	30		M.A.	123
Fore,	Maggie	84		Sallie	119
Forster,	Maggie	40	Franklin,	Bessie	117
Fortner,	Sarah	120		Elizabeth	136
	C.A.	121		Emila	105
	Mary Ann	119		Sarah	50
	Sarah	15		Susan	78
Foster,	Catherine F.	48	Freeman,	Belle	79
Fox,	Amanda	10		Martha	115
	Elizabeth	90	Freemon,	Mary	143
	Emeline	106		Nannie	41
	Emly	8	Fretwell,	Emma	13
	Laura	83	Frizell,	Elizabeth Ann	21
	Sallie	78		Eva M.	10
Fowler,	Bugenie	136		Florence	24
	Cordelia	136		Hattie	20
	May	21		Ingabo	138
	Oct	46		Laura	9-113
	Sarah	7		Maggie	113
	Varina	49		Martha	28
Frady,	Alma	85		Mary M.	26
	Catherine	127		Sarah	100
	Charlotte	43	Fullbright,	Barbary	36
	Ella May	28		Belle	65
	Kansas	57	Fulmer,	Maggie	41
	Manda Allecia	38	Fugate,	Susan	45
	Margaret	44	Gaddis,	Nancy L.	20
	Martha A.	15	Galloway,	Cora M.	54
	Martha C.	89		Lyda C.	127
	Mary M.	19		Paralee	108
	May F.	14	Garrett,	Elizabeth	91
	Nancy	55		Estella	143

Garrison,	Sarah	80	Gipson,		Laura	124
Gather,	Adeline	75			Mary	82-133
Gazaway,	Margaret	149			M.M.	100
	S.I.D.	150			Sarah A.	36
Gennings,	Charity J.	55	NO NAME	------		92
Gibbs,	Catherine M.	125	Golden,		Elizor	72
	E.	83			W.E.	147
	Ida	115	Grant,		Elvira	18
	Josephine C.A.	125			Jane	84
	Margret W.	48			Sarah	126
	Martha	87	Graham,		Lucinda	10-90
	Mary	82-87	Grasty,		Lillie	19
	Mary A.	43	Graves,		Catherine B.	63
	M.A.	53-127	Gray,		Collie	138
	Sarah	115	Green,		Addie	56
	Susan	32			Cielcie Ann	139
	Verlinda	82			Coldellia	135
Gibson,	Cordelia	121			C.E.	33
	Desdimonia	64			Darcus	65
	Emily	68			Emiline	23
	Emma	78			Eugenia	44
	Frankey	60			Hannah L.	68
	Georgia Ann	4			Hester	23
	Holcedonia	42			Jane	102
	Julia	53			Jo Annah	28
	Laura	27			Josephine	95
	Margaret	3-59			Laura	77
	Marthy	113			Laucy Ann	84
	Mary	45			Lacada	81
	M.E.	14			Lavisa	113
	Nancy L.	80			Lillie	28
	Nannie S.	141			Lizzie	56
	Palestine M.	79			Maggie	89
	Pearl	80			Malvina	15
	Polly	105			Mariah	14
	Rachel	20			Margaret M.	9
	Sallie	11			Mary	1-49
	Texanna	148			Meriah	24
Gipson,	Alma	105			Nancy	28-44-135
	Julia A,	45				

Green,	Palestine	135	Hall,	Margaret	25
	Sarah L.	47		Martha H.	50
	V.A.	152		Mary	90
Graham,	Lucinda	10-90		M.A.	83
Grasty,	Lillie	19		M.L.	53
Graves,	Catherine B.	63		Rachel P.	13
Gray,	Callie	138		Sarah	4
Gribble,	Fannie			Sarah L.	29
	Lola	137		Syntha E.	9
	Margaret	24	Hamilton,	Drucilla	89
	Martha	79	Hampton,	Eddie N.	88
	Matilda	46		Erma	146
Grigs,	Marinda	32		Eugenia May	43
Grimes,	Mary	67	Hancock,	Margaret	79
Guilliam,	Elisa	61		Rebecca	125
	Ingabo	68	Handcock,	Emma	31
	Nancy E.	62	Hannah,	Julia A.	30
	Salena	25	Harris,	Belle	8
	Sarah	96		Emeline	34
	Sinthy	145		E.C.	24
Gunter,	Alice	9-36		E.J.	53
	Darcus	64		Fannie	121
	Elmina	76		Florence	132
	Ida	97		Ida	99
	Josephine	81		Mary	24
	Laura	96		Mary C.	35
	Margaret	119		M.E.	119
	Mary	93		Pricilla	43
	Nancy J.	54		Sallie	105-141
	Polly Ann	15		Sarah Jane	134
	Sallie	110	Hasket,	Mary	147
Hadden,	NO NAME -----	38	Hays,	Maud	32
Hall,	Alice	37	Hawkins,	Belle	95
	Amanda	110		Demogna B.	109
	Cordellia	3		Dora	73
	D.B.	113		Josie	48
	Florence I.	85		Julia	102
	G.Lavada	116		Lilian	10
	Eda	4		Mary	111
	Ingrebo C.	52		Mollie	38
	Jency			Pink	69

Hawkins,	Rosa Ann	4	Herske,	Haseltine	78
Haynes,	Mattie E.	123	Hicks,	Francis C.	82
Haaton,	Minnie Gertrude	3		May	34
Hedden,	Etta	16		Rebecca	133
	Minnie	18	Higdon,	Alis	5
	Sallie E.	37		Margaret	141
Hemphill,	Nancy	138		Margarett J.	37
Henderson,	Caroline	144		Martha	4
	Macsie	133		Mollie	37
Henry,	Dovy M.	65		Saphroney	70
	Ellen	98	Hill,	Frances	67
	Emma	136		Levina	107
	Jane	45		Maggie	21
	Lelah	12		Margret	46
	Mary J.	76		Mary	122
	Matilda	15-101		Maude	27
	Melaina	98		Nancy	4
	Mila	112		R.I.	83
	Sarah	112	Hipps,	Edith	94
	Thersa	34	Hix,	J.Elizabeth	71
Hensley,	Jane	68		Mary	87
	Norsisa	68	Holden,	Amanda	27
	Sarah	62		Drusella	12
	Sinda	15		Lillie	6
Henson,	Aliss Jane	20		Martha	82
	Callie	38		Mollie J.	128
	Darcus	143		Octie	134
	Lida	123		Susan	26
	Loreaney	22	Holland,	Connie	22
	L.E.	20		F.J.	45
	Maggie A.	31		Lizzie	145
	Maggie S.	86	Howell,	Annis	87
	Mary	21		Fannie	87
	Mary M.	39-124		Jane	85
	Rebecca E.	49		Tennessee	134
	S.Ella	50	Hoxit,	Jane	17
Herrel,	Phebe.	26	Hooper,	Addie	148
Herrell,	Frances	26		Alma A.	58
	Missouri	131		Amanda	37
Herrin,	Martha	140		Annie	142
				A.E.	68

Hooper,	Callie	37-115	Hooper,	Sarah A.	6
	Catherine	18		Sarah J.	129
	Dillard	111		Sousan	17
	Dora	18-45		Stella	23
	Dosia	84		S.M.	72
	Elizabeth	37-105		Varina	78-132
	Eva	103		Winnie	146
	Fannie	112		Zola	107
	Frona	66	Hornbuckle,	Lucinda	120
	Harrett	47		Minda	35
	Jamima	148	Hoxed,	Nancy	143
	Jane	38	Hoxit,	Belle	150
	Jamimia	149		Dollie	66
	Ibin	149		Mary B.	159
	Laura	83-146-152		Tinie	108
	Laura L.	129	Hoyle,	Emma	102
	Leah	112		Mary	66
	Lizzie	26-118-118		Mollie	40
	Lou	85		N.Virginia	56
	Margaret A.	159	Huffman,	Fannie L.	60
	Margaret J.	72		Hiley	104-141
	Maggie	45-62-93		Mardinia	99
	Maranda	106		Mary P.	149
	Marinda	22		Mary S.	90
	Martha	148		Samantha	60
	Mary	125	Hughes,	Martha	126
	Mary Ann	128		Mary	89
	Mary A.	142		Ruanna	34
	Mary	38-112		Luzena	9
	Mollie	142	Huskins	Catherine	126
	Mollie V.	153	Hyatt,	Addie	86
	M.A.	74-151		Catherine	68
	M.L.	88		Cordelia	101
	Nancy	67		Elizza	49
	Pauline	3		Herriett	53
	Rebecca	55-149		Laura	82
	Rhoda	85		Mariah	145
	Rhoda J.	23		Mary	140-144
	Ruth	67		Mary C.	10
	Ruth A.	72	Hyde,	F.M.	99

Hyde,	Martha	59	Jons,	Elizabeth	122
Iven,	N.C.	61		Ella	114
Inman,	Mattie	118		Ellen	144
Jackson,	Alcey Ann	66		Emma	135
	Margret	92		Emma L.	15
	Mary C.	54		Fannie	149
	Nancy A.	55		Gusta	81
	Nanie	12		Harriet L.	40
Jamison,	Laura L.	143		Hattie	48-50-97
Jarrett,	Mamie	88		Ida	138-144
Jemison,	Delphia	134		Jane	122
	Emma	66		Josie	13
	Kittie	97		Lena	68
	Sarah	100		Lizzie	64-40
Jennings,	Addie L.	75		Lula	10
	Docia	134		Mary A.	46
	Elizabeth	125		Mary C.	30-82
	Ellen B.	101		Mary E.	103
	Margaret	125		Mary M.	60
	Martha	13-64-71		Melvine	28-32
	Mary	125		M.J.	118
	Susan O.	20		Rachel	71
Jenkins,	Bettie	111		Rutha	94-94
	Jane	33		Sallie	114-138
	Lizzie	12		Sarah A.	128
	L.J.	11		Saronias	109
	Margaret	81		Sophia	62
	Marth	64		Sylvania B.	48
	Mary J.	125		Synthia	62
	Nancy	34	Judson,	Melvine	139
Johnson,	M.E.	13	Keener,	Alice Belle	3
	Stacia	137		Ann Eliza	137
Johnston,	E.A.	68		Eliza	29
	Mattie	130		Hattie	7
Jones,	Alma P.	113		M.A.	9
	Angeline	142		Sallie	56-92
	Bethie	136		Sary M.	59
	Caddo	113	Kerkindoll,	Julia	88
	Clarissa	10	Kerkland,	Carolina	84
	C.R.	123	Keever,	Linnie	136
	Elizabeth	46			

Killpatric,	Sarah	79	Leopard,	Martha	19-22
Kimsey,	Emma	96		Mary	101
King,	Emma	118		Myra	59
	Effie Jane	142		Palestine	133
	Fannie C.	131		Sarah A.	108
	Harriett C.	12		Sarah F.	21
	Ida	70	Lester,	Sousan	34
	Josephine	128	Lewis,	Hattie	25
	Josie	95		Martha E.	127
	Laura	109	Lilley,	Mary	57
	Mollie	144	Lindsey,	Elizabeth	37
	Mollie V.	86		Lillie G.	76
Kirby,	Artie L.	26		Maggie	85
	Emily	27	Long,	Caroline	54
Kirkindall,	Mary E.	79		Dora	39
Kite,	Mary E.	30		Elizabeth	85
Knight,	Bettie	49		Elizabeth L.	50
	Elender	151		Emma C.	38
	Fannie	59		Hattie E.	57
	Mary E.	128		Hester	69
Knox,	Caroline	107		Kansa M.	144
	Lizzie	88		Laura Bell	36
Lakey,	Texas	144		Mary A.	74-130
Laney,	Mary	89		Mary J.	103
Lattimore,	Mary	53		Mary L.	27
Lawless,	Kathrine	11		Mollie J.	10
	Polly	11		Nancy J.	127
Leadford,	Elvira	111		N.A.	97
	Laura	136		Rebecca	71
Leatherwood,	Annie C.	38		Roda	47
	Florence May	47		Sallie	88
	Laura Bell	24		Sarah J.	159
Lemmons,	Martha	35		Sarah R.	149
Lemons,	Martha	5		Sary Jane	108
Leopard,	Alice	53	Loury,	Virdie Q.	117
	Cary	152	Love,	Addie	140
	Ellen L.	30		Amanda	138
	Feba	119		Belle	140
	Josephine	101		Chole E.	75

Merrill,	Mary	5
Messer,	Allace	131
	Callie	140
	Charlotte	19
	Cora Belle	78
	Ella	42
	Emma	140-146
	Francis	60
	Ida	126
	Laura	109
	Lavadia	152
	L.J.	64
	Manervia E.	85
	Margaret	64
	Mary	139-136
	Nancy.E.	147
	Racheal	60
	R.A.	42
	Sarah	134
Metz,	Helena	126
Michael,	Lula	140
Middleton,	Chloe	17
	Elzy Magdaline	6
	Jamima	128
	Julia	128
	Maggie	151
	Mollie	152
	Nelly Ann	108
	Sallie	7
	Sereptha P.	142
Mille,	Jennie	86
Miller,	Artic C.	98
	Belle	70
	Mandy	134
	Margaret A.	53
	Milley M.	101
	Naomi	83
	Sarah E.	91
	S.E.	97
	Tennie	4

Mills,	Carisue	97
	Cyntha	111
	Ellen	129
	Eliza M.	79
	Fancy	25
	Frances	39
	Hattie	150
	Isabella	54
	Lizy M.	150
	Malinda	41
	Mary	12-113
	Miley M.	149
	Rebacca	150
	Rhoda Jane	54
	Ruthy	97
	Sarah	19
	Sarah J.	64
	Synthia	95
	Zettie Ann	39
Millsap,	J.A.	79
Mince,	Ellen	61
Mingus,	Sarah	14
Moffit,	Alma	58
	Hiley L.	67
	Margaret	67
	Mary Jane	95
	Zona	142
Monday,	Baty S.	118
	Bettie	77
	Ellen	116
	Laura B.	30
	Martha M.	45
Monis,	Minnie	146
Monteith,	Callie	83
	Mary	43
	M.E.	16
	Otelia	55
Montieth,	Ardella K.	140
	Celinda J.	29

Montieth,	Cleminthine	20	Morgan,	Emma J.	94
	D.J.	65		Florence	45
	Elizabeth M.	126		Nancy	21
	Juda	98	Morison,	Ludia	143
	Martha	153		Lula	59
	Mary	141		Vina	48
	Mary Ann	104	Morris,	L.D.	85
	Mary A.	82-77		Lou	71
	Mary T.	146		Margaret	119
	Sally	49		Margret	129
	Sarah H.	122		Mary W.	97
	Talitha C.	81		Pauline	62
Moody,	Artie	43		Sarah E.	110
	Dellie	130	Morrison,	Magdaline	143
	Dovie O.	81	Morrow,	Nancy	39
	Fannie	97		Nicy	83
	Laura A.	75	Morton,	Elizabeth	138
	Lecie	35		Nancy	91
	Lillie	62	Moses,	Gather	72
	Lou	34	Moss,	Aldie	132
	Loucinda	18		A.D.	133
	Mary	93		Bessie	71
	M.E.	48		Dorthula	26
	Nassie	103		Harriet M.	114
	Nine	41		Margret C.	22
	Rhoda	17		M.J.	79
	Rosana	92·		Sallie	58
	Sallie	50	Muchel,	Sallie	131
	Samantha	21	Mull,	Debby	106
Mooney,	Ida	3		Mary	123
Moore,	Delia	86		Mary E.	95
	Eller J.	146	Munday,	Hattie	3
	Emily	117	Murdock,	Mable	50
	Josephine	84	Murry,	Delle (Casey)	78
	Lou	38		Nancy	78
	Oda (Ida)	115	McCall,	Elizabeth	88
	Mary	7		Malissa	93
	Mary E.	31		Mary	20
Moose,	Esie	56		Mattie	44
				Miley	84

McCambell,	Mary V.	104	Nations,	Mary A.	141
McClain,	Robenia	147		Nancy	14
McConnell,	Malinda C.	2	Neeley,	Alice	48
McCoy,	Harriett	120	Newton,	Lurana	129
	Nannie E.	137	Nicholson,	Alice J.	22
McDade,	Carrie	126		A.A.	78
	Susan	53		Clara	118
McDonal,	Ella	61		L.L.	53
McDonald,	Violet	72		Naoma	145
McDowell,	Hattie	101		Sarah E.	112
	Minta	47		Sarah F.	60
McElray,	Lula	40	Nicols,	N.V.	50
McFall,	George Anna	143	Nicholoson,	Varina	132
McGee,	Laura	94	Norman,	Belle	90
McGuire,	Sally	107		J.E.	19
McKay,	Mary J.	107		Lizzie	7
McKee,	Harriet	33		Mary	54
	Hattie V.	34	Normon,	Cansadie	56
McLain,	H.Frances	12		Emma	12
	Laura A.	30	Norris,	Rebacca	99
	Mattie	94	Norton,	Delzmo	137
	M.E.	114		Mercella	93
McMahan,	Alice	135		Lou	38
	Aveline	62		Octava	68
	Bertha	61		Vinetta	123
	Blanch L.	94	Oocuma,	Anna	75
	Ellis	51	Oocumimer,	Carolina	75
	L.	68	Oolscosty,	--------	37
	Margaret	95	Owee,	Margaret	132
	Matilda	96	Owen,	Adeline	13
	Nancy	55		Charlotte	123
	Sarah	13		Jane	91
	Syntha	1		Margaret	65
Naimon,	Rutha	129		Martha	82
Nations,	Bennie	7		S.M.	92
	Bettie	46	Owens,	Airy J.	84
	Cordelia	122		Angeline	58
	Harriet	80		Canna	145
	L.M.	60		Evaline	75
	Margaret	52		Haseltine C	84
	Mary	114		Linda	13

Owens,	Lula	57	Parker,	Elmina	74
	S.E.	130		E.P.	101
Page,	Bethena	106		Fannie	120
	Elizabeth	142		Hester	91
	Emma	149		Ida	112
	Rena	67		Isabella	103
Painter,	Alice	11		Jane	5-14-89
	Belle	50		Juda	90
	Ellen	111		Lula	132
	Emma	40-148		Maggie M.	109
	Mary J.	117		Martha	111
	Lena	7		Martha E.	39
	Lillie	63		Martha J.	111
	Violet	68		Mary H.	18
Pangle,	Martha	63		Mindie	150
	Mary E.	136		M.T.	91
	Nancy M.	139		Nancy	92
Pannel,	Hannah J.	36		Polly L.	36
	Harriet	127		Roda	143
	Maggie	102		Samantha	150-150
	Sarah	39		Sarah	120
Panter,	Harriett	5		Sarah C.	67
Paris,	Elizabeth	3		Sarah L.	109
	Mary T.	36		Tebitha	150
Parker,	Addie	132		Vashti	56
	Aled	36		Victoria	6
	Allice	110		Vilet L.	86
	Altena	132		Viloa	111
	Angeline	143	Parks,	Sarah J.	82
	Ann	33-110	Parnel,	Catherine	67
	Arilla	71	Parris,	Alice	119
	Arrilla	103		A.E.	97
	Bessie	36		E.J.	109
	Bettie	149		Fannie	45
	Catherine	74		Julia	131
	Charity	26		Laura	22
	Clara	116		Lucinda	106
	Clerica	27		Lucinda E.	124
	Cora	76		Margaret	120
	Cornellie	105		Margaret T.	27
	Elizabeth	77		Martha	39

Parris,	Mary A.	50	Pierson,	Mary	153	
	May	63	Saddie	104	104	
	M.E.	68		S.T.	103	
	Rhoda	81	Pilky,	May	136	
Parson,	America	30	Pinson,	M.E. Mrs.	34	
Partin,	Martha	27	Pinion,	Sarah	99	
	Mary	95	Porter,	Mollie	122	
	Margaret J.	63	Portor,	Sarah E.	60	
	Minnie	93	Potts,	Addie	42	
	Nancy	96		Callie H.	92	
	Rebecca	94		Maggie E.	121	
	Rizie	26		Margret	70	
Passmore,	Eva	57		Margaret	17	
Patterson,	Nancy	53		Martha	114	
	Nannie	115		Mary	56	
Paxton,	Luisey	59		May	75	
	Maggie	24		M.J.	16	
	Sarrah Jane	70		Rebecca	151	
Pearson,	Larrurah A.	70		Susie Jane	153	
	R.Berry	145		S.C.	16	
	Susie	145	Powell,	Mary	44	
Penland,	Jane	56		Sarah	75	
Perkins,	J.P.	138	Presley,	Callie	46	
Philips,	Harriett	6		Ella	10	
	Victory M.	91		Etta	74	
Phillips,	Artie	20		Hester	126	
	Bettie Jane	77		Katharin	140	
	Harriet	42		Ida	55	
	Hattie	7		Jane	21	
	Julia	87		Margarett	110	
	Lavada	110		Martha E.	20	
	L.H.	131		Mary Ann	67	
	Rebecca	79		Nancy	23	
	Rebecca E.	40		Nellie	72	
	Sallie	11		Pink	117	
Pickelsimer,	R.Zella	1		Sarah	138	
Pickens,	Florence	19	Presnell,	Mary	124	
Pierson,	Connie	75	Pressley,	Belle	133	
	Ettie	83		Florence	148	
	Fannie	69		Louisa Jane	123	
				Queen	1	

Pressley,	S.A.	100	Raby,	Jane	140
Price,	Lula E.	16		Love E.	135
	M.E.	106		Maggie	67
	T.L.	74		Mary	13
	Viney	120		Nancy Jane	42
Profit,	Mary	66	Ray,	C.	54
Pruit,	Harriet	5		Rebecha	119
	Mary M.	66	Redley,	Sousan R.	88
Pruitt,	Florence	106	Reece,	Alcester	77
	Sarah	98		Altha	123
Queen,	Allie	82	Reed,	Alice	2
	Amanda C.	120		Anne	134
	Ansa B.	59		Artie	5
	Artie	149		Mary	113
	Elizabeth	39		Pollie	121
	Elvina	35		Rosa	18
	Emma	53		Sarah J.	23-122
	E.C.	41	Reid,	H.L.	45
	Harret H.	130	Reynolds,	Alley	66
	I.	36		Oma	28
	Jane	99	Rhodes,	Martha A.	7
	Laura	43-124-124	Rice,	Bessie	48
	Malinda M.	121	Richards,	Ella V.	88
	Maranda P.	100	Rickman,	Sarah	134
	Margaret H.	51	Rigden,	Mary	45
	Mary	121	Ridley,	Nannie	151
	Mary E.	109		Polly	37
	Mary J.	72-131	Roawland,	Lizzie	80
	Mary M.	111	Roberts,	Mary J.	81
	Martha J.	133		Racheal	15
	Maybelle	22	Roberson,	Bethena	52
	Mollie L.	50	Robeson,	Margaret	124
	M.A.	100	Robinson,	Bertha	25
	M.J.	139		Fannie	107
	Rebecca	40		May Belle	95
	S.A.	149-150	Robison,	Eliza O.	1
	Syntha	18		Harriet	131
	W.E.	88		Maggie	55
Quinn,	Mary	134		Melvina M.	131
Raburn,	Savanah	147		Rachel C.	27

Rochester,	Caroline	85	Sellers,	Nancy	133
	Daisy	58	Seret,	Clarentine	76
	Emma	106	Shaw,	Mary E.	105
	Hattie	32	Shehan,	Elizabeth	141
	Nettie	31	Shelton,	Annie A.	2
	Pennie	77		Belle	140
	Sally M.E.	30		Brilliann	16
Rogers,	Addie	103		Caroline	104
	Alice	135		Emma J.	66
	Ann	47		Isabella	17
	Annie	53-132		Lucinda	119
	Arena	121		Lydia S.	4
	Candas	135		Margaret J.	2
	Belle	128		Martha A.	36
	Druscilla	24		Mary	74
	Fannie E.	84		Mattie May	145
	Harriet	140		Nancy	47
	Lula	96		Nellie	128
	Mellie	87		Oeta	26
	Polly P.	77		Sarah	16-78
	Sallie Viola	97		Sarah E.	95
	Trude	46		Sophiah	17
Runnels,	Nannie	66	Shephard,	Mary	121
Russell,	Ida	148	Sheppard,	Sophia	1
	Lucy C.	91	Sherrill,	Elizzie	108
	Malvina	59		Issubella	49
Ryefield,	Charity A.	84		Laura	49
Sampson,	Sallie	85		Lew L.	52
Sanders,	Josephine	87		Loula	68
	Lona	99		Lou A.	52
	Millie	74		May L.	78
	Susan	130		M.D.	104
Sanford,	Polly	80		P.Mellie	89
Saunders,	Belle	107		Susan	43
	Julia	39	Shook,	Arleasa	96
	Liza	86		Cordelia	97
Scott,	M.E.	57		Docia	142
Seay,	Jenette	115		Laura E.	60
Self,	Martha	124		Margaret	60
Sellers,	Fannie	14		Martha E.	65
	Ruth N.	27		Mary E.	116

Shook,	Matilda	62	Slatton,	Neddie	6
	Nancy J.	47		Olivene	17
	Rachel	151		Victoria	16
	Rebecca	31	Smallwood,	Sarah	89
	Samantha A.	17	Smathers,	Martha	80
Shular,	Ellen	69		Mary	35-44
	Maggie	21		Mary A.H.	103
	Margret	95		Olive	126
	Martha J.	5	Smith,	Abersine	76
	Mary	5		Catherine	100
	Novella J.	108		Dollie	127
	Ruth A.	102		Elmina	146
	Sallie A.	152		Ethel	86
	Sarah Angaline	33		Etta	44
	Tine	76		H.L.	135
Shuler,	Lora	110		J.E.C.	110
	Melvine	96		Laura	129
	M.C.	27		Lena R.	141
	S.M.	135		Maletha A.J.	108
Sih,	Yet	1		Marthey	88
Siler,	Nellie	138		Mary	134
Simons,	Lurruner	63		Sarah	56
Sims,	Stacy	108		Susan	70
Simson,	Analine	52	Sneed,	Mary A.	130
Sisk,	Lillie	153	Snider,	Carrie	76
Sitton,	Lela	29		Etta	96
	Maggie	37		Eva	50
Slatten,	Anna	127		Lillie E.	42
Slatton,	Arvie	145		Lure	9
	Caterine	151		Margret E.	40
	Clarissa I.	108		Mary E.	69
	Dollie	42		Sarah J.	54
	E.M.	9	Sorrels,	C.A.	149
	Haseltine	117		Louisa	76
	Julia	67	Sparks,	Martha	97
	Laura	7		Emma	2
	L.M.	58	Spencer,	Lola	90
	Maud M.	92	Stallcup	Grace	133
	Minnie	115		Mary	31
	Nancy A.	101	Staltcup,	L.	137

Surname	Given	No.		Surname	Given	No.
Stanford,	Ella	51		Stillwell,	Roxil	125
	Margaret	49		Stratten,	Caroline	71
	Samantha	143		Strutton,	Catherine	27
Stapp,	Mary R.	118			Mary	6
Staten,	Susan	74			Roda	123
Steadman,	Mary E.	49		Stuart,	Allis	116
Stephans,	Etta	110			Ida	6
Stephens,	Alis	85			L.J.	103
	Clara H.	73			Sarah	104
	Lousena	74		Styles,	Mollie	122
	Rue	31			Rebecca	102
	Sabra	73		Sutton,	Alice	2-92
	Susan	35			Allice	2
	Teola	110			Catherine	109
	Varina	72			Cherryan	8
Stewart,	Elizabeth	143			Clerosa	95
	Etta	19			Dollie	96
	Laura	26			Hattie	26
	Lucinda	122			Ida	97
	Rutha J.	103			Jane	82-120
	Sallie	26			Lillie	32
	Sarah	107			Lou	28
Stiles,	Caroline	14			Lucy Ann	94
	Elmira	103			Lula	109
	Etta	25			L.C.	46
	Harriet	44			Margaret	136
	Margaret	25			Martha	81
	Martha	63			Mary	110
	Melvina	44			Mary C.	84
	Otelia	63			Menervia	95
	Polly	68			M.M.	32
	Samantha	6			Pollie Ann	91
	Sarah A.	79			Rebecca J.	25
Stillwell,	Belle	30			Sarah A.	32
	Bettie	4		Tally,	Elizabeth J.	109
	Cordilia	30		Tatham,	Ann	63
	Dovey	93			Callie	76
	Elizabeth	38		C	Clurinda	116
	Emma Jane	29			Lilla	24
	Florence	56			Mary	63
	Mary J.	41			Sarah	20

Tatham,	T.C.	22	Turpin,	Jane	130
Taylor,	Della	71		Lily	105
	Dora	19		Sarah	63
	Hix	144		Tennessee	75
	Jane	67	Turner,	Susan	90
	Mary	100-133	Underwood,	Rebecca	86
	Mary A.	141	Upten,	Dulcena S.	8
	Mattie M.	99	Wadkins,	Pollyann	57
Teeters,	Mary	35	Waldroup,	Artie	147
Tekinik,	Ann	59		Florence	89
Tekirih,	Mary	144		Martha A.	140
Terrell,	Mollie J.	137	Walker,	Alice	106
	Sarah E.	11		Docia	147
Thomas,	Annie	29		Lucinda	70
	Indianna	147		Maggie	150
	Magdalien	87		S.J.	114
	Manda	31	Wallace,	Cannie	133
	Rachel E.	58	Ward,	Belzuen	141
Thompson,	Laura	94		Catherine	42
	Louisa	52		Donia	20
	Mary	40-141-146		Elizabeth	96
	S.L.E.	99		Hattie	60
Tompson,	Mary	123		Jane	127
Tilly,	Elizabeth	30		J.U.	104
	Margaret	6		Katie	66
	Mandiney	6		Lenora D.	59
	M.A.	71		Maggie	129
	Rebecca	125		Margaret S.	45
Tilley,	Bell	137		Martha E.	12
	Margaret	6		Pollie	15
	Modenia	115		Sallie	43
Trantham,	Clora	94	Warren,	Ida	22-60
	Sarah	94		Mattie	120
Tritt,	Alace R.	65		Zona	126
	Florence	78	Washington,	Mary	119
	Sarah G.	14	Watkins,	Abigil	99
Tucker	Louise	75	Watson,	Amanda	73
Turk,	Alice	99		Aveline	9
Turpin,	Charlotte	14		A.M.	12
	Collie	94		Becersisa	30

-183-

Watson,	Bessie	72	Webster,	Dialpha	43
	Casie	115		Laura J.	117
	Daisy	39	Wells,	Exie	47
	Darcus	49	West,	Eliza Jane	91
	Elizabeth	18-118		Eliza J.	122
	Eliza	14		Gustus	2
	Hannah A.	15		Louisa R.	118
	Emily	129		Mary	24
	H.A.	139		Mollie	32
	Julia	72		Rebecca	61
	Jane	150	Wiggins,	Amanda E.	73
	Laura	73-114		Annie Bell	61
	Lela	86		Dollie	147
	Lena	104		Matilda	79
	Lou	59		M.A.	52
	L.Arlesa	54	Wike,	Amanda	78
	Margaret	116-123		Annie	71
	Margarett	106		Emma	101
	Martha	40		Julia	124
	Mary	84		Margaret	139
	Mary E.	118		Mariah	19
	Mila	69		Mary A.	72
	Nancy A.	5		Menervia I.	2
	Nancy J.	73		Rebecca	104-126
	Rebecca	109		Sousan J.	149
	Rhoda	81	Wikle,	Adline	106
	Ruth	50		Allie	94
	R.C.	31-75		Brunettie	48
	Sallie	76-121		Neely E.	96
	Sallie	109	Wild,	Luthena	38
	Theadocia	125	Wilkens,	Laura	146
Watts.	Syntha	121	Wilks,	Amanda	34
	Tennie	126		Charity E.	37
Waycaster,	Alice	81		Manervia	141
	Roxie	12		Margaret	34
Webb,	Annie	91		Nancy L.	68
	Lucinda	56		Mary K.	1
	Magdolin	57		Rebecca	42-60
	Rutha	116		Sarah	51

Williams,	Amanda C.	151	Wilson,	Mary	139
	Catherine	78		Mary Ann	28
	Josie	114		Mary J.	81
	Martha J.	15		Mary M.	151
	Mary	152		Matilda P.	24
	Matilda	146		Milly	89
	Polly	4		Minta	73
	Sarah	19		Mollie	11-34
	Saphronia	77		M.I.	123
Wilson,	Alice	44		N.J.	18
	Arminda E.	10		Polina	7
	Beulah	20		Rebecca	138
	Daisy	73		R.Avey	63
	Darthula	29		Salena	153
	Delphia	67		Salina A.	151
	Elizabeth	66-89		Sallie	148
	Elimma	100		Sarah	107-107
	Ella J.	30		Sarah L.	32
	Ellen	144		Stella	8
	Emmy	74	S.J.	89	
	Etta	147		Violet	28
	Florance	113		Violet J.	25
	Ida	82		Zelphia E.	45
	Isabella	49	Wise,	Jane	46
	Jane	3	White,	Martha J.	151
	Julia	72		Susan	114
	Katherine	76		--- ---	36
	Laura	33	Whitmin,	Mary	43
	Laura L.	46	Whitted,	Mary	52
	Lavina	87	Wood,	Amanda	12
	Lillie	56-148		A.M.	35
	Lizzie	153		Darcus	118
	Lora	122		Dovey V.	33
	Maggie	9		Elsie	110
	Margaret	102		Ellen	106
	Margaret	151		Emila	102
	Margaret C.	104		Eva	147
	Martha	137		Fannie	74
	Martha A.	83		Francis M.	130
	Martha J.	57		Isabella	145

www.ingramcontent.com/pod-product-compliance
Lightning Source LLC
Chambersburg PA
CBHW072052020426
42334CB00017B/1474